RICHARD KNIGHT is a former winner of the Travel South USA Young Travel Writer of the Year Award, the prize for which was a trip that gave him his first taste of Highway 61. A devoted jazz and blues fan he has since returned several times, most recently with co-researcher Emma Longhurst to drive the length of the Blues Highway researching this new book.

Richard writes for numerous newspapers and magazines in Britain and the US including *The Times* and *The Sunday Telegraph*. He has written or contributed to several other travel books and is founder of Roots of Rhythm Travel, a specialist tour company for music lovers.

The Blues Highway
First edition September 2001

Publisher
Trailblazer Publications
The Old Manse, Tower Rd, Hindhead, Surrey GU26 6SU, UK
Fax (+44) 01428-607571
info@trailblazer-guides.com
www.trailblazer-guides.com

British Library Cataloguing in Publication Data
A catalogue record for this book is available from the British Library

ISBN 1-873756-43-7

Editor: Henry Stedman
Series Editor: Patricia Major
US proofreader: Heather Glickman
Map research: Emma Longhurst
Cartography: Nick Hill
Layout: Bryn Thomas and Anna Jacomb-Hood
Cover design: Planet Watton
Index: Jane Thomas

**Every effort has been made by the author, contributors and the publisher to ensure
that the information contained herein is as accurate as possible. They are, however,
unable to accept responsibility for any inconvenience, loss or injury sustained by
anyone as a result of the advice and information given in this guide.**

Printed by
Star Standard (☎ +65-861 3866), Singapore

THE BLUES HIGHWAY

NEW ORLEANS TO CHICAGO

A TRAVEL AND MUSIC GUIDE

RICHARD KNIGHT
co-researched with
EMMA LONGHURST

TRAILBLAZER PUBLICATIONS

For Michael Knight, the world's greatest jazz fan

Acknowledgements

The generous support of Tracy Long from British Airways Holidays, Nigel Selby from Hemmingways, Cheryl Hargrove formerly of the Travel Industry Association of America and David White and Sophia Angelis from Southern Comfort helped to get this project rolling.

Sincere thanks are also due to Kevin and Wendy Herridge, Fiona Duthrie, Beverley Gianni, Bruce Morgan, Mary Millar, Tommy Comeaux, Kelly Strenge, Al Elmore, Lenore Barkley, Laura Godfrey, Marcia Weaver, Mary Shepherd, Bill Seratt, Molly and Floyd Shaman, Cheryl Line, Margaret Block, Robert Birdsong, Keith Dockery McLean, Bubba Sullivan, Eddie Mae, Denise DuBois Taylor, Pat Mitchell, Amanda Fuller, Chris Levick, Mary Hendron, John May, Rich Johnson, Karen McFarland, Chris McCafferty, Donna Metz, Fernando Jones and Rev Don Fly for their help and support during our research.

We made and met many friends while researching this book but Rob and Kathy Brown, Greg Woodcox, Tad Pierson, Charlotte Doehler, Ivy McIver and Kat and Steve Angel went way beyond the call of duty.

We are also indebted to Henry Butler, Tabby Thomas, Nathan Williams, Marc Savoy, Rosetta Patton Brown, Eddie Cusic, Charles Evers, Little Milton, Wilson Pickett, Rufus Thomas, Ike Turner, Sam Phillips, Jerry Schilling, Johnny Johnson, Kenny Rice, Gus Thornton, Michael 'Hawkeye' Herman, David 'Honeyboy' Edwards, Michael Frank and Bruce Iglauer for sharing their knowledge of the music of the Blues Highway.

All at Trailblazer have once again done a great job; particular thanks to Bryn Thomas, Henry Stedman, Nick Hill and Heather Glickman. Thanks also to Carol Farley from Portfolio Books for her unflagging encouragement and to Alan Ayres, Dave Tate, David Nicholson, Neema Shah and Paul McLaughlin.

We would also like to thank our families and friends whose support and patience made researching and writing this book possible. We're especially grateful to Jonathan and Judith Longhurst, Michael and Patricia Knight, Lisa Knight, the late Alan Follett and the girls at Granville Road. Finally, I would like to thank my co-researcher, Emma Longhurst, without whom this book would not have been written and with whom researching this book was the happiest journey I've made.

A request

Every effort has been made by the author and the publisher to ensure that the information contained in this book is as up to date and accurate as possible. If you notice any changes or omissions that should be included in the next edition of this book, please write to Richard Knight at Trailblazer (address on p2) or email rich@blues-highway.com.

www.blues-highway.com

Check out our website, blues-highway.com, for book updates, details of how to contact us and for the best jazz, blues, soul and gospel links on the web. Blues-highway.com is being developed into a major music site; log on and let us know what you think.

Contents

Part 3: Mississippi

Part 4: Tennessee

Part 5: Arkansas

Part 6: Missouri

Interviews

Henry Butler New Orleans jazz and blues pianist, p55
Tabby Thomas King of the Swamp blues, p65
Mark Savoy Cajun recording artist, p72
Nathan Williams Zydeco musician, p76
Little Milton Blues musician, p105
Rosetta Patton Brown Charley Patton's daughter, p111
Ike Turner Rock & roll musician, p134
Sam Phillips Founder of Sun Records, p147
Jerry Schilling President of Memphis Music Commission, p157
Johnny Johnson Musical partner of Chuck Berry, p211
Michael 'Hawkeye' Herman Leading blues performer, p238
David 'Honeyboy' Edwards Delta bluesman, p273

Introduction

The story of the birth of American music starts not in New Orleans, where this journey begins, but in West Africa. Men and women from Ghana, Senegal and as far south as Namibia were captured, enslaved and transported to the United States where many were put to work on Southern plantations.

Against this backdrop of forced labor and oppression, slaves found in music temporary escape and a chance to express hope for something better. With most instruments banned, music could be made only with the voice, hands and feet. That music, at first a fusion of the musical traditions of different African tribes and, eventually, a mix of African and New World influences, formed the first tentative notes of what would become jazz in New Orleans and blues in the Mississippi Delta. Jazz and blues went on to underpin the subsequent development of almost all popular music and have played a key role in the cultural and social emancipation of African-Americans.

The voyage from West Africa to New Orleans was, however, just the start of a journey which took jazz and blues around the world. At the end of the bitter Civil War, Southern slaves were freed yet a system of perpetual debt and unfair legislation tied blacks to plantations for many years to come. Slowly, however, the lure of jobs and rights in America's northern cities, most notably Chicago, lured Southern workers north along the 'Blues Highway'. The growing mechanization of the cotton industry prompted yet more to travel as jobs in the South were lost.

A steady stream of north-trekking families grew into the 'Great Migration' which saw hundreds of thousands of black Americans abandon the South during the first half of the twentieth century. By 1943, when Muddy Waters bought his railroad ticket out of Clarksdale, Mississippi, the exodus was reaching its peak.

As these itinerant musicians and families traveled, so they took music with them. Early jazz musicians from New Orleans were among the first to migrate. In the Bronzeville ghetto of Chicago, jazz gave voice to a whole people. Mississippi Delta blues-men roamed north along the Blues Highway, developing a taste for music in every town and city along the way. Memphis, St Louis, Davenport and, finally, Chicago all began to hear the intoxicating rhythms of jazz and blues. That music met other influences and continued to develop. In Memphis, Delta blues, country music from nearby Nashville and Southern gospel music fused to create rock & roll. In Chicago, blues developed into a more refined and urbanized sound and was amplified for the first time to make itself heard in noisy South Side clubs.

The Blues Highway: New Orleans to Chicago traces the development of one people's culture expressed through music and tied, as it is, to one very specific geographic region. That region is the narrow stretch from New Orleans to Chicago as defined by the Mississippi River, Highway 61 and the railroad track.

How to use this book

The Blues Highway: New Orleans to Chicago is a music and travel guide. You'll find detailed and specific information on the music's history, landmarks, venues and artists. But you'll also find detailed information on every aspect of planning and enjoying a successful trip including where to stay, where to eat and even what to see beyond points of musical interest.

Almost all information in this book is found within the relevant sections of the main route guide. So, for example, if you want to read about the roots of zydeco music, you'll need to look in the Lafayette section since that's where zydeco music is played. The planning details in the front section of this book and the 'Who's who of Blues Highway music' in the appendix are the only information sections not contained within the main route guide. There is, of course, a comprehensive index in the back to help you.

MAP KEY

		⛁	Museum	⛴	Ferry service
		▦	Library / bookstore	Ⓜ	Metro station
⌂	Place to stay	⊞	Church	✕	Airport
○	Place to eat	⬛	Cathedral	Λ	Campsite
⊠	Post office	⚘	Casino	⬣Λ	Campsite in State Park
ⓘ	Tourist information	●	Other	🔟	Interstate highway
ⓟ	Music venue	Ⓐ	Bus station	61	US highway
◁	Music landmark	⬛	Railway station	31	State highway

Route planning

This book follows the Blues Highway from south to north for historical reasons and because the story of American music is best told in chronological order. Readers should note, however, that although the book starts in New Orleans and ends in Chicago, it could just as easily be followed from north to south. In fact, each city is tackled in adequate depth to allow readers to use the book for just one city or just one section of the route.

Although music lovers will find every section of the route interesting to explore, several specific route options can be recommended for readers unable to follow the entire Blues Highway. The whole trip could be made in three fairly comfortable weeks but it's a matter of personal choice. Some readers will find three weeks just enough time to check out New Orleans while others will cover the 1000 miles from New Orleans to Chicago in days.

New Orleans to Baton Rouge and Lafayette

The **Louisiana jazz and zydeco trail** from New Orleans to Baton Rouge and on to Lafayette is a great chance to explore the routes of three original American music genres – jazz, zydeco and Cajun music – and allows visitors to soak up the swampy Southern atmosphere.

Early jazz developed in **New Orleans** and the city, forever synonymous with that style of music, has done much to trumpet its noisy past. For jazz lovers, a visit to New Orleans is something of a pilgrimage. New Orleans highlights include: the French Quarter; Congo Square and Louis Armstrong Park; the St Louis cemeteries; the Old US Mint jazz museum; Algiers Point; and, most important of all, the city's many jazz clubs.

Baton Rouge is a quieter, more conservative town known more for blues than jazz. Local stars and out-of-towners keep the city's few good blues bars roaring most weekends.

Lafayette, capital of French-speaking Cajun country, is the place where both zydeco and Cajun music grew up. Cajun music –

a white, folk tradition – is closely tied to the Cajun identity and you'll find music being listened and danced to all over this exuberant town. Zydeco music, a black blues-influenced style of music using accordions and washboards, is a more aggressive, driving sound. Lafayette highlights include: the Vermilionville cultural center; the Acadian Village reconstruction of an old-style Cajun community; the town's swinging restaurant-dancehalls; and zydeco clubs.

Allow at least three nights in New Orleans, one in Baton Rouge and two in Lafayette.

Vicksburg to Memphis and Nashville

The **Mississippi Delta**, Vicksburg to Memphis, is, for many, the most important cradle of musical development in the States. Vast, stark and gripping, Mississippi is a culturally rich state where blues lovers can feel the spirit of Robert Johnson at every lonely crossroads. The Delta – not a geographic entity but a cultural one – is said to be bound by Catfish Row, Vicksburg to the south and the lobby of the Peabody Hotel in Memphis to the north – a distance of 250 miles. From Vicksburg, Highway 61 passes through Greenville, Cleveland and Clarksdale before rolling into Memphis. There are several short diversions from Highway 61 which lead to other important blues sites like state capital Jackson or cotton center Greenwood. Other Delta highlights within easy reach include Indianola, Morgan City, Avalon, Moorhead, Holly Ridge, Leland, Tutwiler and Helena, Arkansas. It's not all neglected grave markers and cottonfields, however. Blues is still lived and played in the Delta; this book will help you find tucked away juke joints and music clubs where raw Delta blues still thrives.

Memphis is itself another enormously important cultural and musical hub. Here, blues was recorded and distributed beyond the Delta. This is also where blues became an ingredient in rockabilly and rock & roll. After blues stars Howlin' Wolf and BB King passed through Sam Phillips' Sun Records studio, rock &

What music where?

Jazz
New Orleans, St Louis, Davenport, Chicago

Blues
Mississippi Delta, Memphis, St Louis, Chicago

Rock & roll
Memphis, St Louis

Soul
Memphis

Gospel
New Orleans, Memphis, Chicago

Cajun
Lafayette

Zydeco
Lafayette

Country
Nashville

rollers like Elvis Presley, Jerry Lee Lewis and Johnny Cash made their names here. The city also made a massive contribution to soul music through the record labels Stax and Hi.

The current music scene in Memphis is as lively as ever; the bars on Beale Street will keep you rocking all night. Memphis highlights include: Beale Street; Sun Studio; Graceland; the National Civil Rights Museum; Al Green's Full Gospel Tabernacle; the Memphis Music Hall of Fame; Memphis Rock 'n' Soul Museum; WC Handy's house; and Jerry Lee Lewis' ranch.

From Memphis, you might also choose to take in **Nashville**, home of country music. Nashville, an engaging and ultra-modern city, is nicknamed 'Music City USA' because of the number of record labels and studios based here. Sometimes it feels like everyone in town is trying to make a buck in the music business. There's live music everywhere. Main highlights include: the Grand Ole Opry; the Ryman Auditorium; Music Row; the Country Music Hall of Fame; RCA Studio B; and scores of downtown music bars. Vicksburg to Memphis – or vice versa – could be driven in a day but four days would be enough to get a good feel for the place.

Allow at last three nights in Memphis and two in Nashville.

Chicago to Davenport and St Louis

A **northern tour** from Chicago to Davenport and St Louis covers the later stages of the Great Migration and, musically, the places where jazz and blues came of age.

In **Chicago** itself blues was adapted by masters like Big Bill Broonzy and Muddy Waters to become the roots of modern rock. A little earlier, jazz was honed by ex-New Orleanians like Louis Armstrong and 'King' Oliver. Today Chicago is blasted nightly by great blues clubs all over town but particularly on the city's sprawling South Side. Highlights include: Bronzeville; blues and jazz clubs; soul food; the 'Maxwell Street' market; the Blues Heaven Foundation; the 'Loop'; and all the more traditional tourist highlights from the Sears Tower to the Lakefront.

Davenport, Iowa, a 175-mile drive west from Chicago, has an important place in the story of jazz; this was home to Bix Beiderbecke. It's also the point where this book picks up Highway 61 heading south or leaves it heading north. Davenport highlights include: the Beiderbecke family home; the Col and Danceland ballrooms; and Arsenal Island.

Further south, **St Louis** was a key staging post for bluesmen heading north to Chicago. Indeed, the city is even better known for its role as a staging post during the American expansion westward. With a deep jazz and blues legacy – Miles Davis, Scott Joplin and Chuck Berry all got started here – St Louis today boasts one of the most lively music scenes anywhere along the Blues Highway. An impressive stock of local talent keeps bars and clubs pumping night after night. Highlights include: Scott Joplin's House; the St Louis Walk of Fame; the Gateway Arch; the Soulard district with its funky clubs and venues; and the University Loop.

Allow at least four nights for Chicago, one for Davenport and three for St Louis.

When to go

Climate

The Blues Highway weaves through two distinct climatic zones: that of the sub-tropical South and the continental Midwest (see temperature and rainfall charts opposite).

The Southern states, particularly Louisiana and Mississippi, are hot and humid all year. Summers can be ferocious and winters mild. New Orleans, particularly, is famous for its stiflingly hot and sticky summers when, in July and August, the intense humidity can be almost choking. Such steamy nights seem to add to the city's lazy and licentious air. Thunderstorms regularly alleviate the dripping humidity. Hurricane season lasts from July to October. Since damaging hurricanes are rare this isn't a reason to stay at home – just keep an eye on long-range weather forecasts. When hurricanes hit they are usually powerful but short-lived.

The continental Midwest sees a greater change between seasons. Summers are dry and can be very hot while winters are often freezing and snowy. Even when bitterly cold, however, winter weather in the Midwest is frequently brightened by clear blues skies.

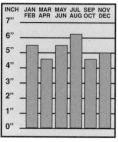

NEW ORLEANS
RAINFALL (INCHES)

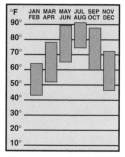

TEMPERATURE (MAX/MIN °F)

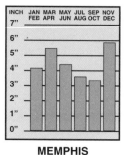

MEMPHIS
RAINFALL (INCHES)

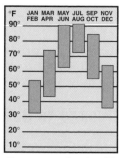

TEMPERATURE (MAX/MIN °F)

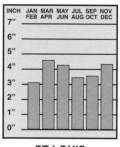

ST LOUIS
RAINFALL (INCHES)

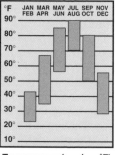

TEMPERATURE (MAX/MIN °F)

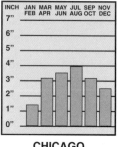

CHICAGO
RAINFALL (INCHES)

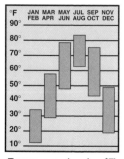

TEMPERATURE (MAX/MIN °F)

Festivals and events

The Blues Highway is famous for its festivals and revelry so it's a good idea to time your trip to coincide with an event. The following section highlights some of the major annual festivals along the Blues Highway. Hotel prices tend to go up markedly when there's something going on in town. You'll find more information about these events on local tourist information websites (see p23).

Note that dates given are approximate and may change from year to year.

January
● **January 8 – Elvis Presley's Birthday, Memphis.** A one-day festival to celebrate the birth of 'the King'; held at Graceland.

February
● **February 1 – Nashville Entertainment Association Extravaganza.** A three-day music festival designed to expose new talent to record label scouts.
● **Shrove Tuesday – Mardi Gras, New Orleans** (see p34). Over 60 parades pass through the French Quarter as a part of a 12-day carnival and drinking frenzy which ends the minute Lent kicks in.

March
● **March 23 – Louisiana Crawfish Festival, New Orleans.** Two days of fairground rides, crawfish cook-offs and live music.

April
● **April 5 – French Quarter Festival, New Orleans**. A two-day music festival staged in thirteen venues around the French Quarter; includes the 'world's largest jazz brunch'.
● **April 18 – GM Gospel Week, Nashville.** Four days of music, seminars and workshops for fans and musicians; climax is a Hall of Fame banquet.
● **April 25 – Festival International Louisiane, Lafayette.** This four-day event is the largest Francophone festival in the States. Founded in 1987, it features traditional Cajun music, cooking, dancing and story-telling.
● **April 28 – New Orleans Jazz and Heritage Festival** (see p43). Held over two weekends at the end of April and early May, 'Jazzfest' is the main event in the New Orleans calendar after Mardi Gras; expect a galaxy of local and international jazz stars.
● **April 29 – Nashville Music Festival.** This one-night benefit concert staged in the Ryman Auditorium draws top country music acts.

May
● **May 5 – Breaux Bridge Crawfish Festival** (see p75). Messy crawfish-eating contests, zydeco music and the famous crawfish queen make this weekend-long event a lively celebration of the coveted crustacean.
● **May 8 – Zoo Blues, Jackson.** A one-day concert held on the meadow at Jackson Zoo featuring nationally-known blues performers.
● **May (second weekend) – Crossroads Blues Festival, Rosedale** (see p122). A two-day blues festival held in honor of Robert Johnson.
● **May 15 – Quad Cities Jazz Festival.** Three days of top jazz, eating and revelry in the hometown of Bix Beiderbecke – not to be confused with the 'Bixfest' itself.
● **May 19 – Jubilee!Jam Music Festival, Jackson.** Jackson's biggest music festival, Jubilee!Jam presents blues, gospel and soul stars in a series of concerts held over three days.

Festivals and events

May (cont'd)

- **May 25 – WC Handy Awards, Memphis** (see p150). The Blues Foundation presents its annual Handy Awards in the Orpheum Theater, Memphis, in this blues version of the Oscars.
- **May 27 – Zydeco Extravaganza, Lafayette.** Held the Sunday before Memorial Day, this one-day concert features some of the best zydeco acts in Louisiana.

June

- **June 2 – Chicago Gospel Festival.** A city-funded free two-day gospel music showcase held outdoors in Grant Park – the first in a series of impressive free music events organized by the City of Chicago.
- **June 2 – Medgar Evers Homecoming, Mississippi** (see p102). BB King and Little Milton play near Jackson to celebrate the life of assassinated civil rights campaigner Medgar Evers.
- **June 8 – Chicago Blues Music Festival** (see p247). This three-day blues extravaganza is one the best in the States; expect to hear some the biggest names in blues.
- **June 14 – International Country Music Fan Fair, Nashville.** A week-long series of country music concerts sponsored by the Grand Ole Opry and the Country Music Association.
- **June 14 – Juneteenth Heritage Jazz Festival, St Louis.** Jazz, blues, gospel and even reggae are represented during this four-day music festival timed to celebrate the end of slavery.

July

- **July 1 – Chicago Country Music Festival.** Grant Park plays host to a two-day country music event featuring some of Nashville's finest.
- **July 6 – Mississippi Valley Blues Festival, Davenport** (see p239). A weekend-long festival featuring some of the most famous names on the current blues circuit.
- **July 15 – Blues on the Fox Blues Festival, Aurora.** A two-day blues showcase presented from several stages in downtown Aurora, a suburb of Chicago. Expect some well-known performers from the Chicago circuit.
- **July 19 – Bix Beiderbecke Memorial Jazz Festival, Davenport** (see p239). Four days of classic jazz and related events to celebrate the life of one-time local Leon 'Bix' Beiderbecke.

August

- **First weekend in August – Sunflower River Blues and Gospel Festival, Clarksdale.** A weekend of classic Delta blues in the one-time hometown of John Lee Hooker and Muddy Waters.
- **August 5 – Peavine Blues Awards, Cleveland** (see p124). The annual Peavine Awards for excellence in Delta blues are presented at Delta State University.
- **August 10 – Elvis Week, Memphis.** A week-long celebration of Elvis Presley's life on the anniversary of his death; expect candlelit vigils at Graceland and music events on Beale Street.
- **August 31 – Chicago Jazz Festival.** International jazz stars perform over several days in Grant Park.

September

- **September 1 – Memphis Music and Heritage Festival.** Two days of music and art held at the Center for Southern Folklore.
- **September 1 – Big Muddy Blues and Roots Festival, St Louis.** The Laclede's Landing district hosts blues bands on five stages over two days.

Festivals and events

September (cont'd)

● **Third Saturday in September – Mississippi Delta Blues and Heritage Festival, Greenville** (see p118). The third Saturday in September sees Greenville inundated for its annual blues festival – one of the best in the States. This celebration of Delta blues features top-flight acts and has been going strong since 1978.

● **September 15 – Baton Rouge Blues Week.** Several downtown venues collaborate to present a week of blues.

● **September 21 – Chicago World Music Festival.** A 10-day series of world music events held at various locations around Chicago.

● **September 24 – Farish Street Festival, Jackson.** The historic Farish Street area of Jackson celebrates its past over two days; features live music, food and art exhibitions.

October

● **October 6 – King Biscuit Blues Festival, Helena** (see p180). Held over the first weekend before Columbus Day, the King Biscuit Blues Festival is one of the best-known in the world. Sleepy Helena bulges to absorb international acts and thousands of fans.

● **October 15 – Grand Ole Opry Birthday Celebrations, Nashville.** A three-day birthday for the Grand Ole Opry during which Opry stars stage several concerts including a special bluegrass roots gig.

November

● **November 16 – WC Handy Birthday Celebrations/Bluestock, Memphis.** A celebration of Handy's life organized by the WC Handy Museum; the event coincides with 'Bluestock', a two-day collection of concerts on Beale Street to celebrate Memphis music.

Costs

Transport costs aside (these are covered in the 'Getting around' section), the Blues Highway is a relatively inexpensive destination. **Hotels and motels** are good value – particularly so in the rural South and Midwest. Expect to pay anywhere from $30 upward for a double room (but double that in cities) or $10-15 for an RV pitch. Hostel dorm beds usually go for around $10-12. Main tourist draws New Orleans, Memphis and Chicago are, predictably, more expensive. Indeed, cheap places to stay are quite difficult to find in New Orleans and very difficult to find in Chicago.

You'll find **food** plentiful and cheap. Just $12 a head will buy a decent meal in any town and, in fact, it would be difficult to spend more in many of the smaller towns along the Blues Highway. For $25 a day per person, you could eat quite well but with few frills. Allow at least $40 a day in larger towns and cities. **Music venue cover charges** – a far more important expense – are generally around the $5 mark unless a well-known act is playing.

Getting there

Direct flights to Chicago are fairly easy to find but to get to New Orleans, Memphis, Nashville or even St Louis, international passengers will need to connect. European flights normally connect at southern hubs Atlanta or Dallas Fort Worth. Flights from Asia usually stopover in Hawaii while flights from Australasia touch down on the West Coast. Once in the US, the comprehensive internal flight network makes getting to the Blues Highway straightforward. The three main **high seasons** for travel are July and August and the Easter and Christmas periods. Airfares will leap at these times. April and November are often the cheapest months.

From within North America

New Orleans, Baton Rouge, Lafayette, Jackson, Memphis, Nashville, St Louis, Davenport and Chicago are all connected by internal air services.

How much?
Prices can be low and flights frequent although it pays to book ahead. Expect to pay $200-$300 for most hops but that can turn into a $1000 bombshell if you expect to grab a seat at the last minute. Smaller airports – like those at Baton Rouge, Lafayette, Jackson and Davenport – are most frequently used by high-paying business customers so can be more expensive. Most airlines offer apex fares which can bring the price down but it's worth trying discount flight specialists and local travel agents for good deals. Students could try youth travel specialists Council Travel (☎ 800-2COUNCIL; 🖥 www.counciltravel.com). In Canada, try Travelcuts (☎ 800-667-2887; 🖥 www.travelcuts.com). Fares will be more expensive around public holidays and major events.

Which airlines?
Air Canada (☎ 800-776-3000); **AirTrain Airlines** (☎ 800-247-8726); **American Eagle** (☎ 800-433-7300); **Canadian Airlines** (☎ 800-247-7000); **Delta Airlines** (☎ 800-221-1212); **Northwest Airlink** (☎ 800-225-2525); **Southwest Airlines** (☎ 800-435-9792); **USAirways** (☎ 800-428-4322).

From Britain and Europe

Intense competition on trans-Atlantic air routes has made flying to the States from Europe relatively inexpensive. London, Paris and Amsterdam are major gateways.

How much?
Return prices start at around £250 and climb quickly from there. While a £250 ticket to Chicago is a distinct possibility – if you shop around, at least – New

Orleans will most likely cost twice that. It usually pays to buy a complete ticket – including any internal transfers – rather than arranging your own add-ons. Discount flightsellers and travel agents regularly offer better deals than the airlines themselves. Try usitCampus (☎ 0870-240 1010; 🖥 www.usit campus.co.uk), STA (08701-600599; 🖥 www.statravel.co.uk) or the Flight Centre (☎ 020-8780 9411).

Which airlines?

Air France (UK ☎ 0845-0845 111; France ☎ 0820-829829; USA ☎ 800-237-2747); **American Airlines** (UK ☎ 08457-789789; USA ☎ 800-433-7300); **British Airways** (UK ☎ 0845-7733377; USA ☎ 800-AIRWAYS); **Continental** (UK ☎ 0800-776 464; USA ☎ 800-231-0856); **Delta Airlines** (UK ☎ 0800-414 767; USA ☎ 800-221-1212); **KLM** (UK ☎ 08705-074074; Netherlands ☎ 20-47477747; USA ☎ 800-447-4747); **Lufthansa** (Germany ☎ 069-255 255; USA ☎ 800-645-3880); **Northwest** (see KLM); **United Airlines** (UK ☎ 0845-8444 777; USA ☎ 800-241-6522); **USAirways** (UK ☎ 0845-600 3300; USA ☎ 800-245-4882); **Virgin Atlantic** (UK ☎ 01293-747747; USA ☎ 800-862-8621).

From Asia

Hong Kong and Tokyo are the two major Asian gateways for flights to the States. Flights from either city to America normally involve a stopover or perhaps a connection at Honolulu in Hawaii.

How much?

Return prices range upwards from around US$1500 – that's 180,000 yen or HK$12,000 – although much cheaper discounted fares are often advertised in the press. As always, it's worth checking out travel agents as well as contacting airlines direct. STA (☎ 03-5391 2922; 🖥 www.statravel.co.jp) has a branch in Japan. In Hong Kong, try Thomas Cook (🖥 www.thomascook.com.hk) or Harvest Travel Services (☎ 852-25117189; 🖥 www.travel.com.hk).

Which airlines?

China Airlines (Hong Kong ☎ 852-2868 2299; Tokyo 813-3436 1661; USA ☎ 800-227-5118); **Japan Air Lines** (Tokyo ☎ 01-2025 5931; USA ☎ 800-525-3663); and **United Airlines** (Tokyo ☎ 01-2011-4466; USA ☎ 800-241-6522).

From Australasia

Getting from Australia or New Zealand to any of the main cities on the Blues Highway means changing planes in Los Angeles or San Francisco.

How much?

Return low-season prices from Sydney to LA hover around the A$1600 mark. Special deal 'add-ons' are sometimes available to extend the flight to Chicago for around A$100. From Auckland, expect to pay around NZ$1900 to get to the West Coast. As always, cheaper fares and deals are sometimes available through travel agents so it's worth shopping around. Try the ubiquitous STA

(☎ 1300-360 960; 💻 www.statravel.com.au) in Australia or Budget Travel (☎ 379 2099; 💻 www.budgettravel.co.nz) in New Zealand. Also look for good value flights advertised in the weekend newspapers.

Which airlines?

Air New Zealand (NZ ☎ 0800-737000; USA ☎ 800-262-1234); **Qantas** (Australia ☎ 13 13 13; USA ☎ 800-227-4500) and **United Airlines** (Australia ☎ 02-9292 4111; USA ☎ 800-241-6522).

Getting around

By car

The United States is one of the most car-dependent nations in the world so, for complete freedom, **car rental** is recommended over public transport. Rental agencies are listed separately for each town along the Blues Highway. Expect to pay around $40 a day or $160 a week for a basic economy car with an unlimited mileage allowance.

A state rental tax of around six per cent will be levied on top of that price. If you pick up the car from an airport, a three per cent airport tax and a small airport surcharge will also appear on the bill. If you plan to drop off the car at a different location from that where you picked it up, you will be asked to pay a 'drop off fee'. **Gas** is the other unavoidable expense. Fortunately, gas is far cheaper in the US than in Europe. At the time of writing, the going rate was hovering at $1.50 per gallon.

National car rental websites

💻 www.alamo.com
💻 www.avis.com
💻 www.budget.com
💻 www.dollar.com
💻 www.enterprise.com
💻 www.hertz.com
💻 www.nationalcar.com
💻 www.thrifty.com

Drivers will need adequate insurance. Your own policy or even your credit card company might protect you but you will need to find out from the rental company exactly what's covered and what excess you might be obliged to pay in the event of an accident. If you're not properly covered – or even if you're not sure – take out the collision damage waiver (CDW) or loss damage waiver (LDW) which will cover you. Air conditioning is an essential extra in the summer. The minimum age for car rental is 21 and the price is usually hiked up for drivers under 25. Renters will need to show a major credit card when collecting the car.

Another option is to sign up with a **drive-away** company (see p31). Drive-away cars are owned by people who need their vehicle delivered from one place to another – usually far apart – but don't want to drive it there themselves. They ask a drive-away firm to find a suitable driver to deliver the car for them. On the plus side, drivers only pay for gas. On the down side, drivers are expected to keep going for eight hours a day so can't dawdle or roam around. For this reason, drive-aways are hardly ideal for exploring the Blues Highway unless you're happy to travel the route without stopping. Drive-away firms are listed in the New Orleans and Chicago chapters.

By RV

For flexibility – and a glimpse of an entire hidden culture which exists on America's freeways – rent an RV or, to Europeans, a 'mobile home'. These multi-wheeled behemoths allow you to travel at your own pace with your home right there with you. It's an enjoyable way to travel and, thanks to the outstanding state park system, it's never hard to find somewhere attractive to camp for the night. The only logistical downside, in fact, is that your RV will also be your car so if you drive into town to check out music joints you'll have to leave your worldly possessions parked outside. Even so, 'RV-ing' is a highly recommended method of traveling the Blues Highway. RV parks and campgrounds are included in this book.

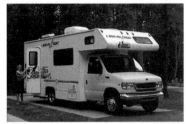

RV rental is fairly expensive. A standard RV – usually a 21-foot truck with enough space to sleep four or five and with an impressive array of mod-cons – will cost between $800-1000 per week. Special offers can make this much cheaper. You'll also have to pay about $85 for a vehicle preparation kit, $35 for personal provisions like pots and pans and $18 per day for the best available insurance which is a necessary expense. That price includes 1000 miles so you might also need to pay for extra 'mileage packs'. One final expense to consider is that these giant machines guzzle fuel. Remember that campgrounds are cheap, however, so you will save some money on places to stay. Cruise America (☎ 800-327-7799) monopolizes the US RV rental business. British readers should contact Hemmingways (☎ 01737-842735), an excellent and very helpful company which organizes RV rental in the States.

By bus

Greyhound Bus Lines (☎ 800-229-9424) runs coaches between almost every major town and city in the States. The comprehensive network and relatively inexpensive ticket prices make up for Greyhound's other shortcomings. While the buses are fairly efficient, long haul journeys are something of an endurance test.

Greyhound serves New Orleans to Memphis (10 hours, $42), Memphis to St Louis (six hours, $44), St Louis to Davenport (seven hours, $62) and Davenport to Chicago (three to four hours, $29). Greyhound bypasses the quiet Mississippi Delta stopping instead in Jackson, Mississippi. To follow Highway 61 through the Delta, use Delta Bus Lines (☎ 662-335 2144) which

WATERFORD

NO

lays on a return trip from Memphis to Baton Rouge once a day. A one-way fare is $66. If you plan to roam further, you might consider buying a Greyhound 'Ameripass' which allows unlimited travel in the States for 60 days for about $540. Ameripasses can be used on Delta Bus Lines.

By train

Amtrak (☎ 800-USA-RAIL), America's national rail network, provides a very limited passenger service. One train, however, follows the route described in this book. Indeed, while many migrant bluesmen traveled north along Highway 61, many more jumped on the Illinois Central railroad line.

The *City of New Orleans* Amtrak train runs through New Orleans, Memphis, St Louis and on to Chicago. The train doesn't go into St Louis but an Amtrak bus service from Carbondale, Illinois, makes the connection. If you take the journey in one go it lasts nearly a day. Trains leave New Orleans at 2.05pm everyday and pull into Chicago at 9.20 the following morning. Tickets are $180.

If you would rather allow time to explore, the *City of New Orleans* route can be broken down into New Orleans to Memphis ($44) and Memphis to St Louis ($69). From St Louis it makes sense to abandon the *City of New Orleans* since faster services connect St Louis to Chicago ($41) three times a day.

By paddlesteamer

Jazz first floated north on paddlesteamers when bands like that of Fate Marable on the Streckfus Line entertained passengers as they cruised up the Mississippi River. Stars as bright as Louis Armstrong and 'Baby' Dodds worked the paddlesteamers and, it's said, Bix Beiderbecke first heard jazz when a Streckfus boat pulled in at Davenport, Iowa. So if you want to travel north the same way jazz once did, you'll need to hop aboard a paddlesteamer. While the Mississippi River is now used to more modern vessels, the Delta Steamboat Company (☎ 504-586-0631, 800-543-7637), based in New Orleans, operates three steamboats for 3- to 11-day cruises. The three boats, *Delta Queen*, *Magnificent Mississippi Queen* and *Grand America Queen*, are beautiful and elegant craft which make a good job of recreating the golden era of steamboatin'. For more information on the Delta Steamboat Company's cruises (see p31).

Hotel price codes

Most US hotels use a fluid pricing system which means the cost of a room varies depending on the season, the day of the week and, to some extent, demand. Frequent special offers confuse the situation further. Rather than quote firm prices that may not apply, this book places hotels and motels in price bands:

❶ – $10-25 ❷ – $26-50
❸ – $51-85 ❹ – $86-120
❺ – $121-180 ❻ – $181-250
❼ – $251+

Prices are per night for a double room.

Information for non-US visitors

Visas and red tape

Non-US travelers will need a **visa** to enter the States with the exception of Australian, Belgian, British, Danish, Dutch, Finn, French, German, Italian, Japanese, New Zealand, Norwegian, Swedish and Swiss nationals whose countries are part of the **visa waiver program**. The program allows stays of 90 days or less without a visa. All foreign visitors are required to fill out and keep an **I-94 arrival/departure record form**. These will normally be handed out on the plane before you land in the States. You will also need a **passport** valid for at least six months after your stay. Other important documents are your **travel insurance policy** – crucial in the litigation-happy US – and a **driver's license** if you intend to hire a car or RV. Drinkers who look remotely in touch with their youth will need to carry some form of **picture ID** in order to buy booze.

Money

The American **currency** is the US dollar ($) which is divided into 100 cents. A 'quarter' is 25 cents, a 'dime' 10 cents and a 'nickel' five cents. Since ATM machines are scattered across almost every street corner, the easiest way for travelers to carry cash is simply to take a credit or debit card from a main international network and withdraw money as it's needed. **Tipping** is a way of life in the States where many waiting and bar staff rely almost solely on tips for their income. One is expected to tip generously and regularly for meals – perhaps 20 per cent – and smaller amounts for cabs, drinks and bell hops.

Exchange rates are as follows:
$1 = Canadian $1.55
$1 = Euro 1.20
$1 = UK£0.70
$1 = Japan ¥120
$1 = Australia $1.90
$1 = New Zealand $2.20

Further information

Since the American tourist trade has a fairly confused system of marketing itself abroad, the best place to find information is online:

Louisiana
💻 www.crt.state.la.us

New Orleans
💻 www.neworleanscvb.com

Lafayette
💻 www.lafayettetravel.com

Mississippi
💻 www.state.ms.us

Jackson
💻 www.visitjackson.com

Tennessee
💻 www.state.tn.us

Memphis
💻 www.memphistravel.com

Nashville
💻 www.musiccityusa.com

Arkansas
💻 www.state.ar.us

Missouri
💻 www.state.mo.us

St Louis
💻 www.explorestlouis.com

Iowa
💻 www.state.ia.us

Quad Cities
💻 www.visitquadcities.com

Illinois
💻 www.state.il.us

Chicago
💻 www.choosechicago.com

Clubs, bars and juke joints

This isn't the place for a potted history of the civil rights movement but it's impossible to understand the origin of blues, jazz and other American music without knowing something about the titanic struggle which African-Americans faced in their fight for equality. Even today, looking deep into the history of black American music means staring into the ugly and often shocking realm of racism.

The South has a reputation for racism and Southern whites are often portrayed as bigoted 'rednecks' in films and on television. In reality, of course, this is itself an unfair caricature. That said, the long history of tension and mistrust between blacks and whites in the South – and, less obviously, north of the Mason-Dixie line – has yet to be forgotten. In truth, it has yet to be resolved. In the Southern states particularly, one finds towns where the black and white populations seem to share little. In such an environment it's hardly surprising to find that rough and ready blues clubs – 'juke joints' – are seldom visited by white people and those who do venture in often feel uncomfortable. This apprehension is understandable but almost always unwarranted.

While it sounds childish to talk in such simple racial terms, however, white readers will need to be sensible. Be aware that you're in someone else's neighborhood and that, frankly, African-American neighborhoods in the US aren't usually on the best side of town. Common sense suggests parking nearby, staying out of trouble and leaving before closing time. This book has omitted only the very roughest joints on the Blues Highway; some pretty disreputable places remain because, quite simply, that's where you'll find the best music. Don't be scared to visit juke joints but, equally, remember that a long history of discrimination and its consequential resentment is hard to overlook.

Louisiana 2

Sweltering Louisiana is not a typical slice of America. Since the French settled the state in 1682, Louisiana has been a place where competing cultures have clashed to create food, language, music and a certain spirit which is unique. The swampy, sultry landscape helps foster Louisiana's exotic air. New Orleans is, for many, the reason to fly south to Louisiana. A truly great city and the source of jazz, New Orleans never disappoints. But the state has far more to offer. Lafayette, capital of Acadiana, is just as exciting. Here Cajun culture and music thrives and zydeco, another original musical form, epitomizes Louisiana's famous *joie de vivre*.

New Orleans

Some cities can be summoned to the imagination by a single sight, smell or skyline. New Orleans can be conjured by one sound – jazz. Ancient, old and new collided to form jazz. That same electric mix gives New Orleans its edge today. No other city in America can boast such intrigue or romance. And no amount of packaging or airbrushing of the 'New Orleans experience' can mask the city's decadent flavor.

History

New Orleans' roots date back to 1682 when French explorer La Salle claimed Louisiana for Louis XIV. In 1717 Scotsman John Law negotiated a royal charter to exploit the region and, one year later, instructed another Frenchman, Jean-Baptiste le Moyne, Sieur de Bienville, to found the settlement of New Orleans.

Law then set about promoting and populating the colony by projecting in Europe a flattering image of Louisiana. Law's publicity of New Orleans was far from accurate; disease was rife and the swampy heat made living hard. But French, German and Swiss settlers began to pour in and the population was further boosted by an influx of freed prisoners, including a good number of whores, and thousands of blacks kidnapped in Africa by French slave traders.

The descendants of white immigrants, many of whom strove to maintain a form of French tradition, became known as Creoles. Two other 'new races' developed as blacks and whites mixed, albeit illegally: Quadroons were one-fourth black, Octoroons one-eighth. These part-black descendants of non-Americans became 'black Creoles'. Many black Creoles emulated whites, so creating their own social niche which survived until after the Civil War.

In 1762, Louisiana and New Orleans were transferred from French to Spanish ownership, so adding another cultural influence to the already heady mixture. France had gained little from its control of Louisiana and used the territory to make Spain an ally in her war against Britain. Spain retained control for 41 years, despite a rumble of resentment and rebellion from the Creoles, until 1803 when Napoleon took back the territory following an agreement made between France and Spain in 1800.

The Louisiana Purchase

Understanding the importance of the Mississippi and its mouth to the westward expansion of the United States, President Thomas Jefferson had by this time begun working towards taking control of the Louisiana territory. His ambition coincided with a growing feeling in Paris that Louisiana was an unnecessary financial burden and one which France would not want to fight to protect.

So when Jefferson made an offer to buy Louisiana, he found Napoleon willing to do business. The United States bought the territory for $15 million and on 20 December 1803 – just under a month after Spain had handed control to France – Louisiana and with it New Orleans came under American control. Louisiana became part of the union nine years later in 1812. In the same year the British made several unsuccessful attempts to seize control of New Orleans.

After the 'Louisiana Purchase', an increasing number of Americans traveled down the Mississippi to New Orleans to find work. Local Creoles resented the invasion and banned Americans from the French Quarter, forcing them to live west of what would become Canal Street. One effect of the division was to protect the French Quarter's European feel.

During this time, blacks in Louisiana, though still abused and exploited, enjoyed certain rights not available in other parts of the United States. Slaves could gather on Sundays to form markets and practise African music and religion. The best known of these markets took place at Congo Square.

In 1861, when America descended into civil war over the issue of slavery, New Orleans was quickly occupied by Union soldiers who remained there, in control of the mouth of the Mississippi, till the end of the war in 1865. The aftermath of the war saw slavery abolished and suffrage extended first to a limited number of blacks and later, after much violent opposition, to all.

On the face of it, the lot of African-Americans was much improved. In practice, however, this post-civil war period marked the start of a long and bloody chapter in the relationship between blacks and whites in Louisiana. White supremacist groups sprang up across the South and blacks became subject to 'Jim Crow' legislation which forced humiliating segregation on all people of color. At the end of the nineteenth century, this charged backdrop gave birth to a then fledgling civil rights movement which would have to wait until 1954 to see an end to Jim Crow laws.

Another important but arguably shameful slice of New Orleanian history was tied up with prostitution. The city had long been famed for the extent of its moral depravation when, in 1897, a city leader named Sidney Story proposed an area of legalized prostitution which became known as 'Storyville' or 'the District'. Here anything went as brothels of all kinds sprang up to meet the varied needs of Storyville clients.

For many, this was a dangerous and desperate place. For early jazzmen, however, this was home. Storyville was officially closed in 1917 but continued to please its patrons, illegally, for many years. In the forties, however, large parts of the area were destroyed. A housing project now stands on the site.

New Orleans today

New Orleans has seen much-needed urban renewal in more recent years. That renewal has been fuelled in part by a growing income from tourism. An oil boom gave the local economy a decent boost in the eighties and a black mayor, 'Dutch' Morial, was elected in 1978. (His son, Marc Morial, is the current mayor.) Despite the addition of a space-age superdome and the all-American towering skyline, however, New Orleans has retained much of its charm. Storyville is dead, but this is still the city of Mardi Gras and music in the streets. It's a good-time, hard-drinking town with a suitably high crime rate and appropriately sultry feel. It is also, of course, the city where jazz grew up; and that, for readers of this book, is the real reason New Orleans is on the map.

History of Jazz in New Orleans

The exact origin of jazz is obscured by time and conflicting accounts. But one thing is certain – it was developed in New Orleans, a city which has been immersed in music for hundreds of years. Of course not all the great names in jazz have emanated from the Big Easy; but, over the years, the city has yielded a remarkable number of true jazz innovators.

From the last years of the nineteenth century when the legendary Buddy Bolden was said to 'call his chill'un home' with a trumpet sound that could be heard 14 miles away on a clear night, to today's jazz scene and latter-day masters Nicholas Payton, Lillian Boutté and the multi-talented Marsalis family, the roll-call of musicians bred in and around New Orleans is, to the true *aficionado* of jazz music, little short of awe-inspiring.

The very street-names in the old city are redolent of the early years of jazz. There are the blues of Basin, Burgundy, Canal and Franklin Streets, the echoes of festive times in South Rampart Street Parade and of haunting melancholy in Perdido. And it was from and in those same streets that a galaxy of great jazz names was to find expression in the music they played and developed. The likes of Ferdinand 'Jelly Roll' Morton, Joe 'King' Oliver, Louis Armstrong, Sidney Bechet, Freddie Keppard, Edward 'Kid' Ory, Johnny Dodds, his younger brother Warren (forever known as 'Baby'), Bunk Johnson, George Lewis and Omer Simeon all pioneered jazz in New Orleans.

The city in which they grew up was a rough one. Crime, violence, prostitution and gambling were part of everyday life. It was a licentious place made exciting by its intermingling of races, creeds, colors and life-styles. To grow up in such an environment was to grow up quickly; survival owed more to low cunning, chance, petty criminality and fleetness of foot than it did to education or the guidance of a good family.

Out beyond the general bustle and hum of the city's Red Light area (Storyville) and the French Quarter lived the moneyed classes in their expensive antebellum mansions around Lake Pontchartrain and the Garden District. There they were shielded from the heat and humidity, the crime and grime and the utter poverty of black New Orleans. The less adventurous of them were, at the same time, deprived of the parades and carnivals, the street-dances and the musical 'cutting contests'. It was from that latter environment that jazz grew.

The way in which that all came about has been the subject of many books and this is the place to do no more than sketch the outlines. However, it is relevant to point out that there was a measure of cultural intermingling between even the most distant points of the class and race divide in those early days of twentieth-century New Orleans. The most obvious meeting point was in music.

Musical fusion

In pre-Civil War New Orleans blacks and whites mixed, at least musically, to a greater degree than anywhere else in the South. Quadroon Balls attracted white men in search of black Creole mistresses, apparently more advanced in the art of sexual pleasure. Black musicians on the other hand would occasionally provide music at white dances. This was no racial Utopia, but it was at least a form of social contact.

Black Creoles occupied at that time a precise place in New Orleanian society; neither black nor white, they straddled two polarized cultures. Most black Creoles tried to emulate white culture to distance themselves from the far less fortunate black population which, at that time, was still largely enslaved. One consequence of this separation was that, for many years, two lines of musical development progressed in New Orleans. Blacks maintained forms of African tradition – musical and religious – at meetings in Congo Square (these carried on until 1855 and, illegally, for some time after) and in church. Black Creoles followed more formal musical paths of opera, symphony and recital.

The dominant catalyst for the musical fusion which led to jazz was cultural – the coming together of blacks and black Creoles. Forced by law to count themselves African, black Creoles found themselves on the black side of town. So untrained blues and parade musicians formed musical partnerships with black Creoles more used to formal music. From the merging of these disparate cultural roots – Spanish, French, German and West African – came the distinctive sounds of a new music which combined the elegance of the *quadrille*, *mazurka* and *schottische* with the earthier rhythms, harmonies, cadences and, above all, syncopation of the 'cakewalk' and of 'the blues', of spirituals and of the worksongs of the plantations. In the bordellos, honky-tonks and sporting houses of Storyville other influences shaped the development of 'ragtime' music, chiefly for the piano.

The evolution of jazz was further boosted by an influx of cheap band instruments in 1898 at the end of the Spanish-American War; Spanish soldiers, retreating to Cuba, simply sold their instruments hurriedly in New Orleans. Many black musicians, previously playing home-made instruments, could now afford the real thing.

Rich folk could certainly hear some of this new music. The festival of Mardi Gras was – and is – the biggest and most famous of the Crescent City's great festivals. It is unlikely that anyone living within 50 miles of New Orleans could have avoided it and its music. But there were also balls and picnics, fashionable outings and excursions at which brass and 'jass' bands were hired to perform. So the various strands of the new music gradually came together.

The end of Storyville

Music was one highlight in the life of a poor young African-American or black Creole in the first two decades of the last century. Those lives could more usually be characterized by hardship. In the words of Paul Eduard Miller, editor of *Esquire*'s famous Jazz Books of the forties, 'every young boy in New Orleans heard so much music that he developed a genuine interest; the parades inspired the kids; they heard music all around them, all the time. They constructed their own home-made instruments or they worked until they had enough money to explore the musical possibilities of pawn-shops and junk-shops. The demand for musicians was heavy and it was for that reason that so many New Orleans jazzmen began playing while they were still mere boys.'

In November 1917 jazz in New Orleans took a dramatic backward step. In an effort to clean up its act and to protect its sailors the United States Navy closed Storyville down. The sporting houses of this previously legalized area of prostitution had of course provided the raucous venues where jazz was nurtured in the Big Easy. The immediate effect was to limit the employment prospects of bartenders, waiters, cab-drivers, pimps and musicians from the black and black Creole sections of society.

Brass bands and jazz funerals

Elaborate, jubilant and musical funeral parades, usually led by brass bands, were an important element in the development of jazz and a chance for young musicians to learn how to play. Early brass bands like the Excelsior, Olympia and Onward brass bands became major local stars and helped a whole generation of pioneering jazzmen to become interested in music. The Onward and Olympia bands still exist. Today the New Orleans brass band tradition also lives on in a small number of very high quality – and highly innovative – new brass bands. The Rebirth Brass Band and the Dirty Dozen Brass Band are the best-known of these but there are several others. Donna's Bar and Grill (☎ 504-596-6914) at 800 North Rampart is the best place to catch up-and-coming brass bands.

To many New Orleanian jazz musicians the end of Storyville signaled a time to move on – and that meant a move north.

Riverboats

For years riverboats had plied their trade up and down the mighty Mississippi from New Orleans. One of jazz music's more influential but less widely known characters, Fate Marable, provided the musical entertainment on the boats. He led his own band from the piano or that rather peculiar riverboat-mounted instrument, the calliope, a set of steam-whistles emitting variously pitched notes and played like an organ from a console.

Adapting his musical styles to match the clientele (classical selections and popular songs for the mainly white paying passengers and jazz on carefully segregated 'colored nights') Marable was able to offer at least temporary employment to some of the most famous up-and-coming jazz musicians from New Orleans. Among those working the riverboats were Louis Armstrong, Henry 'Red' Allen, the great Ellington bass player Jimmy Blanton, the Dodds Brothers, drummer Arthur 'Zutty' Singleton and clarinet player Gene Sedric. Among other famous jazz names to have been influenced by riverboat music was that finest of all cornet players, Leon 'Bix' Beiderbecke. Bix is reputed to have heard his first jazz from the levee at Davenport, Iowa – hundreds of miles up the Mississippi. New Orleanian jazz pioneers took the music from its home in Storyville by train, road and riverboat to Memphis, St Louis, Chicago and the world. Still New Orleans remains a magnet for all true lovers of the music and it revels nightly in its brilliant legacy.

Arrival and departure

By air

New Orleans International Airport is a 20-minute drive west of the city on Airline Highway. The small airport handles flights to around 100 cities though most international passengers will need to connect at larger southern hubs Dallas Fort Worth or Atlanta.

Airport transfers The efficient **Airport Shuttle** (☎ 504-592-0555) delivers passengers to and picks up from all major downtown hotels. Tickets cost $10 and can be bought in advance or from the driver. Cheaper still, look for the **Jefferson Transit Airport Express bus** which follows route E2 downtown for $1.10. **Cabs** charge

Airline offices — New Orleans
● **American Airlines** (☎ 504-712-4000, 800-433-7300; ▤ 504-712-4096), 900 Airline Highway
● **Continental Airlines** (☎ 504-523 8739, 800-525-0280; ▤ 504-529-2716), 225 Baronne Street, Suite 800
● **Delta Air Lines** (☎ 504-828-3950, 800-221 1212; ▤ 504-828-3954), 3850 North Causeway Boulevard, Metairie
● **Northwest/KLM** (☎ 504-674-0706, 800-590-3462; ▤ 504-654-5524), 655 Plantation Boulevard, Mandeville
● **Southwest Airlines** (☎ 504-834-2337, 800-IFL-YSWA; ▤ 504-834-2829), 111 Veterans Memorial Boulevard, Suite 704
● **United Airlines** (☎ 504-465 8181, 800-241-6522; ▤ 504-465 8169), 800 Airline Highway

a set price of $21 from the airport to downtown for two passengers. Each extra passenger incurs an $8 add on. If you've rented a car at the airport, take the I-10 east for downtown (see below for car hire firms based at the airport).

By train

The Union Passenger Terminal at 1001 Loyola Avenue is served by three Amtrak trains (☎ 800-872-7245), the *Crescent, Sunset Limited* and the *City of New Orleans*. The *Crescent* runs between New York and New Orleans via Atlanta. It leaves on Mondays, Thursdays and Saturdays. *Sunset Limited* runs between Los Angeles and Orlando via San Antonio and New Orleans. Pick it up heading west on Mondays, Wednesdays or Saturdays. It heads east through New Orleans on Tuesdays, Thursdays and Sundays. The *City of New Orleans* is of more interest to travelers of the Blues Highway – it traces the migratory route north followed by black workers as they left the south for Chicago. See p22 for more on this train route.

By bus

Greyhound buses (☎ 800-231-2222) share the Union Passenger Terminal at 1001 Loyola Avenue with Amtrak. If you can handle the Greyhound Bus Company's idiosyncrasies, their distinctive red, white and blue machines can get you – eventually – to almost anywhere in America. Nine buses a day leave for Baton Rouge, a two-hour journey.

By car

If you're planning to move on from New Orleans by car you'll either have to rent one (see box) or take a drive-away (see p20). The **Auto Driveaway Company** (☎ 504-737-0266) way out in Kenner at 7809 Airline Highway might be able to help.

By paddlesteamer

To travel north the same way as jazz, you'll need to jump aboard a paddlesteamer. While the Mississippi River is no longer serviced by fleets of bright white steamboats loaded with cotton, the Delta Steamboat Company (☎ 504-586-0631, 800-543-7637), based at 1380 Port of New Orleans Place, operates three

Car rental — New Orleans

- **Alamo** (☎ 504-469-0532, 800-327-9633; ▤ 504-244-7524), 225 Airline Drive
- **Avis** (☎ 504-523-4317, 800-331 1212; ▤ 504-524-6278), 2024 Canal Street
- **Budget** (☎ 504-780-0153; ▤ 504-70-0153), 4841 Veterans Memorial Boulevard
- **Dollar** (☎ 504-467-2285; ▤ 504-466-2087), 1806 Airline Drive
- **Enterprise** (☎ 504-468-3018, 800-736 8222; ▤ 504-468-3043), 1600 Airline Drive
- **Hertz** (☎ 504-568 1645, 800-654-3131; ▤ 504-465 1207), 901 Convention Center Boulevard
- **National** (☎ 504-466-4335, 800-227-7368; ▤ 504-466-9208), 1020 Airline Highway

steamboats for three- to 11-day cruises up and down the Mississippi. The three boats, *Delta Queen, Magnificent Mississippi Queen* and *Grand America Queen*, provide evocative and luxurious journeys up the Mississippi River with good food and live music. Depending on the cruise you choose, stops are made at

New Orleans — events and festivals

● **February/March** – Mardi Gras (☎ 504-566-5003, 800-672-6124). See box on p34 for more information.

● **March** – Black Heritage Festival (☎ 504-827-0112). The second week of March sees the black community's contribution to Louisiana life celebrated in style at the Audubon Zoo.

● **March** – Tennessee William's Literary Festival (☎ 504-581-1144). This three-day series of plays, readings and lectures is held at various French Quarter locations at the end of March.

● **March** – Louisiana Crawfish Festival (☎ 504-271-3836). The end of March also sees New Orleanians pay homage to the mighty crawfish in a fiesta filled with eating, drinking and music.

● **April** – French Quarter Festival (☎ 504-522-5730). Usually held during mid-April, this festival is one of New Orleans' best. Expect a packed schedule of music over one busy weekend.

● **April/May** – New Orleans Jazz and Heritage Festival (☎ 504-861-8686). See box on p43 for more information.

● **June** – Great French Market Tomato Festival (☎ 504-522-2621). Based in and around the French Market over the first weekend in June, the tomato festival celebrates this useful ingredient in fine style.

● **June** – Carnival Latino (☎ 504-522-9927). New Orleans Hispanic Heritage Foundation honors its own in a jubilant festival held along the riverfront.

● **June/July** – Essence Music Festival (☎ 504-523-5652). Big-name acts play the Superdome during late June and early July.

● **December** – New Year's Eve. Always a particularly raucous night in the French Quarter; crowds gather early in Jackson Square to see in the new.

all the main river-towns featured in this book between New Orleans and Davenport. After Davenport, some cruises continue up to St Paul. Prices start at $515 for an 'F' class cabin on a three-day cruise to $7300 for an 'AAA' class cabin on an 11-day cruise.

Orientation

In spite of its sprawling scale, New Orleans is easy to navigate. The city itself occupies a swampy bowl five feet below sea-level framed between the Mississippi River, which flows a further 110 miles into the Gulf of Mexico, and Lake Pontchartrain. The lake, together with the extent of the Mississippi's meanderings at this point, makes the compass almost irrelevant for most locals. Instead, terms are defined by the water which shapes the Crescent City. Downtown,

(Opposite) Top: An old Coca Cola sign hangs from the Royal Pharmacy in the French Quarter, New Orleans. **Bottom:** Blues and jazz buskers compete in Jackson Square, New Orleans (see p44), under the shadow of St Louis Cathedral.

towards the west, is 'downriver'; uptown, towards the east, is 'upriver'; the north side is 'lakeside'; and the southside is, you guessed it, 'riverside'.

The **French Quarter**, or Vieux Carré, is the cultural center of the city built by Europeans fresh off the boat from the Old World. Most visitors see little reason to explore much beyond the Quarter's atmospheric streets. Upriver from here a few skyscrapers and larger hotels mark the **Central Business District**.

Go further upriver to find the striking mansions of the **Garden District** and, just north, **Uptown**. Beyond that you're into the **University** area where you'll find a few clubs and Tulane and Loyola Universities. Travel lakeside from the French Quarter to reach residential **Mid-City** where the Fair Grounds play host to the Jazz and Heritage Festival every year.

Cross the Mississippi to reach the old neighborhood of **Algiers**, so named, apparently, because early immigrants compared the layout of New Orleans to a map of southern Europe.

Getting around

By cab

Taxis are easy to spot and hail in New Orleans so there's rarely a need to book ahead. Rates are $2.10 plus $1 per mile. During special events there's a minimum charge of $3 per passenger. If you need to order a cab try United (☎ 504-522-0629, 800-323-3303) which has a fleet of over 400 cars.

By bus

Bus services in New Orleans are pretty useful once you've figured out the routes; pick up a schedule from the Regional Transit Authority (RTA) at 101 Dauphine Street or 2817 Canal Street. Fares are $1.25 ($1.50 for express buses) plus 20 cents for each transfer. A three-day pass, available from the RTA, is good value at $8.

By streetcar

Made famous by Tennessee Williams' *A Streetcar Named Desire*, New Orleans' 150-year-old streetcar system is today a tourist attraction in its own right. Despite providing a very limited service, streetcars are still used by locals. There are three streetcar lines in operation although one is actually a bus made to look like a streetcar. The St Charles car runs down St Charles Avenue between Claiborne and Canal. The Riverfront car runs between Canal Street and Riverview. The Vieux Carré bus/streetcar rattles round the perimeter of the French Quarter. Fares are $1.20 each way plus 20 cents for each transfer.

(Opposite) Intricate iron balconies, like these at the Royal Café on Royal Street in New Orleans, are a defining feature of French Quarter architecture.

Mardi Gras

Mardi Gras makes New Orleans the party capital of America. This 12-day display of debauchery beats even the hardest party animals. And it's all in the name of religion. The carnival season starts on the Twelfth Night Feast of Epiphany. But the real partying starts on the twelfth day before Mardi Gras (Fat or Shrove Tuesday).

Some 60 parades negotiate the frenzied streets of the French Quarter in the run-up to Mardi Gras. Over a million people line the streets to join the party. Each parade is run by a 'carnival krewe' and each krewe is led by a carnival king and queen. Some krewes invite guest royalty; John Goodman, Billy Crystal, Dennis Quaid and Tom Jones are all recent carnival kings.

Local star Harry Connick Jr has founded his own krewe called Orpheus. Other notable krewes include: Zulu, an all-black parade which was first formed to poke fun at white Mardi Gras; Venus, the first all-female krewe; and Rex which gave the carnival its anthem, *If I Ever Cease to Love*.

Trinkets, necklaces and doubloons are thrown into the crowd from floats as the parades progress through the city. Perhaps the most exciting element, however, is the gaudy but gorgeous costumes which carnival-goers sport over the whole Mardi Gras period. This, together with the fact that the famous drinking dens along Bourbon Street stay open 24-hours a day, gives the city-center a powerful air of reckless hedonism. As always in the Big Easy, the nights are set to a jazz score and the revelers fuelled by Cajun and Creole cooking. This is, without doubt, the mother of American festivals. At midnight on Mardi Gras the revelry suddenly stops as the party-pooping Lenten period kicks in and the streets are quickly cleared.

Party-goers should be aware, however, that life in the 'city that care forgot' is not always as carefree as one might at first suppose. The petty crime rate during Mardi Gras is high. It's also difficult to find accommodations during the carnival so sort out a place to stay well in advance. For more information call ☎ 504-566-5003 or ☎ 800-672-6124 or log on to 🖳 www.new orleanscvb.com.

Future dates for Mardi Gras are February 12 in 2002, March 4 in 2003, February 24 in 2004 and February 8 in 2005.

By ferry

The Canal Street ferry carries cars and foot passengers across the Mississippi from the end of Canal Street to Algiers point. It leaves Algiers at '15 and '45 minutes past the hour and leaves Canal Street at '00 and '30 minutes past the hour. The last boat leaves Canal Street at midnight and returns the following morning. Foot passengers travel free, drivers pay $1 in the Algiers-Canal Street direction only.

By bike

Cycling is a great way to get around the French Quarter's tight streets. Check out French Quarter Bicycles (☎ 504-529-3136) at 522 Dumaine Street where you can rent bikes from $16.50 per day or $4.50 per hour.

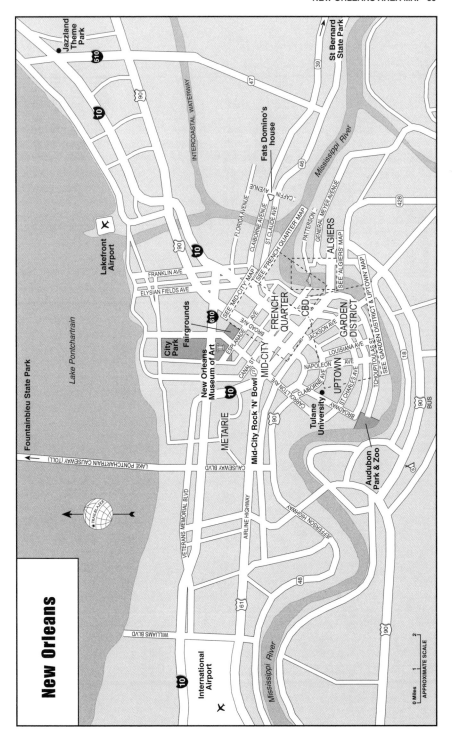

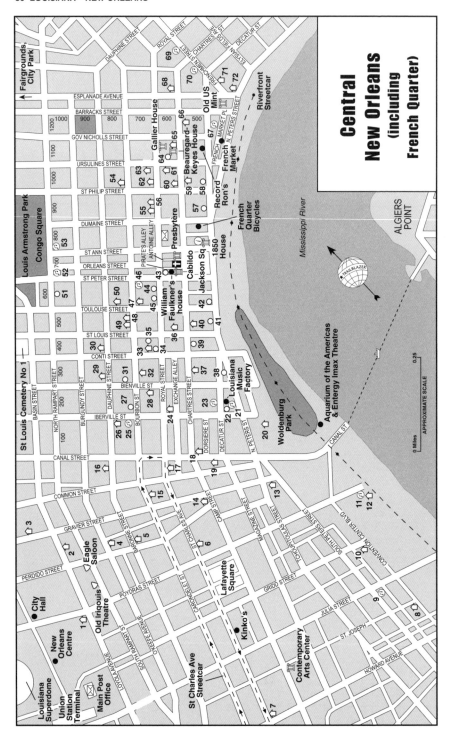

Central
New Orleans
(including
French Quarter)

⌂ WHERE TO STAY

1 Hyatt Regency
2 Holiday Inn – Downtown Superdome
3 Comfort Inn
4 Sleep Inn
5 Comfort Suites
6 Hotel Inter-Continental
7 YMCA International
8 Holiday Inn Select
10 Wyndham Hotel
12 Hilton New Orleans Riverside
13 Windsor Court Hotel
14 La Quinta
15 Hampton Inn
16 Fairmont
17 Courtyard by Marriott
18 Marriott
19 Sheraton
20 Wyndham New Orleans
24 Hotel Monteleone
26 Chateau Sonesta Hotel New Orleans
28 Saint Louis
29 Grenoble House
30 Dauphine Orleans
32 Royal Sonesta New Orleans
33 Saint Ann / Marie Antoinette
36 Omni Royal Orleans
37 W New Orleans
40 Hotel Ste Hélène
47 Hotel Maison de Ville
48 Olivier House Hotel
49 Ramada Inn on Bourbon Street
50 Hôtel St Marie
54 Lafitte Guest Hotel
55 Nine-O-Five Royal Hotel
56 Cornstalk Hotel
59 Hôtel Provincial
60 Chateau
61 Hotel Villa Convento
62 Rue Royal Inn
63 Ursuline Guest House
65 Soniat House
66 Le Richelieu
68 Lanaux Mansion
71 The Frenchman
72 Hotel de la Monnaie

○ WHERE TO EAT

22 Olivier's
27 Mike Anderson's Seafood Restaurant
31 Arnaud's
34 Brennan's
35 Lucky Cheng's
38 Gamay
39 K-Paul's Louisiana Kitchen
41 Crescent City Brewhouse
42 Café Maspero
43 Royal Café
44 Royal Access Internet Café
45 Court of Two Sisters
51 Mama Rosa's
57 Central Grocery
58 Café Sbisa
64 Croissant D'Or Patisserie Francaise

♫ LIVE MUSIC VENUES

9 Howlin' Wolf
11 Pete Fountain's
21 Tipitina's French Quarter
23 House of Blues
25 Storyville District
46 Preservation Hall
52 Funky Butt at Congo Square
53 Donna's Bar & Grill
67 Palm Court Jazz Café
69 Snug Harbour
70 Tin Roof Café

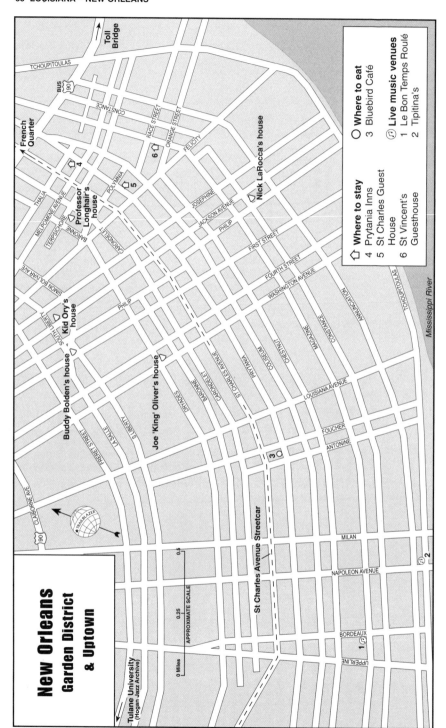

New Orleans
Garden District & Uptown

Tulane University
(Hogan Jazz Archive)

APPROXIMATE SCALE

0 Miles 0.25 0.5

St Charles Avenue Streetcar

Mississippi River

Where to stay
4 Prytania Inns
5 St Charles Guest House
6 St Vincent's Guesthouse

Where to eat
3 Bluebird Café

Live music venues
1 Le Bon Temps Roulé
2 Tipitina's

Professor Longhair's house
Kid Ory's house
Buddy Bolden's house
Joe 'King' Oliver's house
Nick LaRocca's house

French Quarter
Toll Bridge

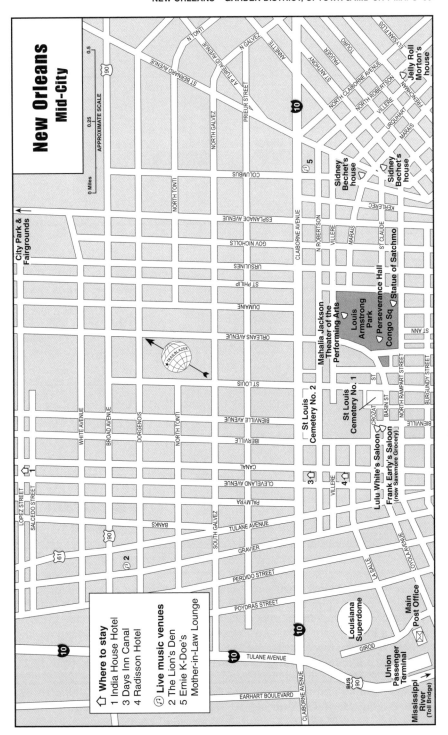

New Orleans
Mid-City

APPROXIMATE SCALE

0 Miles   0.25   0.5

City Park &
Fairgrounds

Where to stay
1 India House Hotel
3 Days Inn Canal
4 Radisson Hotel

Live music venues
2 The Lion's Den
5 Ernie K-Doe's
   Mother-in-Law Lounge

Mahalia Jackson
Theater of the
Performing Arts

Louis
Armstrong
Park

Perseverance Hall

Congo Sq

Statue of Satchmo

St Louis
Cemetery No. 2

St Louis
Cemetery No. 1

Lulu White's Saloon

Frank Early's Saloon
(now Savemore Grocery)

Sidney
Bechet's
house

Sidney
Bechet's
house

Jelly Roll
Morton's
house

Louisiana
Superdome

Main
Post Office

Union
Passenger
Terminal

Mississippi
River
(Toll Bridge)

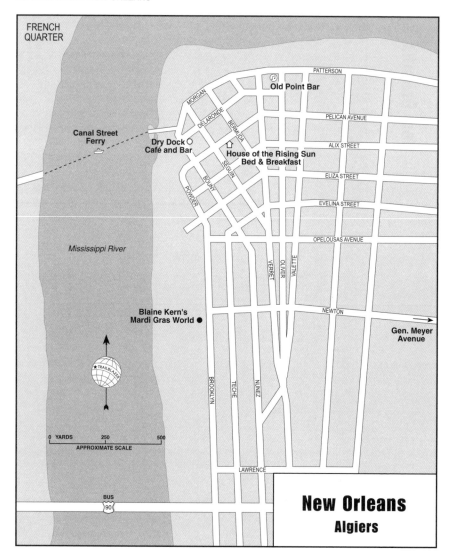

FRENCH QUARTER

PATTERSON

Old Point Bar

MORGAN

DELARONDE

BERMUDA

PELICAN AVENUE

Canal Street
Ferry

Dry Dock
Café and Bar

ALIX STREET

House of the Rising Sun
Bed & Breakfast

SEGUIN

ELIZA STREET

BOUNY

EVELINA STREET

POWDER

Mississippi River

OPELOUSAS AVENUE

VERRET

OLIVER

VALETTE

Blaine Kern's
Mardi Gras World ●

NEWTON

Gen. Meyer
Avenue

★ TRAILBLAZER

BROOKLYN

TECHE

NUNEZ

0 YARDS   250   500
APPROXIMATE SCALE

LAWRENCE

BUS
90

New Orleans
Algiers

Tours

Setting up tours seems to be something of a craze in New Orleans; these are some of the more interesting. **African American Heritage Tours** (☎ 504-288-3478) run extensive van tours of New Orleans ($30) which describe in detail the city's black history. Voodoo Priestess Bloody Mary leads daytime and moonlit **cemetery tours** (☎ 504-486-2080) for $15.

French Quarter Walking Tours with Friends of the Cabildo (☎ 504-523-3939) lead visitors from the 1850 House at 523 St Ann Street on a $10 two-hour historical tour around the Vieux Carré. Tours leave at 10am and 1.30pm. A fascinating **Gay Heritage Tour** (☎ 504-945-6789) leaves Alternatives at 909

Bourbon Street on Wednesdays and Saturdays. Tickets $20. **Gray Line of New Orleans** (☎ 504-587-0733, 800-535-7786) offer, among other things, a 'Secrets of the French Quarter' tour twice daily.

Over in **Algiers**, Kevin Herridge (☎ 504-367 8461) occasionally leads a walking tour focusing on the rich jazz history of that area.

Services

Banks
You're never far from a bank in New Orleans and ATMs accept cards from the major international networks. Free-standing ATM machines are almost ubiquitous; you'll find them in supermarkets and – dangerously – in bars. Major central branches include **Bank One of Louisiana** at 201 St Charles Avenue, **Hibernia National Bank** at 313 Carondelet Street and **Whitney National Bank** at 430 Chartres Street.

Consulates
Lucky diplomats from these nations maintain consular offices in New Orleans:
- **Denmark** (☎ 504-586 8300), 321 St Charles Avenue
- **France** (☎ 504-523-5772), 300 Poydras Avenue
- **Germany** (☎ 504-576-4289), 639 Loyola Avenue
- **Japan** (☎ 504-529-2101), 639 Loyola Avenue
- **Netherlands** (☎ 504-596-2838), 643 Magazine Street
- **Spain** (☎ 504-525-4951), 2 Canal Street
- **Sweden** (☎ 504-897-6510), 2640 Canal Street
- **UK** (☎ 504-524-4180), 321 St Charles Avenue

Communications
- **Post** The main New Orleans post office is at 701 Loyola Avenue but there's a sub-branch at 1022 Iberville Street. Royal Mail at 828 Royal Street is a useful independent post shop.
- **Internet** Since most Americans have their own computers, Internet cafés aren't always easy to find. Try the Royal Access Internet Café at 621 Royal Street. It's expensive; surly staff collect $3 for 15 minutes. Otherwise head over to Kinko's at 762 St Charles Avenue. There's also a free cybercafé in the Contemporary Arts Center at 900 Camp Street.

Tourist information
With tourism such an important part of the New Orleans economy, it's no surprise to find visitors are well looked after in the Big Easy. Go to the Information Center (☎ 504-566-5031) at 529 St Ann Street or contact the New Orleans Metropolitan Convention and Visitors' Bureau (☎ 504-566-5003, 800-672-6124; 🖳 www.neworleanscvb.com).

Record stores
Surprisingly for a city this size and with such a music-loving population, one record store has managed to stay at the top for some years. The **Louisiana**

Music Factory (☎ 504-586-1094; 🖹 504-586 8818; 💻 www.louisianamusicfac tory.com) at 210 Decatur Street is a fertile source of jazz, blues, zydeco, gospel, Cajun and R&B music in all formats. In fact, this is one the great record stores of the Blues Highway and a good place to pick up some sounds for the journey. This is also the best place in town for books on African-American music. The Factory regularly hosts live in-store sets, particularly during Jazz Fest when there are big names playing here almost everyday. **Record Ron's** (☎ 504-524-9444) at 1129 Decatur is fun to explore but the collection here is more local.

Medical emergencies

In any emergency call 911 and ask for an ambulance; New Orleans, like most American cities, has no shortage of hospitals. For general over-the-counter medicines, go to Walgreens at 900 Canal Street.

What to see

Jazz landmarks

Jazz bequeathed New Orleans a hefty legacy in terms of tourism dollars but serious devotees will have to look hard to find evidence of the music's early years. Of course much history was demolished along with Storyville to make way for the desperate 'projects' which occupy that area now. But some early stars' homes and key venues survive. Much of this section deals with how to find them – but don't expect plaques on the walls. You'll need to take a car to find these places and you'll also need to exercise a little caution in the neighborhoods you visit.

The city does make a serious effort to curate its past at the **Old US Mint** (☎ 504-568-6968, 800-568-6869) at 400 Esplanade Avenue which houses a commendable jazz museum (Tues-Sun, 9am-5pm; $5). Here you'll find the story of jazz from its earliest days told with the help of clear notes and prized memorabilia. There's Sidney Bechet's soprano saxophone and a cornet and bugle given to Louis Armstrong to play at the waif's home to which he was banished after shooting a pistol into the air. Bix Beiderbecke's horn and piano are here too.

For further study of jazz in New Orleans, visit the **Hogan Jazz Archive** (☎ 504-865-5688), part of Tulane University, in Joseph Merrick Jones Hall on Freret Street. Curator Bruce Raeburn exhibits just some of the treasures in the archive.

Congo Square and **Louis Armstrong Park** in which it sits are must-see landmarks for jazz lovers. Be careful; the park is dangerous even during the day. Don't hang around. Enter the park where St Ann Street meets North Rampart and walk right to find the gray and slightly awkward **statue of Satchmo** to whom the park was rightly dedicated in 1980. Enter and head left to find what was once Congo Square. Now a deserted brick plaza of sorts, Congo Square could be the actual spot where jazz was born; if not the exact place, Congo Square and the music that was played here by both enslaved and free blacks was, without doubt, critical to the development of jazz.

Perseverance Hall in the north-east corner of the park was played by early jazz greats such as Buddy Bolden. The park is also home to the **Mahalia Jackson Theater of the Performing Arts** named after the great New Orleans gospel singer who made her name in Chicago.

A red-brick grocery store on the corner of Basin and Bienville occupies the site of **Lulu White's Saloon**, perhaps Storyville's most famed brothel, run by composer Spencer William's flamboyant aunt. Many jazzmen played here, Jelly Roll Morton among them. The Savemore Grocery at 1216 Bienville Street was, in a former life, **Frank Early's Saloon**, another noted employer of early jazz pianists. **Jelly Roll Morton's house** was probably located at 1441-1443 Frenchman Street at the corner of Frenchman and North Robertson. This brown house with white windows is now owned by cornet player and jazz historian Jack Stewart. Jelly Roll lived in a number of houses in New Orleans but probably began life here; he would later claim to be the inventor of jazz.

Fats Domino's house at 1208 Caffin Avenue (at the corner of Caffin and Marais) is a sprawling yellow and black, one-story structure. You'll know when you find it by the giant initials 'FD' on the front wall and the stars in the fence. The house is said to be even more outlandish on the inside. Fats grew up in this neighborhood and locals are proud of the fact he chose to stay. The one-time residents of all the other homes in this section are long dead but Fats Domino is, of course, very much alive. For this reason, be discreet.

There's some dispute over exactly where **Sidney Bechet** lived but it was likely to be either at 1507 Marais, a blue-gray house with white shutters, or 1716 Marais next to an empty lot and nearly opposite the Israel Baptist Church on the corner. Head back to 1100 Perdido Street (on the corner of South

New Orleans Jazz and Heritage Festival

First staged at Congo Square in 1970, Jazz Fest has grown to become one of the world's great jazz showcases. These days the event is held over two weekends in late April at the Fair Grounds. Despite attracting some 500,000 visitors, the festival is surprisingly easy to navigate and enjoy; from a logistics point of view, it's a work of pure genius.

Lovers of traditional New Orleans jazz should note that the music on offer is a mix of styles but, unlike some other festivals, almost all the acts are either jazz bands (all types) or belong to some associated genre such as zydeco or blues. The gospel tent is always particularly popular. Non-jazz big names are brought in each weekend to broaden the festival's appeal – in 2000, for example, Lenny Kravitz and Sting appeared – but this is more or less a true jazz festival and, enjoyably, one which is clearly focused on home-grown talent.

The festival spills over into clubs across New Orleans all week as touring New Orleans-based acts come back to play their home crowds. Tickets per day are usually $15 in advance or $20 at the gate. Go to 🖳 www.nojazzfest.com or call ☎ 504-861-8686 for more information.

Ramparts and Perdido) and you'll find what was once the infamous **Eagle Saloon** where the likes of Buddy Bolden and, later, Louis Armstrong honed their craft. Further down South Rampart at 413-415 stands the old **Iriqouis Theater** which was run by Clarence Williams but closed in 1920.

At the turn of the last century **Buddy Bolden** himself lived at 2302 and later 2309 First Avenue between South Liberty and La Salle. Look for a white house with gray trim: that's 2309. Number 2302 is no longer standing. Another true jazz great, **Kid Ory**, lived at 2135 Jackson Avenue between South Liberty and Simon Bolivar Avenue where, today, you'll find just a semi-collapsed shell of a building. Ory's daughter is said to be trying to raise enough money to do the place up.

Louis Armstrong's mentor **Joe 'King' Oliver** once occupied 2712 Dryades Street between Washington Avenue and Fourth, a gray and nondescript house, while a more recent local hero, **Professor Longhair**, once lived at 1740 Terpsichore Street. You'll find his old pad between Baronne Street and Carondelet – it's the two-story brown house with a porch opposite a now empty lot. Original Dixieland Jazz Band leader **Nick LaRocca** lived at 2216 Constance between Jackson Avenue and Philip Street. It's a pale green house with a dark green door decorated with music.

Other highlights

For most visitors, the **French Quarter** or Vieux Carré holds most interest. This is the New Orleans everyone imagines and hopes to find. At the heart of the Quarter, the imposing architecture around **Jackson Square** crowds a peaceful garden. Here accomplished buskers stage the best free gig in town, pausing only for services in the commanding **St Louis Cathedral**. The cathedral was funded by Spanish immigrant Don Andrés Almonaster y Roxas, who arrived in Louisiana penniless but quickly made a fortune in real estate, and was dedicated in 1794. In 1964 Pope Paul VI made the cathedral a minor basilica and, in 1987, Pope John Paul II visited and led mass here. The cathedral opens for mass at 7.30am and closes its doors after a 6pm service.

The cathedral is flanked by the Cabildo to its right and the Presbytère to its left. The **Cabildo**, built in 1799, stands on the site of an earlier, simpler Cabildo which was destroyed by the fire of 1788. The building housed the Spanish leadership in New Orleans however, since 1911, the building has been home to the Louisiana State Museum (☎ 504-568-6968; Tues-Sun 9am-5pm). There's a wealth of material here, tackling the economic and cultural importance of New Orleans since its earliest days, and you'll need to devote several hours to do it justice. The Spanish Council Room is worth seeing since this is where the Louisiana Purchase was signed in 1803. Also part of the Louisiana State Museum, the **Presbytère** was completed in 1813 and used for many years as a courthouse. It now houses collections which chart the changing shape of life in New Orleans.

Bourbon Street is perhaps the best-known thoroughfare in the French Quarter and a symbol of life in the Big Easy. Visitors hoping to find a non-stop, street-long drinking festival won't be disappointed. But for most, Bourbon Street is a victim of its own hedonistic success; too expensive, too crowded, too tacky. Having said that, there's something beautiful about emerging blinking

Voodoo

Voodoo has long had a grip on the imagination of many New Orleanians. Voodoo priestess Bloody Mary of the New Orleans Historic Voodoo Museum believes voodoo was brought to America in the eighteenth century by African slaves. 'Voodoo is thought to be the oldest religion that exists,' she says. 'It's seven to ten thousand years old. But in New Orleans it became part of our Creole tradition. There are certain things we do in New Orleans which are really voodoo customs, not New Orleanian customs. People don't even know the difference any more. Voodoo evolves because it embraces what it finds wherever it goes. It met here with Catholicism and incorporated certain Catholic beliefs.'

Bloody Mary admits voodoo has earned a sinister reputation.

'There are good priests and bad priests in every single religion that exists in the world. Good practitioners and bad practitioners too. It's estimated that about three per cent of the people who're into voodoo still operate at the dark end. But in general that would be considered heretic and quite foolish. Anything you do that's negative will come back at you three times.'

The most influential voodoo queen in New Orleans was Marie Laveau in the nineteenth century. 'Marie Laveau was the real boss of this town,' says Bloody Mary, 'she dealt with a lot of social reform. She had a lot of strength and political pull and she was connected to everyone. She balanced her spiritual and magical life perfectly with her physical life.'

from some Bourbon Street drinking den at seven in the morning to see people making their way to work.

The **French Market** is another of New Orleans' best-loved traditions. Since the days when Indians traded with newly-arrived Europeans, the site of the present-day French Market – between North Peter's and Decatur Streets – has been a center for commerce. The covered butchers' market was built in 1813 but has been taken over by cafés, including the ever-popular, 24-hour Café du Monde, however the farmers' market and flea market still enjoy vigorous business. In the former you'll find all manner of fresh produce available all day while the flea market sells a mix of bargain-priced goodies and touristy tat. A proper trawl can yield some good stuff but you'll have to be patient.

Other jewels in the Quarter include **Gallier House** (☎ 504-525-5661) at 1118-1132 Royal Street, the **1850 House** (☎ 504-568-6968) at 523 St Anne Street and the **Beauregard-Keyes House** (☎ 504-523-7257) at 1113 Chartres Street, all of which are prime examples of nineteenth-century New Orleans architecture which are open to the public. The Gallier House, in particular, offers a fascinating glimpse of life in old New Orleans. Gallier was an architect and equipped his house with the very latest devices for fighting mosquitoes, yellow fever and the heat. **William Faulkner** lived in New Orleans during the early years of his career, renting an apartment at 624 Pirate's Alley. He wrote

Cities of the Dead

Early settlers in New Orleans soon learned the hard way that burying bodies in a town five feet below sea level is no easy task. Graves would immediately fill with water so that, on the day of interment, the coffin would float. The quick-fix solution of puncturing the coffin to make it sink proved unpopular since, on stormy nights, bodies would occasionally be washed out of their graves and float into the streets of the French Quarter.

So New Orleanians began the practice of interring their dead in above-ground vaults. This more practical solution has bequeathed the city over 40 dramatically beautiful cemeteries which are known as the 'cities of the dead'. The grander vaults belong to whole families or certain societies who grouped together to make sure their own would be laid to rest properly.

Many consider Metairie Cemetery to be the most impressive but St Louis Cemeteries 1 and 2 are older and more easily reached from the French Quarter (see below).

for the *Times-Picayune* and worked on his first novel, *Soldier's Pay*, here. The house is now a bookstore open from 10am to 6pm.

St Louis Cemeteries Numbers 1 and 2 in the Tremé district, west of Armstrong Park, are just two of many labyrinthine graveyards in New Orleans and the easiest to reach from the French Quarter. These two cemeteries, dating back to the eighteenth century, are among the most impressive. Voodoo priestess Marie Laveau is said to be buried here; you'll recognize her supposed tomb by its graffiti. The cemeteries are open from 8am to 3pm but since they're overlooked by a fairly sketchy set of housing 'projects', it's not a great idea to wander around alone – you're effectively in a maze.

Art lovers can choose between the **Contemporary Arts Center** (☎ 504-528-3805) at 900 Camp Street or the **New Orleans Museum of Art** (☎ 504-488-2631) in City Park. NOMA (Tues-Sun; 10am-5pm; $6) houses a valuable fine art collection, including a Fabergé hall, but the Contemporary Arts Center (Tues-Sun; 10am-5pm; $3) is arguably the more interesting. Here you'll find thought-provoking multi-media exhibits in a massive 1905 warehouse.

The **Aquarium of the Americas** (☎ 504-8612537, 800-774-7394), where Canal Street meets the Mississippi, is a big draw thanks in part to its collection of sharks – the largest in the States. Cute and cuddly sea otters also help to pull in the crowds. The aquarium is open daily from 9.30am to 7pm and costs $10 for adults, $5 for kids under 12. Next door, the **Entergy IMAX Theater** (☎ 504-581-4629, 800-774-7394) captivates crowds with its five-story 3D screen.

There are, of course, many other historic sites and attractions in New Orleans. Of those not so far mentioned, the **Jazzland Theme Park** (☎ 504-242-2324) at the intersection of I-10 and I-50, a 140-acre Disney-esque sprawl of rollercoasters, might appeal to families. **Blaine Kern's Mardi Gras World** (☎ 504-361-7821, 800-362-8213) at 233 Newton Street on Algiers Point is a great place to go to get a backstage look at the Mardi Gras floats. Kern and family make floats and costumes here in huge warehouses which visitors can explore in organized groups. To get there, take the Canal Street ferry to Algiers and hop on one of the Blaine Kern complimentary minibuses waiting by the wharf.

Where to stay

French Quarter hotels can be fairly expensive; this is, after all, the most charming part of town. But since the Quarter is convenient for the majority of music venues, and because sitting on an intricate iron balcony watching the sun go down behind the Vieux Carré is one of New Orleans' great pleasures, this book focuses on French Quarter accommodations.

Places to stay are organized from the least expensive upwards; prices quoted are approximate and based on high season rates for double occupancy. Rooms are en suite and include air conditioning unless stated otherwise.

See the 'Chain hotels' section for a list of the Marriotts, Holiday Inns and such like. If you plan to save your pennies for cover charges, see the 'Budget options' section. Wherever you plan to stay remember that New Orleans is a busy town and, despite its 30,000 hotel rooms, it gets full. It can be extremely difficult to find somewhere to stay during the city's biggest events – Mardi Gras and Jazz Fest – and prices at these times shoot skyward. Plan and book ahead.

Budget options

There are a handful of budget choices in New Orleans but this isn't the easiest city in which to find a cheap night's sleep and during Mardi Gras or Jazz Fest it's pretty much impossible. Book for a good rate. Hostels include the *YMCA International* (☎ 504-568-9622; **❶**) at 920 St Charles Avenue and the *India House Hotel* (☎ 504-821-1904; **❶**) at 124 South Lopez Street.

There are a number of inexpensive guesthouses which offer a better standard of accommodations. *Prytania Inns* (☎ 504-566-1515; **❷**) based at 1415 Prytania Street runs three great value places on Prytania Street. Otherwise try *St Vincent's Guesthouse* (☎ 504-523-341; **❷**) at 1507 Magazine Street or, best of the lot, the *St Charles Guest House* (☎ 504-523-6556; **❷**) at 1748 Prytania Street. Here you'll find a few 'backpacker rooms' out back. There's a welcome laid-back feel at the St Charles.

The only other course of action for desperate budget travelers is to head for the cheap motel chains which cluster around the airport. You can usually find a room for around $50 out there. Pick up a list from the Convention and Visitors' Bureau. If you've traveled a long way to see New Orleans, though, it seems a shame to banish yourself so far into the city's miserable 'burbs.

Campers could try the *St Bernard State Park* (**❶**) 12 miles south-east of the city on Highway 39. Otherwise check out *Fountainbleu State Park* (**❶**) off Highway 190 on the north-shore of Lake Pontchartrain or *Bayou Segnette State Park* (**❶**) just south of the Mississippi River on Highway Business 90.

French Quarter — mid-range options ($50-120)

One of the best value French Quarter options isn't in the French Quarter at all. The *House of the Rising Sun Bed and Breakfast* (☎/🖹 504-367-8461; 🖳 www.house

oftherisingsunbnb.com; ❸) at 335 Pelican Avenue on Algiers Point is, however, just a few minutes from the Quarter by ferry. Run by Louisiana native Wendy Herridge and her English husband Kevin, this immaculate bed and breakfast has lovely rooms. Kevin Herridge is a respected local jazz historian and an expert on jazz in old Algiers.

Another well-priced option, the *Ursuline Guest House* (☎ 504-525-8509, 800-654-2531; 🖹 504-525-8408; ❸) at 708 Ursulines Street offers a good standard of accommodation. There are three parking spaces – three more than most French Quarter hotels – and there's an attractive courtyard. No kids allowed.

The *Cornstalk Hotel* (☎ 504-523-1515; 🖹 504-522-5558; ❹) at 915 Royal Street is great value. Traditional decor, helpful staff and parking space make the Cornstalk a popular choice. Look out for the impressive 'cornstalk' fence around the hotel – the management will be only too happy to tell you the story behind it.

Just down the road at 905 Royal Street, the plainly-named *Nine-O-Five Royal Hotel* (☎ 504-523-0219, 🖳 www.905royalhotel.com; ❸-❹) is worth investigating. Another 'European-style' French Quarter stalwart, the Nine-O-Five is pretty good value by New Orleanian standards. You might also try the *Hotel Provincial* (☎ 504-581-4995, 800-535-7922; 🖹 504-581-1018; 🖳 www.hotel-provincial.com; ❸) at 1024 Chartres where decent rooms are arranged around a central pool.

The *Hotel Villa Convento* (☎ 504-522-1793; 🖹 504-524-1902; 🖳 www.villaconvento.com; ❹) at 616 Ursulines Street is an endearing place run by three generations of the Campo family. Built in 1833, the Campos have been here for 20 years. There are 23 rooms and the rates include continental breakfast. Similar in price but a small step upscale in standards, the *Rue Royal Inn* (☎ 504-524-3900, 800-776-3901; 🖹 504-558-0566; 🖳 www.rueroyalinn.com; ❹) has

---

New Orleans — chain hotels

- *Comfort Inn* (☎ 504-586-0100), 1315 Gravier Street
- *Comfort Suites* (☎ 504-524-1140), 346 Baronne Street
- *Courtyard by Marriott* (☎ 504-581-9005), 124 St Charles Avenue
- *Days Inn Canal* (☎ 504-586-0110), 1630 Canal Street
- *Hampton Inn* (☎ 504-529-9990), 226 Carondelet Street
- *Hilton New Orleans Riverside* (☎ 504-561-0500) 2 Poydras Street
- *Holiday Inn – Downtown Superdome* (☎ 504-581-1600), 330 Loyola Avenue
- *Holiday Inn – Select* (☎ 504-524-1881), 881 Convention Center Boulevard
- *Hotel Inter-Continental* (☎ 504-525-5566), 444 St Charles Avenue
- *Hyatt Regency* (☎ 504-561-1234), 500 Poydras Plaza
- *La Quinta* (☎ 504-598-9977), 301 Camp Street
- *Marriott* (☎ 504-581-1000), 555 Canal Street
- *Radisson Hotel* (☎ 504-522-4500), 1500 Canal Street
- *Sheraton* (☎ 504-525-2500), 500 Canal Street
- *Sleep Inn* (☎ 504-524-5400), 334 O'Keefe Avenue
- *Wyndham Hotel* (☎ 504-524-8200), 701 Convention Center Boulevard
- *Wyndham New Orleans* (☎ 504-566-7006), 100 Iberville Street

17 stylish but simple rooms available. A relatively quiet location helps the Rue Royal's score. *Le Richelieu* (☎ 504-529-2492, 800-535-9653; 🖹 504-524-8179; ❹-❺) at 1234 Chartres Street is another acceptable though not spectacular option.

Despite labeling itself a 'motor hotel', the *Chateau* (☎ 504-524-9636; 🖹 504-525-2989; ❹) at 1001 Chartres is a charming place with a great courtyard and pool. Also worth considering is the *Olivier House Hotel* (☎ 504-525-8456; 🖹 504-529-2006; ❹) at 828 Toulouse Street with a number of attractive doubles. The *Frenchman* (☎ 800-831 1781; ❹-❺) at 417 Frenchman Street on the southeast fringe of the Quarter is a more elegant option than any of those above and, with rooms ranging from $89, exceptional value. The subtle attention to detail here makes this a first-class hotel. The pool might be little bigger than a bath but you can't have everything.

French Quarter — high-end options ($120-250+)

Another typically New Orleanian vision of dark colors and thick carpeting is the *Dauphine Orleans* (☎ 504-586-1800, 800-521-7111; 🖹 504-586-1409; 🖥 www.dauphineorleans.com; ❺) at 415 Dauphine Street. The better rooms here are excellent. The *Saint Ann/Marie Antionette Hotel* (☎ 504-525-2300, 800-535-9111; 🖥 www.stannmarieantionette.com; ❺) at 717 Conti Street is a more simply furnished affair with 48 light, airy rooms. A little more expensive, the *Saint Louis* (☎ 504-581-7300, 800-535-9111; 🖥 www.stlouishotel.com; ❺) at 730 Bienville Street offers equally pleasant accommodation.

Staff at the *Hotel Ste Hélène* (☎ 504-522-5014, 800-348-3888; 🖹 504-523-7140; ❺-❻), located at 508 Chartres Street, really help to make this a good choice; they're friendly, helpful and full of local knowledge. Otherwise it's an attractive but not exceptional hotel. For a similar price you could stay at the plush *Hotel de la Monnaie* (☎ 504-947-0009; 🖹 504-945-6841; ❺-❻) at 405 Esplanade Avenue though its location opposite the old US Mint is a short walk away from the action.

The *Hotel St Marie* (☎ 504-561-8951; 🖹 504-571-2802; 🖥 www.french quarter.com; ❺) is another reasonable choice in this price range. A further option is the *Lafitte Guest House* (☎ 504-581-2678, 800-331-7971; 🖥 www.lafitteguesthouse.com; ❺) at 1003 Bourbon Street. Rooms in this atmospheric and immaculate New Orleanian townhouse are hard to get in high season.

While the Lafitte is undoubtedly a beautiful slice of New Orleanian opulence, the *Lanaux Mansion* (☎ 504-569-1482; 🖹 504-587-0708; ❺), is arguably still more impressive. Built in 1879 at 547 Esplanade Avenue, the Lanaux Mansion has all the gilt-edged grandeur you would expect from a fine

Hotel price codes

Hotel and motels price bands used in this book reflect the range of prices charged for a double room.

❶ – $10-25	❷ – $26-50	❸ – $51-85	❹ – $86-120
❺ – $121-180	❻ – $181-250	❼ – $251+	

See p22 for more information.

Victorian townhouse in the French Quarter. If you stay here, make sure you ask the owners to show you round the function rooms.

Moving up in price a little more, the *Soniat House* (☎ 504-522-0570, 800-544-8808; ▤ 504-522-7208; ▣ www.soniathouse.com; ❺) at 1133 Chartres is a beautiful and quiet hotel but perhaps a little expensive.

Nudging further up the price scale, the *Chateau Sonesta Hotel New Orleans* (☎ 504-586-0800, 800-766-3782; ▤ 504-586-1987; ▣ www.chateauson esta.com; ❻) at 800 Iberville Street is a large hotel with perfectly adequate but hardly exciting rooms. It's unfortunate that the Chateau Sonesta is located on a dingy stretch of Iberville Street. Its sister property, the *Royal Sonesta Hotel New Orleans* (☎ 504-586-0300, 800-766-3782; ▤ 504-586-0335; ▣ www.royal sonestano.com; ❻) is much better placed at 300 Bourbon Street. It's worth requesting a room at the back overlooking the pool, however, since Bourbon Street gets noisy at night.

A more atmospheric choice for the same price is the *Hotel Maison de Ville* (☎ 504-561-5858, 800-634-1600; ▤ 504-528-9939) at 727 Toulouse Street. You might also try the *Grenoble House* (☎ 504-522-1331, 800-722-1834; ▤ 504-524-4968; ❻) at 329 Dauphine Street. It's an 'all suites' place.

For about the same price, Ramada's *Inn on Bourbon Street* (☎ 504-524-7611. 800-535-7891; ▤ 504-568-9427; ▣ www.innonbourbon.com; ❻) at 541 Bourbon Street is an alternative. But while the building itself is impressive and beautifully maintained, the hotel lacks charm. A more impressive hotel is the *Hotel Monteleone* (☎ 504-523-3341, 800-535-9595; ▤ 504-528-1019; ❻) at 214 Royal Street. With an imposing foyer and attentive staff, the Monteleone lives up to its pedigree; this is one of the oldest hotels in the French Quarter and one which is still in the hands of the family which founded it.

Again similar in price, the *W New Orleans* (☎ 504-581-1200; ▣ www.whotels.com; ❻) at 316 Chartres Street is an ultra-cool place which has recently been completely revamped, though it is unashamedly aimed at the business traveler.

The *Omni Royal Orleans* (☎ 504-529-5333, 800-THE-OMNI; ▤ 504-529-7016; ▣ www.omnihotels.com; ❼) at 621 St Louis Street is a vast AAA four diamond hotel with excellent service, a pleasant rooftop pool and most of the facilities you would expect from a place this size.

Two other hotels which deserve to be mentioned – though both are just outside the French Quarter – are, first, the *Fairmont* (☎ 504-529-7111, 800-527-4727; ▤ 504-522-2303; ❼) at 123 Baronne Street. It's a spectacularly plush place which has retained its élite air despite some ups and downs over a 70-odd year career.

The other hotel which warrants more than a few words is the no-expense-spared *Windsor Court* (☎ 504-523-6000; 800-262-2662; ▤ 504-596-4513; ▣ www.windsorcourthotel.com; ❼) at 300 Gravier Street. Now part of the Orient Express chain of hotels, the Windsor Court is about as good as it gets. The pseudo-British decor might seem a little incongruous but there's no more impressive or opulent hotel in New Orleans. Of course, the prices reflects that.

Where to eat

New Orleanian cuisine is nothing less than a national treasure. Cajun and Creole classics are dished up daily at restaurants all over New Orleans and there's no doubt that people in Louisiana take their food very seriously indeed (see p52 for information on Creole and Cajun cuisine). Since a comprehensive guide to restaurants in the Big Easy could make a book in its own right, this section highlights a few centrally located favorites organized from the least expensive upwards. Many of the live music venues listed on p54 serve bar snacks.

Budget options

The *Bluebird Café* (☎ 504-895-7166) at 3625 Prytania Street serves some of the best breakfasts on the Blues Highway till 3pm every day. Don't even acquaint yourself with this addictive place if you're worried about your waistline. The 'Big Bird Breakfast', for example, includes two eggs, three pancakes and home fries for just $4.95. The Bluebird is always crowded with devotees.

Another good value eatery, this time for lunch or dinner, is *Café Maspero* (☎ 504-523-6250) at 601 Decatur Street. Cavernous but lively, Maspero serves cheap but tasty New Orleans staples such as red beans and rice ($5.75) in ample portions.

Croissant D'Or Patisserie Francaise (☎ 504-524-4663) opposite the Hotel Villa Convento at 615-617 Ursulines Street was opened in 1983 but looks much older. Few tourists find this popular spot which serves various combinations of light snacks – croissants, pie and so on – for around $5. You could also try *Mama Rosa's* (☎ 504-523 5546) at 616 North Rampart for a decent and inexpensive pizza or, cheaper still, grab a *muffeletta* from the *Central Grocery* (☎ 504-523-1620) at 923 Decatur Street where this gargantuan snack was invented in 1906.

If you don't mind heading over the river to Algiers for your meal try the friendly *Dry Dock Café and Bar* (☎ 504-361-8240) at 133 Deleronde Street which has – arguably, because everyone has their favourite – the best red beans and rice in town ($4.95). The Dry Dock also does a good line in alligator po-boys ($5.95).

Mid-range and expensive restaurants

If you want to eat on an iron balcony overlooking the Quarter, but without spending all that money you brought to buy records, try the *Royal Café* (☎ 504-528-9086) at 700 Royal Street. Prices here aren't too bad and neither is the food. The real reason for coming, however, is to enjoy eating on a quintessential French Quarter balcony. Expect to pay from $8 to $18 for an entrée.

Another Vieux Carré stalwart is the *Court of Two Sisters* (☎ 504-522-7261) at 613 Royal Street. An obscure entrance leads into a vast restaurant and courtyard, the latter attractively shaded by swathes of wisteria. A daily $25 jazz brunch from 9am to 3pm provides a chance to familiarize yourself with almost every important Creole dish from jambalaya to andouille gumbo. The buffet is so enormous you'll be given a guided tour by your waiter before you start. The

Crescent City Brewhouse (☎ 504-522-0571) at 527 Decatur Street, a much newer establishment, has made a name for itself with enormous portions, regular live music and four types of home-brewed beer. It's a frenetic place where quantity is clearly deemed more important than quality but, nevertheless, this is a pop-

Cajun and Creole cuisine

Cajun and Creole cuisine, arguably America's greatest contributions to the field of gastronomy, were both pioneered in Louisiana. The two styles are related but different. **Cajun** food is more rustic than Creole cooking, having been developed by Acadians living around Lafayette. It's generally quite hot, meaty and filling. **Creole** cuisine has Spanish as well as French influences because it was cultivated in New Orleans. It's also more complex than Cajun food because more ingredients were available to chefs in New Orleans than those in the country. Creole food is sometimes divided between 'high' and 'low' Creole depending, partly, on the extent of its European influence.

Certain Creole-Cajun dishes crop up time and again in New Orleans and, if you've got a good appetite, you would be well advised to try them all. **Po-boys**, abbreviated from 'poor-boys', are big French bread sandwiches stuffed with shrimps or beef and sold cheap. A **muffuletta** is a mammoth sandwich built to extreme proportions with cheese, salad and Italian hams.

Jambalaya is a delicious and usually spicy rice-based concoction similar to risotto. Seafood, sausage or chicken jambalaya are most common. **Gumbo**, another classic dish, is somewhere between soup and stew; it's thick, filling and you'll find it served almost everywhere. Shrimp, okra and chicken are popular variations. It would be impossible to stay in New Orleans for any length of time without coming across **grits**, usually for breakfast. Grits are ground hominy mashed up to make a liquid-like matter which looks something like semolina.

Red beans and rice, Louis Armstrong's favourite dish, sounds plain but is in fact the most satisfying dish this writer has ever tasted. The beans are kidney beans served up in a thick, spicy sauce often with huge hunks of seasoned **andouille tripe sausage** – which is in itself a local creation. The term **etouffee** refers to a method of cooking shrimps or crawfish slowly and covered in vegetables or tomatoes.

Crawfish, you'll soon discover, are a staple of Louisiana cooking. These mini-lobsters, called 'crayfish' outside the South, are farmed commercially in Louisiana and eaten in almost any dish. Boiled crawfish is something of a delicacy but it's also an acquired taste. If you order this quintessential Louisiana dish you'll be presented with a huge bowl full of the horrible-looking things. There's a way to eat them that's none too pretty either; pull off the head and squeeze the tail to extract what little meat is in there. It's a lot of work for little gain.

Another New Orleans specialty, **pralines**, is a little easier to love. Pralines are a sort of very sweet confectionery made up mostly from sugar, pecans and butter. Local drinks include **Dixie** and **Abita** beers, both brewed in New Orleans and both completely unlike any other American beer, **café au lait** and coffee with **chicory**. Southerners like to eat and it's easy to see why.

ular restaurant. The menu is a mix of Creole, steaks and fried fish; expect to pay around $17 for an entrée. Live jazz is played here every night.

Standard New Orleanian fare with an oceanic spin can be found at *Mike Anderson's Seafood Restaurant* (☎ 504-524-3884) at 215 Bourbon Street. Anderson's, now a chain, serves fresh Louisiana seafood usually thickly coated in breadcrumbs and deep fat fried. You'll pay around $14 for an entrée.

For a slightly more surreal dining experience head over to *Lucky Cheng's* (☎ 504-529-2045) at 720 St Louis Street. Here you'll find excellent 'Asian-Creole' cuisine – including 'Cajun dim sum' – served by large-breasted transsexuals. The food's great (around $15 to $18 for an entrée) and the waiting staff work hard to make sure their guests have a good time. If you don't plan to eat here there's a cocktail bar attached which specializes in house favorites Voluptuous Melons and Pink Pussy. All cocktails are $7.

Olivier's (☎ 504-525-7734) at 201 Decatur Street is one of the best-value restaurants in New Orleans. The prices – around $15 for an entrée – simply don't reflect the outstanding quality of the traditional Creole cooking served here. Try the new potatoes, dill, sour cream and caviar ($6.95) to start. Duck breast in plum and port sauce ($16.95) is an excellent entrée. The restaurant itself is quiet, candlelit and discreet.

Another great Creole restaurant is *Café Sbisa* (☎ 504-522-5565) at 1011 Decatur Street. Sbisa has been here since 1899. The current management has made a great job of preserving and improving the stunning old dining room. Although the modern Creole menu is hard to fault you'll pay around $15-$20 only for an entrée. *K-Paul's Louisiana Kitchen* (☎ 504-524-7394) at 416 Chartres Street is also a New Orleans institution – albeit a much younger one at 20 years old. Celebrity chef Paul Prudhomme has made Cajun food his life's work and here you'll be able to sample his creations – blackened beef, hot Cajun jambalaya – in the comfort of his recently renovated restaurant. Expect to pay around $25 for an entrée.

Arnaud's (☎ 504-523-0611) at 813 Bienville Street is one of the more upscale concerns in New Orleans. An enormous place with six public and 12 private dining rooms, Arnaud's has for 80 years maintained a reputation for consistently excellent French-Creole cuisine. A jazz band plays in the Richelieu Room where there's a $4 cover. Entrées are priced around the $25 mark.

Gamay (☎ 504-299-8800) at 320 Decatur is a new and innovative Creole restaurant opened by chef Greg Sonnier in 1999. Attracting attention immediately, Gamay has quickly become a fashionable addition to the city. Sonnier's dishes (entrées around $25) are firmly rooted in Louisiana cooking but expect a few surprises.

Like Arnaud's, *Brennan's* (☎ 504-525-9713) at 417 Royal Street is impossible to ignore in any restaurant round-up of New Orleans. The Brennan family now owns a number of businesses in New Orleans but this 50-year-old restaurant made their name. Brennan's is famed for its almost impossibly extravagant 'breakfasts'. It would be a shame to miss this Epicurean treat. The food is French-Creole; entrées are priced around $30.

Where to find live music

The most obvious jazz scene in New Orleans is there because it's the sound-track tourists expect. After a few days in town you'll have heard *St James' Infirmary*, *When the Saints Go Marching In* and *Basin Street Blues* hundreds of times; street musicians and café bands across the Quarter belt out such standards with relentless enthusiasm. This is no criticism; many of these bands are outstanding and of course New Orleans should revel in its past.

There is, however, another scene which is altogether more exciting and innovative. Some great musicians are playing the circuit – you have to be good to make a name in jazz in New Orleans – and that circuit boasts some excellent venues. Whether you prefer the standard New Orleanian sound or the cutting edge, you will find jazz flourishing in the Crescent City.

Local jazz stars to look out for include: mesmerizing trumpeter Nicholas Payton; the always entertaining Kermit Ruffins; blind blues and jazz pianist Henry Butler (see opposite); Wynton, Branford and patriarch Ellis Marsalis; Los Hombres Calientes featuring Jason Marsalis; Harry Connick Jr; James Andrews; and Andrews' brother, Trombone Shorty, another popular figure in the New Orleans jazz world.

Live jazz is played in countless venues across New Orleans. This section is a shamelessly subjective hand-picked list of the best. Since jazz joints fade in and out of style it's always worth scouring listings pages to get the latest information. *Offbeat*, a free monthly music magazine, is a good start. Otherwise buy the *Times-Picayune* on a Friday or pick up a copy of the weekly *Gambit*. Expect to pay a cover charge at any of these clubs; the amount varies according to the act and the night of the week but will normally be between $5 and $15.

Clubs

Donna's Bar and Grill (☎ 504-596-6914) at 800 North Rampart is the focal point for the New Orleans brass band revival and an always enjoyable venue. Drop in to hear the Rebirth Brass band if they're in town – you won't regret it. Donna's is slightly rough around the edges and this stretch of North Rampart, opposite Congo Square, is no place to hang around at night so take a cab.

Ernie K-Doe's Mother-in-Law Lounge (☎ 504-947-1078) at 1500 North Claiborne is another must-visit club on the New Orleans scene. K-Doe proclaimed himself the 'Emperor of the Universe' when, in 1961, his giant R&B hit *Mother in Law* climbed to the top of the charts and stayed there for weeks. The club is almost a shrine to the perpetuation of that fleeting fame. Surreal, yes, but mightily good fun and the Emperor makes an amusing host.

The *Funky Butt at Congo Square* (☎ 504-558-0872) at 714 North Rampart – just along from Donna's – is a great jazz club set up with the help of genius pianist Henry Butler. For many visitors to New Orleans, this is how a jazz club should look; small, candlelit and crowded. It attracts a vigorous audience which is kept watered by hard-working waitresses. This is the best and most likely place in town to catch Butler who plays here fairly often. The original Funky Butt (at a different location) was a hard and decadent New Orleans club in the early days of jazz. Like Donna's, the Funky Butt faces Congo Square, a

Interview — Henry Butler

What's your favourite club in New Orleans?
I helped set up the Funky Butt and although I'm a bit disappointed it hasn't been kept up so well, I like playing there. I really helped with it so that other local musicians would have more places to play. I like playing anywhere with a good piano. I play all the clubs in New Orleans.

Is the music scene in New Orleans healthy?
The music scene here is getting better. They're opening some new venues in New Orleans and some musicians will benefit from that. There are lots of musicians in New Orleans, but there are probably not enough clubs for them all to play in. There's generally a good audience for jazz but you can't count on the locals for that. There are a lot of tourists, millions who come to hear music and they support the scene. The locals have their

Henry Butler is a New Orleans jazz and blues pianist

favorites and you can count on them for that, but traditional jazz may or may not be supported by local people.

dangerous part of town, so don't hang around on the street after dark. The much-hyped *House of Blues* (☎ 504-529-2583) at 225 Decatur is either the savior of New Orleans' club scene or a cynical and brazenly commercial caricature. Take your pick. There's normally a pretty full calendar of first-rate acts to help win you round. *Howlin' Wolf* (☎ 504-523-2551) at 828 South Peter's Street is a blues club which, strangely enough, rarely plays the type of Chicago blues pioneered by its namesake. Still if you're after blues not jazz, head here.

Le Bon Temps Roulé (☎ 504-895-8117) at 4801 Magazine Street is a packed Uptown neighborhood joint popular with students. It's a decent enough place made all the better by a regular slot for Kermit Ruffins and the Barbecue Swingers. You'll need to drive or take a cab since it's quite a way from the Quarter.

The Lion's Den (☎ 504-822-4693) at 2655 Gravier Street is owned by Irma Thomas, New Orleans' great soul star. If she's in town and singing here, don't miss it. Much of the time, however, there's no live music. At these times the Den operates as a fairly ordinary neighborhood bar.

The legendary *Mid-City Rock 'N' Bowl* (☎ 504-482-3133) at 4133 South Carrollton is a hybrid between a bowling alley and a live music venue specializing in blues, jazz and zydeco. It sounds like a crass idea – and, in a way, it is – but the place is saved by the quality of the bands it books. That simple rule has kept Mid-City Rock 'N' Bowl going strong for years. Zydeco nights on Wednesdays and Thursdays are particularly rocking; Nathan Williams and the Zydeco Cha Chas (see p76) often play here when they're in town.

The *Palm Court Jazz Café* (☎ 504-525-0200) at 1204 Decatur Street is owned and managed by the eccentric Nina Buck whose husband, George, founded the *Jazzology* record label. Predominantly a restaurant, the Palm Court is also a favorite for lovers of traditional jazz. The house band usually taps out a tame selection of standards but, on occasion, some big names stop by to spice things up. Expect a calm but convivial evening in upscale surroundings.

Pete Fountain's (☎ 504-523-4374) club is housed on the third floor of the Hilton Riverside Hotel at 2 Poydras Street. Clarinetist Fountain first made his name as a jazzman in the fifties. He's now found another niche as purveyor of expensive jazz to crowds of 500 in a bland business hotel. This isn't the most exciting gig in town but few can deny Fountain's great musical skill.

Preservation Hall (☎ 504-523-8939) at 726 St Peter's Street is a strange place but one which jazz lovers feel compelled to visit. Crowds gather early to squeeze into a tight room where they'll catch a glimpse of traditional jazzmen plying their trade. It's rather like watching a living museum exhibit; the décor looks synthetic and some might say the same for the music. But Preservation Hall is credited with keeping traditional jazz alive during its darkest years and that, if nothing else, is one reason to pay your respects.

Snug Harbor (☎ 504-949-0696) at 626 Frenchman Street is a great club – it's stylish, friendly and lines up some of the best modern musicians New Orleans has to offer. Ellis Marsalis regularly plays two Friday night sets. The cover here can be high and it's a good idea to pick up tickets early at weekends when the place frequently sells out.

A new addition to the New Orleans scene, *Storyville District* (☎ 504-410-1000) at 125 Bourbon Street, is the product of a partnership between local restaurant baron Ralph Brennan and Jazz Fest main man Quint Davis. Together, they've created a predictably successful showcase for good food and great music. Storyville District feels just a touch too touristy for some but it's by far the best club on Bourbon Street. And there's more good news: no cover.

The new *Tin Roof Café* at 532 Frenchman Street is a winsome traditional jazz venue with an excellent house band. Family-run and laid-back, the Tin Roof is a good place to hang out while waiting for a later gig to kick off up the road at the more exciting Snug Harbor.

Tipitina's (☎ 504-895-8477) at 501 Napoleon is the 'real' Tipitina's – or 'Tips' as locals call it. The barn-like club was set up for New Orleans piano legend Professor Longhair whose 1953 hit gave the club its name. Tips attracts top acts and a very lively crowd but its location means a drive from the Quarter. Don't park too far from the doors; this isn't an area to wander around alone at night. A visit to Tips is an essential part of the New Orleans experience.

New Orleans — radio stations

Your best bet for jazz and blues is WWOZ at 90.7 FM. This is a community station set up to promote the music of Louisiana although the emphasis appears to be on jazz. WWNO at 89.9 FM plays some jazz. KMEZ at 102.9 focuses on rhythm and blues while WODT at 1280 AM is a great blues channel. You'll find gospel music at WYLD (940 AM), KKNO (750 AM) and WBOK (1230 AM) as well as plenty of good ol' Southern preaching.

Tipitina's French Quarter (☎ 504-566-7095) at 233 North Peter's Street is the flashier, younger brother of the original Tips. A large stage means this smaller club, like the other, can accommodate big acts. Zydeco night is always entertaining; Harry Connick Sr's regular slot is less so.

The *Old Point Bar* (☎ 504-364-0950), at 545 Patterson Street, is across the Mississippi from the French Quarter on Algiers Point. It's a simple enough neighborhood bar but one which books good, funky bands on a regular basis. Since an evening trip over to Algiers is a great way to see the sun set behind the New Orleans skyline, it's well worth a visit.

Moving on — New Orleans to Baton Rouge

From New Orleans the I-10 races west across watery Louisiana to Baton Rouge. The road itself is a staggering feat, bridging as it does over 80 miles of swampland. Highway 61 traces a similar route west but, at this stage, the interstate is a more enjoyable and much faster road.

Baton Rouge

Louisiana's state capital is a functional town built around politics, industry and the state's two largest universities. Despite all this activity the city has a sober feel – it's a straightlaced antidote to New Orleans. The only guaranteed entertainment comes from the capitol, the tallest in America, where Louisiana's famously colorful political life is fought out. A huge port and prosperous petrochemical industry keeps the economy here buoyant but there is little to tempt travelers to stay for long.

That said, Baton Rouge is an attractive city, its center dominated by grand parks, and the evocative plantation country around the capital offers a glimpse of privileged Southern living.

History

When French explorers led by Pierre Le Moyne, Sieur d'Iberville, reached this part of Louisiana in 1699, they found a stake dipped in animal blood – a *baton rouge* – used by Indians to mark the boundary between hunting grounds. The French claimed Baton Rouge but lost the region to Britain in 1736. In turn, the British lost Baton Rouge to the Spanish in 1779.

In 1810 a group of Anglo-Americans seized the fort at Baton Rouge from the Spanish and proclaimed the area an independent republic named West Florida. The republic lasted just 74 days until Americans from New Orleans reclaimed Baton Rouge for Louisiana. The fledgling city was made state capital in 1846. Baton Rouge fell quickly to Union soldiers during the Civil War but was once again capital of Louisiana by 1882. Today, Baton Rouge is a city of over 600,000 people.

Arrival and departure

By air
The **Baton Rouge Metro Airport** (☎ 225-357-4165) is north of downtown off I-110 at 9450 Jackie Cochran Drive. Used mainly by oil executives, the airport is served by American (☎ 225-356-7921), Continental (☎ 225-359-6583), Delta (☎ 800-221-1212), Northwest (☎ 225-355-7693) and USA Air Express (☎ 800-428-4322) airlines.

By bus
Greyhound buses pull up at the bus terminal at 1253 Florida Street (☎ 225-383-3811). There are 13 services a day from here to Lafayette, eight to New Orleans and six to Jackson, Mississippi. **Delta Bus Lines** (☎ 662-335-2144) runs one return service a day from Memphis to Baton Rouge along Highway 61. It stops at Natchez, Vicksburg, Greenville and Clarksdale. A single fare all the way to Memphis from Baton Rouge costs $66.

By car
From Baton Rouge drivers can divert west on I-10 to Lafayette and Cajun country, or shoot north on I-110 to connect with Highway 61 which leads to St Francisville and on into Mississippi.

Orientation

Downtown Baton Rouge stretches out just west of I-110 and north of I-10. Here you'll find the government buildings, library, most businesses and the city's few central clubs. Louisiana State University is a little way south of downtown while Southern University, traditionally an African-American institution, sits some way north of downtown off Highway 61.

Getting around

By cab
Cabs aren't always easy to hail in Baton Rouge particularly after dusk in the downtown area when they seem to dry up altogether. If you plan to book ahead, and it's probably a good idea, try Taxicab Service (☎ 225-667-3600) or Yellow Cab (☎ 225-923-3260).

Car rental
Main Baton Rouge branches include:
- **Avis** (☎ 225-355-4721), Baton Rouge Metro Airport
- **Budget** (☎ 225-355-0312), Baton Rouge Metro Airport
- **Enterprise** (☎ 225-346-5487), 641 Convention Street
- **Hertz** (☎ 225-357-5992), Baton Rouge Metro Airport
- **National** (☎ 225-355-5651), Baton Rouge Metro Airport
- **Thrifty** (☎ 225-356-2576), 2982 Varsity Street

Baton Rouge — festivals and events

● **May** Downtown Baton Rouge businesses get together every May to host the Rhythm and Views Spring concerts in the streets. Expect a mix of zydeco, Latin and reggae music.

● **Mid-September** sees blues celebrated in Baton Rouge's clubs as part of the city's growing 'Blues Week'. Contact the Baton Rouge CVB for more information.

Services

Banks
The main banks in central Baton Rouge are the Union Planters Bank at 339 Florida Street, Bank One at 451 Florida Street and Hibernia at 440 Third Street. Malcolm Travel & American Express at 7744 Florida Blvd is a good place to change travelers' checks.

Communications
● **Post** You'll find the main post office (☎ 225-381-0713) on Florida Boulevard between 6th and 7th streets.
● **Internet** Check your emails for free at the main city library at 7711 Goodwood Boulevard.

Tourist information
The tourist information desk (☎ 225-342-7317, 800-LA-ROUGE) in the lobby of the State Capitol building can supply hotel lists and other useful Baton Rouge literature.

Tours
Since Baton Rouge is fairly easy to explore, an organized tour seems unnecessary. But if you do want to be shown the sights, try one of these companies:
● **Bell Tours** (☎ 225-753 8801) is a family-run firm offering full-day trips.
● **Dixieland Tours** (☎ 225-273-9119, 800-256-8747) provide half- and full-day plantation tours.
● The ubiquitous **Gray Line** (☎ 225-273-0080, 800-441-6962) provides all manner of tours and transfers.
● **Lagniappe Tours** (☎ 225-382-8687) offers tailor-made trips and can provide Spanish-, French- or German-speaking guides.

Medical emergencies
The Baton Rouge General Medical Center (☎ 225-387-7000) is at 3600 Florida Boulevard.

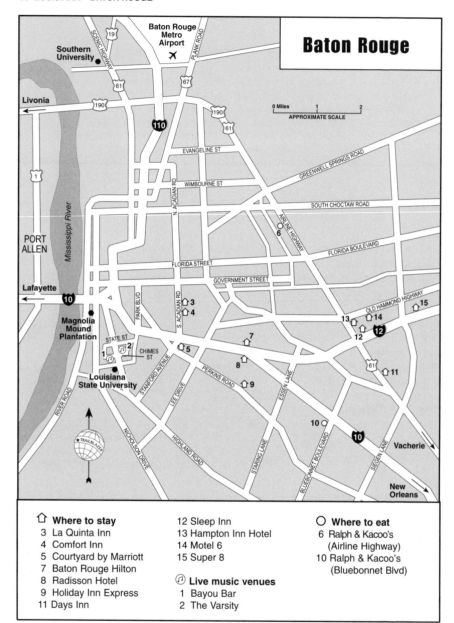

Baton Rouge

Southern University

Baton Rouge Metro Airport

Livonia

PORT ALLEN

Mississippi River

Lafayette

Magnolia Mound Plantation

Louisiana State University

New Orleans

Vacherie

⭑ TRAILBLAZER

0 Miles   1   2
APPROXIMATE SCALE

SCENIC HIGHWAY
PLANK ROAD
EVANGELINE ST
GREENWELL SPRINGS ROAD
WIMBOURNE ST
N. ACADIAN RD
SOUTH CHOCTAW ROAD
AIRLINE HIGHWAY
FLORIDA BOULEVARD
FLORIDA STREET
GOVERNMENT STREET
PARK BLVD
S. ACADIAN RD
OLD HAMMOND HIGHWAY
STATE ST
CHIMES ST
STANFORD AVENUE
LEE DRIVE
PERKINS ROAD
ESSEN LANE
NICHOLSON DRIVE
HIGHLAND ROAD
STARING LANE
BLUEBONNET BOULEVARD
SIEGEN LANE
RIVER ROAD

⌂ **Where to stay**
3 La Quinta Inn
4 Comfort Inn
5 Courtyard by Marriott
7 Baton Rouge Hilton
8 Radisson Hotel
9 Holiday Inn Express
11 Days Inn

12 Sleep Inn
13 Hampton Inn Hotel
14 Motel 6
15 Super 8

🎵 **Live music venues**
1 Bayou Bar
2 The Varsity

○ **Where to eat**
6 Ralph & Kacoo's
(Airline Highway)
10 Ralph & Kacoo's
(Bluebonnet Blvd)

KEY – DOWNTOWN BATON ROUGE (MAP OPPOSITE)

○ **Where to eat**
2 Avoyelles
3 Faye's Subs and Salads
4 Poor Boy Lloyd's
5 Riverside Patty

6 Bamboo Garden
7 Richoux's
9 M's Fine and Mellow Café
10 Black Forest Restaurant

🎵 **Live music venues**
1 Thirsty Tiger
8 Tabby's Blues Box and
Heritage Hall
9 M's Fine and Mellow Café

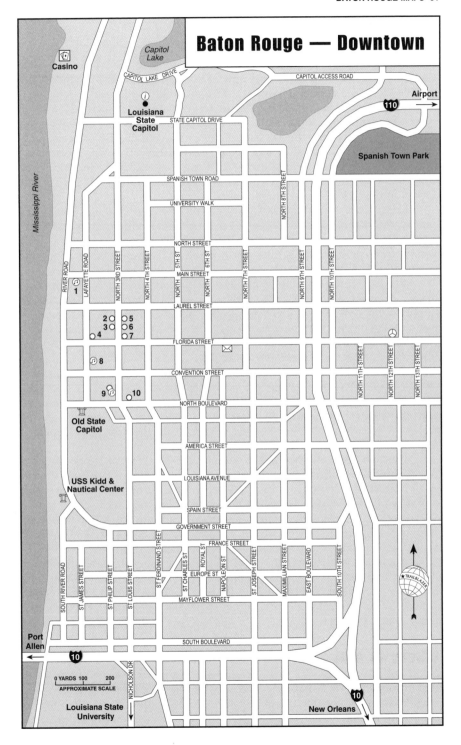

Baton Rouge — Downtown

Casino

Capitol Lake

CAPITOL LAKE DRIVE

CAPITOL ACCESS ROAD

Airport

110

Louisiana State Capitol

STATE CAPITOL DRIVE

Spanish Town Park

SPANISH TOWN ROAD

UNIVERSITY WALK

NORTH 8TH STREET

Mississippi River

NORTH STREET

5TH ST

6TH ST

NORTH 7TH STREET

NORTH 9TH STREET

NORTH 10TH STREET

RIVER ROAD

LAFAYETTE ROAD

NORTH 3RD STREET

NORTH 4TH STREET

NORTH 5TH

MAIN STREET

NORTH 6TH

1

LAUREL STREET

2 5
3 6
4 7

FLORIDA STREET

NORTH 11TH STREET

NORTH 12TH STREET

NORTH 13TH STREET

8

CONVENTION STREET

9 10

NORTH BOULEVARD

Old State Capitol

AMERICA STREET

LOUISIANA AVENUE

USS Kidd & Nautical Center

SPAIN STREET

GOVERNMENT STREET

FRANCE STREET

SOUTH RIVER ROAD

ST JAMES STREET

ST PHILIP STREET

ST LOUIS STREET

ST FERDINAND STREET

ST CHARLES ST

ROYAL ST

EUROPE ST

NAPOLEON ST

ST JOSEPH STREET

MAXIMILIAN STREET

EAST BOULEVARD

SOUTH 10TH STREET

TRAILBLAZER

MAYFLOWER STREET

Port Allen

10

SOUTH BOULEVARD

0 YARDS 100   200
APPROXIMATE SCALE

NICHOLSON DR

Louisiana State University

10

New Orleans

What to see

Few visitors escape Baton Rouge without exploring the **Louisiana State Capitol** (☎ 225-342-7317) on State Capitol Drive. You can't miss it; with 34 stories it's the tallest capitol in America. This monolithic thirties construction is clearly designed to dominate the city, and in that respect it succeeds. Two lift rides take visitors to a 350-ft-high observation deck from which the views over Baton Rouge and down the Mississippi are well worth the risk of vertigo.

The capitol has another, more grizzly distinction. This was the scene of charismatic Louisiana governor Huey P Long's assassination in 1935. Long was a colorful political character who, ironically, conceived the idea of the new capitol in which he was eventually shot.

Long loved to commission great construction projects like that of the capitol. Another of his dreams can be seen made real in the form of the **Baton Rouge Bridge** which, with a clearance of just 65 feet, prevents larger sea-going vessels from progressing further north up the Mississippi (so encouraging business at Baton Rouge port).

The **Old State Capitol** (☎ 225-342-0500) at 100 North Boulevard now houses a museum of Louisiana's political past (Tues-Sun 10am-4pm; $4). It might sound dull but, in Louisiana, politics rivals any soap opera, and the multi-media elements of the exhibition here are impressive. The actual building, which overlooks the Mississippi, is a 150-year-old neo-Gothic beast of a place which most visitors either love or hate.

An unappealing name makes it tempting to skip the **Rural Life Museum** (☎ 225-765-2437; Mon-Sun 9am-5pm; $5) at 4800 Essen Lane, part of Louisiana State University, but think twice. The museum provides a well thought out and structured introduction to rural life in southern Louisiana. Since the State's fortunes have always been tied to agriculture, the story is a compelling one.

The **USS Kidd and Nautical Center** (☎ 225-342-1942) at 305 South River Road features a World War Two destroyer and examples of P-40 and Corsair A-7E aircraft. The center is a cross between a museum and a memorial which might be of interest to some visitors. You might also consider taking a tour to see something of the jungly **swamps and bayous** around Baton Rouge. Several companies offer tours, they include: Alligator Bayou Tours (☎ 225-642-9448); Pure Cajun Swamp Tours (☎ 504-633-9306); and Zam's Tours (☎ 504-633-7881). If, on the other hand, a visit to one of the many elegant **plantation homes** in the area appeals, drive out to: Laura Plantation (☎ 225-265-7690) at 2247 Highway 18, Vacherie; Blythewood (☎ 504-748-5886) at 400 Daniel Street, Amite; or Magnolia Mound Plantation (☎ 225-343-4955) at 2161 Nicholson Drive, Baton Rouge.

Where to stay

Baton Rouge has its fair share of the standard hotel and motel chains which circle most cities; see the 'Chain Hotels' section opposite. If you plan to stay near central Baton Rouge, you'll probably have to settle for one of these places.

Baton Rouge — chain hotels

- *Baton Rouge Hilton* (☎ 225-924-5000), 5500 Hilton Avenue
- *Comfort Inn* (☎ 225-927-5790), 2445 South Arcadian Thruway
- *Courtyard by Marriott* (☎ 225-293-6400), 2421 South Arcadian Thruway
- *Days Inn* (☎ 225-291-8152), 10245 Airline Highway
- *Hampton Inn Hotel* (☎ 225-924-4433), 10045 Gwenadele Avenue
- *Holiday Inn Express* (☎ 225-930-0600), 4924 Constitution Avenue
- *La Quinta Inn* (☎ 225-924-9600), 2333 South Arcadian Thruway
- *Radisson Hotel* (☎ 225-925-2244), 4728 Constitution Avenue
- *Sleep Inn* (☎ 225-926-8488), 10332 Plaza American Drive

Budget options

Those in search of cheap sleep will have to put up with a budget motel. Try the *Motel 6* (☎ 225-291-4912; ❸) at 10445 Rieger Road or the *Super 8* (☎ 225-926-8488; ❸) at 10332 Plaza American Drive.

RV-drivers and campers could head over to the *KOA* (☎ 225-664-7281; ❷) at 7628 Vincent Road in Denham Springs or the *Cajun Country Campground* (☎ 225-383-8554; ❶) at 4667 Rebelle Lane in Port Allen. The KOA has a pool and hot tub and is better than most in this chain, though all things are relative. The Cajun Country Campground has a free Cajun cook-out on a Saturday. Both places seem to have a fairly high proportion of long-term residents.

Bed and breakfast

For a more atmospheric stay than a night in a chain hotel, check out a bed and breakfast. Since almost all the bed and breakfasts in the Baton Rouge area are some way out of town in outlying communities, however, you'll need a car to find them.

Maggie's Place (☎ 225-752-7723; ❸) at 18998 Hoo Shoo Too Road is an unusual establishment with just one guest room. Better still head over to *Pointe Coupee Bed and Breakfast* (☎ 225-638-6254; ❸) at 405 Richey Street in New Roads. This Creole plantation dates back to around 1835 and is a great place to stay if you can grab one of the two rooms available. Book ahead. The *Oak Valley Plantation* (☎ 225-265-2151; ❹) at 3645 Highway 18 in Vacherie is another delightful old place – this one with more rooms. There's an oak-lined path which makes a visit worthwhile even if you don't plan to stay the night.

A little more upscale, the *Garden Gate Manor Bed and Breakfast* (☎ 225-638-3890; ❹) at 204 Poydras Street in New Roads dates back only as far as 1911 but still has ample charm and has been voted one of the South's best historic bed and breakfasts.

Where to eat

Downtown Baton Rouge's Third Street is loaded with little restaurants which are great for cheap snacks; most, however, open only for lunch. Friendly

Avoyelles at 333 Third Street does a mean shrimp po-boy for $5.50. Their house special pasta with parmesan, eggplant and tomato sauce ($6.95) is pretty good too. Opposite at number 336, *Riverside Patty* does a few simple snacks although this is more of a coffee shop. The *Bamboo Garden* (☎ 225-383-5566) Chinese restaurant at 324 Third Street does an all-you-can-eat lunch buffet for $5.75. It's aimed at suits from the capitol so the food's not bad.

Faye's Subs and Salads at 311 Third Street does gargantuan sandwiches for around $6. *Richoux's* (☎ 225-387-0253) at 302 Third Street at the corner of Florida does a beef pot roast for a reasonable $5.50. At 321 North Boulevard, the *Black Forest Restaurant* serves German food everyday for lunch and for dinner by special reservation.

M's Fine and Mellow Café (☎ 225-387-3663) at 143 Third Street, featured in the music venue section, is also a good choice for food. You'll find M's serves some of the best pizza in Baton Rouge for $6-8; try the Mediterranean Delight from the Gourmet Pizza menu. *Poor Boy Lloyds* at 251 Florida Street, also downtown, is a local favourite for cheap lunches. Look out for the collection of Louisiana political bric-a-brac around the walls.

If you're prepared to wander beyond downtown – and in Baton Rouge most people are – you'll find a wide choice of restaurants. The best of these includes *Ralph & Kacoo's* (☎ 225-356-2361) at 6110 Bluebonnet Boulevard (there's another at 7110 Airline Highway). Ralph & Kacoo's serves fresh seafood hidden beneath a mound of batter as is the Louisiana way. It's good stuff and reasonably priced. There's a live jazz band at the Airline Highway restaurant on Sundays between 11am and 3pm.

Another local favourite is *Joe's Dreyfus Store Restaurant* (☎ 225-637-2625) out in Livonia at 2371 Maringouin Road. Set in an old store, as the name suggests, Joe's dishes up classic Creole and Cajun recipes (around $9-10).

Where to find live music

As a large Southern town wedged between Lafayette and New Orleans, Baton Rouge should be a great musical city. But a conservative air and a feeling of being overshadowed by New Orleans have conspired to curtail music in Baton Rouge, which struggles to maintain a limited scene. Interestingly, Baton Rouge is more a blues than a jazz town. Local talent has for years drawn inspiration less from Louisiana than from the Mississippi Delta to the north.

Perhaps the best known of the older generation of Baton Rouge blues stars are Henry Gray and Tabby Thomas. Gray made his name in Chicago, playing with Howlin' Wolf for 12 years, but has since returned to south Louisiana. Actually from Kenner, just outside New Orleans, Gray found prominence on the Baton Rouge scene both before and after his successful stint in Chicago.

(Opposite) The Breaux Bridge Crawfish Festival (see p75) which takes place in May near Lafayette (LA) is a three-day orgy of music, dancing and food. A crawfish-eating contest is the messy highlight.

Interview — Tabby Thomas

How did you first get started with the Blues?
It's a long story. I started singing in the church choir when I was a young boy, then I sung in a quartet and I went from there. I went to San Francisco. I was young, someone heard me singing and told me there was a talent show coming up at a radio station. I went down there for a Sunday audition and they put me on the show. I sung and I won first prize. I had a friend, who when I went to the studio to see about recording, told the producer I was something special – so the producer said 'let me hear you sing'. I was on my lunch hour. I worked down on Market Street in a shoe store. So I sung and the producer said 'cut it' and that record was cut in my lunch hour.

*Tabby Thomas,
King of the Swamp
Blues, is a leading
Baton Rouge
bluesman and owner
of Tabby's Blues Box.*

What's the music scene like in Baton Rouge now?
We've got more here than they have in New Orleans, there's a bunch of them playing, but it's not like it was. You don t get so much real blues, you get guys trying to sing but some of them can't carry a note – they play the guitar too loud and all that.

Is the real old blues going to die out?
It might, everything does sooner or later. Like hard rock – it's evolution. The reason the blues was like it was is because it was primitive. When the slaves came from Africa they didn't have any blues over here, it was a tradition of some of the old African people that came over here and had a longing for their home. In the night when the sun had gone down they were longing for their homeland, they missed their children and their families, and that's how the blues was born. That moaning and that feeling is the sound that prevails in the blues. Not everyone can tell you that – they don't all know it.

How is 'swamp blues' different from other blues forms?
Swamp music is a kind of creation out of blues with a Louisiana flavor to it, some artists are doing it. I'm doing it myself. It's based in the music and the rhythm and the way it's played and sung. Everybody's got a different style. Further up the coast you get a jazzier style but down here it's a railroad thing.

(Opposite) Top: Letting the good times roll to the driving rhythm of zydeco music in Lafayette (La). **Bottom:** Savoy's Music Center (see p77) near Lafayette hosts a Cajun jam session every Saturday morning. Players are expected to bring food and gossip as well as their accordions.

Tabby Thomas (interview p65) has been a dominant figure in Baton Rouge music since he cut a blues record on his lunchbreak in San Francisco.

Other names to look out for include: Tab Benoit, a much-admired younger blues guitarist born in Baton Rouge but based in Houma; gifted harp player Raful Neal; and Chris Thomas King, Tabby Thomas' son and a great guitar player – and actor – in his own right. Baton Rouge also benefits from passing talent playing the circuit in the South; a lot of musicians making their way north from New Orleans find themselves in Baton Rouge.

The best place to start looking for what's on in Baton Rouge is the monthly freebee *Rhythm City* which is itself an integral part of the scene here. Published by photo-journalist and music enthusiast Tommy Comeaux, *Rhythm City* tells you everything you need to know about what's on in Baton Rouge in any given month. Two very different institutions keep music alive at night in Baton Rouge's otherwise anaesthetized downtown. *Tabby's Blues Box and Heritage Hall* (☎ 225-387-9715) at 244 Lafayette Street is the new home of Tabby Thomas and his house band which includes the up-and-coming guitarist John Lisi.

The old Blues Box at 1314 North Boulevard, dingier and smaller than the present place, had for years been a center for blues in southern Louisiana when plans for a new highway forced it to close. Tabby then moved his club downtown to Lafayette Street. It was a brave decision since downtown Baton Rouge is hardly a lively place. Critics claim the new club lacks the charm of the old but it's still a true blues dive – albeit one which attracts a large student crowd. Monday night is zydeco, Tuesday is jam night and on Thursday nights they dish out free draft beer. Music starts at 10pm and goes on till 2pm. Tabby himself, 'King of the Swamp Blues', plays regularly.

The other great club in downtown Baton Rouge is *M's Fine and Mellow Café* (☎ 225-387-3663) at 143 Third Street. This is an altogether more sophisticated set-up than Tabby's and you'll find here a more varied menu of music (and food, which is excellent). The enigmatic M is an eccentric hostess but she has a talent for persuading first-rate artists, particularly jazz stars, to drop by. M's is a gem which, strangely, a lot of locals seem to overlook because of its downtown location. Don't miss it.

Another downtown joint worth checking out is *Thirsty Tiger* (☎ 225-387-9799) at 140 Main Street, a funky little place where owners Steve and Terry Fuller book blues and rockabilly acts most weekends. The *Bayou Bar* (☎ 225-346-1765) at 124 West Chimes Street has been a favourite for LSU students for 40 years; the management sometimes book high-profile blues and zydeco acts. Other popular student hang-outs with regular music include the *Varsity* (225-383-7018) at 3353 Highland Road.

Baton Rouge — radio stations

The main station for blues is KBRH AM 1260/90.3FM. Tabby Thomas has a regular slot. Gumbo 104.5 FM features Louisiana music.

Moving on — Baton Rouge to Lafayette

From Baton Rouge Highway 61 leads north to Mississippi. Some 60 miles west on the I-10, however, sits Lafayette, cultural capital of French Louisiana and home of Cajun and zydeco music. Jubilant Lafayette is an essential chapter in the story of Southern music and an essential excursion from the Blues Highway.

Lafayette

Lafayette is a lounging, low-rise town and cultural nucleus. As unofficial capital of French-speaking Louisiana, Lafayette and its people, Cajuns, maintain traditions and music which are unique. On first impressions, Lafayette itself could be Anywhere, USA. There is no discernable center and the place is riddled with the usual collection of junk food joints and budget motels. Look in the right places, however, and you'll find that Lafayette has something of everything that's great about the South; wild music, friendly people, sleepy days and great food.

Parlez-vous anglais?

Cajun-French continued to develop in Acadiana after the exiled settlers who founded the community established a permanent home here towards the end of the eighteenth century. The isolated nature of Acadiana and the defensive, inward-looking nature of early Acadian settlers conspired to help the language survive.

In the thirties, when roads brought more outsiders to Acadiana and, in schools, French-speaking Cajuns began to be stigmatized for not speaking English, Cajun-French came under threat. Cajuns and their language were at this time looked down on in Louisiana. Rather than continue to subordinate their culture, however, Cajuns began to fight back to save their traditions. Through music particularly, the Cajun spirit and language were kept alive and, in time, both came to be recognized as valuable, legitimate and something to be celebrated.

These days, Cajun culture is stronger than ever and the French-Cajun dialect has enjoyed something of a renaissance. Cajun-French is spoken widely and French is taught alongside English in elementary schools.

The dialect itself is, to the French, very strong and markedly different from the 'mother tongue'. Expressions you might hear in Acadiana include: *c'est tout* – that's all; *fais-do-do* – traditional Cajun dance; *lagniappe* – 'something more'; *joie de vivre* – joy in living; *laissez les bons temps rouler* – let the good times roll; *allons* – let's go.

Lafayette & environs — festivals and events

Cajun country is famous for the regularity and fervor of its festivals; even the humble crawfish and red beans and rice are celebrated. Most festivals feature plenty of live music, whether directly music-related festivals or not, and you can generally rely on lots of food, too. Lafayette fills up for certain festivals like Le Cajun Music awards or the Breaux Bridge Crawfish Festival, so book ahead if your trip looks likely to coincide with a major Cajun party.

- **February** – Mardi Gras, Lafayette and other parishes
- **March** – World Championship Crawfish Cook off
- **April** – Cajun Music Festival, Eunice
- **April** – Festival International de Louisiane, Lafayette
- **May** – Crawfish Festival, Breaux Bridge (see p75)
- **May** – Zydeco Extravaganza, Lafayette
- **June** – Cajun Music Festival, Mamou
- **August** – 'Le Cajun' Music Awards, Lafayette
- **September** – Red Beans and Rice Festival, Fenton
- **September** – Southwest Louisiana Zydeco Music Festival, Plaisance
- **October** – Louisiana Cotton Festival, Ville Platte

History — Lafayette and Acadiana

In 1755 the British Governor of Nova Scotia, Charles Lawrence, ordered the exile of some 18,000 French-speaking Catholic settlers who refused to pledge allegiance to the British crown. His actions forced an entire community to flee by sea to the United States in what came to be known as *Le Grand Derangement*. Many died, but of those who survived most were attracted to Louisiana where they were given land in a series of grants between 1765 and 1785. The region became 'Acadiana' – after an earlier name for Nova Scotia – and its residents 'Acadians' which, in a French-Southern accent, easily corrupts to 'Cajuns'. The community at Lafayette was founded in 1821 by a rich cotton planter named Jean Mouton. Mouton originally named the town Vermilionville, after the river on which it sits, but the name was amended to Lafayette in 1884.

Arrival and departure

By air
Lafayette Regional Airport (☎ 337-266-4400) is a few miles south at 200 Terminal Drive. It's served by American (☎ 337-237-0496), Continental Express (☎ 337-234-9828) and Northwest Airlink (☎ 337-235-6179).

By bus
Greyhounds pull up at 315 Lee Avenue, just a block south of the city bus station. There are frequent Greyhound services between Lafayette, Baton Rouge and New Orleans.

Cajun and zydeco music

To the outsider, **Cajun music** is a type of European-influenced folk music played on fiddles, guitars and accordions to a two-step or waltz rhythm. To academic Barry Jean Ancelet, who describes the origins of Cajun music in a booklet published by the Center for Louisiana Studies, it's a blend of German, Spanish, Scottish, Irish, Anglo-American, Afro-Caribbean and American Indian influences with a base of French Acadian folk tradition.

Displaced settlers carried with them traditions and musical memories from Nova Scotia; when subsequent generations recreated that music in Louisiana it was naturally altered by a new set of influences. Cajun music is almost without exception played by white Acadians.

Although the first Cajun hit was recorded way back in 1928 by Joseph Falcon, the music was virtually ignored outside Louisiana until it was discovered by a wider audience as part of the folk revival of the sixties and seventies. Lots of latter-day Cajun bands keep the music alive in Lafayette where live gigs are easy to find. Lee Benoit, Jay Cornier, Jambalaya, the Lafayette Playboys, Gervais Matte and **Marc Savoy** (see p72) are among the many locally popular acts worth searching for on a Saturday night.

Black Creoles in Acadiana maintain another unique musical tradition, **zydeco**, which shares certain influences with Cajun music. Zydeco is a far more driving, aggressive musical style which owes more to blues and soul than it does to folk. Typically, zydeco music is played with an accordion, a washboard (*frottoir*) and drums.

Few can listen to zydeco without dancing; fewer still can fail to enjoy this ecstatic genre. The story goes that 'zydeco' is a corruption of the word 'haricot'; black plantation workers picking snap-beans would use the rhythm of the snapping to underpin their singing.

Clifton Chenier, who died in Lafayette in 1987 at the age of 62, was the greatest pioneer of zydeco; his influence is still felt and respected today. His son, CJ Chenier, leads the great Red Hot Louisiana Band. A busy touring schedule means it's difficult to catch CJ in Lafayette but if you can, do. Buckwheat Zydeco, led by Stanley 'Buckwheat' Dural Jr, is another of the better-known zydeco acts to have conquered the world from Lafayette. Buckwheat Zydeco has broadened the scope of zydeco music by introducing a rock edge and touring with the likes of U2 and Eric Clapton.

Nathan Williams and the Zydeco Cha Chas is, perhaps, the best zydeco act to appear regularly in Louisiana venues. **Nathan Williams** (see p76) leads a wildly energetic band and enjoys a huge following in the South.

Other zydeco acts to look out for include Lil' Pookie, Beau Jocque and Roy Carrier.

By car

Lafayette sits at the crossroads of the I-10, the I-49 and Highway 90. The I-10 east leads back towards New Orleans, Baton Rouge, Highway 61 and Mississippi. The I-49 threads north into central Louisiana while Highway 90 shoots down to the Gulf of Mexico.

Orientation

Downtown Lafayette, such as it is, sits in the crook created by Highway 90 as it bends south towards Broussard. But the town's attractions sprawl over a much larger area more or less built along Highway 49, the Evangeline Thruway, and the roads west of Highway 90. Opelousas and Eunice are respectively north and north-west of Lafayette; Breaux Bridge and Henderson are east towards Baton Rouge on the I-10.

Getting around

By car

Lafayette is almost impossible to negotiate without a car; the entire city appears to have been shaped by its highways. If you haven't driven to Lafayette, consider renting a car when you get here. The main agencies in town are **Enterprise** (☎ 337-237-2864) at 137 James Comeaux Road, **Thrifty** (☎ 337-237-1282) at 401 Pinhook Road and the **Rent-a-Car Agency of Lafayette** (☎ 337-981-7368) at 3609 Cameron Street.

By cab

Cabs need to be ordered – they're hard to find. Try Yellow Checker Cabs (☎ 337-237-5701), Affordable Cabs of Acadiana (☎ 337-234-2111), AAA Cabs (☎ 337-988-5300) or Cajun Cabs (☎ 337-235-7515).

By tour

There's little point in taking an organized tour if you have your own car but, if you don't, this might be a useful way to get a feel for the area. Of the tour companies operating in and around Lafayette, the best are **Acadia Tours with Alice** (☎ 337-783-5640) at 521 East Third Street, **Class Act Tours** (☎ 337-981-0705) at 102 Westmark Boulevard and **Tour Masters** (☎ 337-643-8481) at 402 North Irving Street, Kaplan.

KEY – LAFAYETTE

○ **Where to eat**
1 Prejean's
8 Café Vermilionville
15 Randol's

♫ **Live music venues**
7 El Sid O's
13 Hamiltons

⌂ **Where to stay**
2 Plantation Motor Inn
3 Motel 6
4 Super 8 Motel
5 Quality Inn
6 Days Inn
9 Best Western Hotel
   Acadiana

10 Ramada Executive Plaza
11 Courtyard by Marriott
12 Holiday Inn Express
14 A La Maison de T'Frere's
16 Le Maison Repos

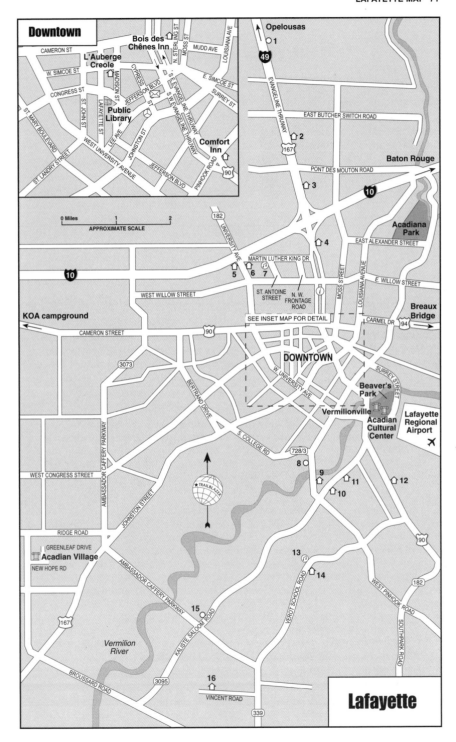

Interview — Marc Savoy

Marc Savoy is a well-known Cajun recording artist, accordion-maker and historian.

What are the origins of Cajun music?
The root of it comes from Canada; the fiddle and triangle probably came from Canada with our ancestors when they arrived here in Louisiana in 1756. A lot of people think the accordion is a Cajun instrument but it wasn't invented until about 1830 so it didn't come with our ancestors. In fact it arrived in about 1850 with the German immigrants. So the music is rooted in Canada, and I guess came from France into Canada in about 1630 and when they were expelled in about 1755 it found its way to Louisiana. Because of the isolation from the mother country, which was what is now Nova Scotia and New Brunswick, this region took on a different branch of the tree of evolution. The influences that were already here, like the African slaves, the Spanish who were governing Louisiana when the Cajuns arrived, the Germans and all the other ethnic minorities, made pretty much a melting pot. It took evolution to produce this thing called Cajun music. As far as where the spirit might come from, all these ethnic minorities I've mentioned, except perhaps the African slaves, didn't have the pepper to make music like Cajun music. I'm foolish enough to think that the spirit that drove the heat and passion of the music came from the heat of Louisiana. You find in these hot, hot regions that music is hot too.

Has Cajun music always been popular?
It's always been popular but until the late sixties it was underground. But it was stigmatized when the Anglos started to invade the area. They did their best to pretend that no such thing even existed. You see they were always down-playing it. So when it was finally discovered by the outside world, and it got to be popular and people started coming here in droves asking 'where's the Cajun music?', that really shook a few people round here.

How was Cajun music discovered by the outside world?
Do you know that Cajun music was discovered in 1964 when a talent scout from the prestigious Newport Jazz Festival came to Louisiana? He negotiated with some people in this area and three old guys went to the festival to represent Cajun music to people who'd never heard it before. It had never been exposed or brought out of the State. They were up against names like Bob Dylan and Joan Baez. Anyone else would have been highly intimidated by that but they didn't even know who Bob Dylan or Joan Baez were. In fact the three of them could hardly speak English. They played with an accordion, fiddle and guitar before 10,000 people. They played a beautiful old Cajun waltz and before it was over the 10,000 people gave these three musicians a standing ovation. When they came home and told me this I felt I had always known that, one day, Cajun music and culture would explode on the world. So I decided I'd get me a music store.

Services

Banks

Main branches are: Hibernia Banks at 213 West Vermilion Street and 112 East Kaliste Saloom and a Whitney National Bank at 911 Lee Avenue.

Communications

● **Post** The main Post Office stands near the corner of Jefferson and East Cypress Streets just across the block from the Southern Pacific railroad depot.
● **Internet** Louisiana's generous library system will allow you to check your emails for free at 301 West Congress Street.

Tourist information

Cajun country has particularly efficient and helpful tourist information offices. In Lafayette, the Visitor Information Center sits in its own landscaped surrounds in the wide central reservation of Highway 49.

Record stores

Savoy's Music Center, a few miles west of Eunice on Highway 190, offers a good, specialist collection of Cajun and zydeco albums. Also try Floyd's Record Shop (☎ 337-363-2138) at 434 East Main Street in Ville Platte.

Medical emergencies

Lafayette's General Medical Center (☎ 337-289-7991) is at 1214 Coolidge Street. There are other major hospitals in town, including the Columbia Medical Center of Southwest Louisiana (☎ 337-981-2949) at 2810 Ambassador Caffery Parkway. Both have ER departments.

What to see

City highlights

Cajuns are very aware of their history, perhaps because they have had to struggle to keep their identity alive. So in Lafayette, cultural capital of French Louisiana, it's no surprise to find that history carefully documented.

Vermilionville (☎ 337-233-4077; daily 10am-5pm; $8) at 1600 Surrey Street is a 'living history' museum set on the banks of the Bayou Vermilionville in the dense forest of Beaver Park. You can easily spend half a day here exploring early Cajun life with the help of costumed actors and expertly recreated buildings. The **Acadian Cultural Center** (☎ 337-232-0789; daily 8am-5pm; free) is nearby at 501 Fisher Road. Here you'll find a detailed explanation of the fascinating but tragic events which led to this patch of Louisiana becoming home to French-speaking settlers from Canada.

Acadian Village (☎ 337-981-2364; daily 10am-5pm; $6) at 200 Greenleaf Drive is another, though smaller, reconstructed Cajun community. Normally less crowded than Vermilionville, Acadian Village gives almost as impressive an insight into Lafayette's past but it is quite a few miles from town.

Where to stay

Budget options

Of the cheap motel chains, *Motel 6* (☎ 337-233-2055; ❷) at 2724 Evangeline Thruway is probably the best value. Since Lafayette is so spread out it doesn't really matter that the Motel 6 is a few minutes drive from anywhere useful. Another option is the *Super 8 Motel* (☎ 337-232-8826; ❸) which is a few blocks away at 2224 Evangeline Thruway. The *Plantation Motor Inn* (☎ 337-232-7285; ❷) at 2810 Evangeline Thruway is also pretty inexpensive. Campers can choose between the *KOA* (☎ 337-235-2739; ❷) at 537 Apollo Road or the far more attractive *Acadiana Park* (☎ 337-291-8388; ❶) at 1201 East Alexander Street where ranger Joe Thibodeaux can answer any question on Lafayette you care to throw at him.

Bed and breakfast

For some reason Lafayette has more than its fair share of chain hotels; these are, as always, listed in a separate box. But the town also has more than its fair share of outstanding bed and breakfasts. They believe in the best traditions of Southern hospitality in Lafayette and you will find each of these recommended bed and breakfasts offers elegant accommodation and extravagant Cajun breakfasts. Since prices fluctuate according to demand, and because these establishments all charge a broadly similar amount, assume all these bed and breakfast's rates fall into the ❸ category.

One of the best places to stay in Lafayette is *A La Maison de T'Frere's* (☎ 337-984-9347) at 1905 Verot School Road. The exceptionally friendly French-speaking hosts here are famed for their 'Oh La La' breakfast which features several courses, each more appealing than the last. It's quite a treat. *A Bois des Chênes Inn* (☎ 337-233-7816) at 338 North Sterling Drive is arguably a more upscale place which has scooped some pretty impressive write ups in bed and breakfast guidebooks. There are five beautiful suites available and, again, the breakfast is traditionally Cajun.

L'Auberge Creole (☎ 337-232-1248) at 204 Madison Street is a smaller and more intimate place with just three rooms for rent. Each room is decked out in genuine antiques; the owners have clearly paid great attention to detail.

Lafayette — chain hotels

- *Best Western Hotel Acadiana* (☎ 337-233-8120), 1801 Pinhook Road
- *Comfort Inn* (☎ 337-232-9000), 1421 Evengeline Thruway
- *Courtyard by Marriott* (☎ 337-232-5005), 214 Kaliste Saloom
- *Days Inn* (☎ 337-237-8880), 1620 North University Avenue
- *Holiday Inn Express* (☎ 337-234-2000), 2503 Evangeline Thruway
- *Quality Inn* (☎ 337-232-6131), 1605 North University Avenue
- *Ramada Executive Plaza* (☎ 337-235-0858), 120 Kaliste Saloom

Another quality bed and breakfast, *Le Maison Repos* (☎ 337-856-6958), stands at 218 Vincent Road. Again, Le Maison Repos is a small family-run place located a little way out of town in a semi-rural setting.

Where to eat

Cajun's eat out a lot – and they take their food as seriously as their French heritage would suggest. Typically, Cajun food is spicy, plentiful and rustic. Seafood is a specialty and, in season, you'll find crawfish in almost every dish.

Mulate's (☎ 337-332-4648) at 325 Mills Avenue in Breaux Bridge is one of the three main restaurant-dancehall institutions in the Lafayette area. Like the others, Prejean's and Randol's, Mulate's has turned the Cajun experience into relatively big business. Some locals resent the place for that but there's no denying the food is good and the music colorful. Expect to pay around $15 for an entrée.

Randol's (☎ 337-981-7080) at 2320 Kaliste Saloom is, if anything, a bigger and more lively Cajun dancehall and restaurant with live music every night. Dinners here (again, around $15 for an entrée) are huge even by Louisiana standards. The $18 seafood platter is worth tackling if you're feeling particularly hungry. You'll be presented with a mass of crawfish, shrimps, catfish, crabs and seafood gumbo – almost all of it coated in some form of batter.

Prejean's (☎ 337-896-3247) at 3480 Hwy 167 North is the other well-known Cajun restaurant to feature live music every night. Prejean's has good food and books lively bands. If you don't feel like dancing, you can watch the

---

Peace, love and crawfish

Love Louisiana, love crawfish. The two are inseparable. Nowhere is this more obvious than at the Breaux Bridge Crawfish Festival held every May. The festival has become one of the biggest draws in the calendar of south-west Louisiana thanks to its endearing blend of the bizarre, the amusing and the downright entertaining. There's crawfish racing, a crawfish queen and a crawfish-eating contest. The rules of the latter demand contestants guzzle as much boiled crawfish as they can within 45 minutes. If you throw up – and people do – you're disqualified. The record stands somewhere around 40lb. Every year the organizers attract a rich line-up of star bands, both Cajun and zydeco, which makes the festival a key event for music-lovers and well worth visiting even if, after a couple of weeks in Louisiana, you've come to hate crawfish. Plenty of beer and cheap crawfish gumbo add to the carnival atmosphere which lasts over three days.

Campers can park their RVs near the festival which is always held in Parc Hardy in Breaux Bridge. For more information contact the Breaux Bridge Crawfish Festival Association (☎ 337-332-6655; 💻 www.bbcrawfest.com). If you're wondering why the ugly crawfish is so revered in Louisiana, the crawfish industry is worth $120 million and employs over 7000 people.

frenetic two-stepping from the sidelines as you tuck into steaming heaps of boiled crawfish and shrimp etouffe.

Other restaurants worth checking out for Cajun cooking include the rather more stylish *Café Vermilionville* (☎ 337-237-0100) at 1304 West Pinhook which serves refined Cajun dishes in a 200-year-old property listed on the National Register of Historic Places.

At *Enola Prudhomme's Cajun Café* (☎ 337-896-7964), 4676 Evangeline Thruway, you'll find consistently excellent Cajun meals served with the Prudhomme twist; Enola is the sister of Paul Prudhomme, a celebrity chef in New Orleans.

For a less polished but arguably far superior taste of real Cajun cooking, drive out to Eunice where you'll find *Ruby's* on the corner of Walnut and Second. Just a few dollars will buy you a plateful of traditional, provincial Cajun cuisine. You can't be too picky at Ruby's, however, since the menu is very limited depending on what the chef has chosen to create that day.

Where to find live music

Cajun music is easier to find than zydeco in Lafayette; and searching for the latter is more likely to take you to less salubrious venues. But while Cajun music is culturally important and certainly interesting, it's zydeco which really rocks this town. To visit Lafayette without dancing the zydeco would be to miss the point.

Of the many venues which lay on live **Cajun bands**, the most popular for outsiders are the competing *restaurant-dancehalls* Mulate's, Prejean's and Randol's. All three attract a lively if older crowd for regular weekend *fais-do-*

Interview — Nathan Williams

How would you describe zydeco music?
I've been playing zydeco for almost fifteen years. Zydeco is a local kind of music and the word means 'snap bean'. It's totally different from Cajun music, it's got a lot of blues in it, Caribbean sounds and all sorts of different stuff. My kind of zydeco has got a bit of R&B and reggae. Zydeco's caught on because it's enjoyable music.

Where are the best places to go to hear zydeco?
Zydeco is taken all over the world now as well as all over the country but it's not always that well supported in Louisiana. The Rock and Bowl in New Orleans (see p55) is my most favorite place to play, it's a fun place to go. My brother's got a club in Lafayette, El Sid O's (see opposite), and that's where I really started from. It's been open about 15 years. That's a fun place to go, too.

Nathan Williams of 'Nathan Williams and the Zydeco Cha Chas' is one of zydeco's most successful artists.

dos and both are described in more detail in the 'Where to eat' section on p75.

Arguably a more exciting taste of Cajun musicianship can be heard at the **Liberty Center for the Performing Arts** (☎ 337-457-7389) in Eunice, north-west of Lafayette. A live radio and TV show, the *Rendezvous des Cajuns* is staged here every Saturday night at six. The show features plenty of music, cooking and joke-telling – mostly in French.

Another true Cajun stronghold is **Marc Savoy's Music Center** which stands a few miles west of Eunice on Highway 190. Marc Savoy hosts a jam in his music store every Saturday morning from nine in the morning till around midday. Visitors are welcome to watch but you'll find almost everyone present is there to play. The jam session has become a community fixture; people bring food for one another, catch up on gossip and get their accordions fixed. At any one time some 15 musicians, mostly sat on ageing sofas, contribute to the sound. Marc and his son join in on accordion or piano. The age range of those involved is amazing; the larger Cajun dancehalls tend to attract a stately crowd of pensioners but Marc Savoy's jam session proves that Cajun music is played and enjoyed by people of every age.

Zydeco is popular for festivals and events so, depending on when you're in town, it's always worth checking the paper to see who's around. Despite the great interest in zydeco bands, however, actual zydeco venues are not only scarce but they're difficult to find, slightly rough around the edges and rarely frequented by white locals. By far the best of them is *El Sid O's* (☎ 337-235-0647) at 1523 Martin Luther King Drive and St Antoine Street. El Sid O is in fact Sid Williams – Nathan's brother. Sid runs a great joint where you'll be welcomed enthusiastically and encouraged to dance. The music here is always fantastic, not least because Sid's connections allow him to pull in the best bands around from Buckwheat Zydeco to his own little brother. A simple soul food menu is also available. There's music here every weekend till late.

A dingier club, *Hamiltons*, has raucous zydeco most weekends. You'll find it at 1808 Verot School Road. Local journalist Steve Landry, a zydeco fan, recalls how in the eighties Hamiltons would put on a 'whites night' to allow white people to listen to zydeco in what is, basically, a black club.

For an even more adventurous zydeco experience, drive out towards Opelousas to find the *Offshore Lounge*. This bizarre place is little more than a shack but, if you can find it on a weekend, you'll be in for some great music. Roy Carrier plays here regularly. From Opelousas head towards Eunice on Highway 190 for six miles. Look out for a Chevron garage and turn right

Lafayette — radio stations

Lafayette's two most Cajun music-friendly radio stations are KJCB at 770 AM and KRVS at 88.7 FM. You should also be able to pick up KBON 101.1 FM from Eunice and KVPI 1050 AM from Ville Platte.

Mississippi 3

With just 2.5 million people in an area six times the size of Massachusetts, Mississippi has plenty of space. Much of this vast and wide open state is devoted to agriculture. The state capital, Jackson, is the state's largest city by far but even Jackson has a sleepy feel. The Mississippi River forms the meandering western boundary of the state and it's this region, the Mississippi Delta, which is described in the following chapter. The Delta, stretched out under a fierce sun, is the cradle of blues and among the most culturally interesting and important regions in the country. Bad press and movies have at times branded Mississippi a backward place resistant to change. Perhaps it is. But music lovers won't want to leave this state and its mix of Southern elegance, endless horizons and, of course, the blues.

Lafayette and Baton Rouge to Natchez

If you've diverted from Baton Rouge to Lafayette, the best way to re-join the Blues Highway is to take the I-49 to Opelousas, Highway 190 to Livonia then head north on minor roads through soft and sylvan Louisiana landscape to New Roads where a free ferry takes cars across the Mississippi River to St Francisville.

If you didn't divert to Lafayette, pick up Highway 61, the Blues Highway, north of Baton Rouge and follow it into Mississippi. Natchez is 90 miles from Baton Rouge.

St Francisville is a small, attractive town which sees little action except passers-by travelling between Mississippi and Louisiana. There's an enticing café, the *Magnolia* (☎ 225-635-6528), at 5687 Commerce Street. It's open daily for lunch between 10am and 4pm and for dinner at weekends. The owners usually book a local band for Friday nights and an out-of-town act for Saturday nights.

As Highway 61 weaves into Mississippi the road races past dense forest, across which one can see for miles, before it slows to meet Woodville. Again, this is a tiny place but, unlike St Francisville, one which has nothing at all to offer passing traffic save, perhaps, a certain 'middle of nowhere' appeal with its rusty, towering water-tank casting a long shadow over the town's

Delta blues

Blues emerged from the Mississippi Delta around the turn of the last century. Early blues was played in other regions, most notably Texas, but Delta blues shaped the development of the genre and carried it north to black Chicago, then to Europe and finally to a world audience.

To trace the origins of this most influential music, however, one must look beyond Mississippi to the west coast of Africa. Here, slaves were captured and shipped to the United States where many thousands were put to work on vast Southern cotton plantations. Since slaves were drawn from many African countries from Senegal, Ghana and Nigeria down to Angola, these unwilling imports found themselves thrown together with people from different tribes with markedly different traditions and, more to the point, strange musical styles.

This mix led to the genesis of blues. Few instruments meant most slaves had only their own bodies with which to make music. So the human voice and clapped rhythms were developed as musical tools, another important factor in the creation of Delta blues.

Other social factors also helped provoke the invention of blues. Even after the Civil War when slaves were freed, most African-Americans in the South were tied by debt to plantations which operated a system of sharecropping which left workers perpetually poor. Life was hard and opportunities were few. So blues developed as a way to escape that painful existence, if only for a few hours in a dusty juke joint on a Saturday night. Blues was, and is, music for dancing. It's also a form of communication, a way to spread news, a vehicle for tackling complicated issues and emotions and a chance to improve the lives of a poor and marginalized people.

In the Delta itself, Henry Sloan is thought to be one of the very first to play Delta blues as we would recognize it. Almost nothing is known about Sloan except that a young Charley Patton followed his every move and was inspired to learn the guitar. Patton, of course, is generally considered to be the most influential bluesman of all. He inspired contemporaries like Tommy Johnson and, in time, younger musicians like Son House and Robert Johnson. They in turn passed the blues onto the next generation, to men such as Muddy Waters, who would take the blues north as they joined the mass exodus of blacks from the south during the forties and fifties. The musical progression can be followed further into rock & roll, rock and pop.

Chicago would eclipse the Delta as the place where blues moved forwards. The big labels like Chess were based in Chicago and much of the South's musical talent had rattled north along the Illinois Central Railroad to Chicago. The electrified sound, the future of blues, was pioneered in Chicago's noisy south side clubs.

Blues hasn't left the Delta altogether. Lots of musicians stayed and continue to stay. Some others are drifting back to the South. Any Mississippi bluesman will tell you that young African-Americans in the South ignore blues and listen only to rap; that live music is a rarity in juke joints and that the future of blues is in doubt. The Delta is home to a lot of ghosts, that's certainly true. But blues does still drift across the Delta on a Saturday night and there is interest from the younger generation. Guitarist Johnny Billington's blues education program in Lambert and Clarksdale proves that. The Delta is, without doubt, the historic cradle of blues and, as such, will never be far from the heart of the music.

deserted streets. This is the kind of place where people stare, taciturn, from under their John Deere caps and dogs stretch out in the backs of broken down pick-ups.

Natchez

Littered with antebellum mansions reeking of unrestrained excess, Natchez is and always has been a place of sharp contrasts. The town is too far south of the Delta to have made much impression on the development of blues. But one can learn a lot about the South in Natchez. As the one-time commercial capital of the cotton industry, there were once more millionaires living here than anywhere else in America. Today the town is still dripping in Southern charm and elegance, its finery only slightly dulled by time.

History

The early years of Natchez were bloody. French settlers established a fort here in 1716 but clashed with the indigenous Natchez Indians who, after massacres on both sides, were annihilated. The British took over from 1764 to 1779 when the Spanish took control. In 1798 the United States Territory of Mississippi was founded.

By this time the potential of the rich floodplain around Natchez was being realized in the form of cotton production. The invention of the cotton gin helped but the industry was fuelled mainly by the mass import of slaves. After the Louisiana Purchase in 1803, the Mississippi River could be used to transport cotton to the Gulf of Mexico for shipment worldwide. Natchez became a major river-town port and a center for the cotton trade.

A sort of 'sub-town' developed around the riverboat landings which became known as 'Natchez-under-the-Hill'. In conspicuous contrast to the affluence above, Natchez-under-the-Hill grew to become one of the most bawdy, dangerous and turbulent places anywhere along the Mississippi River. The place drew in gamblers, thieves, fighters and whores but terrified more legitimate riverboat passengers.

Many people in Natchez became enormously wealthy until the Civil War raged and the slave trade ended. Fortunes were lost and plantations crippled. In time, however, Natchez began to recoup its wealth – the cotton industry persevered and many slaves, though freed, were kept bound to plantations by debt – until the early years of the twentieth century when the 'boll weevil' destroyed the town's cotton and with it its prosperity.

Those years of extreme wealth bequeathed Natchez a remarkable collection of antebellum architecture which, through tourism, have gone some way to restoring the town's fortunes over the second half of the twentieth century.

Arrival and departure

By bus
Delta Bus Lines coaches pull up at 103 Lower Woodville Drive (☎ 601-445-5291). One Memphis-bound bus and one Baton Rouge-bound bus pass through Natchez everyday.

By car
Natchez sits on the Blues Highway, 61, 90 miles from Baton Rouge and 70 miles from next stop Vicksburg. Natchez also marks the start of the Natchez Trace scenic route which cuts diagonally across the state to Nashville, Tennessee, and marks the path of flight taken by the Natchez Indians as they were hunted by early French settlers.

Orientation

Unlike Lafayette, Natchez has a very clearly defined downtown area which lies west of Highway 61 on the high bluffs overlooking the Mississippi River. Downtown is bound by Martin Luther King Street to the east and Broadway to the west. Natchez-under-the-Hill huddles under the bluffs closer to the river's edge and the Lady Luck Casino.

Getting around

By cab or car
Cabs aren't easily hailed in Natchez so it's worth calling ahead. Try Natchez-Vidalia Taxi Service (☎ 601-442-7500). For car rentals call Enterprise (☎ 601-442-4600) or U-Save Auto Rental (☎ 601-445-8910).

By tour
Natchez Historic City Tours (☎ 601-445-9300) at 508 Orleans Street takes busloads of visitors on a whistle-stop tour of main landmarks. **Black Heritage Tours** (☎ 601-445-8309) and **Open Arms Tours** (☎ 601-442-4865) both lead engaging, specialized tours investigating African-American history in Natchez.

Services

Banks
There's an ATM at the Natchez Visitors' Reception Center at 640 Canal Street, a Britton & Koontz Bank on the corner of Main and Commerce streets and, cunningly, a United Mississippi Bank ATM at the Lady Luck Casino and another at 20 Sergeant S Prentiss Drive.

Communications
● **Post** The main US Post Office is at 214 North Canal Street.

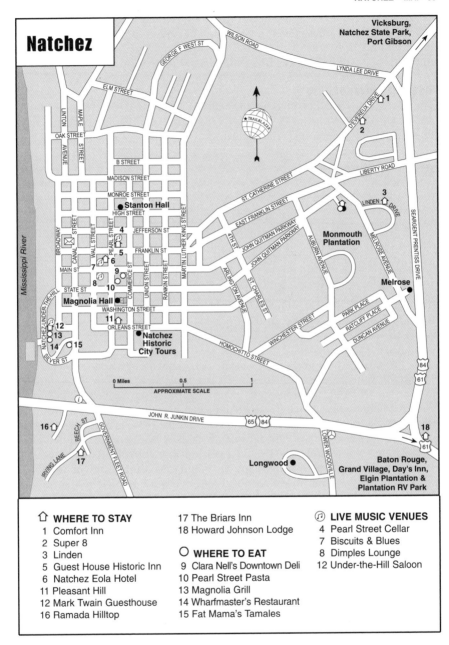

Natchez

Vicksburg,
Natchez State Park,
Port Gibson

Baton Rouge,
Grand Village, Day's Inn,
Elgin Plantation &
Plantation RV Park

⌂ **WHERE TO STAY**
1 Comfort Inn
2 Super 8
3 Linden
5 Guest House Historic Inn
6 Natchez Eola Hotel
11 Pleasant Hill
12 Mark Twain Guesthouse
16 Ramada Hilltop

17 The Briars Inn
18 Howard Johnson Lodge

○ **WHERE TO EAT**
9 Clara Nell's Downtown Deli
10 Pearl Street Pasta
13 Magnolia Grill
14 Wharfmaster's Restaurant
15 Fat Mama's Tamales

♫ **LIVE MUSIC VENUES**
4 Pearl Street Cellar
7 Biscuits & Blues
8 Dimples Lounge
12 Under-the-Hill Saloon

● **Internet** The George W Armstrong Library at 220 South Commerce Street has free Internet access. Otherwise try the visitors' center at 640 South Canal Street.

Tourist information

Natchez is well geared up for tourism with a spanking new visitor center (☎ 601-

446-6345, 800-647-6724) at 640 South Canal Street. Apart from information and hotel reservations, the center offers Internet access, a bookstore and a 20-minute film, *The Natchez Story*, which explains the origins of the town and the importance of cotton and the Mississippi River to its fortunes.

Medical emergencies

The town's two main hospitals are the Natchez Regional Medical Center (☎ 601-443-2100) at 54 Sergeant S Prentiss Drive and the Natchez Community Hospital at 129 Jefferson Davis Boulevard.

What to see

During the depressed thirties, a group of local women formed the 'Natchez Pilgrimage' (☎ 601-446-6631, 800-647-6742) which has grown to become the major tourism draw in town. Three times a year over spring, fall and Christmas, ladies of the Pilgrimage and the Garden Club show visitors round the town's major historic homes while clad in traditional pre-Civil War dress.

Fourteen of these homes are open year-round for visitors. The most interesting of these include **Stanton Hall** at 401 High Street. Built in 1857 by cotton trader Frederick Stanton, the home is as lavish as any home could be during the mid-nineteenth century. You'll find the ladies who act as guides in the house are brimming with knowledge but rather over-protective of the place; don't touch the bannisters!

Another of the great homes is the octagonal **Longwood** at 140 Lower Woodville Road. Designed in 1859 by Philadelphia architect Sam Sloan for cotton mogul Dr Nutt, the enormous pile is supposed to represent the best of Eastern architecture. In fact, it's an incongruous and unfinished behemoth. But it's an interesting one; indeed, the very fact that the place is unfinished makes it a diverting case study of mid-nineteenth century building techniques. Work on the home was curtailed by the Civil War during which Nutt lost his wealth and with it the means for completing his grand vision for Longwood.

Some of the other more beautiful and evocative homes in and around Natchez are: **Monmouth**, dating back to 1818, at 36 Melrose Avenue; **Melrose**, built between 1841 and 1845, at 1 Melrose-Montebello Parkway; and the Greek-revivalist **Magnolia Hall**, built circa 1858, at 215 South Pearl Street. Expect to pay around $6 for entry and a tour in any of the historic homes of Natchez. Opening hours tend to fall between 9am and 4pm at all homes.

Natchez-under-the-Hill is worth exploring for its quaint appeal; head down Silver Street off Broadway to find it. There are a couple of bars, some decent restaurants, a great view over the Mississippi River and the **Lady Luck Casino** (☎ 800-722-LUCK) which occupies a grand, old-style paddlesteamer on the river.

Mississippi law dictates that casinos are legal in the state only if they float on the river. This is why there are casinos all along the Blues Highway, which traces the Mississippi. Most Blues Highway casinos are fairly shabby Las Vegas wannabes and the Lady Luck is no exception. The boat itself looks attractive from the outside but inside it's hot, cramped and, frankly, depressing. There's almost no feeling of fun; punters simply stuff cash into slots like automatons.

Native American history has been rather overshadowed by subsequent events in Natchez but the **Grand Village** (☎ 601-446-6502; Mon-Sat 9am-5pm, Sun 1pm-5pm; free) at 400 Jefferson Davis Boulevard makes a good stab at documenting the way of life of the successful Natchez Indians who once prospered here. There's a museum, a recreated village and ceremonial burial mounds.

Where to stay

Budget options

Bargain-hunting travelers will struggle a little in Natchez. Campers can choose between the adequate but over-priced *Plantation RV Park* (☎ 601-442-5222; ❷), which is 1.5 miles south of Natchez on Highway 61, or the recommended *Natchez State Park* (☎ 601-442-2658; ❶) which is off Highway 61 North on Wycliffe Road. The park has recently been overhauled so the camping sites and amenities are brand new and spacious.

One of the least expensive motels in town is the *Super 8* (☎ 601-442-3686; ❷) at 271 D'Evereux Drive.

Mid-range options ($50-120)

One of the better value possibilities is the *Mark Twain Guesthouse* (☎ 601-446-8023; ❷-❸) at 25 Silver Street. This Under-the-Hill hotel has just three rooms; ask for number one which has a balcony overlooking the Mississippi. The hotel is above a bar, the Under-the-Hill Saloon, so this isn't the always the most restful place in town.

For a fairly opulent option which won't make too big a dent in your travel fund, try one of Natchez's many bed and breakfasts. *Pleasant Hill* (☎ 601-442-7674; ❸) at 310 South Pearl Street and *The Briars Inn* (☎ 601-446-9654; ❸) at 31 Irving Lane both offer a reasonable level of accommodation and are within striking distance of downtown Natchez.

A more upscale bed and breakfast, the *Linden* (☎ 601-445-5472, 800-254-6336; ❹), occupies the historic antebellum home at 1 Linden Place. If you feel like digging a little deeper into your pockets, the Linden provides a genuine and genuinely impressive taste of wealthy Natchez living. The *Monmouth Plantation* (☎ 601-442-5852, 800-828-4531; ❹) at 36 Melrose Avenue is similarly impressive and a much larger residence. The *Guest House Historic Inn* (☎ 601-442-1054; ❹) at 201 North Pearl Street is convenient, well-appoint-

---

Hotel price codes

Hotel and motels price bands used in this book reflect the range of prices charged for a double room.

❶ – $10-25	❷ – $26-50	❸ – $51-85	❹ – $86-120
❺ – $121-180	❻ – $181-250	❼ – $251+	

See p22 for more information.

Natchez — chain hotels

- *Comfort Inn* (☎ 601-446-5500, 800-221-2222), 337 D'Evereux Drive
- *Days Inn* (☎ 601-445-8291, 800-524-4892), 109 Highway 61 South
- *Howard Johnson Lodge* (☎ 601-442-1691), 45 Sergeant S Prentiss Drive
- *Ramada Hilltop* (☎ 601-446-6311, 800-256-6311), 130 John R Runkin Drive

---

ed and has helpful staff but it isn't quite so evocative a retreat as the Monmouth or the Linden.

The *Natchez Eola Hotel* (☎ 601-445-6000, 800-888-9140; ❹) at 110 North Pearl Street, now owned by Radisson, is the main downtown Natchez hotel. Each of the 130 rooms is very well maintained and the two in-hotel restaurants, Juleps and Café LaSalle, are more than adequate. The Eola is in a great position if you want to be in the heart of the downtown area although, unless there's some major event going on, downtown Natchez is pretty quiet.

Where to eat

At its best, Natchez offers some of the finest dining in Mississippi. Starting at the other end of the price scale, however, you'll find a few good lunch joints downtown.

Budget options
Clara Nell's Downtown Deli at 408 Main Street is a straightforward sort of place with excellent – and enormous – salads, sandwiches and soups. It's open for breakfast and lunch till 5pm. Over at *Fat Mama's Tamales* (☎ 601-442-4548) at 500 Canal Street you'll find red-hot chili tamales dished up perfunctorily. For American-Italian food try *Pearl Street Pasta* (☎ 601-442-9284) at 105 South Pearl Street.

Mid-range and expensive restaurants
Head under the hill to find the simple but friendly *Magnolia Grill* (☎ 601-446-7670) at 49 Silver Street where great baked catfish goes for $15. Just along at 57 Silver Street, the Ballard family's *Wharfmaster's Restaurant* (☎ 601-445-6025) serves up good steaks and fish dishes for a similar price. The restaurant stands on the site of a warehouse which collapsed into the Mississippi.

For a real gastronomic experience, however, you'll need to book in for dinner at one of the great antebellum homes which doubles as an exclusive restaurant. Most are very expensive and, in true Southern tradition, you will be expected to share one long table with around 20 other guests. The best of these places are the *Monmouth Plantation* (☎ 601-442-5852) at 36 Melrose Avenue and *Elgin Plantation* (☎ 601-446-6100) at 1 Elgin Plantation Road. Dress up and book ahead.

Where to find live music

Natchez might lie on 61 but this is not a blues town. There are a handful of places which occasionally host live gigs. **Biscuits & Blues** (☎ 601-446-9922) at 315 Main Street is by far the best bet; there's music here till 11pm at weekends. It's hardly a Delta juke joint like those you'll find further north, but it's a pleasant place which does book some fairly big name acts from time to time.

You might also investigate the cavernous **Pearl Street Cellar** at 211 Pearl Street, **Dimples Lounge** (☎ 601-445-9464) near Biscuits & Blues at 324 Main Street and the **Under-the-Hill Saloon** (☎ 601-446-8023) at 25 Silver Street which has music till late at weekends. The bands here are often local and normally play rhythm and blues or covers. This last place is the most atmospheric with views over the Mississippi to Louisiana.

Moving on — Natchez to Port Gibson to Vicksburg

Highway 61 picks up speed as it runs north from Natchez past thick, lush forest. Occasional trailers and wooden homes line the sides of the road. The first town between Natchez and Vicksburg, a 70-mile journey, is Fayette. Unless you need to use the small supermarket or gas station there's very little reason to do anything other than accelerate past the place.

Port Gibson is more interesting. During the Civil War Union general Ulysses S Grant apparently declared the place 'too beautiful to burn' when he orchestrated a critical battle here in 1863.

The town is packed with historic homes though none can compete with those in Natchez. Still, it's a pretty enough place and worth nosing round. If you stop here for lunch, the **Old Depot Restaurant & Lounge** at 1202 Market Street is an absolute gem. The menu verges on soul food with 'sloppy beef po-boys' for $5.95 and all kinds of steaks and burgers.

Vicksburg

The 'Mississippi Delta' is, to readers of this book at least, a cultural region rather than a geographic one. It's said to extend from Catfish Row in Vicksburg, Mississippi to the lobby of the Peabody Hotel in Memphis, Tennessee. So when you roll into Vicksburg from the south, you're rolling into the Mississippi Delta. This is the land of juke joints, cotton fields, long straight roads, wide open skies, deserted crossroads and – of course – the blues.

Vicksburg itself has an uneasy relationship with its own blues history. Most locals seem more keen to extol the virtues of a backroom where *Coca Cola* was first bottled than the fact Willie Dixon, perhaps the greatest of all blues composers and a key figure in American culture, was born here back in 1915. Today the town is known not for blues but for the pivotal Civil War battle fought here in 1863. Almost all tourism in town is built around that event.

Even among the African-American community in Marcus Bottom, there's very little music going on. One reason for this is the fact that a mayoral ordinance forces bars in Marcus Bottom to close at 10pm.

Most businesspeople in the area can no longer attract live bands to play such short gigs. There's no doubt Vicksburg is an essential stopover on the Blues Highway, but those in search of blues will find more luck deeper in the Delta. Civil War buffs, however, will be more than satisfied.

History

Modern Vicksburg was established in 1811 by the Reverend Newit Vick and quickly become a commercially and strategically important river-town. Indeed, the town's position on the Mississippi River was deemed so strategically important that during the Civil War President Abraham Lincoln was moved to state, 'Vicksburg is the key. The war can never be brought to close until that key is in our pocket'.

So in 1863 General Ulysses S Grant masterminded a complex attack on Confederate stronghold Vicksburg in order to win that key. He met fierce resistance and a long, bloody series of battles ensued. Vicksburg eventually came under siege and remained so for 46 days until, on 4 July 1863, the town was forced to surrender to Grant. A jubilant Lincoln declared, 'the Father of Waters again goes unvexed to the sea'.

History of music in Vicksburg

From the blues and jazz point of view, Vicksburg's most notable claims include the fact that blues legend **'Little Brother' Montgomery** took up residency here in around 1920 and soon influenced a young **Willie Dixon**. Dixon went on to become a key blues composer and, as producer at Chicago's Chess Records, one of the more instrumental figures in blues history. 'Little Brother' Montgomery, who was just 11 when he left home in Liberty, Mississippi to make his way as a professional blues pianist, created the complex 'Vicksburg Blues' which standardized the 12-bar format.

In 1988 Willie Dixon visited Vicksburg High School where he attributed his early blues influences to 'Little Brother' Montgomery and said, 'When you start getting information about American music – all American music – you'll find the blues are at the roots of it all'.

According to respected local historian Gordon Cotton, there is also a case that the origin of the word **'jazz'** lies in Vicksburg. The great Duke Ellington and others, including Vincent Lopez, have credited Vicksburg with conjuring the word. The story goes that in the days of early ragtime, a talented Vicksburg drummer named Charles Washington discovered a particular gift for syncopated rhythm. He would launch into episodes of overstated syncopation to the command from the bandleader 'Now, Chaz!'. So in time that style of rhythm came to be called 'chaz' which then corrupted to 'jazz'. It might not be true, but it's a good story.

No introduction to jazz and blues in Vicksburg would be complete without reference to two cherished but now defunct local institutions – the **Red Tops** and the **Blue Room**. During the fifties and sixties, the Vicksburg-based all-black Red Tops, led and managed by drummer Walter Osborne, was the most popular dance band in the South. Even during segregation, the universally admired Red Tops would perform for white or black audiences. Few Southern bands could make the same claim. The Blue Room (see p90) made an equally bold statement during its life from 1937 to 1972.

Arrival and departure

By bus
Greyhound services use the main terminal at 1295 South Frontage Road (☎ 601-638-8389).

By car
Vicksburg sits at the crossroads of the I-20 between Jackson and Shreveport, and Highway 61 which leads north to Greenville. Jackson, the state capital, is just 20 miles away.

Getting around

By car or cab
Enterprise Rent-a-Car (☎ 601-638-3866) operates from 1800 South Frontage Road. Try the J&B Cab Co on 601-636-0099.

By tour
Red Carpet Tours (☎ 601-634-8641) offer detailed tours of Vicksburg by minibus; tours leave at 9.30am Monday to Saturday and 1.30pm on Sunday. For an altogether different perspective, **hydro-jet boat tours** (☎ 601-638-5443) are available for $16 from the wharf at the river end of Clay Street. The boat explores the Mississippi and Yazoo Rivers for one hour while a guide explains the importance of the waterway in the Civil War.

Services

Communications
● **Post** The main US Post Office is at 3415 Pemberton Square Boulevard.
● **Internet** Try the library at 700 Veto Street.

Tourist information
The main Convention and Visitors' Bureau (601-636-9421, 800-221-3536) is downtown at the corner of Washington and Clay streets. There is also a State Welcome Center off the I-20 just by the bridge over the Mississippi. The CVB is actually more useful but there is at least free coffee at the Welcome Center.

Medical emergencies
Head for Parkview Regional Medical Center (☎ 601-631-2131) at 100 McAuley Drive.

What to see

Music landmarks

Under the eccentric ownership of Tom Wince, the **Blue Room** became a fabled nightclub not just in Mississippi but around the world. Wince, about whom almost everyone in Vicksburg has a story, somehow attracted a steady stream of the greatest names in blues and jazz to his small club in what was, and still is, a quiet, tucked away town. Louis Armstrong, Louis Jordan, BB King, T-Bone Walker, Count Basie, Dinah Washington, Ray Charles and many others played here.

In creating the Blue Room, Wince turned himself into one of the most admired black businessmen in the South at a time when the odds were firmly stacked against the African-American community. The club's dance-floor was black-only but whites could watch from the balcony upstairs. Fighting and bawdy behavior were stamped out by Wince who would leap across the bar, pistol in hand, to throw out troublemakers.

Wince started the Blue Room in 1937 with a $10 investment. According to a story in a 1972 edition of the *Vicksburg Sunday Post*, the club closed that year because of 'urban renewal'. The Blue Room was located on the corner of Mulberry and Clay Streets. There's nothing to see there now. In fact, the only reminder of the man or the club stands at City Cemetery in the form of Wince's flamboyant grave which bears the inscription, 'An internationally known nightclub owner who established and operated the famous Blue Room night-club from 1937 to 1972'. Wince died in 1978 at the age of 68.

Marcus Bottom, sometimes called Douglas Park, is a predominantly black and run-down part of town, itself something of a blues landmark in that it's where Willie Dixon and 'Little Brother' Montgomery lived. It's also a place where the blues is lived today. Marcus Bottom is a rough neighborhood and its few remaining bars very rarely see white visitors. Clubs like the Do Drop Inn, Sam's and Kathy Singleton-Green's El Morocco rarely see bands these days either and rely instead on jukeboxes. Marcus Bottom doesn't even appear on Vicksburg maps. To find it, follow Halls Ferry Road between the I-20 and Cherry Street. Unless a local helps you, checking out Marcus Bottom bars is, frankly, dangerous.

Mississippi or Yazoo?

In the early years of the twentieth century Vicksburg's importance as a river-town was catastrophically ended when the mighty Mississippi River changed its course. Vicksburg had sat on a sharp bend. The river eventually, and inevitably, channeled a new course of least resistance so cutting off the bend to leave Vicksburg sitting on an 'oxbow lake'. The US Army Corps of Engineers, which has long struggled to tame the Mississippi and still has its largest testing station in Vicksburg, diverted the Yazoo River to run past Vicksburg and into the Mississippi's new course.

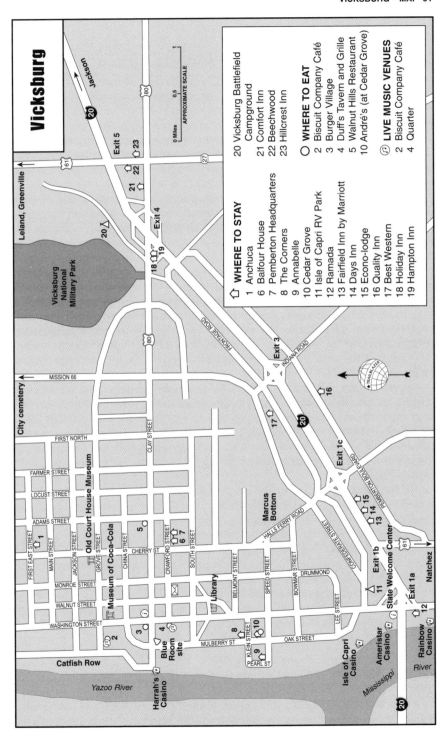

Vicksburg

WHERE TO STAY

1 Anchuca
6 Balfour House
7 Pemberton Headquarters
8 The Corners
9 Annabelle
10 Cedar Grove
11 Isle of Capri RV Park
12 Ramada
13 Fairfield Inn by Marriott
14 Days Inn
15 Econo-lodge
16 Quality Inn
17 Best Western
18 Holiday Inn
19 Hampton Inn
20 Vicksburg Battlefield
   Campground
21 Comfort Inn
22 Beechwood
23 Hillcrest Inn

WHERE TO EAT

2 Biscuit Company Café
3 Burger Village
4 Duff's Tavern and Grille
5 Walnut Hills Restaurant
10 André's (at Cedar Grove)

LIVE MUSIC VENUES

2 Biscuit Company Café
4 Quarter

The Mississippi Delta's southern boundary is **Catfish Row** in Vicksburg. Catfish Row was the bawdy side of town where blues was played and fights were frequent. There is no Catfish Row in Vicksburg today but according to local blues historian Earnest MacBride, Levee Street stands on the same site. The river, tracks and run-down warehouses make Levee Street an evocative part of town. A couple of clubs have come and gone here over the past few years.

Other highlights

The biggest draw in Vicksburg is the immaculate **National Military Park** (☎ 601-636-0583; daily 8am-5pm; $4 per car) which curves around the north and east of town. Tours are self-drive and start from the visitor center which is just off Clay Street near the I-20.

Every nuance of the battles and siege which raged here is chronicled in the form of carefully maintained markers and memorials which line the narrow 16-mile-long route around the site. Each regiment on both sides has its own marker and each state an elaborate memorial. A 15-step marker map is available from the visitor center, it takes about two hours to follow. Since it requires a certain amount of imagination to understand the battles fought here, you might consider booking a guide to join you in your car. They charge $20 but really help to bring the whole thing alive.

A separate museum in the north-west corner of the park houses the salvaged warship **USS Cairo**. The iron-clad Cairo was used like a river-going tank to crawl up the Mississippi under fire until it hit a mine and went under.

For a wider overview of Vicksburg's history, visit the **Old Court House Museum** (☎ 601-636-0741; Mon-Sat 8.30am-4.30pm; $3) at 1008 Cherry Street. Curators Gordon Cotton and Jeff Giambrone have made a great job of presenting Vicksburg's history from pioneer times to the present. There are sections on music, African-American heritage and, of course, cabinets full of Civil War memorabilia. A newspaper cutting tells one of Vicksburg's favourite stories about a reunion for elderly Civil War veterans from both sides. Arguments broke out and the old men started fighting and beating each other with their walking sticks.

The arguably more obscure but popular **Museum of Coca-Cola** (☎ 601-638-6514; Mon-Sat 9am-5pm; $2.95) stands at 1107 Washington Street in the old Beidenharn Candy Company building. This is where Coke was first bottled in 1894 by the enterprising Joseph Beidenharn. Beidenharn's invention allowed him to transport the drink to rural areas and later allowed Coca-Cola to ship their product worldwide. The museum displays old bottling equipment and Coca-Cola merchandise and memorabilia from the early twentieth century. Vicksburg has four major **casinos**: Harrah's (☎ 601-636-3423) at 1310 Mulberry Street; Isle of Capri (☎ 601-636-5700) at 3990 Washington Street; Ameristar (☎ 601-638-1000) at 4116 Washington Street; and the Rainbow (☎ 601-636-7575) at 1380 Warrenton Road.

Where to stay

Like Natchez, Vicksburg is a small antebellum town which attracts large numbers of visitors. For this reason Vicksburg, like Natchez, boasts lots of first-class bed and breakfasts set in historic homes. If you're not on too tight a budget, and you're bored of chain hotels, try one. Vicksburg also has so many hotel rooms for such a small place that it can be fairly easy to negotiate a good deal.

Budget options

The best camping is found at *Vicksburg Battlefield Campground* (☎ 601-636-2025; **❶**) at 4407 Frontage Road. If that's full, try the *Isle of Capri RV Park* (☎ 601-631-0402; **❶**) which has 24-hour security and is attached to the casino.

The cheapest motels are the *Hillcrest Inn* (☎ 601-638-1491; **❷**) at 40 Highway 80, *Beechwood* (☎ 601-636-2271; **❷**) at 4449 East Clay Street and the *Econo-Lodge* (☎ 601-636-7881; **❸**) at 3308 Pemberton Square Boulevard.

Mid-range options ($50-120)

Balfour House (☎ 601-638-7113, 800-294-7113; **❹**) at 1002 Crawford Street was built in 1835. Balfour was used by several generals during the Civil War and wartime owner Emma Balfour kept a diary of the siege from within the house. When current owners Bob and Sharon Humble restored the place in 1982 they discovered a cannonball lodged in the wall.

The Corners (☎ 800-444-7421; **❹**) at 601 Klein Street is one of the most elegant of Vicksburg's bed and breakfasts. Each of the 15 rooms is immaculate and unique; they're spread between the main house and a separate lodge on the grounds. Entertaining owner Cliff Whitney joins his guests for a shared gourmet breakfast every morning.

Nearby *Annabelle* (☎ 800-791-2000; **❹**) at 501 Speed Street has the added advantage of a pool which in summer really counts for something. Owners George and Carolyn Mayer provide an enthusiastic welcome.

The Greek-revivalist *Anchuca* (☎ 601-661-0111, 1 888-686-0111; **❹-❺**) at 1010 East Street dates back to 1830 and has been lovingly restored. The decor is sumptuous and there's a welcome pool.

The *Pemberton Headquarters* (☎ 601-636-9581, 1 877-636-9581; **❹-❺**) at 1018 Crawford Street is an interesting building. The price is a little higher than average but it's a beautiful place and, as Pemberton's Headquarters, its rooms are sought after by Civil War buffs.

Cedar Grove (☎ 601-636-1000, 800-862-1300; **❺**) at 2200 Oak Street is the largest and most elaborate bed and breakfast in town. With 30 rooms it's verg-

---

Vicksburg — chain hotels

- *Best Western* (☎ 601-636-5800, 800-528-1234), 2445 North Frontage Road
- *Comfort Inn* (☎ 601-634-8438, 800-228-5150), 3959 East Clay Street
- *Days Inn* (☎ 601-634-1622, 800-329-7466), 2 Pemberton Place
- *Fairfield Inn by Marriott* (☎ 601-636-1811, 888-424-1811), 20 Orme Drive
- *Hampton Inn* (☎ 601-636-6100, 888-568-4044), 3332 Clay Street
- *Holiday Inn* (☎ 601-636-4551, 800-847-0372), 3330 Clay Street
- *Quality Inn* (☎ 601-634-8607, 800-221-2222), 2390 South Frontage Road
- *Ramada* (☎ 601-638-5750), 4216 Washington Street

ing on hotel status and as such lacks the intimacy of some smaller establishments. But it's a gorgeous, plush establishment and a magnificent 1840s antebellum property.

Where to eat

For cheap eats the best place in town by far is *Burger Village* at 1220 Washington Street where you'll find outstanding home-cooked Southern food from gumbo to red beans and rice. This isn't the Ritz but the food is great and for just a few dollars you can't go wrong.

Just along Washington Street at 1100, the *Biscuit Company Café*, featured below for blues, serves huge lunches and dinners – mostly fried fish or pasta – for $8 to $12. If you're too hungry even for that place, you could try one the casino's Las Vegas-style all-you-can-eat buffets. The Veranda Buffet in the *Ameristar Casino* is a good one; prices start at $6.95.

Back on Washington Street, *Duff's Tavern and Grille* at number 1306 is just a shade more upscale. It claims to be an 'English-style pub' reminiscent of an 'English country manor', although why anyone sitting yards from the Mississippi River in the heart of blues country would want to dine in an English country manor is hard to fathom. The menu is varied and the prices pretty reasonable.

For a significantly more upscale dining experience, book in at *Andrés* at the Cedar Grove Mansion (☎ 601-636-1000) at 2200 Oak Street. Cedar Grove is an attractive antebellum home and the food served here is very good; expect to pay around $20 for an entrée. A piano player helps conjure a convivial atmosphere while chef André works some magic in the kitchen.

However, none of these places, with the possible exception of Burger Village, can claim such quintessential Southern charm as the *Walnut Hills Restaurant* (☎ 601-638-4910) at 1214 Adams Street just off Clay Street. Walnut Hills lays on a traditional Southern 'round table' lunch until 2pm after which an *a-la-carte* menu is available for the evening. The round table is great fun; random configurations of diners are placed at large tables together while dozens of waitresses load them till they creak with dishes like country fried steak, mustard greens, okra and tomatoes, creamed potatoes and blackberry cobbler. For just $9.65 one can gorge on these treats till sated. It's a very sociable event and you'll soon find yourself making friends around the table. Sunday is the best day to go when locals dressed up for church meet here after the service.

Where to find live music

There are very few live music venues in Vicksburg. The *Biscuit Company Café* (☎ 601-631-0099) at 1100 Washington Street (the entrance is actually on Grove Street around the corner) regularly hosts blues gigs on Wednesdays, Fridays and Saturdays. It's a fairly ordinary restaurant-bar with a fairly ordinary band, the Blues Dudes, but it's the only viable live music venue in town.

Another club, the *Quarter*, operates above Duff's Tavern and Grille at 1306 Washington Street but it's more of a dance-techno place.

Moving on — Vicksburg to Jackson

State capital Jackson has played a major role in blues history and is a rewarding diversion from Highway 61; take the I-20 east from Vicksburg for 45 miles. This stretch of the I-20 is a road in need of repair but it's still a quick journey. The route leads through Edwards and Bolton. Both are backwaters frozen somewhere in the fifties; you won't even find a cup of coffee in these places. But, interestingly, Delta blues pioneer Charley Patton spent his earliest years on a plantation between the two towns.

Jackson

Mississippi's capital is a big city which feels like a small town. And it's soaked in blues history, much of it overlooked. The place seems staid, solid and somehow tired, as if the state's stormy past has worn it down. It's a contradictory city where shabby juke joints on run-down residential streets crowd wide, empty boulevards overshadowed by monumental civic buildings in which the state's legislature slowly grinds on. For blues lovers, Jackson is fertile ground.

History

When Mississippi was admitted to the Union in 1817, Natchez, commercial hub of the cotton industry, was named capital. Four years later, however, it was decided the state capital should occupy a more central location and a spe-

---

Jackson — events and festivals

● **April** – International Crawfish Festival. Held at Smith Park, this event proves there's still some way to travel north before one finally escapes the crawfish.

● **May** – Zoo Blues. Early May sees the zoo used to stage a blues festival. Call 601-960-1565 for more information.

● **July** – Mississippi Gospel Gathering. Downtown Jackson hosts a series of gospel concerts given by groups from all over the South.

● **July** – Jackson Music Awards. Gongs are given to winners in various music categories including blues, gospel and rhythm and blues.

● **September** – Festival Latino. Central and South American communities celebrate their culture through music, dance and food.

● **September** – Farish Street Festival. This annual event is designed to honor Farish Street as the commercial and cultural nucleus of the African-American community in Jackson. Call 601-372-1262 for more information.

● **October** – Mississippi State Fair. One of the biggest fairs in the South.

cial committee settled for a trading post on the Pearl River called LeFleur's Bluff. The name was later changed to Jackson in honor of General Andrew Jackson, a hero of the revolutionary war and a president of the United States. During the Civil War the town was burnt three times by Union soldiers. Of the major civic institutions which stood here, only the Governor's mansion, City Hall and the Capitol survived.

History of blues in Jackson

Farish Street, still a major thoroughfare in the African-American community, has set the scene for many substantial contributions to blues. **Henry C Speir**, who worked as a part-time talent scout from his music store on Farish Street, organized the great Robert Johnson's first recordings, delivered Charley Patton to Gennet Records and discovered the likes of Skip James.

Lillian McMurray set up **Trumpet Records** from her furniture store on Farish Street and gave breaks to blues legends Elmore James and Sonny Boy Williamson II. Further up the street, the recently-restored **Alamo Theater** launched Otis Spann's career after a talent contest.

According to blues historian Greg Woodcox, Jackson was a main stop on the **'hobo blues route'** between Memphis, Dallas and later Chicago. Early itinerant musicians would hitch rides on trains between these cities, taking blues with them as they traveled. This made Jackson a regular port of call for young, wandering blues players. Jackson has been home to several other important **blues labels**, including **Ace**, and is currently base for **Malaco** records.

Arrival and departure

By air

Jackson International Airport (☎ 601-939-5631) sits east of town by junction 52 of the I-20 on Airline Boulevard. It's served by Delta, American Eagle, Southwest, Northwest Airlink and Continental Express.

By train and bus

The main passenger rail station is at 300 West Capitol Avenue (☎ 601-355-6350). There are daily Amtrak services to New Orleans and Chicago. Greyhound buses use the terminal at 201 South Jefferson Street (☎ 601-353-6342).

By car

Jackson sits on two major interstate arteries, the north-south I-55 and the east-west I-20. New Orleans is 185 miles south, Memphis 208 miles north and Vicksburg 45 miles east.

(Opposite) Top: Farish Street was once the commercial hub of African-American life in Jackson (Ms) and a key blues center. Charley Patton, Robert Johnson and Sonny Boy Williamson II found recording contracts here. **Bottom:** Owner Mary Shepherd tends the bar at Club Ebony (see p111) in Indianola (Ms) where BB King plays a 'homecoming' concert every year.

Orientation

Much of Jackson lies inside the loop created by the I-55 and the I-220 but the distinct downtown area is bound by High and Court Streets to the north and south and Farish and Jefferson Streets to the east and west.

Farish Street runs through an inner-city African-American belt and is home to almost all the blues history in Jackson. Much of downtown Jackson is devoted to political and civic buildings; little happens here after dark. Hotels and motels are clustered along Highway 80 between Terry Road and the I-220.

Getting around

By car

For car rental, try **Alamo** (☎ 601-936-4010), **Avis** (☎ 601-939-5853), **Hertz** (☎ 601-939-5312) or **National** (☎ 601-939-5713) at the airport. Otherwise contact **Enterprise** (☎ 601-948-0062) at 700 South State Street.

By cab

You won't find many cabs cruising downtown after dark so you will need to call ahead if you plan to take a cab out to a blues venue or restaurant. Contact Citi-Cab Co (☎ 601-355-8319), Deluxe Cabs (☎ 601-948-4761) or Veterans Cabs (☎ 601-355-8319).

Services

Banks

There are several main bank branches with ATMs downtown including the Deposit Guaranty National Bank at 200 East Capitol Street.

Communications

● **Post** The main US Post Office is downtown at the intersection of Capitol and Lamar Streets.
● **Internet** The Eudora Welty Public Library on the corner of State and Mississippi Streets has Internet access.

Tourist information

For information on Jackson, log on to ▣ www.visitjackson.com or call ☎ 800-354-7695.

(Opposite) Club flyers flap in the slight breeze of a fiercely hot afternoon in New Orleans (see pp25-57).

Jackson

WHERE TO STAY

3 Hilton
4 Motel 6
5 Fairfield Inn by Marriott
6 Courtyard by Marriott
7 Hampton Inn
10 Days Inn
11 Ramada Inn
12 Comfort Inn
13 Best Western Metro
14 La Quinta Inn
15 Super 8

WHERE TO EAT

1 Amerigo
8 Poets

MUSIC VENUES

2 Red, Hot & Blue
9 The Kitty Kat Klub

Ross Barnett Resevoir

Timberlake Campground

SPILLWAY ROAD

OLD FANNIN ROAD

LAKELAND ROAD

Jackson International Airport

475

Pearl River

Le Fleurs Bluff State Park

APPROXIMATE SCALE

0 Miles   2

80

468

475

20

49

NATCHEZ TRACE PARKWAY

LAKE HARBOUR DRIVE

PEAR ORCHARD ROAD

OLD CANTON ROAD

WHEATLEY RD

RIDGEWOOD DRIVE

RIDGEWOOD ROAD

OLD CANTON RD

FANNIN ROAD

FLOWOOD DRIVE

Canton

220

COUNTY LINE ROAD

HANGING MOSS ROAD

NORTHSIDE DRIVE

BRIARWOOD

MEADOWBROOK

LAKELAND DRIVE

BAILEY AVENUE

WOODROW WILSON AVENUE

MILL ST

GALLATIN ST

RIVERSIDE DR

FORTIFICATION ST

STATE ST

WEST ST

JEFFERSON

55

NORTH STATE STREET

SEE INSET MAP

LIVINGSTON RD

RIDGEWAY

SEE 'DOWNTOWN JACKSON MAP'

CAPITOL STREET

ELLIS AVE

ROBINSON STREET

LYNCH ROAD

TERRY RD

RAYMOND ROAD

BELVEDERE DR

MCDOWELL ROAD

WOODY DRIVE

Brookhaven

20

15

55

14

13

11

10

12

20

Vicksburg

Zoological Park

220

CLINTON BLVD

MEDGAR EVERS BLVD

49

80

18

KEY

DOWNTOWN JACKSON MAP (BELOW)

WHERE TO STAY

2 Poindexter Park Inn
6 Sun N Sand Motel
7 Millsaps-Buie House
10 Edison Walthall Hotel
12 Holiday Inn Express
13 Old Capitol Inn
14 Days Inn

WHERE TO EAT

9 Elite
11 Hal & Mal's

LIVE MUSIC VENUES

1 Queen of Hearts
3 Subway Lounge
4 Jazzy's
5 Field's
8 Crowne Plaza Hotel
11 Hal & Mal's

Medgar Evers Home

RIDGEWAY ST

MIAMI ST

MISSOURI

MARTIN LUTHER KING JNR DR

Greenwood

MARGARET WALKER ALEXANDER DRIVE

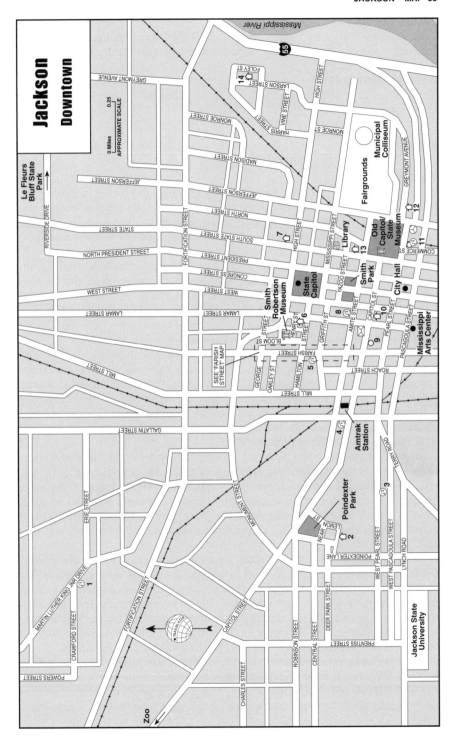

Record stores

Check out the Parkway Record Shop at 3724 Parkway Avenue; you'll find a vast collection of old records and tapes and knowledgeable staff.

Medical emergencies

The University of Mississippi Medical Center (☎ 601-960-1926) is at 2500 North State Street.

What to see

Blues landmarks

Blues in Jackson grew up on **Farish Street**, for years the center of black commerce and entertainment. So far little effort has been made to preserve that history, however. Worse, Farish Street is in steep decline. This made local blues historian Greg Woodcox determined to record the history of this once critical strip of stores and clubs for the benefit of the local community.

With a brief to let 'local kids know Elmore James came from their street' and to make them 'proud of their neighborhood', he enlisted the help of prominent blues scholar and writer Gayle Dean Wardlow. Together, they set up the outstanding **Farish Street Blues Museum** at 405 Farish Street (☎ 601-944-0000), the first serious attempt to document the Street's influence. Don't miss one of Mississippi's best blues monuments.

This description of the music landmarks on Farish Street starts where Amite Street meets Farish and works north from there as far as Oakley Street. Number 225 Farish Street, marked 'Ross Furniture Company' in faded letters, was the site of **Speir's Music Store** until the late twenties when it moved down the street to 111. According to Gayle Dean Wardlow, H C Speir was 'the godfather of the Delta blues' and 'to twenties and thirties country blues what Sam Phillips was to fifties rock & roll'.

A white businessman, Speir set up his music store in the black neighborhood to sell records, guitars and wind-up Victrolas. He began scouting for talent, calling himself a 'talent-broker', and quickly proved to record companies he had a fine ear for what would sell. He found Tommy Johnson in 1927, Charley Patton in 1929 and Skip James in 1931. Speir supplied talent to several 'race labels' including ARC, Victor, Columbia, OKeh, Paramount, Vocalian and Gennett.

Speir bought his own recording equipment on which to cut demos and made extra money charging $5 to let people cut their own 'vanity' records. He installed the equipment above his store and, from then on, a stream of country blues singers passed through Farish Street hoping Mr Speir could help them get on record. In 1935 one Robert Johnson tried out for Speir who contacted Ernie Oertle, an ARC agent, and arranged for Johnson to make his way out to San Antonio, Texas, where he cut his first sides in a hotel room.

Gayle Dean Wardlow befriended Speir before his death in 1972. Wardlow believes Speir never fully understood the significance of his work in the twenties and thirties and that, without him, many of the greatest Delta blues pioneers would never have reached an audience bigger than their local juke joint.

Just two doors down from the old Speir Music Shop, number 241 Farish Street is the former home of **Ace Records**. Established by Johnny Vincent in 1955, Ace Records specialized in rock & roll and rhythm and blues, recording the likes of Earl King and Huey Smith & the Clowns. Vincent closed Ace in 1960 but subsequently resurrected the company and sold it in 1997. In the next block, set back from the road, **Field's** juke joint puts on live blues some weekends. Another bar, Big Al's Recovery Room, is next door.

Big Al's Recovery Room is the first business in a block property which is divided into five distinct sections. The end two sections of the building, collectively number 309, once housed Lillian McMurray's furniture and record shop and with it **Trumpet Records**. McMurray approached Speir in 1950 and asked his advice about starting a blues label. Speir suggested it might work so McMurray, another white trader on the black side of town, launched Trumpet Records and set about recording Sonny Boy Williamson II (Rice Miller) and several gospel artists. She went on to record Elmore James who laid down his most famous track, *Dust My Broom*, on Trumpet Records. Willie Love and Big Joe Williams also recorded at 309 Farish Street.

Further up Farish Street at 333, the revamped **Alamo Theater** (☎ 601-352-3365) stands out from its dilapidated neighbors. The Alamo was well known for its talent searches which launched the careers of, among others, Otis Spann, who went on to make a

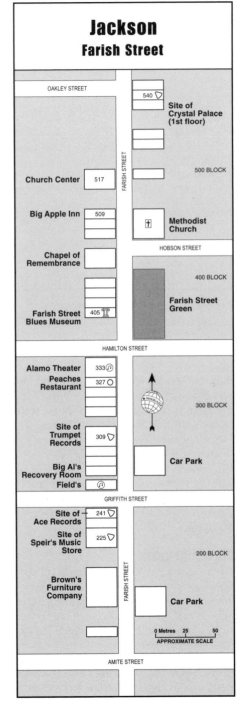

Jackson
Farish Street

The Medgar Evers Homecoming

Medgar Evers was a pivotal figure in the early years for the civil rights movement in Mississippi. Through the late fifties and early sixties his conviction and bravery did much to establish the National Association for the Advancement of Colored People (NAACP) in this most racially troubled state.

On 12 June 1963, Evers was assassinated in front of his own home by a racist named de la Beckwith. The killing further stained race relations in the state but focused national and world attention on the cause of the NAACP.

Medgar Evers' brother, Charles, himself a respected local politician and radio boss, has organized a 'homecoming concert' in his brother's memory every year since 1963. For the past 27 years BB King, a friend of the Evers family, has played at the concert. Charles Evers says the homecoming 'shows how far we've come. At first people were afraid to come to it, since then it's grown bigger and better every year'. The concert is held in the first week in June. BB King combines the trip with his annual pilgrimage back to his own hometown, Indianola.

The Medgar Evers story did not end in 1963; his killer remained free for over 30 years, despite compelling evidence of his guilt, until the Mississippi legal system brought him to justice in the nineties. That story has been made into a faithful and compelling movie starring Alec Baldwin and James Woods.

name as Muddy Waters' pianist, and Dorothy 'Misty Blue' Moore. The Alamo, an impressive and attractive building, fell into disrepair until 1996 when a group of locals raised funds for its restoration. The theater is now active; the talent search is back, jazz and blues is played every third Friday and in 2000 Jackson's first black mayor, Harvey Johnson, used the venue to deliver his 'State of the City' address.

Some way further on next to number 540, opposite the left turn into Oakley Street and above Birdland, the **Crystal Palace** was an important venue in the twenties and thirties. A host of huge stars played here, including Louis Armstrong and Duke Ellington. One can still see the sign on the side of the building.

Other highlights

An imposing building in its own right, the **Old Capitol** (☎ 601-359-6920; Mon-Fri 8am-5pm, Sat 9.30am-4.30pm, Sun 12.30-4.30pm; free) at 100 South State Street now houses the outstanding **State Museum**. The museum is commendably frank about issues such as slavery, Jim Crow legislation and the civil rights movement, all of which have contributed to painful episodes in Mississippi's history.

One of the most bitter of those episodes was the murder of civil rights campaigner **Medgar Evers** (see above) whose modest home at 2332 Margaret Walker Alexander Drive (☎ 601-977-7839) is open to visitors by appointment.

For a deeper insight into the history of African-Americans in Mississippi, head for the **Smith Robertson Museum** (☎ 601-960-1457; Mon-Fri 9am-5pm, Sat 9am-12pm, Sun 2pm-5pm; $1) at 528 Bloom Street. Located in what was Jackson's first school for blacks, the museum explains the entire story of Mississippian African-Americans from slavery onwards.

The new **State Capitol** (☎ 601-359-3114; Mon-Fri 8am-5pm; free) at 400 High Street, built in 1903, is worth exploring as much for its elaborate decor as for the opportunity to see Mississippi government in action. The American eagle is said to face away from Washington in Southern defiance. Other interesting highlights include the **Mississippi Arts Center** (☎ 601-960-1515; Mon-Sat 10am-5pm, Sun 12-5pm; $5) at 201 East Pascagoula Street, with a vast collection of material much of which relates to Mississippi, and **City Hall** at 219 South President Street which dates back to 1847 and is perhaps Jackson's most attractive civic building.

Where to stay

All the main chain hotels are in Jackson but beyond those there is a very limited choice of accommodations.

Budget options

Campers should head for *LeFleur's Bluff State Park* (☎ 601-987-3985; ❶) at 2140 Riverside Drive, the best camping around Jackson, or the *Timberlake Campground* (☎ 601-992-9100; ❶-❷) which has a pool and tennis court. To find it take exit 98B from the I-55 onto Lakeland Drive and, after three miles, go left onto Fannin Road for three or four miles. The campsite is on the banks of the Ross Barnett Reservoir.

Jackson has quite a number of cheap motels, many of which can be bargained down in price if it's a quiet night. The *Super 8* (☎ 601-982-1044, 800-228-5151; ❸) at 2655 I-55 South and the *Motel 6* (☎ 601-956-8848, 800-851-8888; ❸) at 6145 I-55 North are worth trying if you've got a car. You might also investigate

---

Jackson — chain hotels

- *Best Western Metro* (☎ 601-355-7483), 1520 Ellis Avenue
- *Comfort Inn* (☎ 601-922-5600), 2800 Greenway Drive
- *Courtyard by Marriott* (☎ 601-956-9991, 800-321-2211), 6820 Ridgewood Court
- *Days Inn* (☎ 601-352-7387, 800-329-7466), 804 Larson Street
- *Fairfield Inn by Marriott* (☎ 601-957-8557), 5354 I-55 North
- *Hampton Inn* (☎ 601-956-3611), 465 Briarwood Drive
- *Holiday Inn Express* (☎ 601-948-4466), 310 Greymont Avenue
- *Hilton* (☎ 601-957-2800, 888-263-0524), 1001 East County Line Road
- *La Quinta Inn* (☎ 601-373-6110, 800-531-5900), 150 Angle Street
- *Ramada Inn* (☎ 601-944-1150, 800-265-9399), 1525 Ellis Avenue

Hotel price codes

Hotel and motels price bands used in this book reflect the range of prices charged for a double room.

    ❶ – $10-25   ❷ – $26-50   ❸ – $51-85   ❹ – $86-120
    ❺ – $121-180   ❻ – $181-250   ❼ – $251+

See p22 for more information.

the outstandingly retro *Sun-n-Sand Motel* (☎ 601-354-2501; ❷) at 401 North Lamar Street or the *Econo-Lodge* (☎ 601-353-0340; ❸) at 2450 Highway 80 West.

Mid-range options ($50-120)

The three best bed and breakfasts are the charming *Millsaps-Buie House* (☎ 601-352-0221, 800-784-0221; ❸-❹) at 628 North State Street, the central and larger *Old Capitol Inn* (☎ 601-359-9000, 888-359-9001; ❸) at 226 North State Street and, best of the three, the *Poindexter Park Inn* (☎ 601-944-1392; ❸) at 803 Deer Park Street. Owned by blues enthusiast Marcia Weaver, this 1907 house is elegant, comfortable and very good value. Weaver played a large part in the restoration of the Alamo Theater and knows the local blues scene very well.

If you plan to head more upscale, try the *Edison Walthall Hotel* (☎ 601-948-6161, 800-932-6161, 🖹 601-948-0088; ❹) at 225 East Capitol Street. This stately institution is surprisingly good value and very well placed in the heart of downtown.

Where to eat

There's no shortage of restaurants in Jackson but very few are downtown. *Elite* (☎ 601-352-5606) at 141 East Capitol Street is one of those that is. This cozy diner-style restaurant has been dishing up great steaks, specials and soul food for 50 years. Just $7.50 will get you a satisfying set menu. The service is a touch too fast – don't head here for a lingering, romantic meal – but the food is hard to beat.

For classic down-home cooking in the heart of the blues district, try *Peaches* at 327 Farish Street next door to the Alamo Theater. Peaches is a great place with outstanding food and is easily the most enjoyable restaurant in town for music lovers; you can feel the blues on Farish Street as you eat good home cooking.

Hal & Mal's (☎ 601-948-0888) at 200 South Commerce Street, mentioned also on p106, doubles as a popular restaurant. The menu is more or less New Orleanian with po-boys for around $6, red beans and rice for $7 and grilled catfish for $13.25. There's even a mufeletta. Hal & Mal's is also a 'brew pub' which means diners feel obliged to drink horrible homemade beer with their meal.

An Italian restaurant, *Amerigo* (☎ 601-977-0563) at 6592 Old Canton Road, provides respite from standard Southern fare with classic Italian pasta and pizzas. It's a decent place with a wide menu (expect to pay around $12 for an entrée) but it lacks charm.

Poets (☎ 601-982-9711) at 1855 Lakeland Drive is better from that point of view and there's regularly music and dancing here. Like Hal & Mal's, the menu has a definite New Orleanian twist; the oysters Bienville give the game away. Entrées go for around $15; try the soft shell crab for $13.95.

Where to find live music

The best sources of listings in Jackson are *The Planet*, a free weekly, and Thursday's *Clarion-Ledger*. Jackson boasts two of the coolest juke joints in Mississippi, the Subway Lounge and the Queen of Hearts.

Interview — Little Milton

What does it mean to you to play the Medgar Evers homecoming concert?
Mississippi is my home state and the Delta's where I'm from. I come back often and always for the Medgar Evers homecoming. To go back and honor someone who gave his life for people who were denied their rights is something I've been doing for several years and as long as I'm alive I'm happy to do it. Charles Evers is doing something to keep the people's memory of his brother alive. All the entertainers who participate in this are probably thinking the same thing. BB King and I do it every year. We're dedicated and committed.

Do you think early blues musicians would be surprised if they knew how far blues has come?
The people that started it way before my time, they would be proud. I'm sure back then they had no idea. They tell you the blues is strictly black music, just for you so it's segregated. You grow up believing this. That's the rub, there's no such thing as one group's music. Music belongs to whoever can feel it, enjoy it and understand it.

Can you define blues?
Many have asked for my definition of the blues but there isn't a definition. When you say 'blues' some people think 'poor' or 'ignorance'. But really it's about everyday life, realism. You can be rich and still have the blues. It doesn't mean you have to be sad. It's about everyday situations that most of us go through, that's what makes it so meaningful. It's going to live forever. It's been here forever and it's staying here forever. When we're all gone there'll always be someone to step in and keep it warm.

Little Milton, from Inverness, Mississippi has been a leading blues star since he recorded for Sun in the early fifties. Along with BB King, he is a regular at the Medgar Evers homecoming concerts.

Jubilee!JAM

This three-day concert is held downtown every May and has been going from strength to strength since it started out in 1986. Organizer Richard Hudson attracts a better line up every year. Highlights in 2000 included Isaac Hayes, Government Mule, R L Burnside, Bobby Rush and Johnny Billington. Tickets go for $15 on the gate. For more information, log onto ⌨ www.jubileejam.com or call 601-335 -FEST.

Subway Lounge (☎ 601-352-6812) at 619 West Pearl Street is hard to find – it's in a quiet residential street – but worth the effort. A guy with a torch watches clubgoers' cars so look out for him if you're having trouble finding the place. The club is one shabby basement room decorated with fairy lights. At weekends a wild house band belts out powerful, bawdy blues to whoops of delight from the densely packed crowd. It's electric. If you want to carry on drinking after two in the morning, when the bar closes, arrangements can be made through a hatch in the side of the house next door. There's a $5 cover at weekends.

The *Queen of Hearts* (☎ 601-352-5730) at 2243 Martin Luther King Jr Drive is a harder, rougher place with intermittent blues often from local guitar man King Edward. This is an improvised neighborhood juke joint and as such it's an exciting place to hear blues. The barbecue's pretty good too.

Another accomplished local blues guitarist, the gentlemanly Jesse Robinson, plays regularly in the more upscale surroundings of the *Crowne Plaza Hotel* (☎ 601-969-5100) at 200 East Amite Street. It's not an ideal showcase for Robinson's great talent but, after the Queen of Hearts, you might find the thickly-carpeted Crowne Plaza a welcome contrast.

Hal & Mal's (☎ 601-948-0888) at 200 South Commerce Street hosts regular live music, much of it blues, jazz or rhythm and blues. Bands here tend to be locally famous or well known in the South but this place has attracted some much bigger stars in its time – Lionel Hampton and BB King to name just two. Hal & Mal's is an enjoyable venue and one which creates an excellent environment in which to listen to live music. But there's little of the authenticity and atmosphere which make the Subway Lounge so charged.

Fields (☎ 601-353-1400) on the corner of Farish and Griffiths Streets has live blues some weekends and most Mondays. It's a funky juke joint and the fact it's on Farish makes it all the more appealing.

The Kitty Kat Klub (☎ 601-362-6860) at 1221 Ridgeway Street also has blues most weekends. One other venue worth investigating is the restaurant *Red, Hot & Blue* (☎ 601-956-3313) at 1625 East County Line Boulevard. Blues is played here fairly regularly but, since this is a restaurant, it's hardly the most exciting venue in town.

For jazz try the appropriately named *Jazzy's* (☎ 601-353-5200) at 426 West Capitol Street. The weekend jam session is worth every cent of the $2 cover.

Deep Delta

Head north from Jackson on the I-55 towards Winona and you'll find yourself rolling into the heart of the Mississippi Delta. Driving through the Delta is a profound experience; every town, every crossroads, every rusting railroad wagon brings home the blues. No music better reflects its environment.

This section explains key Delta blues landmarks in the relatively compact area between Greenville and Greenwood clustered around Highway 82.

Greenwood to Avalon

Greenwood is a strange town. It claims to be the second largest cotton market in the US after Memphis but the town feels permanently sleepy, dripping in sweat and lethargy under the burning Mississippi sun. If you're travelling from Winona, turn right before Greenwood to head up a narrow road to Avalon.

Avalon was home to the great **Mississippi John Hurt** who is buried here in St James's Cemetery. It's difficult to find the grave and there's rarely anyone around to ask. Go east at Avalon along a track for three miles till you reach a smaller track with a gate across it. Head up here for about a mile and look for the cemetery to the left. Hurt played an unusually soft and lyrical brand of blues but despite recording thirteen sides for OKeh in 1928 lived almost all his life unknown outside Avalon. He worked as a farm laborer until 1963 when he was 'discovered' and brought to national attention. He died just three years later.

Robert Johnson's graves

Even in death the legendary Robert Johnson (see p108) is something of an enigma. His certificate of death shows he was buried at the Mount Zion Church in Morgan City in 1938. But others, including 'Honeyboy' Edwards, claim Johnson's sister had the body moved, perhaps to Payne Chapel in Quito. So there are now two grave markers. To make matters more confusing, both markers were laid down in the nineties so no-one alive could remember the exact location of either grave.To find Payne Chapel in **Quito**, take route 7 all the way through Itta Bena and travel south for about four miles. Quito is not signposted but after crossing a small bridge by a large, brown house (said by some to be the Three Forks building), turn right immediately up a track which leads past a couple of shacks to **Payne Chapel**. The track is opposite a run-down business building called 'Hardwicke Etter Ginning Systems'. The grave marker is to the left of the church towards the back of the cemetery. An Atlanta-based rock band called *The Tombstones* placed the marker here in 1991. From Quito drive south on Highway 7 for several miles to reach **Morgan City**.

Robert Johnson

The legend of **Robert Johnson** is the greatest of all blues myths. Johnson made a colossal contribution to the development of blues and stretched the blues guitar far beyond its previous scope. In his short life Johnson recorded few tracks but those classics he did cut, including *Terraplane Blues*, *Hell Hound on my Trail* and *Sweet Home Chicago*, are among the most enduring in blues history.

But while his recorded legacy reveals genius as a musician and songwriter, mythology maintains that to achieve this almost supernatural talent, Johnson 'went down to the crossroads and sold his soul to the Devil'. Whether you believe this or not – and many people do – it's certainly true that Johnson went quickly from being a second-rate guitarist, failing to impress older bluesmen like Son House, to perhaps the most dazzling and influential guitar player in the Delta.

Johnson's death is equally mysterious. Several versions of the story exist. Only one man in a position to know the truth is still alive. David 'Honeyboy' Edwards (interviewed on p273) was with Robert Johnson when he died. So this is how Honeyboy remembers it.

Johnson had been playing a juke joint called **Three Forks** a few miles out of Greenwood near Quito. He played a regular gig there for several weeks during which time he started an affair with the owner's wife.

Johnson had a weakness for women almost as lethal as his weakness for whiskey. One night, while playing a set with **Sonny Boy Williamson II**, a girl handed Johnson an open bottle of whiskey. As he was about to take a drink, Sonny Boy knocked the bottle out of Johnson's hand. 'Don't never take a drink from an open bottle – you don't know what could be in it,' he yelled.

Sonny Boy, like others, had sensed growing tension that night as Johnson showed his affection for the married woman. Johnson reacted angrily to Sonny Boy and when a second open bottle was handed to him, he drank. As the two bluesmen started their second set, Johnson became increasingly incoherent and eventually stopped playing and went outside for air. At about this time, David 'Honeyboy' Edwards showed up with his guitar and found Johnson desperately ill. Johnson was taken to a friend's home.

Honeyboy describes visiting him there in his book, *The World Don't Owe Me Nothing*. 'People couldn't call the doctor. What black person had any money then? So he just died for attention. And here I thought he would just get over it. But Robert died. He was buried by Wednesday. They say at the end he was crawling around like a dog, and howling. That's the way they say he was.' Johnson had been poisoned by whiskey laced with strychnine.

The road is perfectly straight, passing fields, farms and telegraph poles, and the landscape is absolutely flat. At Morgan City, which is just a few wooden buildings, the road bends right. At this point a track leads left signposted 'Mathew's Brake Wildlife Refuge'. Follow this to reach the **Mount Zion Church** just a little way on the left. It's a squat, white place sitting on a patch of cropped grass. It's hard to imagine a more peaceful site. There's no shade and no sound. The road is close, conjuring Johnson's lyric from *Me and the Devil Blues*: 'You may bury my body, ooh, down by the highway side/So my old evil spirit can catch a Greyhound bus and ride'

The marker was donated in 1991 by Columbia Records who were persuaded by California-based blues disciple Skip Henderson. It's a tasteful and fitting four-sided marker which bears the beautiful line, 'His blues addressed a generation he would never know and made poetry of his visions and fears'.

Where the Southern cross the Dog

Head east on Highway 82 then south for a couple of miles on route 3 to reach **Moorhead**. When in 1903 W C Handy 'discovered the blues' listening to a 'lean, loose-jointed Negro' at the railroad station in Tutwiler, Mississippi (see p132), he was intrigued by the hobo's repetition of the line 'Goin' where the Southern cross the Dog'. In fact the line refers to the point where the Yazoo & Mississippi Valley railroad, nicknamed the 'Yellow Dog', crossed the Southern railroad. That point is in Moorhead.

To find it, head into town and turn right immediately before the railroad tracks onto North Southern Avenue. The road ends by a wooden bandstand and, from here, you'll be able to see the railroads cross. A state sign marks the spot. The Yellow Dog line does not run anymore but a 35-yard section remains.

Back by the railroad crossing on the main drag, Roberts County Store and the *Yellow Dog Café* are open for business. The café is surprisingly kitsch; a sign over the bar reads 'Howdy folks! What'll it be?'. There's a juke joint, the Cotton Inn, on the corner of

Moorhead: intersection of Yazoo & Mississippi and Southern railroads.

Washington and Olive Streets. Despite the impression given by chipboard over the windows, it's open most weekends. Moorhead was also home to Grand Ole Opry star Johnny Russell as a sign at the town limits shrieks.

Indianola and BB King

Continue east on 82 and you'll get to **Indianola**, a larger town than any since Greenwood and the boyhood home of blues great **BB King**. Born here in 1925, King began his recording career in 1949 and quickly established himself among the blues élite. He has since grown to become the greatest living bluesman and the undisputed ambassador of blues. King fills the world's most

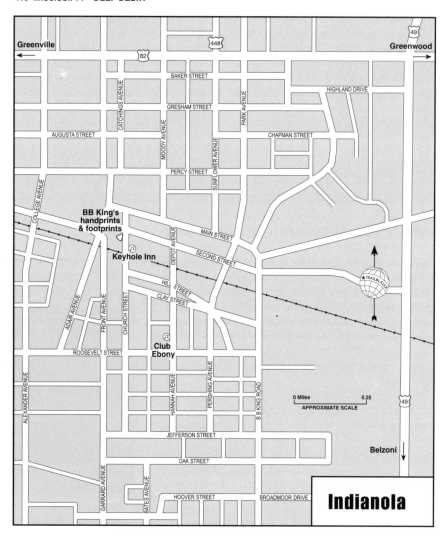

prestigious concert halls and has earned the respect and admiration of each subsequent generation of musicians. Another legend of blues, the magnificent **Albert King** (no relation), was also born in Indianola just two years before BB.

Indianola honors BB King in two ways. At the corner of Church and Second Street you will find his handprints and footprints in the cement. Further up Second Street, at about the point where downtown descends into a run-down black neighborhood, BB King Road leads right towards some cotton gins.

Two Delta juke joints have endured over the years in Indianola. One is the *Keyhole Inn*. To get to it turn right off Second Street onto Church Street and cross the railroad line. It's the green shed-like building immediately on the left. The Keyhole is run by Mary Price but rarely has live bands these days; locals rely on the jukebox instead. The Keyhole was redecorated in 2000 and, at the time of writing, there was no sign over the door which made it harder to find.

The other place is Mary Shepherd's *Club Ebony* at 404 Hannah Avenue. BB King plays here once a year when he heads into Mississippi for the Medgar Evers Homecoming concert (see p102). The club is a small place which, predictably, fills to the roof for King's concert. If you're ever going to catch a BB King concert, this would be the place to do it. It's a far cry from Carnegie Hall.

Holly Ridge and Charley Patton

As Highway 82 nears Leland a turn-off leads to the tiny, desolate community of **Holly Ridge** to the right of the road. **Charley Patton** is buried here. It's hard to exaggerate Patton's influence on blues. Born in 1891 in Edwards, Mississippi, he became the first truly great Delta bluesman and shaped the form of Delta blues for all later musicians. He is, in fact, the father of country

Interview — Rosetta Patton Brown

Did you live with your father?
No, I never lived with him. My mother raised me, but he would come to see me all the time. He had girlfriends so Mum wouldn't let me stay with him, she was afraid that he'd mistreat me. I was born and raised down here and I saw him often. I remember that he was a good man to me, I don't think he bothered nobody but I guess if someone bothered him he'd try to protect himself. He was always making music, going from place to place, I've got some of his records.

He was making music from before I was born. Mamma said he used to hold me on his lap and pluck the guitar. She used to say 'don't do that, don't sing the blues to the baby'. She thought I would take heed and be more interested in that than being a nice quiet girl. That's the kind of woman she was, she didn't like no rough stuff.

Did you know how important your father's music was?
Dad's music must have been important because they're still playing the records. I'm proud of him and the way he made his living. He'd try to get people to go his way. I didn't hear my father in clubs, just at the house when he called. I missed him so much. I'd be so glad to see him when he came, and he was glad to see me. I have some of his records and I play them sometimes. Dad played nothing but the blues. People like that, it has a feeling, it touches you. A lot of people used to try to claim they were him. One day he was on a train and there was an old fat man saying, 'I'm Charley Patton' and waving a guitar. My Dad walked up to him and said 'no you're not, I am'.

Rosetta Patton Brown, Charley Patton's daughter, still lives in Mississippi.

blues and therefore one of the most important figures in American cultural history.

Patton also defined the life of a bluesman; he traveled constantly, had eight wives, drank, smoked and ended up in jail at least once. Patton's daughter, Rosetta, is interviewed on p111. In true blues style, Patton's grave is obscure and difficult to find. Follow the road into Holly Ridge past a large research center on the right. At the T-junction where the Holly Ridge store (Patton used to play outside this place) stands on the left, take a left turn and follow the road to the **New Jerusalem Church**, half-hidden on the left. The cemetery is so overgrown and unkempt you can't see it from the road. Patton's grave is near the back, marked by a tombstone donated in 1991 again with the help of Skip Henderson. This is a beautiful place but it does seem ironic that such a giant of original American music should end up in a seemingly forgotten cemetery.

Leland

Before rolling into Greenville, Highway 82 crosses Highway 61 at **Leland**. This small town is just now waking up to its own blues legacy. **James 'Son' Thomas**, **Little Milton** (see p105), **Willie Foster**, **Boogaloo Ames** and **Eddie Cusic** all came from Leland. A mural on Fourth Street depicts these and other local greats around a Highway 61 sign. It features on this book's cover.

People here seem genuinely – and rightly – proud of their rich blues past. A group calling itself the Leland Blues Project has been established to organize the Highway 61 Blues Festival (the inaugural concert in 2000 headlined Little Milton, Willie Foster and Eddie Cusic) and to create a blues museum in the Old Temple Theater on the corner of Broad and Fourth Streets. The blues festival is up and running but the museum will take a little longer to establish. Contact the Leland Blues Project on ☎ 662-686-2063.

Greenville

Greenville, like many towns in Mississippi, has few specific attractions to recommend it. There's just that mood, unique to the Delta, which makes the place so hypnotic. And if you're in town to find the blues, Greenville will put a spell on you. Nelson Street, which runs at right angles from the levee, is steeped in the Delta blues. It's hard to miss the fact that Las Vegas has moved into Greenville, building giant casinos on pontoons. The town has several of these monsters; rows of gamblers stand inside, pumping dimes into greedy machines. But the casino industry has brought jobs to the impoverished state of Mississippi, and an unexpected jackpot for Greenville.

History

The town was founded in 1828 and named after revolutionary war hero Nathanial Greene. Greenville occupies the highest site on the Mississippi between Memphis and Vicksburg and so was stormed by Union soldiers during the Civil War. Resistance from residents prompted Union troops to burn the town but it was later rebuilt because of its geographic importance. Greenville has since grown into a major river-port and a commercial hub for the Lower Mississippi Delta with a population approaching 50,000.

History of blues in Greenville

As the largest city in the Mississippi Delta, Greenville was a natural stopover for traveling bluesmen. Nelson Street, a main artery through the black community, became a magnet for itinerant musicians. Little Milton sang about Annie Mae's Café in the club Perry's Flowing Fountain while Willie Love captured the spirit of the strip's juke joints in *Nelson Street Blues*.

Apart from Little Milton (see p105), clubs along Nelson Street have fostered local bluesmen Willie Foster and James 'Son' Thomas while stars from across the South have passed through on their way to Chicago. BB King, Howlin' Wolf and Ray Charles all knew Nelson Street well in the early years of their careers. Several old Delta bluesmen still perform in the area. Look out for Eddie Cusic, Boogaloo Ames and T-Model Ford.

Arrival and departure

By air

The **Mid-Delta Regional Airport** (☎ 662-334-3121) lies a few miles north of Greenville off North Broadway. Northwest Airlink runs daily commuter flights between Greenville and Memphis.

By bus

Delta Lines buses use the terminal at 1849 Highway 82 East. One Baton Rouge-bound and one Memphis-bound bus pass through everyday along Highway 61.

By car

Greenville sits on the banks of Lake Ferguson, a sharp meander in the Mississippi, some 10 or 15 miles west of Highway 61 on Highway 82. Jackson is 100 miles east, Memphis 125 miles north.

Orientation

Downtown Greenville is bound by Walnut and Theobald Streets to the west and east and Nelson and Central Streets to the north and south. Casino Row, where the gambling boats are permanently moored, runs parallel to Walnut Street along the levee. Nelson Street is traditionally the blues street in Greenville though, today, there are more venues along Walnut.

Getting around

A car is almost essential for negotiating Greenville which like most places has very limited public transport.

For **car rental** contact Avis (☎ 662-378-3873) at 166 Fifth Avenue or Enterprise (☎ 662-334-4498) at 437 Highway 82 East.

Services

Banks
There are plenty of banks scattered around Greenville but head for the Jefferson Bank at 1645 South Martin Luther King Boulevard if you have trouble finding one.

Communications
● **Post** The main US Post Office is at 305 Main Street.
● **Internet** Check emails at the main library at 302 Main Street.

Tourist information
The Washington County Convention and Visitors' Bureau (☎ 662-334-2711) is located at 410 Washington Avenue.

Record stores
Greenville's main record store is on Walnut Street, just a few properties along from the Sandbar. It isn't a specialist blues place. For a great selection of books on blues, race and Mississippi, however, visit the McCormick Book Inn (☎ 662-332-5038) at 825 South Main Street. Owner Hugh McCormick really knows his stuff and can tell you a lot about the local scene. He even has an impressive collection of blues records and a sculpted head by James 'Son' Thomas, famous not just for his blues guitar but for these strange clay creations.

Medical emergencies
Head for the King's Daughters Hospital (☎ 662-378-2020) located downtown at 300 South Washington Avenue.

What to see

Blues landmarks
Nelson Street itself is Greenville's blues landmark. This is where blues in Greenville was, and is, pioneered, played and enjoyed. At one time there were far more juke joints along this street than there are today. Nelson Street was dealt a blow in 2000 with the death of Perry Payton, owner of Perry's Flowing Fountain which was for years the dominant and most respected blues club in Greenville. Payton witnessed some of the greatest names in blues perform on his small stage.

This is a rough part of town. Clubs, often ramshackle hole-in-the-wall joints, come and go with the seasons. But a couple of clubs endure. Blues lovers should explore Nelson Street, the place is saturated in Delta blues, but take care; this is a run-down side of town where visitors should be discreet and respectful. Get local advice before heading down here on a Saturday night.

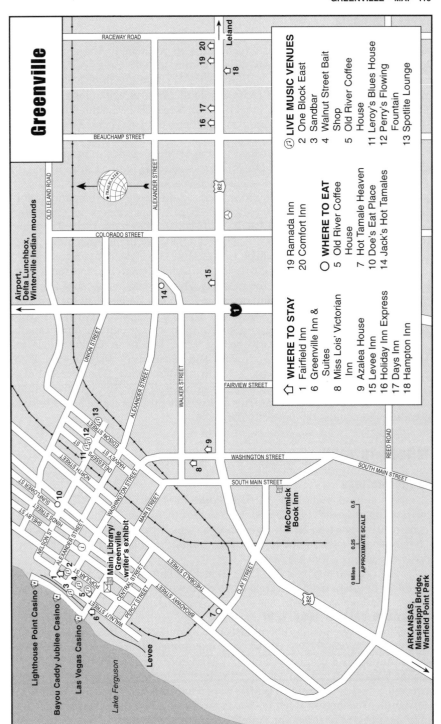

Greenville

RACEWAY ROAD

Leland

BEAUCHAMP STREET

OLD LELAND ROAD

ALEXANDER STREET

Airport,
Delta Lunchbox,
Winterville Indian mounds

COLORADO STREET

82

UNION STREET

WALKER STREET

ALEXANDER STREET

FAIRVIEW STREET

EDISON STREET

HARVEY STREET

NORTH STREET

DELESSEPS ST

ST

WASHINGTON STREET

WASHINGTON STREET

SOUTH MAIN STREET

SOUTH MAIN STREET

REED ROAD

SHELBY ST

NELSON ST

HINDS STREET

SURFLOWER ST

ALEXANDER STREET

MAIN STREET

THEOBALD STREET

CLAY STREET

POPLAR ST

McCormick
Book Inn

82

Main Library/
Greenville
writer's exhibit

CENTRAL STREET

PERCY STREET

BROADWAY STREET

WALNUT STREET

Levee

Lake Ferguson

Lighthouse Point Casino

Bayou Caddy Jubilee Casino

Las Vegas Casino

ARKANSAS,
Mississippi Bridge,
Warfield Point Park

APPROXIMATE SCALE

0 Miles   0.25   0.5

WHERE TO STAY
1 Fairfield Inn
6 Greenville Inn &
   Suites
8 Miss Lois' Victorian
   Inn
9 Azalea House
15 Levee Inn
16 Holiday Inn Express
17 Days Inn
18 Hampton Inn
19 Ramada Inn
20 Comfort Inn

WHERE TO EAT
5 Old River Coffee
   House
7 Hot Tamale Heaven
10 Doe's Eat Place
14 Jack's Hot Tamales

LIVE MUSIC VENUES
2 One Block East
3 Sandbar
4 Walnut Street Bait
   Shop
5 Old River Coffee
   House
11 Leroy's Blues House
12 Perry's Flowing
   Fountain
13 Spotlite Lounge

Other highlights

Greenville is one of the best points along the Mississippi River from which to see the massive **levee system** which tames it. Amazingly, the levee is both longer and taller than the Great Wall of China. In 1927 the levee catastrophically collapsed at Greenville leading to the devastating floods of that year which destroyed vast areas of Delta farmland. You can walk along the top of the levee at the point where it's met by Main Street. The **'Casino District'** is in the same area; three large casinos operate here, the Las Vegas, Bayou Caddy Jubilee, and Lighthouse Point casinos.

Greenville has long been seen as one of Mississippi's more progressive towns. Back in the forties *Delta Democrat Times* editor Hodding Carter Jr won the Pulitzer prize for his editorials against racial prejudice. At that time, of course, his was a brave voice. Carter's office stood on the corner of Main and Walnut Streets. Several other influential writers began their careers in Greenville, including Shelby Foote, Ellen Douglas and William Alexander Percy. These and other local literary heroes are celebrated at the **William Alexander Percy Memorial Library's writers exhibit** (☎ 662-335-2331) at 302 Main Street.

As the largest city in the Mississippi Delta, Greenville's fortunes have long been tied up with the cotton industry. **Deer Creek**, just west of Highway 61 between Leland and Hollandale, claims to boast the most fertile soil anywhere in the world except the Nile Valley. You'll see fenced off patches of crops across the area; these are research stations set up by agricultural corporations.

One other site well worth seeing while you're in Greenville is the **Winterville Indian Mounds State Park and Museum** (☎ 662-334-4684; Wed-Sat 8am-5pm; $1) off Highway 1 North at Winterville. The sacred burial mounds found here are among the best examples of prehistoric Indian culture anywhere in the United States. The mounds themselves make an eerie sight standing tall against the perfectly flat Delta.

Where to stay

Budget options

Campers should make for *Warfield Point Park* (☎ 662-335-7275; ❶) a few miles south of Greenville. To find it, go to the junction of the Highways 82 and 1, then drive west on 82 for five miles, at which point you'll pick up signs. They offer tidy sites by the river but the military feel of the place, taken seriously by staff, is a touch irritating.

The *Levee Inn* (☎ 662-332-1511; ❷) at 1202 Highway 82 East is the cheapest motel in town. It's a basic place but good value.

Mid-range options ($50-120)

There are just two bed and breakfasts in Greenville itself, both on leafy South Washington Avenue. They are the charming *Azalea House* (☎ 662-335-0507; ❸-❹) at number 548 on stately South Washington Avenue. Owners Willis and Donna Winters go to great lengths to make their guests comfortable. The other Greenville bed and breakfast is *Miss Lois' Victorian Inn* (☎ 662-335-6000; ❸) at 331 South Washington Avenue. The eccentric and eponymous owner will be only too pleased to show you round her elaborate home.

Greenville — chain hotels

- *Holiday Inn Express* (☎ 662-334-6900), 2428 Highway 82 East
- *Comfort Inn* (☎ 662-378-4976), 3080 Highway 82 East
- *Days Inn* (☎ 662-335-1999), 2500 Highway 82 East
- *Hampton Inn* (☎ 662-334-1818), 2701 Highway 82 East
- *Ramada Inn* (☎ 662-332-4411), 2700 Highway 82 East

Another good bed and breakfast, *Deer Creek* (☎ 662-686-9525; ❸), is out at 203 Deer Creek Drive in Leland. One of the better downtown hotels is the new *Greenville Inn & Suites* (☎ 662-332-6900; ❹) at 211 Walnut Street. This is a very comfortable and friendly place just a short walk from the clubs in Walnut Street and close to the water. Also consider trying the convenient *Fairfield Inn* (☎ 662-332-0508; ❹) at 137 North Walnut Street.

Where to eat

It might at first seem odd to think that people travel for miles to eat out in Greenville. But one restaurant, *Doe's Eat Place* (☎ 662-334-3315) at 502 Nelson Street, tempted even Bill Clinton to make a special visit. Doe's Eat Place serves some of the best down-home food in the Delta and steaks to rival any restaurant in the South. The restaurant itself is a tumbledown place in the black Nelson Street neighborhood

Doe Sr started the business in 1941 after the 1927 flood had destroyed his grocery on the same site. He was a white man but ran a honky-tonk for blacks only in the front of the building and a restaurant for whites out back. His steaks and hot tamales quickly became famous so Doe closed the honky-tonk and focused on the restaurant.

Despite its humble appearance, Doe's has a huge following of discerning steak fans. It's now run by his sons, Charles and 'Little' Doe. They're still there cooking steaks in the front room where everyone can watch this great Delta tradition unfold. The price is good, the food better and the ambience unbeatable.

Other places to try for down-home Mississippi cooking include *Jack's Hot Tamales* at 1211 East Alexander Street, *Hot Tamale Heaven* at 614 South Theobald Street and the *Delta Lunchbox* at 1298 Highway 1 North. The *Old River Coffee House*, featured in the live music section, also serves good food. The huge 'Highway 61' rolled tortilla sandwich with perfectly-smoked Boston butt is a bargain at $5.95.

Where to find live music

While Nelson Street is traditionally the home of blues in Greenville, recently revitalized Walnut Street has a few cool venues too. Less intrepid visitors might prefer these; Nelson Street can at times feel pretty menacing. Like most juke joints, those on Nelson Street are generally okay once you're in them. It's wandering the street itself after dark which can lead to problems.

The best of Nelson Street's juke joints is *Perry's Flowing Fountain* which, despite the recent passing of founder Perry Payton, is still open for business. You'll find the place at 816 Nelson Street opposite the Southern Cotton Oil Inc building. One side of the place is Annie Mae's Café made famous by Little Milton. Blues here is usually provided by the jukebox but there are occasional live gigs. In its glory days, the Flowing Fountain presented a steady stream of great blues names. It's a tidy place with a good atmosphere. There are a few other bars along Nelson Street which you might like to check out. These include *Leroy's Blues House* at number 800, near Perry's, and the *Spotlite Lounge* further up the street.

On Walnut Street head for the *Walnut Street Bait Shop* (☎ 662-332-0315) at number 128. Owner Brad Jordan has turned this place into a funky and likeable little club. One wall is decorated with newspaper cuttings pasted around a photograph of Robert Johnson. Katie Mae's Soul Food Café is attached. There's supposed to be live music here Thursdays to Saturdays but, in practice, the schedule can be quite sporadic.

The cavernous *Sandbar*, over the road at number 129, has blues some weekends but country music is more commonly played here. Further along, the *Old River Coffee House* (☎ 662-335-7580) at 138 Walnut Street is a newer and cooler place with a quasi-Latin feel. There's live music most weekends for a $3 cover.

One Block East at 240 Washington Street is a more dingy place but there's live music here several nights a week. Rock bands appear more often than blues acts but the open mic session on Sundays can attract an interesting mix of performers. Of the casinos, the *Bayou Caddy Jubilee* and *Las Vegas* occasionally present live blues.

Lillo's Restaurant (☎ 662-686-4401) on Highway 82 near Leland regularly books local piano legend Boogaloo Ames.

Mississippi Delta Blues & Heritage Festival

Greenville hosts one of the oldest blues festivals in the Delta on the third Saturday of every September.

Established in 1978 in a cotton field, the festival is now a major event attracting visitors from all over the world and top performers from the worlds of blues and gospel. A mini-festival called 'Little Wynn' takes place on Nelson Street on the Friday before the main event. The entire week before, 'Blues Week', features events and gigs building up to the festival itself.

Tickets are $15 in advance or $20 on the gate. For information, visit 🖳 www.deltablues.org or call organizers Mississippi Action for Community Education (MACE) on ☎ 662-335-3523.

Moving on — Greenville to Cleveland

Under a vast and unpredictable sky, Highway 61 runs unswerving past cotton fields, telegraph poles and little else. This is archetypal Delta country and it's easy to picture early bluesmen pioneering country blues on these immense farms. The Mississippi River is some miles west and won't be seen again for quite a while.

Cleveland

Despite a student population of some 9000, Cleveland is a small, quiet Delta town which oozes charm and blues in equal measure.

Dockery Farm, just a short drive east on Highway 8, is the very place where Delta blues was born; Henry Sloan, Charley Patton and others worked here in the early years of the twentieth century. You don't have to be a blues fan to find Cleveland easy to like – the relatively buoyant economy and friendly locals make this a vibrant town.

History

Cleveland's history, like its fortunes, has long been tied to cotton production. This otherwise serene Delta town became an important hub for cotton growers who would arrange to sell their harvest on Cleveland's Cotton Row. As a true Delta town it is perhaps no surprise to find that the story of Cleveland is little more and certainly no less than the story of cotton and of blues.

History of blues in Cleveland

Most music scholars agree that the Delta blues was invented near Cleveland on **Dockery Plantation**. The details are cloudy but **Charley Patton** grew up here learning at the feet of **Henry Sloan** who played a rhythmic guitar style which Patton later developed into blues.

That contribution is hard to underestimate. Robert Palmer, in his definitive book *Deep Blues*, claims, '...he [Patton] inspired just about every Delta bluesman of any consequence. He is among the most important musicians twentieth century America has produced'. Charley Patton's daughter, Rosetta, lives in the Delta not far from Cleveland; she is interviewed for this book on p111. Keith Dockery McLean, widow of Joe Rice Dockery who inherited the plantation from his father, still lives on the farm; she is interviewed on p123 in the section on Dockery.

Another great American musician, **WC Handy**, also found inspiration in Cleveland. In 1905 he witnessed an early blues band playing at the Cleveland Courthouse. He was so taken by the music he made the now famous declaration: 'An American composer is born'. Handy's contribution to African-American music is itself colossal.

Listening to early Delta blues records reveals the extent to which this area, the heart of the Delta, was the cradle of the blues. Charley Patton's *Pea Vine Blues* describes the so-called **'Pea Vine' railroad** which carried cotton through Dockery, Boyle and Skene on its way west to Rosedale and the Mississippi River. Another Patton classic, *Tom Rushen Blues*, refers to County Deputy Sheriff **Tom Rushing** whose family vintners still stands. The state prison at **Parchman** played a part in many blues musicians' lives. **Bukka White** reflects on his time there in *Parchman Farm Blues*. **Rosedale** found its way into Robert Johnson's *Traveling Riverside Blues* with the lyric, 'Lord, I'm going to Rosedale, gonna take my rider by my side/we can still barrelhouse baby, 'cause it's on the riverside'.

Of the many local juke joints famous among bluesmen, the **Harlem Inn**, now defunct, was one of the best. Here the enterprising management presented a stream of blues greats throughout the forties and fifties.

Arrival, departure and getting around

Cleveland stands at the crossroads of Highway 8 between Ruleville and Rosedale and Highway 61, the Blues Highway, between Greenville and Clarksdale. The town itself is compact and easy to navigate but out here in the wide open Delta you'll need a car. For **car rental** contact Enterprise (☎ 662-843-9649) at 210 North Davis Avenue. The **bus terminal**, served by Delta Bus Lines, is at 809 North Davis Avenue

Orientation

Cleveland is easy to get around. The business district is framed by Sharpe and Fifth Avenues. Most businesses and cheaper accommodations are strung out along Highway 61, or Davis Avenue as it becomes in Cleveland. Rosedale is some 18 miles west of town on Highway 8, Dockery is five miles east on the same road.

Services

Banks
Cleveland's main banks are the Cleveland State Bank at 128 North Sharpe Avenue, the Valley Bank at 100 East Sunflower Road or the Union Planters Bank at 129 South Sharpe Avenue.

Communications
● **Post** The US Post Office is at 210 South Chrisman Avenue.
● **Internet** There's free Internet time available at the Bolivar County Library at 401 South Court Street.

Tourist information
Call the Cleveland-Bolivar County Chamber of Commerce (☎ 662-843-2712, 800-295-7473) on Third Street.

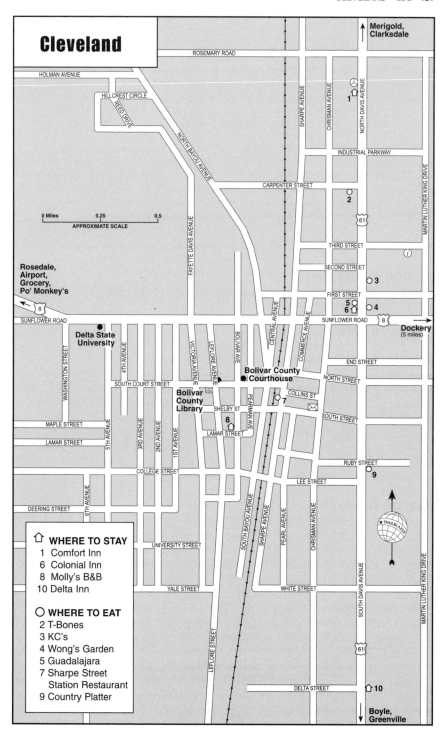

Cleveland

ROSEMARY ROAD

HOLMAN AVENUE

HILLCREST CIRCLE

REED DRIVE

NORTH BAYOU AVENUE

SHARPE AVENUE

CHRISMAN AVENUE

NORTH DAVIS AVENUE

MARTIN LUTHER KING DRIVE

INDUSTRIAL PARKWAY

CARPENTER STREET

FAYETTE DAVIS AVENUE

0 Miles   0.25   0.5
APPROXIMATE SCALE

1

2

61

THIRD STREET

SECOND STREET

Rosedale,
Airport,
Grocery,
Po' Monkey's

8

SUNFLOWER ROAD

i

3

FIRST STREET

5
6
4

SUNFLOWER ROAD   8

Dockery
(5 miles)

WASHINGTON STREET

Delta State
University

4TH AVENUE

VICTORIA AVENUE

LEFLORE AVENUE

BOLIVAR AVE

CENTRAL AVENUE

COMMERCE AVENUE

END STREET

SOUTH COURT STREET

Bolivar County
Courthouse

Bolivar
County
Library

PEARMAN AVE

NORTH STREET

COLLINS ST

7

SHELBY ST

8

LAMAR STREET

SOUTH STREET

MAPLE STREET

5TH AVENUE

3RD AVENUE

2ND AVENUE

1ST AVENUE

LAMAR STREET

RUBY STREET

COLLEGE STREET

LEE STREET

9

DEERING STREET

6TH AVENUE

SOUTH BAYOU AVENUE

SHARPE AVENUE

PEARL AVENUE

CHRISMAN AVENUE

TRAILBLAZER

UNIVERSITY STREET

⌂ **WHERE TO STAY**
1 Comfort Inn
6 Colonial Inn
8 Molly's B&B
10 Delta Inn

○ **WHERE TO EAT**
2 T-Bones
3 KC's
4 Wong's Garden
5 Guadalajara
7 Sharpe Street
Station Restaurant
9 Country Platter

YALE STREET

WHITE STREET

LEFLORE STREET

SOUTH DAVIS AVENUE

MARTIN LUTHER KING DRIVE

61

DELTA STREET

⌂ 10

Boyle,
Greenville

Rosedale and the Crossroads Blues Festival

Some 18 miles west of Cleveland on Highway 8, Rosedale is a small river-town with its own blues legacy. As wandering African-Americans traveled north to Chicago, they would camp by the Mississippi River to avoid the police.

So Rosedale probably saw as many early bluesmen pass through as did Cleveland, a fact reinforced by Robert Johnson's *Travelling Riverside Blues* which names the town. The Crossroads Blues Society (🖳 www.crossroadsblues.org), run by Leo McGee, organizes the **Crossroads Blues Festival** over the second weekend in May. Leo also owns the River Run Café at 1310 Main Street where Highway 8 hits Highway 1. Drop in to find out more about the festival. Rosedale is also home to Bug's Lounge juke joint (see p125).

Medical emergencies
Head for the Bolivar Medical Center (☎ 662-846-0061) at 901 Highway 8 East.

What to see

Cleveland Courthouse
Cleveland Courthouse, where WC Handy experienced his blues revelation, is now the **Bolivar County Courthouse** on Court Street. It doesn't look like a blues venue but here, in 1905, Handy apparently heard a Delta blues band perform and was inspired by what he heard. Handy called himself the 'Father of the Blues'; he didn't invent the form but he did much to promote it through his own smooth compositions like *Memphis Blues*, *St Louis Blues* and *Yellow Dog Blues*. An historic marker opposite the courthouse commemorates Handy although, at the time of writing, it had been stolen.

Rushing Winery
The old Rushing Winery is out near Merigold. Take Highway 61 north from Cleveland towards Merigold and, shortly before reaching South Street on the left, go right down a narrow road for a couple of miles until you reach the white, dilapidated building.

The winery has been closed since 1990. Blues devotees cherish the place because its one-time owner and County Sheriff, Tom Rushing, was the subject of Charley Patton's *Tom Rushen Blues* in which Patton warns of the Deputy Sheriff with the line, 'Laid down last night hopin' I would have my peace/I laid down last night hopin' I would have my peace/But when I woke up, Tom Rushen [sic] was shakin' me'.

Tom Rushen Blues is a good example of the way in which early blues records served as a form of news communication for African-Americans. Patton wasn't just making music; he was warning others to avoid Tom Rushing as they traveled to that part of the Delta.

Dockery Plantation

Take Highway 8 east from Cleveland for about five miles to reach the Dockery Plantation on the left. From the road one can see the old cotton gin, bearing the family name, the commissary and the Baptist Church which once served the spiritual need of the plantation's many poor, black workers. Charley Patton, pioneer of Delta blues, became one of those workers after his father moved the family there in 1897. Will Dockery founded the plantation in around 1895. He cleared the land, built a home and began farming. The business grew quickly, not least because Dockery developed a reputation for paying his workers fairly if not generously. In 1936 Will Dockery died leaving the plantation to his son, Joe Rice Dockery. By then the plantation had become a huge concern. Joe Rice Dockery's widow, Keith Dockery McLean, still lives in the beautiful old plantation home which stands overlooking the Sunflower River.

'Back in the twenties and thirties,' says Keith Dockery McLean, 'we knew nothing about the blues being played on the plantation. When Lomax came to Dockery to record for the Library of Congress in the forties, that was the first we heard about it. I knew black musicians would play concerts at the courthouse but Mr Dockery was very surprised when Lomax arrived and asked him about Charley Patton. The plantation system has changed a lot since then. Mechanization and the invention of the cotton-picker lost a lot of people their jobs. That led to the black migration north. I mean, when I first came to live at Dockery there were probably 2000 people working here.'

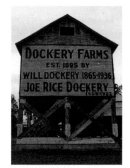

Old cotton gin at Dockery Plantation

The plantation is now rented to different farmers; one large company farms most of it. Mrs Dockery McLean is well-read on the subject of blues and is proud of her husband's reputation for treating his black workers fairly. While she doesn't mind people pulling over to take photographs of the cotton gin and plantation entrance, she asks blues fans to respect her privacy.

Other Blues landmarks

Parchman Penitentiary, one-time home to a number of blues musicians, is quite a drive north from Cleveland on Highway 49. The prison itself is still open for business which is one reason why there's little point making the trip. While one can see the prison from the road, signs warn against stopping 'except in an emergency' and there's really little to see. Bukka White is one of the prison's most famous former residents but other bluesmen, including Son House and Sonny Boy Williamson, have spent time inside the now famous institution. Folklorist Alan Lomax recorded Bukka White here in 1939 for the Library of Congress.

In 1998, Cleveland established the Peavine Blues Awards (see p124) and with it the **Mississippi Delta Blues Hall of Fame** which is being set up on the Delta State University campus in the Charles W Capps Jr Archives and Museum building. In the past **Chrisman Avenue** was the Nelson Street of Cleveland; a number of music venues stood here but these have long since faded into oblivion.

The Peavine Blues Awards

A group of local blues enthusiasts and the Cleveland-Bolivar County Chamber of Commerce set up the first Peavine Awards for 'artistic excellence in the Mississippi Delta Blues' in 1998. The awards are given annually in August.

The first year's awards were given posthumously to Charley Patton, Willie Brown and Tommy Johnson, all Dockery residents and Delta blues pioneers. The 1999 awards were given to Robert Johnson, Robert Jr Lockwood and the St Louis-based bluesman Henry Townsend. A fund in Robert Johnson's name has also been set up to promote blues education and 'scholarly research' into the blues.

Where to stay

There are few places to stay in Cleveland; all the best options are presented here in order of expense.

For a cheap sleep check in at the *Delta Inn* (☎ 662-846-1873; **❶-❷**) at 1139 Highway 61 South. You get what you pay for, of course, but if your budget is tight this is the place to try. The *Colonial Inn* (☎ 662-843-3641; **❷**) on Highway 61 next to the Guadalajara Mexican restaurant is a little more expensive but probably better value. Another slight step up, the *Comfort Inn* (☎ 662-843-4060; **❷-❸**) on Highway 61 at 721 North Davis near Rosemary Road is, as its name suggests, a little more comfortable.

By far the best place to stay in Cleveland – indeed, one of the most enjoyable bed and breakfasts anywhere on the Blues Highway – is *Molly's* (☎ 662-843-9913; **❸**) at 214 South Bolivar Avenue. There are only four rooms so book ahead. Molly's is run by Molly and Floyd Shaman who've turned their attractive home into a truly unusual place to stay. Floyd is a nationally known sculptor who has found time to use his considerable talent to decorate the property. Each room is unique; themes range from melons to North Africa. Breakfast, too, is approaching art. Molly's is comfortable, quiet and great fun.

Where to eat

For a small town Cleveland has a surprisingly wide choice of good restaurants. One of the best-loved of these is Jimmy Williams' *Country Platter* (☎ 662-846-7051) at 700 Ruby Street on the corner of Ruby and Highway 61. A filling, down-home buffet attract legions of lunchtime visitors in search of proper Southern cooking for just a few dollars. Smothered pork steak with yams and greens is a specialty. Like all the tastiest Southern recipes, the greens have been cooked for hours and caramelized so that any goodness that might once have lurked in the leaves has long since evaporated; it tastes fantastic.

Incongruously, perhaps, there's a very good Mexican restaurant, *Gaudalajara* (☎ 662-846-6965), at 307 North Davis Avenue. There's a great combination dinner (one enchilada, one burrito and one taco with rice and beans) for just $6.50. Park in the Colonial Inn carpark to get to the restaurant. If it's global cuisine you're after you might try *Wong's Garden* (☎ 662-846-6313) at 316 North Davis Avenue. The lunch buffet here is great value for just $5.

Steak lovers should seek out *T-Bones* (☎ 662-846-0806) at 308 East Carpenter Street. Vegetarians would be well-advised to steer well clear of this place where truly enormous steaks are the standard fare. It's not cheap, steaks are around the $16 mark, but the quality is high. A new and welcome addition to Cleveland's restaurants is the ill-named *Sharpe Street Station Restaurant* (☎ 662-846-0000) at 201 South Sharpe Avenue. You'll find excellent and reasonably-priced seafood and pasta with a clear New Orleanian influence.

The best restaurant in Cleveland, however, is *KC's* (☎ 662-843-5301) on Highway 61 just past Sunflower Road; look out for a California-style Spanish mission replica looking as out of place as any building could. Chef Wally Joe and his wine-aficionado brother Don have created a nationally noted restaurant in what is, let's face it, a fairly unlikely location. Food critics from across the country have praised the outstanding menu which combines influences from as disparate gastronomic regions as California, Europe and China. The wine list is one of the best in the South. Expect to pay around $20 for an entrée; that's fairly expensive by local standards but good value anyway.

Where to find live music

Cleveland's most dependable live music venue is the *Airport Grocery* (☎ 662-843-4817) on Highway 8 West towards Rosedale. Owner Jonathan Vance books blues acts as often as he can, including the late harmonica legend Willie Foster whose 1999 album for Mempho Records was recorded live here. This is a relaxed and friendly venue with good Southern food which has been dishing up blues, hot tamales and catfish hoagies since the sixties.

The Airport Grocery is Cleveland's best venue but it isn't a juke joint. For that, head out to *Po' Monkey's*. This is one of the most appealing juke joints anywhere in Mississippi. Imagine all a juke joint should be – ramshackle, wild and in the middle of a cotton field – and Po' Monkey's will surpass your expectations. Po' Monkey's real name is William Seaberry. He's a giant of a man who will make you welcome. There's seldom a band here but on Thursday nights a DJ keeps the packed joint jumping. Most other nights Po' Monkey's is a strip-joint. The roof is made waterproof by trash bags, the decor is from the fairy lights and bottle-tops school of interior design and the dancing is frenzied.

It's not the easiest place to find. Drive out towards Rosedale on Highway 8 and turn right soon after passing the Airport Grocery into a road signposted to the 'Bayou Academy'. Carry on along this road, which quickly gets worse, for five miles until you've crossed four stop signs. Shortly after the fourth, turn right onto a bumpy gravel track until you reach the tumbledown shack which is Po' Monkey's. You'll see lights across the flat fields long before you reach the place.

Rosedale's *Bug's Lounge* is another juke joint worth seeking out for a taste of real Delta partying. Drive into downtown Rosedale on Main Street and take a right just before reaching the courthouse. The street name isn't marked. Follow the road till it hits Bruce Street; Bug's is on the corner. Live acts rarely appear but a jukebox keeps the place lively.

A rather different venue, the *Performing Arts Center* (☎ 662-846-4626) at Delta State University, presents a generally impressive series of musical events, some of which have a blues or jazz connection.

Moving on — Cleveland to Clarksdale

Clarksdale makes a convincing claim to be the blues hub of the Delta and this raggedy 37-mile stretch of 61 between Cleveland and Clarksdale has to be as evocative as any section of the Blues Highway.

The route trundles past **Merigold**, near Tom Rushing's Winery, and **Mound Bayou**. Mound Bayou was established in 1887 by former slaves as a haven for African-Americans. **Winstonville**, just a few miles further on, once boasted another Harlem Inn, this one bigger and better known than that which once drew crowds in Cleveland. Winstonville's Harlem Inn, which stood near the corner of Maxin Street and Highway 61, burned down in 1989 but there are said to be plans to rebuild it.

Further north again, **Shelby** is a larger community which hides a couple of juke joints. The Do Drop Inn and the Windy City Blues House both stand on Lake Street which runs parallel to Highway 61. The Do Drop Inn is an olive green building with music most weekends. The Windy City, on the corner of Lake and Second, has occasional music. Both joints can be rough.

After Shelby, Highway 61 leads past the small community at **Duncan** where poverty-stricken streets seem to show the blues still being lived rather than played. From Duncan it's just a short cruise in to Clarksdale.

Clarksdale

Easily the most blues-rich town in the Mississippi Delta, Clarksdale represents to many the essence of the music. Today, Clarksdale is a fairly lively community which has been coaxed into celebrating its musical past by the slow realization that it occupies a crucial place in blues history.

The town itself appears to have changed little since the fifties when rising stars like Ike Turner began moving north to Memphis to see a certain Mr Phillips at Sun Records; the back streets are still crowded with hole-in-the-wall bars and shabby juke joints.

History

Clarksdale was founded in 1848 by one John Clark. Clarksdale quickly grew to become one of the Delta's main trading towns and a hub for the surrounding cotton industry. After the Civil War, Clarksdale, like many Delta towns, suffered as plantation owners struggled to maintain their freed workforces and cotton yields dipped. Clarksdale persevered. It's still an important commercial and cultural hub to the northern Delta region.

History of blues in Clarksdale

During the thirties, forties and fifties, Clarksdale became the blues nucleus of the Mississippi Delta. This was the place to make it as a musician. John Lee Hooker, Sam Cooke, Jackie Brenston and Ike Turner (interviewed on p134) were born and raised here. Many other influential bluesmen made names for themselves in Clarksdale's Fourth Street juke joints. Son House, Muddy Waters, Bukka White and Robert Nighthawk are just a few names from the celestial list of local talent.

Clarksdale is also a key city in the story of the musical migration north to Chicago. It was from here that Muddy Waters jumped on the Illinois Central railroad in 1943 to make his way north to Bronzeville, Chicago. Many more would follow. On 26 September 1937 Clarksdale witnessed one of the most tragic episodes in blues history – the untimely and controversial death of legendary singer Bessie Smith after a car accident on Highway 61 near Coahoma.

Arrival, departure and getting around

Highway 61 skirts downtown Clarksdale as it makes its way north to Memphis. From Clarksdale, Highway 49 leads south-east Tutwiler while Highway 6 shoots east to Oxford, Mississippi's academic bastion. Passenger trains stopped picking up here in the sixties but **buses** pull in at 1604 State Street. For taxis try the City Cab Co (☎ 662-624-9288) or Jerry's Cabs (☎ 662-624-9222).

Orientation

Highway 61, called State Street in Clarksdale, runs along the southern edge of town. Sunflower Avenue, which runs parallel to the Sunflower River, leads from 61 to downtown Clarksdale which is broadly the few streets north and east of the old Illinois Central railroad tracks which bisect the town. Everything south of the tracks is the African-American side of town and so the area of most interest for blues lovers. Martin Luther King Jr Boulevard, formerly Fourth Street, is the main thoroughfare through the black community.

Clarksdale — events and festivals

- **April** Muddy Waters Day
- **May** Robert Johnson Day

- **August** Sunflower River Blues and Gospel Festival

Services

Banks

There are several ATMs in Clarksdale but head for the main bank downtown on Third Street if you're having trouble finding one.

Communications

● **Post** The main post office is on the corner of Third Street and Sharkey Avenue in the Federal Building.

● **Internet** Head for the Carnegie Public Library, former home of the Delta Blues Museum, at 114 Delta Avenue.

Tourist information

Clarksdale isn't the most user-friendly place but you could try hunting for information at the Clarksdale-Coahoma County Chamber of Commerce (☎ 662-627-7337, 800-626-3764) at 1540 DeSoto Avenue (Highway 49).

Record stores

The **Delta Blues Museum** in the old freight depot on Edwards Street has an excellent selection of blues books and some recordings. The **Stackhouse Record Mart** at 232 Sunflower Avenue offered an interesting collection of records, CDs and general blues paraphernalia until it closed in 1998 when owner Jim O'Neal moved to Kansas City. At the time of writing the place was apparently on the verge of reopening.

Medical emergencies

The main hospital in town is the Regional Medical Center (☎ 662-627-3211) at 1970 Hospital Drive.

What to see

Delta Blues Museum and Blues Alley

In 1979 the original **Delta Blues Museum** was established in the Carnegie Public Library. While the intention was no doubt admirable, the exhibition was inadequate. The displays had the feel of a high school project and the space given to the museum was far too tight. So it was welcome news when in October 1999 the Delta Blues Museum (☎ 662-627-6820; Mon-Sat 9am-5pm; free) announced its move into the old freight depot on Edwards Street, or 'Blues Alley'. The museum houses the old collection – including one of BB King's 'Lucille' guitars – at one end of the bright, gentrified space but now

---

(Opposite) A squat shack stands alone in a Delta field under the vast Mississippi sky.

boasts changing exhibits, rehearsal space, a shop and blues-related art as well. The rehearsal area is used to give blues workshops to local school-age children. Free concerts take place at the attached open-air stage on selected Fridays throughout the summer.

Blues Alley, the new address of the Delta Blues Museum, has recently been renamed as part of a general nod to Clarksdale's blues roots. This used to be Edwards Street. The section of Yazoo Avenue between Blues Alley and Third Street has been christened **John Lee Hooker Lane** in honor of one of Clarksdale's more illustrious bluesman. Just along from the old freight depot, now the museum, the old passenger terminal has also enjoyed a recent makeover. It's used for civic functions and can be rented. The frosted glass hatch between the main room and the kitchen used to be the ticket booth. So this is where Muddy Waters, and many like him, must once have stood in line waiting to buy a ticket to Chicago.

Riverside Hotel (GT Thomas Hospital)
The Riverside Hotel (☎ 662-624-9163) at 615 Sunflower Avenue is the current incarnation of the GT Thomas Hospital for blacks where Bessie Smith died. Smith was among the most influential of all blues singers whose popularity in the twenties and thirties was almost unprecedented for a black performer. Her hard drinking and daring sexual affairs with both men and women helped foster the mystique which surrounded her. In 1937 Smith was making her way to a gig in Clarksdale when her car crashed on Highway 61. She later bled to death at the GT Thomas hospital.

The incident still causes a good deal of controversy since some believe Smith was first taken to the white hospital where she was refused treatment. By the time she reached the black hospital it was too late to save her. There appears to be no hard evidence for the story which most blues scholars now claim to be fiction. The current owner of the Riverside Hotel, Frank 'Rat' Ratliff, claims his mother, who turned the hospital into a hotel in 1944, knew what really happened. She told Frank but Frank's telling no-one.

Today the Riverside Hotel, a labyrinthine place, welcomes long-term residents and blues devotees in roughly equal measure. Frank Ratliff prefers not to rent out 'Bessie's Room', number two, but will show it to anyone who stops by to ask. A poster of Bessie covers the bed. John F Kennedy chose to stay at the Riverside when he visited Clarksdale; he stayed opposite Bessie's in Room 2a.

Frank Ratliff's mother, the late Mrs Z Hill, knew many of the great names in blues who would stay here on their way through town. Ask Frank to tell you the story about Ike Turner who came to live at the Riverside when he was just a boy. Mrs Hill made the uniforms for his first band.

(Opposite) Top: A section of Yazoo Avenue in Clarksdale (Ms) has been renamed John Lee Hooker Lane in honor of the 'Boogie Man' who was born here in 1920.
Bottom: The Red Top Lounge juke joint (see p134) has been a fixture in Clarksdale for nearly 60 years.

Other blues landmarks in Clarksdale

Ike Turner's enduring fame has recently been for all the wrong reasons. In the fifties, however, Turner was a central figure on the Memphis music scene and a true blues-rock innovator. his band recorded Jackie Brenston's *Rocket 88* for Sun in 1951. Most rock academics name that song the first ever rock & roll number. **Ike Turner's house** where the boy-wonder grew up still stands at 304 Washington Street. Another talented local boy, **Sam Cooke**, grew up in a house on the corner of Seventh Street and Illinois Avenue.

By the time you reach Clarksdale, chances are you've spent enough time in the Delta to find out that communities up and down Highway 61 claim to know the whereabouts of the **crossroads** where Robert Johnson sold his soul to the Devil. In Clarksdale they'll tell you it's the intersection of Highways 61 and 49. To reinforce the point they've erected two huge, dueling iron guitars over the now-busy interchange. Tacky, yes. Accurate, no. The fact is, of course, that the myth is just that – a story. And even if it did happen, no-one alive could know where. Still, it seems rude not to at least stop by and take a photograph.

Blues landmarks — out of town

In 1903 **WC Handy** famously 'discovered the blues' at the railroad station in Tutwiler (see p132). At the time, Handy was living in Clarksdale in a house on the corner of Blues Alley and Issaquena Avenue. An historic marker denotes the spot. **Wade Walton's Barbershop** stands near the marker. Wade Walton was a well-known local harmonica and guitar player whose barbershop became something of an institution on the Blues Highway. People would drop in just to hear him play. Sadly, Wade Walton died in 2000 and, at the time of writing, the famous barbershop still looked closed. Another defunct blues institution in Clarksdale is **WROX Radio** at 317 Delta Avenue. Much-loved blues DJ Early Wright broadcast blues and gospel over the WROX airwaves from 1947 to 1998. Passing blues fans would drop in to meet the man whose knowledge of the local music scene was encyclopaedic.

Perhaps the greatest ever bluesman, and certainly the brightest star of the Chicago blues scene, **Muddy Waters** grew up near Clarksdale on the **Stovall Plantation**. Waters, born McKinley Morganfield in 1915, moved to the plantation from Rolling Fork to be looked after by his grandmother after his mother died in 1918. As a boy, the budding star learned harmonica but he didn't pick up the guitar till he was 17.

Muddy Waters, who apparently earned his nickname from playing in muddy streams, was determined to escape the hardship and poverty of plantation life. In 1943, already an accomplished musician who had recorded for Alan Lomax and the Library of Congress, Waters traveled to Chicago where he would became the leading blues musician of his generation and an inspiration to blues and rock musicians worldwide.

To find Stovall, take Oakhurst Road west out of Clarksdale. It turns into Stovall Road after a few miles. The vast plantation leads away to the left of the road after around eight miles. When you reach eight tiny houses on the left of the road before the Stovall Farms office, you've found the place. Sadly, however, Muddy's house has gone. It didn't collapse or burn; the House of Blues

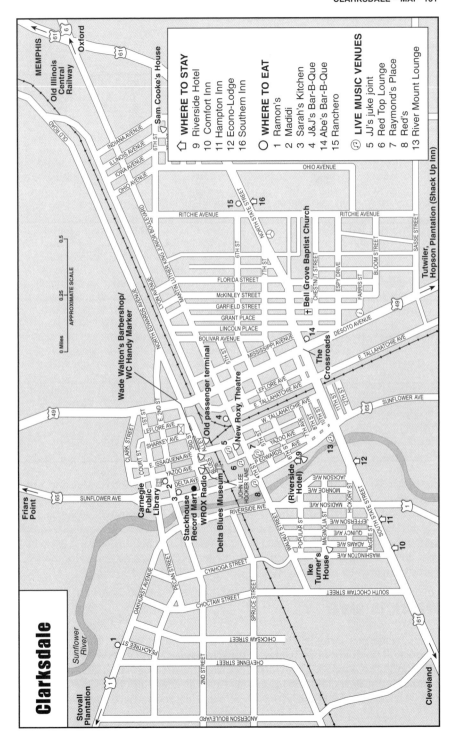

Clarksdale

WHERE TO STAY
9 Riverside Hotel
10 Comfort Inn
11 Hampton Inn
12 Econo-Lodge
16 Southern Inn

WHERE TO EAT
1 Ramon's
2 Madidi
3 Sarah's Kitchen
4 J&J's Bar-B-Que
14 Abe's Bar-B-Que
15 Ranchero

LIVE MUSIC VENUES
5 JJ's juke joint
6 Red Top Lounge
7 Raymond's Place
8 Red's
13 River Mount Lounge

Tutwiler

In 1903 a certain **WC Handy** sat waiting for a train in Tutwiler, Mississippi. A man sat down beside him. Handy watched as this 'lean, loose-jointed Negro commenced plunking a guitar.' 'His clothes were rags,' wrote Handy, 'his feet poked out of his shoes. His face had on it some of the sadness of the ages. As he played, he pressed a knife on the strings...and the effect was unforgettable'. W C Handy had discovered the blues.

The bluesman went on to sing the line 'Goin' where the Southern cross the Dog' which, Handy discovered, referred to the point where the Yazoo & Mississippi Valley railroad, nicknamed the 'Yellow Dog', crossed the Southern railroad in Moorhead (see p109). Tutwiler has another claim to blues fame which draws music lovers across the cotton fields from Clarksdale: **Sonny Boy Williamson II**, Rice Miller, is buried here.

To reach Tutwiler, a small and dusty Delta community, drive southeast on Highway 49 for around 15 miles. The station at Tutwiler is no longer standing but sections of the foundations can be seen next to the old track and a set of benches. Artist Christine Barnard has painted an outstanding mural on the walls opposite.

The last frame in the mural shows a map to Sonny Boy Williamson's grave. It's actually a little confusing. Take Second Street out of Tutwiler and, after passing the last few houses on the right, go right into Bruister Road. Carry on for a mile, past Gibbons Road till Bruister Road turns into Prairie Place. The graveyard is 150 yards along on the right. Whitfield Church stood here till April 2000 when it burnt down. Sonny Boy's grave is set apart from the rest towards the back. There's normally a pile of harmonicas and some bottles of whiskey left in his honor. Sonny Boy's sisters' graves are to the left of his; both sisters died in a tragic fire in 1995. Tutwiler's only juke joint is the **Purple Palace** on Hancock Street.

franchise leased it from the plantation in 1996, packed it into crates and now ships it around America to spice up stage sets at concerts. The franchise soon expires, however, so it remains to be seen whether the cabin will come back to Clarksdale. If you want to get a feel for Muddy's childhood home, it was the last one in the line of buildings. Howard Stovall, the plantation heir, is executive director of the Blues Foundation in Memphis which administers the WC Handy Awards (see p150).

Where to stay

Like Cleveland, Clarksdale has surprisingly few places to stay. Hardcore blues lovers will no doubt hope to stay at the *Riverside Hotel* (☎ 662-624-9163; ❷) at 615 Sunflower Avenue. This simple boarding house offers no-frills rooms in a genuinely blues-soaked environment. Another cheap option is the *Southern Inn* (☎ 662-624-6558; ❷) at 1904 State Street. Most rooms here are en-suite. The

Econo-Lodge (☎ 662-621-1110; ❷) at 350 South State Street is low-cost but, of course, low-grade as well.

James Butler, owner of the Hops Plantation off Highway 49 by the junction with the new Highway 61, has turned his farm buildings into something of a living blues museum. A barn has been transformed into a club with occasional music and an outbuilding has been made to resemble a plantation workers' cabin and labeled the *Shack Up Inn* (☎ 662-624-5756; ❸). The shack has one double bedroom, a microwave, stereo, piano, fridge, bathroom and lounge area. There's even a rocking chair and a string on the porch.

Stepping up in price and quality, the *Comfort Inn* (☎ 662-627-5122; ❸) at 818 South State Street and the *Hampton Inn* (☎ 662-627-9292; 3/4) at 710 South State Street are pleasant if plain choices. The nearest bed and breakfast, *Uncle Henry's Place* (☎ 662-337-2757; ❸-❹) is miles away in Dundee, Mississippi.

Where to eat

Down-home Delta cooking is easy to find in Clarksdale. *Sarah's Kitchen* (☎ 662-627-3239) at 208 Sunflower Avenue serves good, cheap Southern food. Blues acts are occasionally booked to play here.

J & J's Bar-B-Que at 407 Martin Luther King Jr Boulevard, a newer place, is quickly getting a reputation for excellent smoked food and barbecue. There are plans to organize live blues events here, too. However, most locals will tell you that *Abe's Bar-B-Que* (☎ 662-624-9947) at 616 State Street does the best barbecue in town. In fact, Abe's is something of an institution which sells its own barbecue sauce to devoted fans. This is still a cheap place. At the time of writing, Abe's was considering relocating to a site alongside the new Highway 61 bypass which is being built to take traffic past Clarksdale.

Of the few more 'upscale' restaurants in town, *Ramon's* (☎ 662-624-9230) at 535 Oakhurst Avenue and *Ranchero* (☎ 662-624-9768) at 1907 North State Street are recommended. Both offer decent, filling dishes for reasonable prices.

The finest food in Clarksdale is served up at *Madidi* (☎ 662-627-7770) at 164 Delta Avenue. Madidi was opened in 2001 by Hollywood superstar Morgan Freeman and a local lawyer. You'll find gourmet treats like sweet potato crusted salmon and peppered veal chop for marginally sub-Hollywood prices.

Where to find live music

Clarksdale has scores of juke joints – probably more than any other Delta town – but live music is increasingly rare. Most rely instead on jukebox entertainment. Blues can be found but you'll need to ask around; the helpful staff at the Delta Blues Museum know which clubs to try. As with all Delta towns, juke joints come and go. You only need to plug a jukebox into a bare cement room and you can claim you're standing in a juke joint. Equally, established places can go under almost overnight.

Issaquena Avenue is a wide and raggedly evocative street in the heart of what was once labeled the 'New World' area. At one time Issaquena was a

Interview — Ike Turner

Do you miss Clarksdale now you live in California?
I remember my childhood in Clarksdale very well, and I go back to see folks there quite often. It's come a long way since I was a kid.

A lot of things are still the same, there are buildings there that were new when I was a kid that are leaning over now. Makes me feel pretty old. I don't miss Clarksdale itself but I do miss the people that live there. Thing is I like to keep busy and Clarksdale's a little settled.

Ike Turner (right), born in Clarksdale, played key roles in the Memphis and St Louis music scenes. His band recorded 'Rocket 88' in 1951, the first ever rock & roll record.

Would you still have been a bluesman if you hadn't come from the Mississippi Delta?
That's a good question but I doubt it. It's because I was there that I got started with the piano.

A lot of people think I'm a guitar player, but really I play piano. There were a lot of influences down in the Delta, a lot of reasons to get into music. I got started with the piano there and so I became a musician.

major blues thoroughfare. Now the place feels almost abandoned, the dilapidated New Roxy Theater a reminder of livelier times. **JJ's** juke joint at number 339 is still open for business. It's a low-key kind of place but it's well worth dropping in.

On the next street over, Yazoo Avenue, **Raymond's Place** at number 407 is another popular Clarksdale club which lays on live bands from time to time. Raymond's occupies the site of the old Big J's. Bobby Blue Bland got started here.

Further along Yazoo at number 377, the *Red Top Lounge* (also known as Smitty's) is an enduring club which has been going since the forties. There's rarely live music here either, although you'll find a DJ at weekends.

Red's, on the corner of Martin Luther King Jr Boulevard and Sunflower Avenue, is a great place. If a film crew chose to mock up a traditional Delta juke joint, this is how it would look if they got it right: frayed around the edges, battered and oozing blues. Red's opens at weekends and host bands from time to time. The surviving Jelly Roll Kings, Sam Carr and Big Jack Johnson, have been known to play here when passing through town.

The *River Mount Lounge* at 911 Sunflower Avenue was for a long time one of Clarksdale's more upscale clubs but at the time of writing the place looked as if it had gone under.

One other juke joint which might be worth checking out is the *Country Blues Lounge* in Lyon at 1695 Robertson Road; there's actually no number but

Clarksdale — radio stations

WROX 1450 AM, former home of veteran blues DJ Early Wright, focuses on gospel music but still airs some blues.

Also try **WWUN 101.7 FM** for occasional blues slots.

if you follow Roberston Road from Highway 61 for two miles to Rodgers Road you'll find the club on the corner. It's a big old barn-like place on the edge of a field which may or may not have been abandoned depending on who you ask. The views across the cotton fields from here make the trip worthwhile whether or not you get to see inside one of the area's more enigmatic establishments.

For a more spiritual musical experience than most juke joints can offer, slide over to the *Bell Grove Baptist Church* at 831 Garfield Street. The preacher, Reverend Willie Morganfield, is Muddy Waters' cousin. Expect a fiery sermon and some fine singing.

Moving on

Clarksdale to Helena (Arkansas)
Helena, across the Mississippi River in Arkansas, is a short diversion from Highway 61 and an important cradle of blues.

A fast section of Highway 61 leads north-east from Clarksdale for 15 miles to Rich. Take a left here on Highway 49 to cross the river into Arkansas.

Turn to p177 for information on Helena.

Helena to Tunica to Memphis
From Helena head back across the bridge to Mississippi to pick up Highway 61 from Rich, a small town.

Just a few miles beyond Rich, look out for **Lula**. It's worth turning off the highway at Lula to find the Washbucket Launderette at 254 North Front Street. It's easy to find; Lula is tiny. There's a cool mural inside the launderette depicting bluesmen Lonnie Shields, Bennie Jones and Sam Carr.

After Lula, 61 leads straight to **Tunica**, the self-styled 'Casino Capital of the South'. Tunica was until relatively recently a small town in one of the poorest counties in the States. Then giant casino firms were invited in to create an enormous gambling Mecca well placed to attract customers from Tennessee and Arkansas as well as Mississippi. There are 10 main players including the Hollywood Casino, with its piles of movie-related artifacts, Bally's, Grand Casino, Harrah's and Sam's Town, made to look like a street in a Western film. All these casinos and others present live entertainment every night and from time to time a decent blues or soul act will pop up, so check out the schedules.

The Horseshoe Casino (☎ 800-363-7666) has a blues museum, **Bluesville**, within its complex. You'll find a respectable collection of memorabilia so it's worth dropping in.

For Tunica **tourist information** contact the Convention and Visitors' Bureau (☎ 662-363 3800) at 13625 Highway 61 North. Old Tunica still exists but there's little to see.

Beyond Tunica Highway 61 races past Robinsonville before slowing to meet the surge of traffic orbiting Memphis.

Memphis

A vibrant, prosperous and instantly likeable city of 615,000 people, Memphis has been a music hub since Delta refugees began drifting through in the first decades of the twentieth century. With flattened thirds in major chords, these wanderers precipitated a great made-in-America discovery: fusing blues, gospel and country music creates rock & roll. Of all the musical genres threaded together by the Blues Highway, more meet in Memphis than anywhere else; it's this rich union which gives the city its edge. Modern Memphis makes much of its musical past. After the lonely, beautiful Delta where blues is so often buried, Memphis is a welcome festival of great clubs, first-rate performers and cherished landmarks.

History

The earliest European settler to see the present site of Memphis was Spaniard Hermando DeSoto who passed through in 1541. But the high bluffs over the Mississippi would wait a further 198 years before the French erected a fort in 1739. The Spanish occupied the site from 1795 to 1797 at which point Americans took over, building Fort Adams to consolidate their territorial gain.

In 1819 a judge from Nashville led the development of a settlement here, naming it 'Memphis' after the ancient capital of Egypt. Memphis soon became a boisterous pioneer town where chancers and gamblers operated beyond the gaze of the law. Memphis fell to the North early in the Civil War, making it a natural base for war profiteers who smuggled contraband to both sides. The town's fortunes continued to improve immediately after the war when vast shipments of cotton poured into Memphis to be shipped directly to Britain.

Under this layer of frantic commerce a problem festered; Memphis suffered from terrible sanitation which, during the long, hot summers, would make the town almost intolerable. In 1867, 1872 and 1878 that persistent problem was blamed for successive cholera and yellow fever epidemics which killed thousands and caused many thousands more to abandon the once-booming city. Memphis was declared bankrupt, its charter revoked.

African-Americans, who appeared largely resistant to yellow fever – perhaps thanks to natural immunity carried with them from Africa – set the pace in the subsequent drive to rebuild and repopulate the city. Labyrinthine drainage ditches were dug to improve the city's sanitation.

Robert Church, a former slave, was a key figure in the rebirth of Memphis which was for some years pioneered by freedmen. Cotton continued to provide Memphis with wealth and, towards the end of the nineteenth century, a burgeoning hardwood market contributed to the city's fast-improving coffers.

Beale Street became the pulse of the African-American community in both culture and commerce. In 1908 when a young WC Handy settled on Beale Street, it was already a center for African-American music. For much of the century Beale Street would act as a magnet for musical talent and innovation. From the bluesmen Sam Phillips recorded before Elvis to Stax and its squadron of soul greats, Memphis would make a mighty contribution to American music.

Civil rights and urban renewal

The civil rights movement suffered its most painful blow in Memphis when on 4 April 1968 Dr Martin Luther King Jr stood on the balcony of the Lorraine Motel to address a crowd in support of striking sanitation workers. As he spoke an assassin took aim and killed him. The event led to shock, anger and violence in Memphis, America and the world.

In the seventies and eighties Beale Street and the black neighborhood around it fell into steep decline. Businesses moved out and developers looked to the area for profitable regeneration. Protests, campaigns and a concerted effort to respect the spirit of Beale Street forced the city to spend some $500 million restoring rather than rebuilding the area. The result is a Beale Street lined with bars and clubs which trumpet the musical history of the area. Some lament the commercial intrusion and feel for one-time residents who are now priced out of their own neighborhood. Many more are pleased to see blues history cherished and so many musicians employed.

History of music in Memphis

Blues

When bandleader and composer WC Handy gravitated to Memphis in 1908, Beale Street was a lively strip of stores and bars and the heart of the black community. Although music was already a fixture on Beale Street, Handy was one of the first to bring blues to Memphis.

Handy was the first to publish a blues composition with flattened thirds and sevenths in the style he had heard in the Mississippi Delta. That composition, *Memphis Blues*, was originally titled *Mr Crump*, a campaign tune commissioned by mayoral candidate EH 'Boss' Crump. Crump was elected and Handy's tune became a hit.

Labeled the 'Father of the Blues', Handy quickly followed up his success with such classic compositions as *St Louis Blues* and *Beale Street Blues* before moving to New York to set up his own music publishing business. His place in American musical history is assured.

Over the next few decades bluesmen poured into Memphis from the Delta; that mass northward migration of Southern blacks made Memphis, and more specifically Beale Street, a musical boomtown and a key arena in which bluesmen would cut their teeth. Memphis had established itself as a potent musical hub with influence far beyond Tennessee.

In the twenties Beale Street favored the lighter blues of 'jug bands' such as the Memphis Jug Band and Gus Cannon's Jug Stompers. These groups played blues after a fashion but their style owed as much to the jocular music of minstrel shows as to Delta blues. Later Muddy Waters, Albert King, Bobby 'Blue' Bland, Memphis Minnie, Memphis Slim, Furry Lewis, Howlin' Wolf and – perhaps most famously – BB King all found on Beale Street an education in the blues and a chance to project the music of the Delta to a wider audience.

Towards the end of the forties a young radio station employee, one Sam Phillips (interviewed on p147), resolved to record some of the blues he was hearing in Memphis. Phillips opened the Memphis Recording Service and forged relationships with labels RPM and Chess. He recorded BB King, whom he sent to RPM, Howlin' Wolf, Jackie Brenston, Ike Turner and others before creating his own label, Sun, in 1951.

Rock & roll

For Sun, Phillips continued to record blues artists but began looking for a 'white man who could sing with the spontaneity of black artists'. The cold fact was that in fifties America, black music sold only to black audiences. It seemed that the blues had to be filtered through white lungs before it could reach a white audience. Sun would record a raft of white artists some of whom mixed blues, country and gospel to create something new – rock & roll.

Of the great names Sun recorded, Elvis Presley's remains dominant. Presley was discovered by Phillips aged 18 and remained with the label for one year before Sun sold the rocketing star to RCA for just $35,000. Phillips maintains that his decision to sell Presley was a good one; that cash from RCA paid a lot of Sun's debts. Other great rock & rollers to share the Sun rosta include legends Jerry Lee Lewis, Carl Perkins, Johnny Cash and Roy Orbison.

Soul

Blues and rock & roll made Memphis one of the musical capitals of the world; the city's blues and rock & roll heritage is truly extraordinary. But another genre, soul, also contributed a string of stars to Memphis' already overloaded talent pool. In the sixties the Hi and Stax soul record labels opened for business in Memphis, harnessing the flair of a further throng of soon-to-be stars. Steve Cropper, Booker T & the MGs, Eddie Floyd, Isaac Hayes, Otis Redding, Al Green and Wilson Pickett (see p176) were all unleashed on the world through these labels.

Arrival and departure

By air

Memphis International Airport (☎ 901-922-8000) is a 15-minute drive south of downtown along I-55. All the main US carriers service the airport; the Dutch carrier KLM flies non-stop to Amsterdam where passengers can connect to destinations around the world.

Airport transfers There's no easy bus route from the airport to downtown. Number 32 heads in the right direction but it's slow, infrequent and requires a transfer half-way. Taxis are far more convenient but expensive; expect to pay $25 one-way. Yellow Cabs (☎ 800-796-7750) provides a cheaper minivan transfer.

By train

Memphis Central Station has recently enjoyed a much-needed revamp but the 1914 building at 545 South Main Street is still home to Amtrak (☎ 215-824-1600). The *City of New Orleans* service from Chicago to New Orleans and back passes through daily.

By bus

Greyhound buses use the terminal at 203 Union Avenue (☎ 901-523-2440); it's a shade better than most Greyhound stations. From Memphis, Greyhound runs several services a day east to Nashville, north to St Louis and south to Jackson, Mississippi. Delta Bus Lines (☎ 662-335-2144) runs one coach a day down to Baton Rouge and back along Highway 61.

By car

Memphis is the northernmost tip of the Mississippi Delta and a major cross-roads. From here, the I-40 leads east to Nashville and west to Little Rock, Arkansas. Highway 61 and the I-55 which traces it runs south into the Delta and north into Missouri towards St Louis.

Orientation

Memphis extends a long way east from its core on the bluffs over the Mississippi; a car is very useful for exploring beyond the relatively compact downtown. Downtown Memphis itself, the heart of which is framed by the trolley loop along Main Street and Riverside Drive, is easily navigated on foot. Beale Street, the former African-American ghetto and blues nucleus of Memphis, runs east-west off South Main Street.

At the north end of downtown around North Parkway, an area some-times called 'the Pinch', there's another cool cluster of bars and restaurants. Midtown Memphis, north and east of downtown, is an increasingly popular residential area of minor interest to visitors. Graceland is a 20-minute drive south of downtown not far from the I-55 on, you guessed it, Elvis Presley Boulevard.

Memphis — events and festivals

● **January 8** – Elvis Presley's birthday is celebrated at Graceland

● **April** – Spring Festival on Beale Street

● **April** – Africa in April celebrates a different African country each year and focuses on African-related culture, music and art

● **May** – Memphis in May events include the Beale Street Music Festival and a giant barbecue cooking contest

● **May** – WC Handy/Blues Foundation Blues Awards at the Orpheum Theater

● **August** – Elvis week; the King is celebrated citywide

● **September** – Memphis Music & Heritage Festival featuring plenty of blues

● **October** – International Blues Talent Search on Beale Street

● **November 16** – WC Handy birthday celebrations and Bluestock

Getting around

By cab

It's not too difficult to hail a cab in Memphis but if you would prefer to call ahead, try **City Wide Cabs** (☎ 901-324-4202) or **Premier Cabs** (☎ 901-577-7777).

Car rentals in Memphis

● **Avis** (☎ 901-345-2847), 2520 Rental Road
● **Budget** (☎ 901-398-8888), 2650 Rental Road or 1678 Union Avenue
● **Enterprise** (☎ 901-525-8588), 426 Union Avenue
● **National** (☎ 901-345-0070), 2680 Rental Road

By bus

Few visitors bother to wrestle with the local bus service which is frustrating and limited, despite claiming to be 'city-wide'. For bus information, contact the Memphis Area Transit Authority (☎ 901-722-7171).

By trolley

Marginally more useful than the buses, Memphis' trolley system trundles down Main Street from the Pyramid to Calhoun Avenue then back up along Riverside Drive. Most of the old trolleys were imported from Portugal and their antique air does make them attractive. The price is good, too: 50c a trip, half off at lunchtime.

By tour

For readers of this book one Memphis tour firm is likely to stand out above the rest; Tad Pierson's **American Dream Safaris** (☎ 901-527-8870; 🖳 americandreamsafaris.com) is for music lovers a brilliant idea perfectly executed.

The ever-cool Tad takes small groups on music-orientated jaunts in his 1955 pecos beige Cadillac, signed inside by the likes of Sam Phillips, Rufus

Thomas and Pinetop Perkins. Tailor-made trips are available and four standard itineraries are on offer: 'Greatest Hits', a ride around Memphis; 'Delta Day Trip', a spin through Mississippi as far as Clarksdale; Sundays' 'Gospel Church' trip which includes a service at Al Green's tabernacle and lunch; and 'Saturday Night Juke Joint', a chance to check out Beale Street and Wild Bill's club with Tad as your companion. Prices range from $50 upwards. The fact is, of course, that you could find all these places yourself, but it's more fun turning up in a '55 Cadillac and Tad is a knowledgeable guide.

Other tour companies in Memphis include: **Blues City Tours** (☎ 901-522-9229); **Heritage Tours** (☎ 901-527-3427); **Sample Memphis** (☎ 901-541-5215); and **Unique Tours** (☎ 901-527-8876).

Services

Banks
There's no shortage of banks or ATMs in downtown Memphis; most also offer currency exchange. If you do have trouble finding cash there's a conveniently located ATM on the corner of Main Street and Beale.

Communications
● **Post** The most central US Post Office stands at 1 North Front Street.
● **Internet** The downtown library at 33 South Front Street has free Internet access. It's closed at weekends.

Tourist information
For Tennessee information as well as specific Memphis help, head for the Tennessee State Welcome Center at 119 North Riverside Drive. A more convenient Memphis-only information center is located in the Police Museum at 159 Beale Street. Call ☎ 901-543-5333 for telephone help or log on to 🖥 memphistravel.com.

Record stores
Beale Street is home to several record or record and souvenir stores where you'll find a good collection of Memphis music, gospel and general blues.

There's a more interesting store, **Shangri-La Records** (☎ 901-247-1916), at 1916 Madison Avenue. Shangri-La specializes in Memphis music and has a decent stock of rare and used records.

These guys also produce the *Kreature Comforts* guide to Memphis, a cheeky but geeky stab at presenting Memphis for aficionados – buy one.

Medical emergencies
Memphis has become a major player in the healthcare business; with 23 hospitals and 2,650 doctors, it's as good a place as any to get ill. The Baptist Memorial Hospital (☎ 901-227-2727) at 899 Madison Avenue is the world's largest private hospital and a key Memphis employer. St Jude's Children's Hospital (☎ 901-495-3300) at 501 St Jude's Place is generally thought to be one of the world's best.

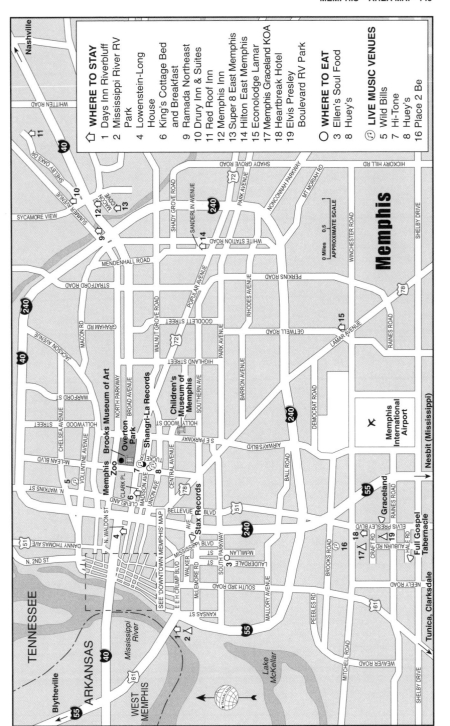

⇧ WHERE TO STAY
1 Days Inn Riverbluff
2 Mississippi River RV Park
4 Lowenstein-Long House
6 King's Cottage Bed and Breakfast
9 Ramada Northeast
10 Drury Inn & Suites
11 Red Roof Inn
12 Memphis Inn
13 Super 8 East Memphis
14 Hilton East Memphis
15 Econolodge Lamar
17 Memphis Graceland KOA
18 Heartbreak Hotel
19 Elvis Presley Boulevard RV Park

◯ WHERE TO EAT
3 Ellen's Soul Food
8 Huey's

♫ LIVE MUSIC VENUES
5 Wild Bills
7 Hi-Tone
8 Huey's
16 Place 2 Be

Memphis
Downtown

⌂ **WHERE TO STAY**
4 Memphis Marriott
Downtown
5 Comfort Inn Downtown
6 Sleep Inn at Court Square
12 Holiday Inn Select
13 Best Western Benchmark
15 Talbot Heirs Guesthouse
16 Peabody Hotel
17 Radisson Memphis

○ **WHERE TO EAT**
1 North End
3 Cozy Corner
7 Yellow Rose Café
9 Café Samovar
10 Huey's Downtown
11 Rendezvous
14 Automatic Slim's Tonga
Club
20 Arcade

♫ **LIVE MUSIC VENUES**
1 North End
2 High Point Pinch
8 Map Room
10 Huey's Dowtown
18 Last Place on Earth
19 Ernestine's & Hazel's
21 Marmalade

What to see

Graceland

Home to Elvis Presley for 20 years, Graceland sits 10 miles south of downtown on Elvis Presley Boulevard. The boy-wonder from Tupelo bought Graceland for $100,000 in 1957 aged just 22. He paid cash. One of his first alterations was a high wall erected around the perimeter of the property to deflect the gaze of adoring fans; the Wall of Love became a famed canvas across which the King's admirers still daub evidence of their affection.

The house itself, an imposing but not ostentatious place, retained and still retains an air of solid, Southern taste. Inside, however, Elvis indulged his whim for outlandish interior design. Graceland's rooms and corridors were subjected to a series of radical overhauls until, in 1977, Elvis died and Graceland was frozen in the seventies.

From the design point of view, Graceland could hardly have been fossilized at a worse time. But the King's taste in decor aside, today's Graceland experience is very far from the tacky pilgrimage many make it out to be. It is in fact a moving celebration and a slick piece of organization.

Visiting Graceland Entry to Graceland (☎ 901-332-3322) costs $19.50 for the full tour or $10 for the house only; it's open daily 9am-5pm. Visitors buy tickets at the plaza across the road from Graceland and are handed audio-guides before being ferried to the front door by bus. The tour is led virtually by Priscilla via audio-tape.

Starting in the **hallway**, you get a glimpse of the **dining room** to the left and **living room** to the right. Like many rooms in Graceland – and, indeed, Graceland itself – both are smaller than most visitors expect. Priscilla explains that Elvis and the rest of the 'Memphis Mafia' would share meals around the long table with the King himself sitting at the head. The **music room** and Elvis's piano can be seen beyond glass partitions at the end of the formal living room, perhaps the most sober of the main function rooms.

Moving down the hallway, visitors get a peek into the King's **kitchen** where, Priscilla tells us, Elvis could often be found whipping up a fried peanut butter and banana sandwich; understandably his favourite snack. The kitchen is fairly ordinary although the yellow and chrome fitted units and gadgets were no doubt state of the art in the seventies. A mirrored staircase then leads down to the **TV and pool room** where Elvis would relax, play tunes and watch three TV stations at once. Upstairs the **Jungle Room** is perhaps Elvis's most bizarre creation. A sort of Africa theme-room, this was apparently his favourite of Graceland's weird dens.

Outside the tour moves on to **Vernon Presley's office** where Elvis' father managed his son's affairs. A video loop shows a clip of Elvis being interviewed in the office on his return from Germany where he famously served as a GI. In the interview he is asked about a girl he met there, the daughter of an Air Force officer. She is, of course, Priscilla. Elvis replies with a bashful grin.

From there the tour leads to the **racquet sports room** which is now lined with an amazing collection of gold and platinum discs from record label subsidiaries around the world. Then on to the **Trophy Room** which houses cabinets full of prime Elvis memorabilia such as jump-suits, movie props, sheriff's badges and, of course, the legendary **Hall of Gold** – a corridor plastered with gold discs, the largest private collection in the world. Finally, Priscilla guides the by-now hushed crowd to the **Meditation Garden** where Elvis and his family are buried and where fans still post flowers and notes daily.

Back at the plaza, visitors can explore **Sincerely Elvis**, a collection of personal memorabilia, the **Auto Museum**, a fascinating hoard of cars, bikes, and the King's jets, the *Hound Dog II* and the *Lisa Marie*. The *Lisa Marie* is particularly interesting; with gold fixtures, thick carpets and seats for all his friends, Elvis called it a 'flying Graceland'.

Sun Studio

Sun Studio (☎ 901-521-0664; daily, 10am-6pm; $7.85) at 706 Union Avenue was opened in 1950 by **Sam Phillips**. This is where blues legends Ike Turner, BB King, Little Milton and Howlin' Wolf cut tracks before Elvis Presley, Carl Perkins, Jerry Lee Lewis, Johnny Cash and Roy Orbison kicked off the rockabilly and rock & roll revolution. More recently, big names like Paul Simon and U2 have recorded here in the hope of soaking up a little of Sun's soul.

Today Sun is occasionally a working studio by night and always a Memphis attraction by day. The place itself is small; there's an office, an engineer's room and, of course, the studio. Given that there's little to see, the tour is clever and completely engrossing. A guide explains the history of the place and plays rare out-takes and recordings to illustrate the studio's illustrious past. Though still in use, the studio looks very much like it did in the fifties; the original microphone used by Elvis Presley to record *That's All Right Momma* is still standing in the corner.

The guide gives a good impression of the extent to which those early rock & roll stars developed the music together – they were part of the same club and influenced one another. Extracts from the 'Million Dollar Quartet', an impromptu 1956 jam session featuring, among others, Elvis Presley, Carl Perkins, Jerry Lee Lewis and Johnny Cash, is interesting evidence of that. A music store next door sells much of the music featured on the tour, including the Million Dollar Quartet, and a small café serves peanut butter and banana sandwiches and other rock & roll snacks.

Stax Records

In 1960, just a few years after Sun's stars had shot to fame, Estelle Axton and Jim Stewart opened **Stax Records** at 926 McLemore Avenue. Stax made Memphis soul a worldwide hit through such performers as Otis Redding, Wilson Pickett and Booker T and the MGs. Stax aficionados claim the particular shape of the recording studio helped created the Memphis sound which kept Stax at the top for years. The Stax building was demolished in the late eighties – there's nothing to see at 926 McLemore Avenue now except a vacant lot – but hardcore Stax fans regularly swing by the site where there is, at least, a marker.

Interviewed for this book, Wilson Pickett, one of soul's greatest stars and a Stax artist, believes Memphis to have been instrumental in the birth of R&B. 'I don't think anywhere can beat it,' he says, 'and it's still here, Memphis music

Interview — Sam Phillips

When you look back to the fifties were you aware how important the music you were recording was going to be?
I was very much aware of the fact that the things I wanted to do were not being done. I felt that we needed a white person of some sort that would not attempt to copy a black artist, but would have the spontaneity and the feel that black artists have when they sing. The sort of gutbucket thing I was getting out of the Delta was so spontaneous. When I ran into Elvis I knew that this guy had the most beautiful voice I ever heard. If I recorded Elvis Presley trying to sing like Dean Martin or Frank Sinatra – and those are great pop singers – it would have been the worst thing in the world. I doubt if you would ever have heard of Elvis.

Sam Phillips founded Sun Records, discovered Elvis Presley and recorded blues stars from BB King to Howlin' Wolf.

I really felt to pull this off we had to get out of this black music or white music thing. To hell with that, man. I want to hear music from the heart. I don't care what color you are – and I don't to this day. The one thing I knew was that I could not give up easily. But I didn't have money – I was using the little money I had and what I was making before I opened the 706 Union and later Sun Records. I believed in what I was attempting but I had to be realistic enough to know that it wasn't going to be an overnight conversion. The question was: could I hang on long enough to prove it one way or the other?

When you recorded black artists, did you run up against opposition from your own white community?
I sure did. I was trying to prove a certain point but there was a lot of opposition even to the idea of what we were doing. I didn't agree with them but it wasn't a surprise to me. It did take a lot of true understanding of human nature, especially in the South where they were out in the open with their feelings about blacks. Up north they were coy enough to hide it to a great extent. I'm not speaking disparagingly of the people in the north, I'm just saying that Southern people are so much more upfront – be they right or wrong.

Was Elvis an immediate hit?
He was locally a big hit and we didn't do anything artificially because I didn't want to kid myself. I wanted to know the truth one way or the other. Out in the hinterlands it was really something we had to stay with patiently and work at. At first I was really disappointed with the response I'd got on Elvis' release outside of Memphis. But I had this feeling that what I was trying to do was different and that it either had to be a huge success or a real flop. If I could just survive financially and emotionally and continue to work as many hours as I had been, then I really believed that I was on to something that was so needed for young people. Kids didn't have anything then. Teenage years back then were just rough because you didn't have anything that you could call your own.

(Continued on p148)

Interview – Sam Phillips (cont'd)

Do you think the musical revolution which took place in Memphis, and of which you were a part, could have happened anywhere else?
I'd never say that it couldn't have happened elsewhere. But the Delta is so rich with so many vibes. The vibes are just incredible. For people that go from New Orleans up Highway 61 to Chicago, Memphis is right in the middle and right on the river. We've got the greatest river in world right here at our front door. It's just something very special, nice and muddy; untamed and untrained. Even the Corps of Engineers hasn't been able to handle it. It made great land and it saved a lot of people from starving. It made slaves out of a lot of us. But we had a bit to eat. There's a spirit that goes all the way up Highway 61 as far as it goes and on into Chicago. But there's nothing like Memphis, Tennessee. I mean I love New Orleans, St Louis, Chicago – they're great towns. But Memphis, Tennessee, I don't know of a better place to be on this Earth. So anyone that reads your book, I can tell them, there's a magic – there s a feel. They'll see more than just the beautiful cottonfields.

What do you think of Beale Street and Graceland today?
I've been asked so many times if I think Graceland's been over-commercialized. Well no doubt to a degree it has been, but the people of this world need to know more about Elvis – that man was responsible for so much good. Jack and Priscilla and Lisa-Marie who run Graceland have had a tough job keeping people from abusing it. I don't know that anyone could have done it better.
    As for Beale Street, I think it's great. Some people are going to abuse anything by over-commercialization, but did you know that in Memphis we have spent an awful lot of money helping it to be a real safe place for tourists and everyone? It's a Mecca for Memphis people too, you know a lot of times you don't go to see what's nearest your own home but they do here. There are nights when Beale Street is just ram-packed jammed. I do want us to keep the tradition of what Beale Street is all about.

ain't going nowhere. One time it looked a bit shady for R&B but now a lot of disc jockeys and different packaging has saved it. There's a lot of other popular music out there now but we're holding in there pretty good'.

Beale Street

At the height of segregation, Beale Street was the main commercial thoroughfare of the black community where most whites were as unwelcome as blacks were on Main Street, the hub of white commerce. The corner where the two streets meet was, of course, interesting. Further down Beale Street whites were allowed to see shows in the Palace Theater on Thursday nights but were otherwise kept from the area. The Palace Theater gave, among others, BB King and Rufus Thomas their breaks, but was knocked down in the sixties.
    The **Orpheum Theater** has occupied the corner of Main and Beale Streets since 1895 when it was built for opera. The Orpheum burned down and was re-built in 1928. Today's Orpheum, restored to its 1928 grandeur, is home of

the WC Handy Blues Foundation awards (see box p150). Lined with stores, bars, clubs and juke joints, Beale Street was a rough and bawdy place by night. Crowds would come in search of music, prostitutes, cheap whiskey or all three. Many early bluesmen busked Beale Street – the so-called 'Sidewalk University'. Their increasingly refined Delta blues would later play an important part in the birth of rock & roll.

In the sixties Beale Street businessmen began to drift to the suburbs as part of a wider decline affecting downtown Memphis. Within years Beale Street looked ready to be leveled by bulldozers to make way for 'urban renewal'. But while many buildings were knocked down, a drive to preserve the spirit of Beale Street persuaded the City to turn Beale into an entertainment district reflecting its past but making business sense in the present. The plan worked.

Today, Beale Street is again a lively strip of stores, bars and clubs. Crowds fill the street at weekends and there's plenty of music most nights. Clubs are described in the section on live music on p156. Beale Street has been criticized for somehow cashing in on its past; and it is true that whether planned or not the old black community around Beale has to some extent made way for the new entertainment district. But today's Beale is not quite the sanitized blues theme park some claim it to be; head here on a Friday or Saturday night and you'll find real blues, raucous partying and plenty to drink.

Arguably the two most famous stores on Beale Street were Lansky's and A Schwabs. Lansky's, purveyor of bizarre suits to Elvis and others, has been replaced by Elvis Presley's Memphis (see p156). **A Schwab's Dry Goods Store** at 163 Beale Street, however, has been a constant on Beale since it opened in 1876. Schwab's is an eccentric, rambling place

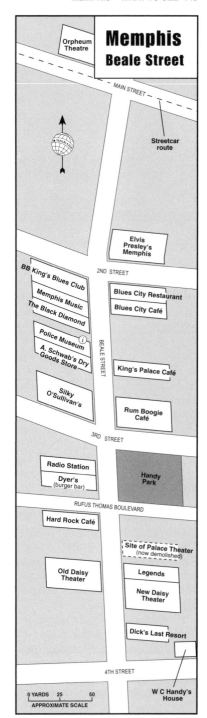

The Handy Awards

Founded in 1980 to 'promote and preserve blues music around the globe', the Memphis-based Blues Foundation hands out WC Handy Blues Awards every May at the Orpheum Theater. The 24 separate categories include Blues Entertainer of the Year, Blues Song of the Year and Blues Album of the Year.

Since its creation in 1979, the awards show has grown to become the most important night in blues and a major event for Memphis. The event is well worth attending, it's a slick production and an extravagant blues showcase. Stars in town for the awards often appear unannounced at clubs up and down Beale Street so it's a good weekend to be in Memphis whether or not you get a seat in the Orpheum. Also look out for after-show jam sessions.

with a nice line in voodoo paraphernalia and as diverse and incongruous a collection of stock as could be imagined. The motto here is 'If you can't find it at Schwab's, you're better off without it'. Schwab's played its part in early blues, too, selling jukebox hits and even loaning records to hard-up local radio stations.

A short walk east of Schwab's, **Handy Park** on the north-side of Beale Street was dedicated to the 'Father of the Blues' in 1931; the statue was added in 1960. Handy Park has traditionally been center stage for buskers and bluesmen on Beale Street. **WC Handy's house** (☎ 901-522-1556; Tues-Sat 10am-5pm, Sun 1-5pm; $2) at 352 Beale Street, where the composer lived from 1905 to 1918, is now preserved as a small museum thanks to the efforts of blues historian Harry Godwin. In fact, Handy lived in this house but not at the current location; originally at 659 Jennette Place, the house was moved to Beale Street in 1985. The organizers have squeezed sackfuls of valuable Handy memorabilia into a tiny space and the staff here are hugely knowledgeable about the man and the history of Beale Street.

Memphis Rock 'n' Soul Museum

Just a short walk south of Beale Street, the **Gibson Guitar** building (☎ 901-543-0800) at 145 Lt George W Lee Avenue gives guitar buffs the chance to see Gibson's instruments in the making (tours $10). But the real reason for rocking up here is to check out the outstanding **Memphis Rock 'n' Soul Museum** (☎ 901-543-0800; Sun-Thurs 10am-6pm, Fri-Sat 10am-8pm; $6) which is located in the Gibson building.

Part of the Smithsonian Institute, the Rock 'n' Soul Museum treats visitors to a learned, accurate and exceptionally entertaining history of the origins and influence of Memphis music. Personal audio-guides allow visitors to absorb the museum – and its music – in their own time. It's worth watching all the introductory film; it includes excellent interviews with prominent Memphis music insiders and explains the context of the museum well. There's a gift shop with a decent collection of Memphis music attached.

Memphis Music Hall of Fame

An older but no less interesting museum, the Memphis Music Hall of Fame (☎ 901-525-4007; daily 10am-6pm; $7.50), stands at 97 South Second Street. This amazing place gives complete biographies for Memphis music legends; many also have on display personal memorabilia, artifacts and even instruments. The Memphis Music Hall of Fame has the largest collection of Elvis Presley memorabilia outside Graceland and the largest collection of WC Handy memorabilia in the world. There's also the original Sun Records recording equipment, presented in a recreation of Sun Studios, and a massive exhibition on the great Stax and Hi soul labels.

Lewis Ranch

For a more esoteric look at a Memphis music legend, you might consider making an appointment to visit the Lewis Ranch in Nesbit, Mississippi, a short drive south from Memphis. Home to a certain Mr Jerry Lee Lewis – the 'Killer' himself – the ranch (☎ 601-429-1290; Mon-Fri 10am-4pm by reservation; $15) is nothing if not surreal. Why Mr Lewis would want to invite random tourists to traipse round his living room is hard to imagine. But he does and they do.

Jerry Lee's music was and is inspired, of that there's no doubt, but today a trip to his ranch is a rather sad experience. It feels like Graceland's poor cousin. Where Graceland has the 'Hall of Gold', Jerry has a sort of 'Corridor of Gold'. While the Elvis Auto Collection has some 22 vintage Cadillacs, Rolls Royces and Ferraris, the 'Killer's Kar Kollection' looks like a used car lot. Indeed, the highlight of the trip is the piano-shaped pool and a piano in the lounge on which Lewis learned to play. A trip to the Lewis Ranch is recommended, and Jerry Lee Lewis' colossal contribution to music is enough to ensure that people do visit, but don't expect either to meet the man or to find another rock & roll mansion like Graceland.

Full Gospel Tabernacle

Soul legend Al Green, who spurned the music industry for a more righteous path some years back, preaches at the Full Gospel Tabernacle at 787 Hale Road. His amazing voice – responsible for classics *Let's Stay Together* and *Take Me to the River* – is just as impressive in the service of the Lord as it was for Hi Records. Reverend Green likes to preach on the pitfalls of his empty showbiz lifestyle and the role of the family. Whatever the theme, however, the music is always exceptional and visitors are made welcome. Be aware that Reverend Green isn't always preaching. Services are held every Sunday at 11am and last several hours.

National Civil Rights Museum

The National Civil Rights Museum (☎ 901-521-9699; Mon-Sat, 9am-5pm, $6, free Mon 3-5pm) at 450 Mulberry Street is one of the most poignant, shocking and insightful anywhere in the world. It tracks the civil rights movement from its earliest days to student sit-ins, freedom rides, the march from Selma to Montgomery and all the many other defining campaigns of the fifties and sixties. If you see just one thing in Memphis, see this. Appropriately, the museum is housed in the shell of the Lorraine Motel where Dr Martin Luther King Jr was

---

Memphis cotton

Visitors to Memphis get little sense of the fact that this city's vast fortune has been built on cotton. And that fortune is still being built. The Memphis region has some 66,000 farms generating cotton crops with a retail value in excess of $18 billion every year. Memphis is today the largest cotton market in the world, trading nearly half of America's cotton crop.

---

assassinated. Inside, the museum displays a clever mix of storyboards, artifacts and interactive features to explain the all-too-often tragic struggle for equality.

Following the pre-determined route around the museum eventually leads you to the bedroom of Dr Martin Luther King Jr and the balcony on which he was standing when he was killed. It's a good idea to take the audio-guide offered by the entrance; it's difficult to get the full effect of the material on display without it.

Other highlights

Mud Island (☎ 901-576-7241; daily 10am-8pm in summer; Tues-Sun 10am-5pm at other times; $8), reached by taking the monorail or walkway from Riverside Drive, is an enormous complex of parkland and attractions. There's an impressive Mississippi River Museum and a scale model of the lower Mississippi which feeds into a 'Gulf of Mexico' big enough to swim in. For anyone journeying along the Blues Highway, the model provides an interesting précis of the trip. You'll also find a 5000-seat theater, the original *Memphis Belle* bomber aircraft and a collection of restaurants and gift shops.

Blues lore dictates that while the southern tip of the Mississippi Delta is found on Catfish Row in Vicksburg the northern boundary is the lobby of the **Peabody Hotel** in Memphis, Tennessee. The Peabody, at 149 Union Avenue, is the city's finest hotel and one of the best-known in the South. Today, the lobby of the Peabody is better known for the ducks which live in its fountain.

Back in the thirties, general manager and keen huntsman Frank Schutt placed decoy ducks in the fountain to amuse his guests. The ploy worked and the 'Peabody Ducks', now replaced by real ones, have become a Memphis tradition. Every morning at 11 the ducks are brought down from their penthouse apartment and encouraged to waddle along a red carpet to the fountain where the splash around till 5pm at which point they're returned to their palatial enclosure. A 'duckmaster' oversees the procession which always attracts a massive crowd of duck-fancying tourists.

September 2000 saw the much-admired **Center for Southern Folklore** (☎ 901-525-3655; daily 10am-10pm; free) move from Beale Street to 119 South Main Street. The address is a little misleading; it's actually in Pembroke Square at Peabody Place opposite the Market on Main grocery store. The Center celebrates the Southern contribution to art and music with films, occasional live performances and well-chosen exhibits. The staff are very well informed. For fine art head over to the **Memphis Brooks Museum of Art** (☎ 901-544-6200;

Tues-Sat 10am-4pm; Sun 11.30am-5pm; free) at 1934 Poplar Avenue in Overton Park, itself an attractive forest haven just a few miles from downtown. Brooks has a broad collection of art spanning many centuries.

Travelers with kids in tow might choose to check out the **Children's Museum of Memphis** (☎ 901-458-2678; Tues-Sat 9am-5pm, Sun 12-5pm; $5) at 2525 Central Avenue. This 'child-sized city' presents hands-on exhibits designed to appeal to both children and their parents. The effect is fairly dull for parents but exciting for kids. Arguably a better alternative for pint-sized travelers, **Memphis Zoo** (☎ 901-276-WILD; daily 9am-8pm during the summer; $7) at 2000 Galloway makes an imaginative stab at recreating natural habitats for hundreds of rare and exotic animals. As always, the chimps draw the biggest crowds.

Where to stay

Budget options

Campers could try the *Elvis Presley Boulevard RV Park* (☎ 901-332-3633; ❶) at 3971 Elvis Presley Boulevard, the *Memphis Graceland KOA* (☎ 901-562-9386; ❷) at 3691 Elvis Presley Boulevard or the *Mississippi River RV Park* (☎ 901-946-1993; ❶) at 870 Cotton Gin Place.

The cheapest beds in town are at the *Lowenstein-Long House* (☎ 901-527-7174, ▤ 901-527-9811; ❶) at 217 North Waldron Street. A sort of bed and breakfast with a hostel attached, the Lowenstein-Long House offers dormitory beds in a large townhouse. Private rooms are available.

Nudging up in price, there are a number of cheap motels. The best value of these are: the *Red Roof Inn* (☎ 901-388-6111; ❷) at 6055 Shelby Oaks Drive; *Memphis Inn* (☎ 901-373-9898, ▤ 901-388-3790; ❷) at 6050 Macon Cove; *Super 8 East Memphis* (☎ 901-373-4888; ❷) at 6015 Macon Cove; and the *Econo-Lodge Lamar* (☎ 901-365-7335; ❷) at 3456 Lamar Avenue.

Mid-range options ($50-120)

One of the better and more convenient downtown options, though one which should probably feature in the chain hotels box (see p154), is the *Sleep Inn at Court Square* (☎ 901-522-9700, ▤ 901-522-9710; ❸-❹) at 40 North Front Street. It's just yards from a trolley stop and offers comfortable if ordinary rooms within walking distance of Beale Street.

Bed and breakfast options are surprisingly limited in Memphis, a town where accommodations are more or less monopolized by the big brands, but there are two characterful places worth investigating. *King's Cottage Bed and Breakfast* (☎ 901-722-8686, ▤ 901-725-0018; ❸-❺) at 89 Clark Place is an attractive private house. A guest kitchen and a piano in the lounge help make visitors feel at home, as do the friendly and helpful hosts. The convenient midtown location is another plus. Out of town in Nesbit, Mississippi, just a short drive south from Memphis, the *Bonne Terre Country Inn* (☎ 662-781-5100; ❹) offers more typically Southern hospitality on a beautiful 100-acre estate. With a whirlpool and fireplace, the rooms here are a real treat.

If it's kitsch you want – or you're a die-hard fan of the King – the only place to stay is the *Heartbreak Hotel* (☎ 901-332-1000, ▤ www.heartbreakho-

Memphis — chain hotels

- *Best Western Benchmark* (☎ 901-527-4100), 164 Union Avenue
- *Comfort Inn Downtown* (☎ 901-526-0583), 100 North Front Street
- *Days Inn Riverbluff* (☎ 901-948-9005), 340 West Illinois Street
- *Drury Inn & Suites* (☎ 901-373-8200), 1556 Sycamore View
- *Hilton East Memphis* (☎ 901-767-6666), 5069 Sanderlin Avenue
- *Holiday Inn Select* (☎ 901-525-5491), 160 Union Avenue
- *Memphis Marriott Downtown* (☎ 901-527-7300), 250 North Main Street
- *Radisson Memphis* (☎ 901-528-1800), 185 Union Avenue
- *Ramada Northeast* (☎ 901-685-0704), 5225 Summer Avenue

tel.net; ❹) across the road from Graceland at 3677 Elvis Presley Boulevard. The Heartbreak Hotel is owned and operated by the team behind Graceland and Elvis Presley's Memphis on Beale Street. Like many of the places along Elvis Presley Boulevard, free Elvis movies are aired 24 hours a day. The Heartbreak Hotel, however, has the added advantage of a heart-shaped pool and a high level of service. Like its sister businesses, the hotel somehow avoids bad taste despite its tacky premise.

High-end options ($120-250+)

Despite the Heartbreak Hotel's heart-shaped pool, the *Talbot Heirs Guesthouse* (☎ 901-527-9772, 🖹 901-527-3700, 🖳 www.talbothouse.com; ❺-❻) at 99 South Second Street is the most unusual hotel in Memphis. It's also one of the very best. Each of the nine rooms here is completely different. Room nine is fifties retro, room six has a marble floor and plantation shutters and room five has a four-poster bed which looks like a picket fence. All rooms have separate kitchens (stocked with goodies) and a private bathroom.

The *Peabody Hotel* (☎ 901-529-4000, 🖳 www.peabodymemphis.com; ❼) at 149 Union Avenue is the pride of Memphis, a 120-year-old institution which flaunts all the Southern opulence it can muster. More to the point, perhaps, the lobby of this fine hotel is said to be the northern boundary of the Mississippi Delta, not the geographic delta but the cultural delta which spawned the blues. Other visitors drop by to see the Peabody ducks described in more detail on p152. The hotel itself has 486 sumptuous rooms, several excellent restaurants, an athletics club, shops, an extravagant ballroom and all the other amenities one would expect to find in a leading hotel. Unlike so many large hotels, however, the Peabody has plenty of charm.

Where to eat

If Memphis has its own cuisine, other than fried peanut butter and banana sandwiches, it's barbecue; ribs are a staple and barbecue sauce recipes are jealously guarded. Whatever style of food you go for, you'll find most people in Memphis have little time for calorie counting.

Budget options

Ellen's Soul Food (☎ 901-942-4888) at 601 South Parkway East on the corner of Macmillan Street is a Memphis institution and the best place in town for tasty down-home cooking. There are no frills here, just great food. Diners sit in red plastic bucket seats chomping on meatloaf, fried pork and the like. Expect to pay around $5 for a main course. Don't miss the banana pudding for dessert.

For more classic American cuisine, head over to the *Arcade* (☎ 901-526-5757) at 540 South Main Street at the intersection with GE Patterson Avenue (previously Calhoun Avenue). An authentic forties diner with a long bar, booths and all-day breakfasts, this is the most immediately loveable restaurant in town. A 'great balls of fire' meatball sandwich will set you back $5.50; a plateful of eggs, bacon and home fries is the same price. Over-indulgers could try the Arcade's special $1 hangover cure – a slice of cold cheese and a Budweiser.

Dyer's (☎ 901-527-3937), opposite Handy Park at 205 Beale Street, is an old-style burger bar which claims to use its own type of 'famous grease' to create its distinct burger flavor. It sounds revolting but the burgers are good. Dyer's is also fairly cheap; a generous double cheeseburger goes for just $3.45 and is arguably a more effective hangover cure than that offered at the Arcade. Still at the cheaper end of the scale, *Cozy Corner* at 745 North Parkway is thought by many to dish up the best ribs in Memphis. It's a controversial claim in a town where barbecue is considered fine art but the food here is consistently excellent.

Downtown at 56 North Main Street, the *Yellow Rose Café* (☎ 901-527-5692) serves great Southern food – meat and slow-cooked, sweet vegetables – to lunching office workers. This is comfort eating at its best; the portions are huge, the waitresses are kind old ladies and it's hard to spend more than $7. Breakfast is served from 6.30-10.30am.

All branches of *Huey's*, a popular local burger restaurant chain, are recommended for cheap, tasty eats. Huey's downtown is at 77 South Second Street (☎ 901-527-2700) while the original branch is out at 1927 Madison Avenue (☎ 901-726-4372). Apart from serving the 'World famous Huey Burger' for just $3.80 and excellent red beans and rice for $3.95, Huey's has live music on Sunday nights. If you're bored of your burger, Huey's let's customers shoot cocktail sticks into the ceiling and graffiti the walls.

If you need a break from burgers, barbecue and fried breakfasts – the three main food groups in the Memphis diet – you could try the *Café Samovar* (☎ 901-529-9607) at 83 Union Avenue. With an Armenian-Russian menu and 14 different types of Martini, it's certainly very different. Main dishes are great value; try the Belorussian Blini for $5.95.

Mid-range and expensive restaurants

Several of Beale Street's clubs double as good restaurants. The *Rum Boogie* (☎ 901-528-0150) at 182 Beale Street offers a loosely Creole-Cajun menu and Memphis barbecue in a noisy, spirited setting. The deep-fried shrimps are a good choice at $11.95; there's also gumbo, po-boys and the like.

BB King's (☎ 901-524-5464) at 143 Beale Street serves burgers and bar snacks. The 'Lucille' burger, named after BB's famous guitar, is worth a closer look at $6.50. A better Beale Street option for food is the *Blues City Café* (☎ 901-

526-3637) at number 138. The Blues City restaurant, separate from the club area, serves first-class steaks and fish but is by some way more expensive than its neighbors. Expect to pay at least $15 for an entrée. *Elvis Presley's Memphis* (☎ 901-527-6900) at 126 Beale Street serves the King's favourite, peanut butter and banana sandwiches, for $5.75 and other Elvis-related foodstuffs such as a giant 'Graceland salad' for $6.25 and, of course, generous cheeseburgers for $7.25. Each of these restaurant-venues is described in more detail in the live music section below.

The *North End* (☎ 901-526-0319) at 346 North Main Street, easily reached on the trolley, is a cozy neighborhood restaurant a block away from the Marriott Hotel. Part drinking den (there are beers here from all over the world) and part restaurant, the North End isn't exactly a posh place but it does offer an interesting menu of wild rice blends, stuffed potatoes and salads. By the time the chef has thrown on heaps of cheese and dressings, the food here becomes rather less healthy than it sounds but it is a friendly place and a chance to escape the more obvious downtown and Beale Street choices.

Rendezvous (☎ 901-523-0145) at 52 South Second Street is generally thought to serve the best barbecue in town and is therefore Memphis' best-loved restaurant. They have been serving up charcoal-broiled ribs here since 1948 – and they FedEx cartons of ribs all over the USA to needy customers – but despite the hype and the obscene portions, the food is a little disappointing. It seems few share that sentiment, however, since Rendezvous is always very busy.

For a more varied menu in a refined and stylish setting, *Automatic Slim's Tonga Club* (☎ 901-525-7948) at 83 South Second Street serves a strange blend of Southern and, despite the name of the place, Caribbean dishes. The effect seems to work, whatever the origins. Entrées here are outstanding and very good value at around the $15 mark. The Jamaican jerk duck, tuna capriccio and Australian lamb chops are recommended.

Where to find live music

The Memphis music scene is audibly healthy. Blues is kept alive by a string of local stars. Look out for Preston Shannon, Little Jimmy King, Ruby Wilson, Blind Mississippi Morris, RL Burnside and Mose Vinson among many others. Soul and R&B is played in several clubs – often by veterans of the Stax episode – while gospel lives on, not least in the church of soul star-turned-preacher Al Green. Strangely, however, the fifties-style rock & roll which brought Memphis to the world's attention is seldom heard in Memphis today.

Friday's *Commercial Appeal* is the best source of entertainment listings in Memphis. Even here in the so-called 'home of the blues', it's worth planning ahead to find good live acts. Beale Street is almost always happening but beyond that strip of clubs, the town can be fairly quiet on weeknights. Blues rules in Memphis and most of the venues listed in this section reflect that fact. Cover charges are usually around the $5 mark but increase for major acts.

Beale Street is the main drag for music in Memphis. Strolling down Beale Street from Main Street, *Elvis Presley's Memphis* (☎ 901-527-6900) is on the left at number 126; there's a statue of Elvis outside. Located in the former Lansky's clothes store, once patronized by the King himself, Elvis Presley's Memphis is a large and polished operation with music most nights. Bands here are generally high-energy, rock & roll-style acts. The place is pleasant enough but it feels just a bit too corporate for some tastes. There's no cover but drinks aren't cheap.

Further down at 138 Beale Street the *Blues City Café* (☎ 901-526-3637) is a well-known blues showcase for local and national talent. While the quality of blues here is almost always high, today the Blues City Café places at least as much emphasis on the restaurant side of the business as it does on music. However the restaurant and venue sections are separate so at least the club's

Interview — Jerry Schilling

Is the Memphis music scene just about the past or is it still innovative?
We have such a strong heritage, people come here to hear blues. And we do have great blues singers. But Memphis thrives on new things. I've not been back here long enough to discover everything yet, but there is a big thing happening here. Hip hop and rap is big here, we're the third most important producer of it in the country behind LA and New York. Then there are bands like the North Mississippi All Stars, a unique combination of blues, rock and soul. It would be great if there was a genre of music that comes out of here that's part heritage and part future.

If Elvis had been born elsewhere would he have made it the way he did?
I don't feel that at that time there could have been any other place in the world where Elvis would have wound up with a recording contract. He had to find Sun Records and Sam Phillips. Sam had a unique way of getting the sound to the world. His studio was an open place. Anybody could go in there and record. They might not have got called back. But I don't think there was another recording studio in the South that would record black people and white people at the same time under the same management.

Why did Elvis stay in Memphis?
There was a part of him that was rooted here. As complicated as his life became he still cared about the simple, real things. He truly loved it here.

Are you surprised by how enduring Elvis' legend is – would he be?
I lived with Elvis for eleven years and we worked, ate and entertained together. He had some pretty slow years – he had seven years without a hit record. There were a lot of career disappointments regarding material and movies he was doing. What's happened since he left us? Well, he knew he was special and that people had a special feel for him. He questioned that from time to time – what does this mean? What am I supposed to do with this? He was a thinker. This iconic image is crap. I have said that I don't think his legacy should be a white jumpsuit and peanut butter sandwiches, and it was that way for about ten years. Fortunately now I think people are going back to his work and his potential. Unfortunately a lot of great people aren't appreciated until they're lost – so the person who deserves the appreciation is not around to receive it.

(Continued on p158)

Interview –Jerry Schilling (cont'd)

Do you think the popular image of Elvis is fair?
I think what is missed is the intelligence. The fans who love him just have a feeling for him. But the average person who's not a fanatic forgets how Elvis worked so hard. He was good and he knew what he was doing. It weren't no accident. He was gifted, but he worked at it. I often had the good fortune to sit up all night talking with him and if I had only one wish it would be to do that one more time. I learned more about politics and religion from that man than I ever learned in all my years at school and college. Also people didn't get to see him in the studio so don't realize that he was one of the greatest producers of all time. He picked the material, he picked the band. He was the most underrated producer in history and he had all the right instincts to have been a film director. I don't want the world to think that Elvis was just some good-looking guy with a good voice, a happy-go-lucky who got hung up on drugs and that's the story. It's much, much deeper than that.

Do you like the way Graceland is run?
I had a lot of conversations with Priscilla when she decided to open. It was a hard thing to do. There are things that bother me in other areas but as far as Graceland goes, I think it's wonderful.

Jerry Schilling, President of the Memphis Music Commission, was a close friend and confidante of Elvis Presley.

low-down bluesy atmosphere remains undiluted. Red lights, dingy corners and cheap beer contribute to the experience. Almost opposite at 143 Beale Street, **BB King's Blues Club** (☎ 901-524-5464) is a must-visit joint for blues lovers. Opened in 1991 by the 'Beale Street Blues Boy', BB King's has struck a fine balance; it's a fun place for the uninitiated with music of a high enough quality to satisfy any blues fan. Local stars like Preston Shannon and Little Jimmy King play here often while larger acts – including BB King himself – stop by several times a year. Some complain that BB King's attracts too many random tourists and as such loses some of its authenticity as a music venue. But wait till the food's been cleared away and the band's rocking; BB King's can get as wild as any club in Memphis.

The **Black Diamond** (☎ 901-521-0800) at 153 Beale Street is a slightly shabbier set-up than BB's; tinsel and fairy lights decorate the walls and drinkers are wedged in around sparse wooden tables as they listen to powerful blues performed on a tiny stage. The close mood and confined dancefloor make the Black Diamond a charged and likeable place. A relative newcomer to Beale Street, this club has quickly found a place for itself by booking good bands and dishing up decent Southern food.

On the other side of the road at number 162, **King's Palace Café** (☎ 901-521-1851) is another venue worth checking out. It's not one of Beale Street's best clubs but good acts do appear here and the service is friendly.

At 182 Beale Street the two-storey *Rum Boogie Café* (☎ 901-528-0150) is one of the bigger clubs on Beale with live music every night. It's always packed with diners, drinkers and dancers. Music in the main club is usually energetic R&B or soul rather than straight blues although the Boogie Blues Band, which appears frequently, plays a highly entertaining mix of all three. Famous musicians' guitars hang from the ceiling and the walls are hidden behind Memphis music memorabilia including a Highway 61 sign. A Stax sign hangs over the stage. Both would make great bar trophies but, naturally, we don't encourage theft and, anyway, they're probably fairly well fastened.

The *Blues Hall* 'club within in a club' inside Rum Boogie is a more hardcore blues stage in the style of a juke joint. You could almost be in another place altogether. Almost opposite at 183 Beale Street, *Silky O'Sullivan's* (☎ 901-522-9596), a huge Irish theme pub, features good-time piano music most nights and blues acts from time to time.

If you carry on east along Beale the after-dark feel of the place begins to grow steadily more seedy despite the unfortunate presence of a *Hard Rock Café* on the corner of Rufus Thomas Boulevard. There are, however, three more venues still to discover. *Legends*, at 326 Beale Street, is a cavernous and unpretentious blues hall and drinking den. The back of the place seems to be little more than a warehouse. Legends feels a shade rougher than most Beale Street venues although some would see that as a good thing.

Just a few steps further on at number 330, the *New Daisy Theater* (☎ 901-525-8979) is another huge venue – 900 seats – and an under-rated Beale Street stalwart where BB King made his name. There's often a great jam party here after the Handy Awards ceremony.

A little further on again, *Dick's Last Resort* (☎ 901-543-0900), while predominantly a bar-restaurant, has live blues and R&B from time to time.

While it would be easy to satisfy your musical curiosity on Beale Street, one of the best clubs in Memphis is some miles away at 1580 Vollintine. *Wild Bill's* (☎ 901-726-5473) is a small, simple place with a mighty atmosphere and great music till the small hours on Fridays, Saturdays and Sundays. Some nights it's blues, other nights it's R&B. Well-known local musicians frequently sit in. Wild Bill, a big, gray-haired man, runs a slick operation; there's rarely any sort of trouble.

A handful of other clubs keep Memphis music alive outside Beale Street. *Marmalade* (☎ 901-522-8800) at 153 East GE Patterson Avenue is a lively and popular R&B joint with music every weekend. *Hi-Tone* (☎ 901-278-8663) at 1913 Poplar Avenue is a recommended bar-cum-music venue with bands at sporadic times and of markedly different styles. Call ahead to find out what's coming up.

The Last Place on Earth (☎ 901-545-0007) at 345 Madison Avenue is a more contemporary place and a chance to check out up-and-coming Memphis talent. *The Map Room* (☎ 901-579-9924) at 2 South Main Street is a trendy, convivial and conveniently located coffee shop which features blues or cover bands most weekends.

Ernestine's & Hazel's (☎ 901-523-9722) at 531 Main Street has 'singing round the piano'-style music nights every weekend. Larger bands appear

Memphis — radio stations

Rufus Thomas, the first Sun Records artist to record a hit and a pioneer of Southern funk, co-hosts a soul and blues show on **WDIA 1070AM** on Saturday mornings.

Thomas has been on the Memphis blues and soul scene since the forties. Interviewed for this book, he told us: 'Memphis has made more of a contribution to music than any other one city in the whole world and that includes New York. There are people who have tried to keep it from going where it is today and they're still trying to keep the blues down. But the more you knock the blues down, the faster it gets up again'.

Another local station, **WEVL 89.9FM**, plays jazz, blues and Memphis music everyday.

from time to time. Ernestine's & Hazel's is a cozy down-home place with great Southern food.

You might also check out the *Place 2 Be* at 1035 East Brooks Road, a soul and R&B club, the *North End* (☎ 901-526-0319) at 346 Main Street, right on the trolley loop, for its Sunday night jazz, *High Point Pinch* (☎ 901-555-4444) at 111 Jackson for its Wednesday night open mic and *Huey's* (☎ 901-726-4372) at 1927 Madison Avenue, the famous Memphis burger bar, for Sunday night jazz and blues. The downtown branch of Huey's at 77 South Second Street also has music on Sundays but Madison Avenue regularly gets the best bands.

Moving on — Memphis to Nashville

Nashville, like Lafayette in Louisiana, is another important and worthwhile diversion from the Blues Highway.

Nashville is home to a particular style of music: country. Nashville is an easy 210-mile drive from Memphis; head east on the I-40 through Jackson and across the Tennessee River.

(Opposite) Elvis Presley's Graceland (top, see p145) stands in stark contrast to Jerry Lee Lewis' ranch (bottom, see p151) just south of Memphis in Nesbit (Ms) where 'the Killer' lounges in a piano-shaped pool.

Nashville

Millions of tourists – many clad in 10-gallon hats and cowboy boots – pile into Nashville, the capital of Tennessee, every year. But few come to see the capitol. Nashville draws crowds because it's the home of country music. Nicknamed 'Music City USA', it's also a record industry center to rival New York and Los Angeles. Music publishers, studios, and record labels are scattered across the city. Country music alone employs some 25,000 people and hopeful songwriters, session musicians and wannabe Garths arrive on Greyhound buses daily.

While the business side of music here is largely hidden, Nashville is an exuberant city where live music is easy to find. First-time visitors are often surprised; it's tempting to imagine Nashville to be a sort of cowboy town but it is in fact an ultra-modern metropolis which looks more like Gotham City than Tombstone.

History

Native Cherokee, Chickasaw and Shawnee Indians first saw Europeans in middle Tennessee in 1710 when French fur-trader Charles Charleville scouted the area and established a trading post. Settlers wouldn't build a permanent base here until 1779, however, when Briton Colonel James Robertson moved his settlement from North Carolina to the bluffs which he named 'Nashborough' in honor of General Francis Nash. In 1784 that name was changed to the less British 'Nashville'.

Despite clashes with indigenous Indians, the settlement prospered. Andrew Jackson became one of Nashville's earliest heroes when in 1812 he led the defense of New Orleans against the British. In 1829 he became the seventh president of the United States. Some years later another Nashvillian, William Walker, achieved international fame when he attempted to unite Central America into one country under his presidency. His great ambition failed although he did become president of Nicaragua – the only US citizen to become leader of another country – until his execution in Honduras in 1856.

A few years earlier in 1843 the Tennessee state capitol was moved to Nashville from Knoxville. That new honor signaled a period of growth, prosperity and building in Nashville.

During the Civil War, Nashville was identified by both sides as a key city; its position on the Cumberland River and a major rail crossroads gave it great

---

(Opposite) **Top:** Tad Pierson's 1955 pecos-beige Cadillac is a familiar sight on the streets of Memphis. **Bottom:** Sam Phillips' Sun Records launched BB King, Howlin' Wolf, Elvis Presley, Johnny Cash and many others into the musical firmament. Now open for tours, visitors can sing into the same microphone used by 'the King' to record his first hit.

strategic importance. Union soldiers seized the city. The Confederate's 1864 attempt to take Nashville was their last offensive action in the war. The war left Nashville damaged but the economy recovered, in part thanks to growing printing and wholesale businesses, and Nashville bounced back relatively quickly.

The post-war period saw particular growth in education; in 1866 the first private school for blacks, Fisk University, opened. In 1873 the respected Vanderbilt University was founded.

Country music came to shape the city's image from the twenties when record companies began to build studios here. Today Nashville is a city of over 500,000 people and one of the music industry's most important headquarters in the United States.

History of music in Nashville

Nashville has produced gospel stars, nurtured Elvis Presley (who recorded over 200 hits in Nashville's RCA Studio B) and even attracted blues performers. But country music is by far the most significant contribution Nashville has made to music and the reason it is labeled 'Music City USA'.

White rural workers, whose musical traditions were steeped in British and Irish folk, began to drift into Nashville in search of employment away from the fields during the first years of the twentieth century. Nashville slowly emerged as a natural base for music of the white, rural south and south-east. As that music grew in popularity, so a music industry grew up in Nashville to exploit it.

Nashville had become the undisputed center of country music by the twenties. In 1925 the Grand Ole Opry radio show was established by the National Life and Accident Insurance Company as a country music showcase. It now claims to be the world's longest-running radio show. Today, country music is a massive industry earning billions of dollars every year – a far cry from its rather innocent, even simple, image.

The term 'country music' is a broad one. It encompasses traditional 'bluegrass' music from the Appalachian mountains, 'country and western' music – and with it the largely Hollywood-inspired tradition of the 'singing cowboy' – and the contemporary, more refined style of country music practised by today's big stars. The most commercial of these stars are enormously successful.

In recent years a subtle backlash against the more corporate end of country music has provoked a steady increase in the popularity of bluegrass and more cutting edge country styles.

Arrival and departure

By air
Nashville International Airport is about 10 miles east of downtown off the I-40 at exit 216A. Continental, Delta, Northwest, KLM and United are among the airlines which serve Nashville. Most long-haul passengers will have to go via the larger hub at Atlanta.

Airport transfers The Metropolitan Transit Authority (☎ 615-862-5950) provides regular bus connections between the airport and downtown; tickets for the express service are $4, the journey taking 20 minutes. Avoid the cheaper 'local service' which takes twice as long.

A taxi fare from the airport to downtown should be around $15 plus 50 per cent extra for each additional passenger.

By bus

Greyhound buses use the terminal at 200 Eighth Avenue South (☎ 800-231-2222) which is just a few blocks south from Broadway. There are frequent daily services back to Memphis and New Orleans.

By car

Since Nashville sits at the intersection of the I-40, the I-24 and the I-65, it's a principal transport axis and is easy to reach from almost anywhere in the mid-south. To continue north or south on the Blues Highway, however, you'll need to re-trace your path back along the I-40 to Memphis to pick up Highway 61.

Orientation

One of the most attractive features of Nashville is its compact and walkable downtown. Downtown actually sits on a bluff on the west side of the Cumberland River. The state capitol occupies the highest point on the bluff and downtown fans out around that building to the south.

Most bars, clubs and restaurants of interest are lined up along Second Avenue, Broadway and the intersection of the two. Music Row lies west of downtown over the I-40 and, a little further on, the Vanderbilt and Hillsboro districts are the most enjoyable suburban communities.

Opryland and the so-called 'Music Valley' in which it sits are some miles east of downtown on Briley Parkway.

Getting around

By cab

Cabs aren't that useful downtown but you'll need one to get to Music Valley

---

Nashville — events and festivals

- **February** – Nashville Entertainment Association Extravaganza
- **April** – GM Gospel Music Week
- **April** – Nashville Music Festival
- **May** – Tennessee Jazz and Blues Society Concert Series

- **June** – International Country Music Fan Fair
- **June** – Chet Atkins' Musician Days
- **October** – Fall Music Festival
- **October** – Grand Ole Opry Birthday Celebration

if you don't have a car. Try **Music City Taxis** (☎ 615-262-0451) or **Yellow Metro Cabs** (☎ 615-256-0101).

By bus

The Metropolitan Transit Authority runs a fairly extensive service from the transit center at Deaderick and Fourth; fares are $1.40. Call ☎ 615-862-5950 for route information.

By tour

Grand Ole Opry Tours (☎ 615-889-9490) offers guided trips around Opryland, the Ryman Auditorium and Music Row. The more tongue-in-cheek **NashTrash Tours** (☎ 615-226-7300) bills itself a 'musical comedy show' and includes a gossip-orientated spin past stars' homes.

Car rentals in Nashville

The main car rental outfits in Nashville are:
● **Avis** (☎ 615-361-1212) at the International Airport;
● **Budget** (☎ 615-366-0822) downtown at 1406 Broadway;
● **Enterprise** (☎ 615-254-6181) downtown on Division Street and at the International Airport;
● **National** (☎ 615-361-7467) at the airport and at the Opryland Hotel;
● **Tennessee Cars** (☎ 615-885-1632) at 2425 Lebanon Road;
● **Thrifty** (☎ 615-361-6050) at 1315 Vultee Boulevard.

Services

Banks

ATMs are easy to find across downtown and at all malls; American Express (☎ 615-385-3535) at 4400 Harding Road and SunTrust (☎ 615-748-4832) downtown offer currency exchange as do most downtown bank branches.

Communications

● **Post** The US Post Office is downtown on Broadway between Ninth and Tenth Avenues.
● **Internet** Kinko's (☎ 615-244-1000) at 212 Broadway, open 24-hours, is the most convenient place for Internet access downtown; the charge is 20 cents per minute.

KEY TO MAP BELOW

⌂ **WHERE TO STAY**
1 Bordeaux Motel
2 Motel 6
3 Knight's Inn
4 La Quinta
5 Best Western Metro Inn
6 Days Inn
7 Carole's Yellow Cottage
8 Opryland KOA
9 Holiday Nashville Travel Park
10 Holiday Inn Express Music Valley
11 AmeriSuites Music Valley
12 Ramada Inn & Suites
13 Holiday Inn Select Opryland
14 Embassy Suites
15 Super 8
16 Holiday Inn Express
17 Comfort Inn
18 Music City Motor Inn
21 Commodore Inn & GH
23 Hillsboro House

◯ **WHERE TO EAT**
22 Pancake Pantry
26 Belle Meade Brasserie

♪ **LIVE MUSIC VENUES**
19 Douglas Corner Café
20 Sutler
24 F Scott's
25 The Bluebird Café

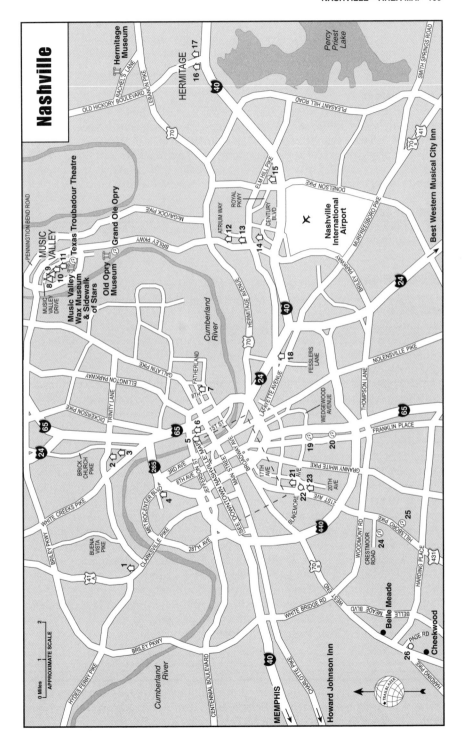

Nashville

Tourist information

Head for the giant glass and steel Nashville Arena on the corner of Broadway and Fifth; there's a visitor information center (☎ 615-259-4747, 🖳 www.nashvillecvb.com) in the foyer.

Record stores

Ernest Tubb's Record Shop (☎ 615-255-7503) at 417 Broadway is a massive place with a vast range of CDs and music-related gifts and books. There's a sculpture of Tubb, who died in 1984, inside the shop.

Just along the street at 409 Broadway, the **Lawrence Record Shop** (☎ 615-256-9240) is a smaller place with a good collection of vinyl and unusual records. Both stores offer an impressive collection of country music.

Medical emergencies

Nashville's General Hospital (☎ 615-862-4000), highly regarded in Tennessee, stands at 72 Hermitage Avenue.

What to see

Grand Ole Opry

For fans of country music, a trip to the **Grand Ole Opry** (☎ 615-889-3060; evening shows $18) is almost a pilgrimage. A radio show with a large live audience, the Opry is country music's most prestigious – and most entertaining – showcase.

In 1925 the National Life & Accident Insurance Company established a radio station with the callsign WSM, an abbreviation of the company slogan 'We Shield Millions'. WSM used local country and bluegrass musicians to create a sort of barn dance over the airwaves. The show was introduced by a 30-year-old radio star, George D Hay, who, despite his relative youth, gave himself the nickname 'The Solemn Old Judge'. Three years later he labeled the show 'The Grand Ole Opry'. It has since become America's longest-running radio series.

The Grand Ole Opry has moved to a succession of increasingly spacious venues, including the famed Ryman Auditorium, and in 1974 it settled in the current 4400-seat theater in Opryland which was built specifically as a radio studio. The show is broadcast live on WSM 650 AM every Friday and Saturday night; five half-hour slots feature some twenty or so country music stars every show. A half-hour section is also shown on TV on The Nashville Network (TNN). TNN also tapes the popular **Prime Time Country** TV show here from Mondays to Thursdays. Tickets for the studio audience are free; call ☎ 615-457 PTC4 for details and reservations. To find the theater, located at 2804 Opryland Drive, head east on the I-40 and north on Briley Parkway to reach Opryland, part of the giant 'Music Valley' development. Exit Briley Parkway at junction 11 for the theater.

The same road will take you to the **Grand Ole Opry Museum** (☎ 615-889-3060; daily 10.30am-6pm; free) at 2802 Opryland Drive. Built around personalities rather than the music itself, the exhibits celebrate Grand Ole Opry stars past and present such as Patsy Cline, Roy Acuff, Minnie Pearl, Little Jimmy Dickens, Jim Reeves, Reba McEntire and Garth Brooks.

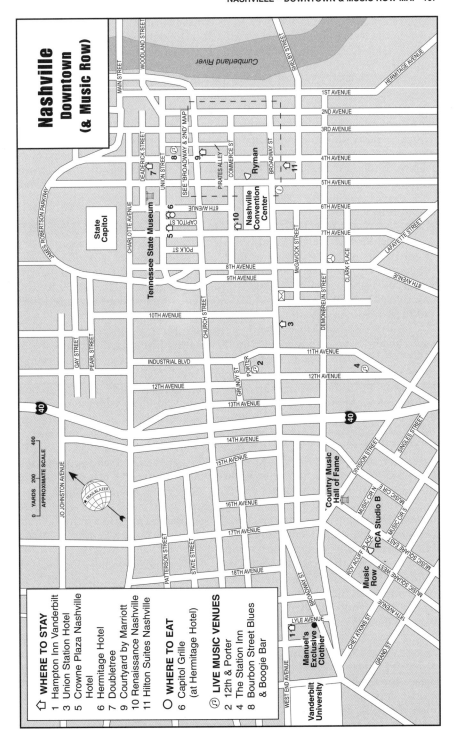

Before the Grand Ole Opry moved to its current location, it was staged down-town in the **Ryman Auditorium** (☎ 615-254-1445; daily 8am-4pm; $6.50) at 116 Fifth Avenue North. Built as a tabernacle for religious performances in 1892 by retired riverboat captain Thomas Ryman, the auditorium quickly gained a rep-utation for excellent acoustics. In 1904, after Ryman died, the auditorium began to attract a wider range of performers and by the thirties it had a reputation as one the best-known stages in the South. In 1943 the Grand Ole Opry moved here, earning the auditorium the moniker 'the mother church of country music'. Though a fairly dull structure from the outside, the auditorium is still an active and revered venue. By day, music fans tour the premises to soak up some of its history. You'll find displays on Thomas Ryman and the country music greats who played here. There's even the chance to stand on the stage, guitar in hand.

Music Row

Nashville's Music Row is the tight collection of streets south of Division Street which includes Music Circle and Music Square. This is the music industry ghetto of Nashville; the streets are lined with studios, record label offices, pub-lishers and agents. Just a brief loop around Music Square will take you past the tinted offices of Ascap, Sony, MCA, EMI, Polygram and Gaylord Entertain-ment, the Nashville monolith which owns everything from Opryland to the Wild Horse Saloon.

A roam around Music Row is interesting for a glimpse of the suits and suites behind the glamour but also for the **Country Music Hall of Fame** (☎ 615-256-1639; daily 9am-5pm; $10.50) at 4 Music Square East. At the time of writing, there were plans afoot to move the Country Music Hall of Fame to a new loca-tion. Call the Nashville Convention & Visitors' Bureau on 615-259-4700 to find out the latest. At any rate, the old Hall of Fame could do with a revamp; the panels explaining the history and nature of country music are clear and help-ful – and the memorabilia here is impressive – but the place feels very dated.

Artifacts of most interest include Elvis Presley's gold Cadillac, apparent-ly his favourite, from 1960. The King installed a gold-plated telephone and tel-evision in the back and the ceiling is lined with gold records. Tasteless, yes, but magnificent all the same. Elsewhere, Elvis' gold piano from Graceland draws gasps from visitors. Elvis Presley, of course, recorded more than his fair share of smash hit country records as well as those classified as gospel or rock & roll. Considerable space is devoted to many of country's other great stars; the Hank Williams collection is particularly good.

Tickets for the Country Music Hall of Fame include admission to **RCA Studio B**, just a short walk away at 26 Music Square West. Studio B is to Nashville what Sun Studio is to Memphis. The 'Nashville Sound' was pio-neered here and with it the unique system of musical notation which all Nashville musicians must understand before they can find session work.

This is also the studio where Elvis Presley recorded from 1957, shortly after he was sold to RCA from Sun, to 1977 when he died in Memphis. Like the tour at Sun, a guide escorts visitors into the studio to explain its musical history. This means the quality of the tour depends almost completely on the nature of the guide, since there's little to see except recording paraphernalia and a studio room; but most are enthusiastic, knowledgeable and keen to answer questions.

Rawhide

If a stay in Nashville brings out the cowboy in you, you'll need to get hold of the right gear to look the part. Not surprisingly, perhaps, Nashville is home to several well-known western wear stores. The best of these are Dangerous Threads (☎ 615-256-1033) at 105 Second Avenue North or the interesting Manual's Exclusive Clothier (☎ 615-321-5444) at 1922 Broadway.

For boots try Robert's Western Wear (☎ 615-256-7937), also a music venue, at 416 Broadway.

Other music landmarks

Other music-related points of interest in Nashville include the **Music Valley Wax Museum** (☎ 615-883-3612; daily 8am-10pm; $3.50) at 2515 McGavock Pike where 50 country music stars have been hewn from wax along with their trademark sequin-coated jackets and crocodile-skin boots. The adjacent Sidewalk of Stars allows you to compare your hand and footprints with those of 250 stars who have immortalized theirs in cement.

Another Music Valley attraction for die-hard country fans is the **Texas Troubadour Theater** (☎ 615-885-0028) at 2414 Music Valley Drive where the *Ernest Tubb Midnite Jamboree* is staged for radio every Saturday night from midnight to 1am. The show, like the Grand Ole Opry, is broadcast on WSM 650 AM. Expect a mix of famous and not-so-famous country musicians. Entrance is free; doors open at 10pm.

Other highlights

Tennessee's **State Capitol**, downtown on Charlotte Avenue, was designed by Philadelphia architect William Strickland and was completed in 1859. Strickland is interred within the building in the northeast corner. The capitol's 150-year-old interior has largely been restored to its original splendor; the library is particularly impressive. Open Mon-Fri, 9am-4pm, there's no admission charge but, for security reasons, visitors must spend a minimum 30 minutes in the building.

Another free and popular downtown attraction, the **Tennessee State Museum** (☎ 615-741-2692; Tues-Sat, 10am-5pm, Sun, 1-5pm; free), stands on Fifth Avenue between Union and Deaderick Streets. A vast collection of exhibits from prehistoric times to the twentieth century chart the human story of the state of Tennessee in careful detail.

Andrew Jackson, a Tennessee hero and the seventh president of the United States, retired to his Nashville mansion, the Hermitage, in 1837. The mansion itself, part of a 1500-acre cotton plantation, was built in 1821. Today the **Hermitage** (☎ 615-889-2941; daily, 9am-5pm; $9.50) is a conscientiously preserved museum, interesting both as an historic Nashville home and as an introduction to the life of Andrew Jackson. Visitors are shown a film about Jackson's life before exploring the home and its grounds. The Hermitage is found some 12 miles east of downtown north of exit 221 of the I-40.

The self-proclaimed 'Queen of the Southern Plantations', **Belle Meade** (☎ 615-356-0501; 9am-5pm Mon-Sat; $8), west of downtown at 5025 Harding Road, is indeed a fine mansion and the epitome of elegant Southern tradition. Built by John Harding in the mid-nineteenth century, Belle Meade became a 5400-acre plantation and leading stud farm.

Cheekwood (☎ 615-356-8000; Mon-Sat, 9am-5pm, Sun, 11am-5pm; $9), another great Nashville home, is a twenties mansion built for the Cheek family, heirs to the Maxwell House coffee empire. Today the home is used as an arts center with changing exhibitions, mostly modern, workshops and art classes. The 55-acre grounds, beautifully cultivated, feature a woodland sculpture trail and water garden.

Where to stay

There's no shortage of hotel rooms in Nashville, a city littered with hotels and motels, but the vast majority of these belong to the main chains of the sort found in any city.

Budget options

Campers can get close to the Grand Ole Opry action at the *Opryland KOA* (☎ 615-889-0282; ❷) at 2626 Music Valley Drive, pretty good for a KOA, or the *Holiday Nashville Travel Park* (☎ 615-889-4225; ❶-❷) at 2572 Music Valley Drive. Both are enormous places.

Competition from the sheer number of motels in Nashville makes it possible to get a cheap night's sleep pretty easily. Look out for coupons and special offers. Some of the cheapest motels in Nashville are: *Super 8* (☎ 615-889-8887; ❸) at 720 Royal Parkway; *Music City Motor Inn* (☎ 615-255-2604; ❷) at 526 Murfreesboro Road; *Motel 6* (☎ 615-227-9696; ❷) at 311 West Trinity Lane; the excellently named *Knight's Inn* (☎ 615-226-4500; ❷) at 1360 Brick Church Pike; and the *Bordeaux Motel* (☎ 615-242-5000; ❷-❸) at 3230 Clarksville Highway.

Mid-range options ($50-120)

A handful of bed and breakfasts offer an escape from the mainstream. *Carole's Yellow B&B* (☎ 615-226-2952; ❹) at 801 Fatherland Street is a 100-year-old home within striking distance of downtown. With only two rooms it's worth

---

Hotel price codes

Hotel and motels price bands used in this book reflect the range of prices charged for a double room.

❶ – $10-25	❷ – $26-50	❸ – $51-85	❹ – $86-120
❺ – $121-180	❻ – $181-250	❼ – $251+	

See p22 for more information.

booking ahead. *Hillsboro House* (☎ 615-292-5501; ❹) at 1933 20th Avenue South is well-located in the cool Hillsboro suburb with its coffee shops, bookstores and Pancake Pantry.

Also in Hillsboro the *Commodore Inn & Guest House* (☎ 615-269-3850; ❹-❺), 1614 19th Avenue South, is a larger place with a full kitchen available for guests to use. There are other bed and breakfasts in and around Nashville which might be worth exploring; call ☎ 615-331-5244 for the About Tennessee bed and breakfast booking service which has around 100 properties on its books.

High-end options ($120-250+)

Downtown Nashville also offers a handful of singular and very impressive hotels for those in search of a memorable place to stay. The *Renaissance Nashville* (☎ 615-255-8400, ▤ 615-255-8202; ❺), 611 Commerce Street, is a towering ultra-modern structure with over 600 rooms. It's built for business but the Renaissance is more comfortable – and more enjoyable – then other blander business hotels. Another hotel about which one could make a similar claim, the *Doubletree* (☎ 615-244-8200; ❺), stands at 315 Fourth Avenue North. The Doubletree doesn't quite have the gleaming presence of the Renaissance but it's very convenient for downtown nightlife and reasonable value.

A big step up from both in terms of style, elegance and individuality, the *Hermitage Hotel* (☎ 615-244-3121; ❺) at 231 Sixth Avenue is traditionally Nashville's best hotel. Built in 1910 it has enjoyed a colorful history and, in 1995, a complete restoration. The lobby is worth seeing even if you don't intend to stay.

The *Union Station Hotel* (☎ 615-726-1001; ❺-❻) at 1001 Broadway occupies Nashville's defunct railway station and in doing so eclipses the

---

Nashville — chain hotels

- *AmeriSuites – Music Valley* (☎ 615-872-0422), 220 Rudy's Circle
- *Best Western Metro Inn* (☎ 615-259-9160), 99 Spring Street
- *Best Western Music City Inn* (☎ 615-641-7721), 13010 Old Hickory Boulevard
- *Comfort Inn – Hermiage* (☎ 615-889-5060), 5768 Old Hickory Boulevard
- *Courtyard by Marriott* (☎ 615-256-0900), 170 Fourth Avenue North
- *Days Inn* (☎ 615-254-1551), 211 North First Street
- *Embassy Suites* (☎ 615-871-0033), 10 Century Boulevard
- *Hampton Inn – Vanderbilt* (☎ 615-329-1144), 1919 West End Avenue
- *Hilton Suites Nashville* (☎ 615-620-1000), 121 14th Avenue South
- *Holiday Inn Express – Hermitage* (☎ 615-871-4545), 1414 Princeton Place
- *Holiday Inn Express – Music Valley* (☎ 615-889-0086), 2516 Music Valley Drive
- *Holiday Inn Select – Opryland* (☎ 615-883-9770), 2200 Elm Hill Pike
- *Howard Johnson Inn* (☎ 615-352-7080), 6834 Charlotte Pike
- *La Quinta* (☎ 615-259-2130), 2001 MetroCenter Boulevard
- *Ramada Inn & Suites* (☎ 615-83-5201), 2425 Atrium Way
- *Sheraton Crowne Plaza* (☎ 615-259-2000), 623 Union Street

Hermitage. Look up as you enter to see a majestic Tiffany glass ceiling. Behind the reception the old railway board shows departure times. Elegantly and expensively restored, the Union Station Hotel, with over 100 suites, is in itself a Nashville landmark. It's hard to believe the building was scheduled for demolition when hoteliers bought it in 1986.

Where to eat

Nashville's restaurant scene is almost, but not quite, as varied as one would expect from a city this size. There are surprisingly few really upscale places; to compensate, however, Nashville boasts plenty of good value, good time restaurants where the portions are huge and the atmosphere buzzing. Many of the venues listed in the 'Live Music' section also offer meals.

Budget options

For a cheap but good lunch try the *Sbarro Italian* self-service on the corner of Commerce and Second streets. Pizza, pasta and salads are served quickly and at very reasonable prices.

For a more authentic slice of Nashville, however, head over to Hillsboro village for a plateful at the *Pancake Pantry* (☎ 615-383-9333) on the corner of 21st and Wedgewood. Pancake Pantry is famed in Nashville for the quality of its breakfasts and the cool crowd who eat here. In fact it's such a popular place there's often a line to get in, but it's easily worth holding out for a table. Mountainous $6 breakfasts are served all day to eager customers crammed into seventies-style wooden booths.

Downtown Nashville has a number of large, themed restaurants. The best of these include the *Old Spaghetti Factory* (☎ 615-254-9010) at 160 Second Avenue. Ironically, perhaps, the place really does feel like a factory where people are mass-fed by automaton-like waiting staff. The food's okay, however, as are the prices. One could make similarly half-hearted comments about the *Nascar Restaurant* (☎ 615-313-7223) at 305 Broadway. The 'Pit Pig Sandwich' for $7.99 is undeniably tasty, however, and kids love the Nascar stuff strewn about the place.

The *Market Street Brewery & Public House* (☎ 615-259-9611) at 134 Second Avenue North makes an inexplicable but commendable attempt to recreate the delights of the traditional English boozer. You can even indulge in some 'bangers and mash' for $8. It lets down its claim to authenticity by its failure to show European soccer on the TV instead of baseball.

Mid-range and expensive restaurants

At 166 Second Avenue North, *Melting Pot* (☎ 615-742-4970) is a pleasant fondue restaurant with set dinners for $30 per person. For Japanese try *Ichiban* (☎ 615-254-7185) at 109 Second Avenue. Ichiban is a great little place with an almost impossibly extensive menu, attentive staff and high quality food.

Steak lovers could try *Prime Cut* (☎ 615-242-3083) at 170 Second Avenue North. The steaks here are good and gargantuan. Expect to pay around $20 for a 28oz steak – if you can eat one that size. *Capitol Grille* (☎ 615-345-7116) in the Hermitage Hotel at 231 Sixth Avenue North has maintained consistently high standards since its opening. Prices are surprisingly good considering the standard of the Southern-American menu and the graceful setting.

Another upscale option is the *Belle Meade Brasserie* (☎ 615-356-5450) at 101 Page Road with good wines and outstanding 'new American' entrées from around $15.

Where to find live music

The energetic nature of Nashville's music scene is one of the city's most endearing features; countless downtown venues present live bands most

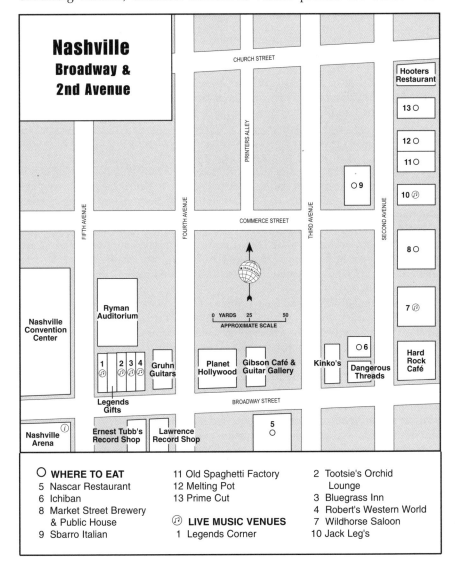

Nashville
Broadway &
2nd Avenue

Songwriters' nights

Music hopefuls pile into Music City USA daily in search of their big break.

The best of these would-be stars will test their work on audiences at songwriters' nights in the Bluebird Café, Sutler and the Douglas Corner Café. If you want to catch tomorrow's big names, or you want to try your own luck, get to these venues early on the appropriate nights to make sure the talent scouts and producers from Music Row haven't taken all the seats.

weekends. Country and bluegrass dominate, of course, but blues and jazz fans will occasionally find something to suit their tastes too. For local listings, track down the free *On Nashville* published every Wednesday by the *Tennessean* newspaper or *Nashville Scene*, also free, published on Thursdays.

Both the **Grand Ole Opry** and **Texas Troubadour Theater** showcase country music; the Grand Ole Opry is the place to go to hear some of the biggest names in Nashville. Both venues are described in more detail in the preceding section. Another venue which constitutes a musical landmark, the Ryman Auditorium, is also worth investigating for live concerts.

Since there are so many places to catch live music in Nashville, this is necessarily a rather partial list of recommendations. Several downtown clubs are clustered along Broadway between Fifth and Second and along Second Avenue. Tackling them from the corner of Fifth and Broadway, **Legends Corner** (☎ 615-252-4968) at 426 Broadway is the first you'll find. Legends is a laid-back place and a popular club; there's live music everyday, often light-hearted country, and no cover charge. Tips buckets are passed round. Record sleeves line the walls and vinyl discs are embedded in the table tops. Expect plenty of dancing.

Just along at 422 Broadway, **Tootsie's Orchid Lounge** (☎ 615-726-0463) is famous in country music circles; Opry stars would drink in here before shows at the Ryman Auditorium. There's live country music most nights till 2am. Signed photographs of country music stars cover every inch of wall space.

Continue east on Broadway to reach the **Bluegrass Inn** (☎ 615-726 2799) at 418 Broadway. Head here to catch live bluegrass acts nightly till 3am.

Next door at number 416, **Robert's Western World** (☎ 615-244-9552) is an amusing place where the walls are lined by cowboy boots behind which shine bright, pastel lights. The effect makes the place look like a shrine to cowboy boots – which, perhaps, it is. Live music – country, of course – carries on till the small hours.

Around the corner on Second Avenue, the **Wildhorse Saloon** (☎ 615-902-8200) at number 120 is to country music what the House of Blues chain is to blues; it's a giant bar-restaurant with a country music theme and regular live performances. The 3300-square-foot dancefloor is used for mass line dancing lessons every afternoon while inverted plastic horses stampede across the ceiling. For all its lack of character, however, when the music's good the place rocks; a dancefloor that size could hardly do anything else. Watch out for the over-zealous security who make getting in to the Wildhorse Saloon harder than crossing an international border.

A little more laid back, *Jack Leg's* (☎ 615-255-1933) at 152 Second Avenue is an up-and-coming music venue which presents some quality acts.

There are a number of other outstanding clubs scattered across Nashville's suburbs. The *Station Inn* (☎ 615-255-3307), a squat one-room club tucked away at 402 12th Avenue South, is a respected bluegrass hangout for serious devotees. There's live music every night from Tuesday to Saturday at 9pm and an excellent, foot-stomping bluegrass jam session on Sunday nights. More and more musicians join the jam till there's a wide circle of fiddle players and guitarists contributing to the collective sound.

Bluebird Café (☎ 615-383-1461) at 4104 Hillsboro Pike Road is a tiny club incongruously located in the Greenhills shopping mall. The place does, however, have far greater influence than its appearance would suggest; as a well-known arena for new singers and songwriters to test their work, the Bluebird has launched the careers of some of Nashville's greatest. There's a songwriters' night on Sundays and an open mic on Mondays. Get there early to make sure you get in; this is an exceptionally popular and very small venue.

Sutler (☎ 615-297-9195) at 2608 Franklin Road is another old-style club in a seemingly odd location. Look for the 30 Lanes Bowling Alley to find it; Sutler is next door. There's live music Monday to Saturday nights. It's not always country; jazz and blues musicians occasionally perform here, too.

The *Douglas Corner Café* (☎ 615-298-1688) at 2106 Eighth Avenue South is another dingy, low-key place with great music. It doesn't look much but the Douglas has presented some of the most dazzling of Nashville's country stars in recent years: Garth Brooks, Trisha Yearwood and Alan Jackson have all performed here. The writers' showcases, like those of the Bluebird, are respected and often observed by talent scouts.

Blues and jazz fans could try the *Bourbon Street Blues & Boogie Bar* (☎ 615-242-5837) at 220 Printers Alley, another hub of lively bars. Otherwise try *F Scott's* (☎ 615-269-5861) at 2210 Crestmoor, a more refined jazz lounge than the Bourbon Street Bar.

For alternative rock and occasional country, check out *12th & Porter* (☎ 615-254-7236) at 114 12th Avenue North; this stylish venue has a great open mic night on Mondays.

Nashville — radio stations

The mighty WSM, founder of the Opry, broadcasts on 650 AM as anyone in Nashville could tell you.

Also try WSIX 97.9 FM for country music and WMOT 89.5 for jazz.

Moving on — Nashville to Memphis to Arkansas

From Nashville there's little alternative but to re-trace one's route back to Memphis in order to pick up the Blues Highway heading north into Arkansas and on up to St Louis or south into the Mississippi Delta. Helena, the most interesting blues town in Arkansas, is described in the Arkansas chapter but connects to the route geographically near Clarksdale on p135 of the Mississippi chapter. To pick up the route north from Memphis, skip to p182 of the Arkansas chapter for a description and explanation of the route from Memphis to West Memphis and north to Blytheville.

Arkansas 5

This next leg of the Blues Highway is a second excursion into the state of Arkansas for travelers heading north. To the south, Helena, across the Mississippi from Highway 61, was home to blues greats Sonny Boy Williamson II and Frank Frost and is still home to the legendary King Biscuit Time radio show. Arkansas is a rural state and its riverside counties have much in common with the vast, stark Mississippi Delta. Helena, however, is one of the few Arkansas towns to boast any significant blues history.

Helena

Note – Helena connects to the route on p135 in the Mississippi chapter.

Quiet and forlorn, Helena is a town which has for years been in decline. Before World War II, Helena was a flourishing port attracting bluesmen to its Elm Street clubs. Despite its fading economic status, however, Helena is a likeable place; people seem genuinely pleased to receive tourists and the town's blues legacy is enormous.

The King Biscuit Blues Festival, held every October in honor of local hero Sonny Boy Williamson II, is one of the most popular blues events in the South attracting over 130,000 visitors a year.

History

As a busy river-port, Helena was, in its early days, a prosperous place admired by Mark Twain and crowded with Victorian architecture. The Battle of Helena on 4 July 1863 was a key fight in the Civil War. Union soldiers defended the town from a Confederate attack and eventually overpowered the Southern forces. Along with Gettysburg and Vicksburg, the fall of Helena was a decisive blow against Lee's men. Helena continued to thrive as a port until the sixties when decline set in as trade was taken away by the rail and road freight industries.

History of blues in Helena

Some of the greatest names in Delta blues passed through Helena looking for work or a place to play. Some, like Sonny Boy Williamson II, made it a permanent base.

In 1941 Sonny Boy teamed up with Robert Jr Lockwood, Robert Johnson's stepson. Together they approached Helena's KFFA radio station with the idea to play live on air in return for advertising their upcoming gigs. The local Interstate Grocer Co sponsored the show, pushing its King Biscuit Flour brand, and the 'King Biscuit Time' blues show was born.

The show did much for the careers of its stars, later joined by others including Pinetop Perkins, but also proved that there was a demand for a dedicated blues show on radio. King Biscuit Time endured for 28 years in its live format, although Sonny Boy came and went over that time till his death in 1965, and still continues today. Now it's broadcast from the Delta Cultural Center by original presenter Sonny Payne.

Multi-instrumentalist Frank Frost, who died in 1999, was another blues star who chose to make Helena his home. In 1962 he formed the Jelly Roll Kings with Sam Carr and Big Jack Johnson. Frost was a popular figure in Helena – a street is named after him – and a gifted bluesman. His profile was further boosted when he featured in the blues movie *Crossroads*.

Arrival, departure and getting around

With no bus station or railroad, you'll need a car to get to and around Helena. It's an easy town to navigate and all the main blues sites are within walking distance of the town's three bed and breakfasts. For taxis call the Helena Cab Company (☎ 870-338-8806).

Orientation

Helena's quaint downtown comprises little more than the few streets on either side of Cherry Street, the town's main business thoroughfare. Elm Street, now a hushed place, was once a lively strip of clubs and the hub of the African-American and blues communities in Helena. From the bridge, Biscoe Street leads straight into town, making it easy to find Elm Street to the right. Cherry Street is a left off Elm.

Services

For an **ATM** find the First National Bank downtown on Cherry Street. The main **post office** is at 617 Walnut Street and the helpful **Helena Public Library**, with Internet access, is at 623 Pecan Street.

Tourist information is available from the Arkansas State Tourism bureau just over over the bridge opposite the Best Western. In case of a medical emergency, contact the **Helena Regional Medical Center** (☎ 870-338-5800) at 1801 Martin Luther King Drive.

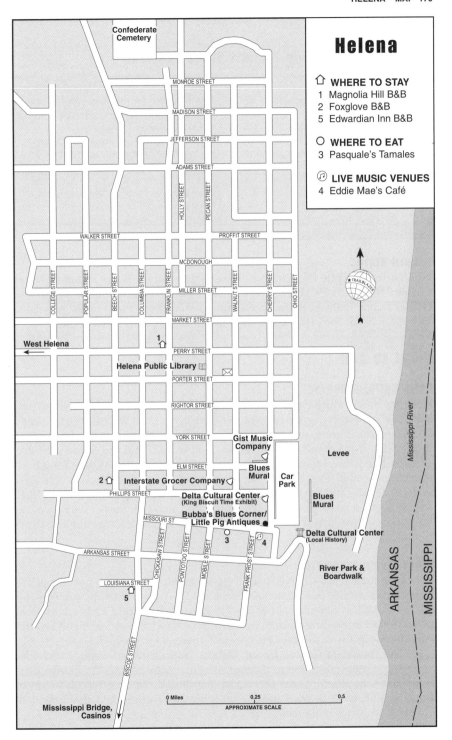

Helena

⌂ **WHERE TO STAY**
1 Magnolia Hill B&B
2 Foxglove B&B
5 Edwardian Inn B&B

○ **WHERE TO EAT**
3 Pasquale's Tamales

♫ **LIVE MUSIC VENUES**
4 Eddie Mae's Café

Confederate Cemetery

MONROE STREET
MADISON STREET
JEFFERSON STREET
ADAMS STREET
HOLLY STREET
PECAN STREET
WALKER STREET
PROFFIT STREET
MCDONOUGH
COLLEGE STREET
POPLAR STREET
BEECH STREET
COLUMBIA STREET
FRANKLIN STREET
MILLER STREET
WALNUT STREET
CHERRY STREET
OHIO STREET
MARKET STREET

West Helena

1 ⌂
PERRY STREET

Helena Public Library

PORTER STREET

RIGHTOR STREET

YORK STREET

Gist Music Company

ELM STREET

Blues Mural

2 ⌂ Interstate Grocer Company

PHILLIPS STREET

Car Park

Delta Cultural Center
(King Biscuit Time Exhibit)

Bubba's Blues Corner/
Little Pig Antiques

MISSOURI ST

CHICKASAW STREET
PONTOTOO STREET
MOBILE STREET
FRANK FROST STREET

○ 3
♫ 4

ARKANSAS STREET

LOUISIANA STREET
5 ⌂

BISCOE STREET

Levee

Blues Mural

Delta Cultural Center
(Local History)

River Park & Boardwalk

Mississippi River

ARKANSAS

MISSISSIPPI

★TRAILBLAZER

Mississippi Bridge, Casinos

0 Miles   0.25   0.5
APPROXIMATE SCALE

King Biscuit Blues Festival

Established in 1986 as a one-day, one-off event to celebrate Helena's blues heritage and, in particular, the contribution of one Sonny Boy Williamson II, the KBBF has grown into a three-day blues extravaganza presenting the best in live blues over five stages in front of some 130,000 visitors – a lot of people for a small town like Helena.

Stars like Robert Jr Lockwood, Pinetop Perkins, Frank Frost, Sam Carr and Little Milton have all supported the festival over the years.

The event is always held over the weekend before Columbus Day in October. For more information contact the Helena Tourism Promotion Commission (☎ 870-338-9144) at 413 Cherry Street.

Record stores

Hidden in the Little Pig Antiques store at 105 Cherry Street, **Bubba's Blues Corner** (☎ 870-338-3501) is one of the Delta's best-stocked blues music stores. Owner Bubba Sullivan knows pretty much everything about blues in Helena; if the store's not too busy he's always happy to share his knowledge.

What to see

Delta Cultural Center

Helena's outstanding Delta Cultural Center (Mon-Sat, 9am-5pm, Sun, 1pm-5pm; free) is split across two downtown sites just a short walk from each other. Local history is presented at 95 Missouri Street in the old Pacific railroad depot. The displays focus on the great flood of 1927 and the cotton industry. At 141 Cherry Street two stores have been renovated to form space for a first-rate blues exhibit. The story of the King Biscuit Time blues show is told here in great detail – and the show itself is now broadcast from here between 12.15 and 12.45 Monday to Friday. Inside you'll find some excellent interactive features like a video-linked piano which explains the fundamental musical structure of basic blues.

Other music landmarks

Down the road at 307 Cherry Street the **Gist Music Company** is a well-stocked music store which has furnished Helena's bluesmen with instruments for years. Sonny Boy bought his harmonicas here as did almost all his many imitators. It's an interesting place to nose around – it radiates old-fashioned charm – but like so many stores on Cherry Street, there is a vaguely desolate air.

The **Interstate Grocer Co** on Walnut Street between Phillips and Elm Streets is a blues monument of more marginal interest; this company sponsored the King Biscuit Blues show and distributed the King Biscuit brand of flour. The business is gone and the building looks gutted but the 'Interstate Grocer Co.' sign is still emblazoned across the crumbling walls.

The Delta tradition of blues **murals** is flourishing in Helena where two fairly recent creations adorn downtown walls. There's one on the corner of Cherry Street and Elm Street, an appropriate site between the traditional black and white business arteries, and another behind the Delta Cultural Center on Missouri Street. This second mural which runs along the railroad bank is quite a work of art.

A final landmark and an important one to local blues lovers is **Frank Frost Street** which meets Missouri Street almost opposite Walnut Street. Eddie Mae's Café stands at the corner. Frank Frost was a gifted blues musician whose reputation extended far beyond the South though he chose to stay in the Delta.

Where to stay

The *Best Western Inn* (☎ 870-572-2592; ❸-❹) at 1053 Highway 49 West is a very ordinary hotel with surly staff but it's one of the few places to stay in Helena so it's worth trying if you're stuck.

Much better are the three outstanding bed and breakfasts all close to downtown Helena. *Foxglove* (☎ 870-338-9391; ❸) at 229 Beech Street is a cosy 1900 Southern mansion with comfortable rooms and the sort of convivial charm so wholly lacking at the Best Western. The *Edwardian Inn* (☎ 870-338-9155; ❸) at 317 Biscoe Street has similar high standards and wonderful breakfasts.

The pick of the bunch, however, is *Magnolia Hill* (☎ 870-338-6874; ❸-❹) at 608 Perry Street. Owners James and Jane Insco have lavishly refurbished this 1895 cotton merchant's mansion to make it one of the most elegant bed and breakfasts in the region.

Both the *Lady Luck* and *Country* casinos over the bridge in Mississippi – from the road you can't miss the giant flashing guitars over the entrance – have rooms for around $80 but that price fluctuates a lot. Accommodation here is adequate but hardly exceptional.

RV-drivers can park in the patrolled casino lot for free; it's the only **camping** option in the area.

Where to eat

Other than a couple of fast-food chains and the neon-clad Lady Luck and Country *casinos* just over the bridge on the Mississippi side of the river, culinary opportunities are very limited in Helena.

Eddie Mae's Café at 121 Missouri Street is a club during the evenings but a quiet café by day serving inexpensive Southern staples like burgers and fried fish. Try the catfish dinner for $5.

Just up the road at 211 Missouri Street, *Pasquale's Tamales*, with the slogan 'tastes so good you'll suck the shucks', has a loosely Mexican fast-food menu with a few New Orleanian additions like muffeletta. Pasquale's claims to ship its famous tamales all over America.

Helena — radio stations

KFFA, the station behind 'King Biscuit Time', broadcasts on 1360AM. Sonny Payne, the original King Biscuit Time host, still presents the show from a booth in the Delta Cultural Center every weekday at 12.15pm.

Eddie's Place (☎ 870-338-7746) at 303 Valley Drive is a no-frills barbeque restaurant with tasty ribs and hickory-smoked hams.

If none of these appeals, try the *South China* (☎ 870-572-4450) Chinese restaurant at 849 Sebastian Street in West Helena. There's an all-you-can-eat dinner buffet for just $6.25.

Where to find live music

There's just a slim chance of finding live blues in Helena other than during the King Biscuit Blues Festival in October. There is only really one blues joint operating in town and that's *Eddie Mae's Café* at 121 Missouri Street. Eddie Mae, the late Frank Frost's girlfriend, runs a no-nonsense place with a well-stocked jukebox, a pool table and good food. Eddie Mae herself is a charming lady but these days she very rarely presents live blues bands.

Moving on — Memphis to Blytheville

This second Arkansas stretch of the Blues Highway, from West Memphis to Blytheville, is an attractive 65-mile drive through rural Arkansas. There's no music history to speak of and even the towns encountered en route are rather nondescript. But the route is framed by expansive farms interrupted by giant grain silos and cotton gins, rusting trucks and idyllic barns. Imagine any decade from 1930 to 2000 and you'll see little to contradict or confirm that vision; this region is timeless.

West Memphis

From Memphis the I-55 crosses the Mississippi into Arkansas and the town of West Memphis. There isn't a great deal to recommend West Memphis itself; eclipsed by its neighbor and overlooked by most tourists, the town offers little except a few shops, restaurants and, strangely enough, one of the largest greyhound racing tracks in the United States. This latter attraction, the **Southland Greyhound Park** (☎ 870-735-3670), is located at 1550 North Ingram Boulevard. You might also want to visit **Delta Farms Tours** (☎ 870-732-5776) for a chance to see how cotton and catfish are farmed.

To get onto Highway 61 from West Memphis, take route 77 north through Marion then take a right just before the intersection with the I-55. This road leads directly to Blytheville. It's a prettier, slower alternative to the I-55, lined with bullet-riddled signposts and sagging farmhouses.

Wilson

Some 30 miles on from West Memphis, Highway 61 leads through the tiny town of Wilson. The town itself is a quiet community built around farming but it also happens to be a region rich in Native American history. An interested townsman and amateur archaeologist, Dr James K Hampson, retrieved and preserved countless Native American artifacts which are now housed in the **Hampson Museum** at the junction of Highway 61 and Lake Drive. The museum is no bigger than a classroom but the material here, much of it collected from the nearby Nodena site, is fascinating.

Blytheville

Moving on from Wilson, it's just a short drive into the town of Blytheville and the border with Missouri. Blytheville is a town in need of a little Prozac in its water supply; hushed, inward-looking and just plain strange, it hardly lives up to its slogan – 'Where Southern Hospitality Begins'; 'Where Southern Hospitality Ends' might be more accurate. It is, at least, a reasonably large town with some useful services for people passing through.

Services

There's a **library** on the corner of Walnut and Fifth where one can get Internet access. For more **information** on Blytheville, visit the Chamber of Commerce (☎ 870-762-2012) at 124 West Walnut (there are plans to move the Chamber of Commerce to a new center further along on Walnut).

What to see

Points of interest include the **Ritz Civic Center** (☎ 870-762-1744) at 306 West Main Street, an old vaudeville theater which has been renovated for modern stage shows, and the **Blytheville Heritage Museum** (☎ 870-763-2525) on Main Street which makes a gallant stab at recording the town's past. The art-deco **Greyhound Station** on the corner of Walnut and Fifth is more interesting than most; it was built in 1939 and has remained the same ever since.

Where to stay

Places to stay include: *Best Budget Inn* (☎ 870-763-4588; ❸) at 357 South Division; *Comfort Inn* (☎ 870-763-7081) at 1520 East Main; *Economy Inn* (☎ 870-763-8139; ❷) at 1003 South Division; and the *Royal Inn* (☎ 870-762-1136; ❸) at 1214 South Division.

Where to eat

For food, try *Pastime Billiards* at 211 West Main Street where, through thick clouds of grease, you can just make out surly staff flipping burgers. More conventionally enjoyable restaurants include *Poor Boy's Café* at 405 North Franklin for good value snacks, the *Great Wall Chinese Restaurant* at 301 Access Road and *Bon Appetit* at 414 Chickasawba Street.

Moving on — Blytheville to New Madrid (Missouri)

Highway 61 continues to track the I-55 north from Blytheville and into Missouri to New Madrid, a journey of 60 miles past the ordinary small towns of Hayti and Portageville. At New Madrid the highway almost meets a bend in the Mississippi on which this quiet but pretty town sits.

Missouri's stretch of the Blues Highway is an unforgettable spin through some of America's most attractively soft and fertile farming land. From the Arkansas border, a succession of small towns build to the great city of St Louis, a jazz and blues powerhouse and one of the most geographically important gateways in America.

St Louis has cast its musical influence across the state as far as Kansas City, another musical Mecca but one far beyond the bounds of the Blues Highway, and into neighboring Illinois. Missouri has played a critical role in the migration of African-America music by delivering Southern musicians and music to Chicago and the waiting North.

The 220-mile drive to St Louis from New Madrid, the southernmost town on the Missouri stretch of Highway 61, is an increasingly attractive spin past John Deere dealerships, farms and more modest towns.

The most interesting of those towns – Cape Girardeau and Ste Genevieve – are described in some detail in this section; other, smaller communities are left for the reader to explore.

New Madrid

New Madrid claims to be the oldest American city west of the Mississippi River. When the town was built in 1789 almost constant earthquakes rocked the new community for two years. These days it's a mellow, picturesque and friendly place where little appears to happen beyond the constant charge of the Mississippi's waters negotiating the 20-mile-long 'Bessie's Bend' meander.

Visitor information is available from the Chamber of Commerce (☎ 877-748-5300) at 560 Mott Street or from inside the Higgerson School Historic Site at 300 Main Street. The old school, a one-room affair which operated for 40 years till 1968, is one of several **attractions** worth pausing to explore. Others include: the New Madrid Historical Museum (☎ 573-748-5944), 1 Main Street, with engaging displays on the earthquakes and the Civil War; the

Hunter-Dawson State Site (☎ 573-748-5340), 312 Dawson Road, an 1858 antebellum home in outstanding condition; and, best of all, the Mississippi River
Observation deck which stands 120 feet above the waters where Main Street
meets Levee Road. From here one can enjoy epic views up and down the river
and across to Illinois.

From here Highway 61 creeps north while the I-55 races past in the same
direction. You have the choice, of course, but 61 is a more scenic drive. Farms,
fields and fences continue to peel away to the horizon as the road leads
through Miner and Benton before rolling into Cape Girardeau some 60 miles
beyond New Madrid.

Cape Girardeau

The largest of the south Missouri stretch of river-towns, Cape Girardeau provides lively respite from the quaint but quiet towns which neighbor it. This is
no musical powerhouse but it's a charming place and worth a visit.

Orientation

This is a small town and an easy one to get to know; downtown Cape
Girardeau is compact, wedged as it between the Mississippi and Sprigg Street,
and easy to explore on foot.

The Trail of Tears State Park is north of downtown, also on the river,
while the highways out of town shoot past the town's western perimeter.

Services

The **post office** is downtown at 320 N Frederick Street. For **Internet** access
visit the public library on North Clark Avenue.

Tourist information is available from the Cape Girardeau Convention &
Visitors' Bureau (☎ 573-335-1631 or 800-777-0068) at 100 Broadway, useful for
hotel lists and local tips.

In the event of a **medical emergency**, head for Southeast Hospital (☎ 573-
651-5555) at 1701 Lacey Street or St Francis Hospital (☎ 573-331-5110) at 211 St

City of Roses Music Festival

Mid-October sees the City of Roses
Music Festival attract a mix of artists
to Cape Girardeau's bars and restaurants and open-air stages. Organizer
Bill Shivelbine makes sure he gets a
wide range of musical styles from
classical to rock to blues – Snooky
Pryor played here in 2000.

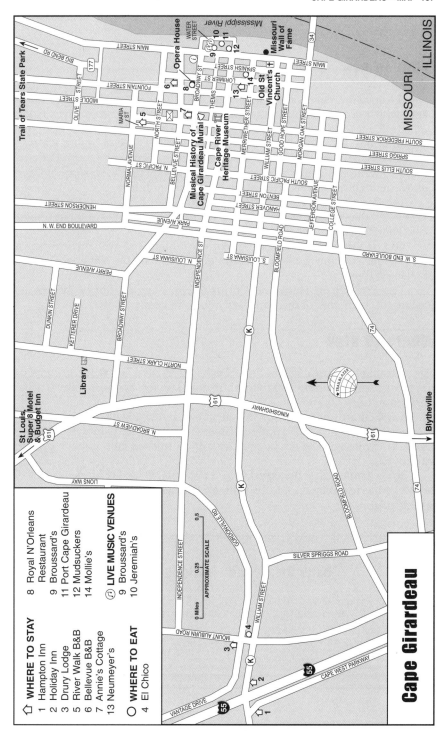

ILLINOIS

MISSOURI

Mississippi River

Trail of Tears State Park

BIG BEND RD

177

MAIN STREET

WATER STREET

Opera House

Missouri Wall of Fame

34

MAIN STREET

9
10
11
12

SPANISH STREET

FOUNTAIN STREET

MIDDLE STREET

OLIVE STREET

6

8

BROADWAY ST

LORIMIER ST

THEMIS

13

Old St Vincent's Church

MARIA ST

5

NORTH STREET

7

Musical History of Cape Girardeau Mural

Cape River Heritage Museum

MERIWETHER STREET

SOUTH FREDERICK STREET

NORMAL AVENUE

N. PACIFIC ST

BELLEVUE STREET

WILLIAM STREET

GOOD HOPE STREET

MORGAN OAK STREET

SPRIGG STREET

SOUTH ELLIS STREET

HENDERSON STREET

N. W. END BOULEVARD

PARK AVENUE

SOUTH PACIFIC STREET

BENTON STREET

HANOVER STREET

JEFFERSON AVENUE

COLLEGE STREET

PERRY AVENUE

N LOUISIANA ST

INDEPENDENCE ST

S. LOUISIANA ST

BLOOMFIELD ROAD

S. W. END BOULEVARD

DUNKIN STREET

BROADWAY STREET

KETTERER DRIVE

NORTH CLARK STREET

Library

61

K

KINGSHIGHWAY

74

61

Blytheville

St Louis, Super/8 Motel & Budget Inn

61

N BROADVIEW ST

LIONS WAY

K

SILVER SPRIGGS ROAD

BLOOMFIELD ROAD

74

INDEPENDENCE STREET

GORDONVILLE RD

0 Miles   0.25   0.5

APPROXIMATE SCALE

WILLIAM STREET

MOUNT AUBURN ROAD

3

4

K

2

CAPE WEST PARKWAY

55

1

VANTAGE DRIVE

TRAILBLAZER

WHERE TO STAY

1 Hampton Inn
2 Holiday Inn
3 Drury Lodge
5 River Walk B&B
6 Bellevue B&B
7 Annie's Cottage
13 Neumeyer's
8 Royal N'Orleans
 Restaurant
9 Broussard's
11 Port Cape Girardeau
12 Mudsuckers
14 Mollie's

ⓘ LIVE MUSIC VENUES

9 Broussard's
10 Jeremiah's

○ WHERE TO EAT

4 El Chico

Cape Girardeau

Francis Drive. For **car rental**, contact Enterprise (☎ 573-339-7800) at 2008 North Kingshighway. For **taxis** call ☎ 573-335-5533.

What to see

One of Cape Girardeau's more appealing attractions is the **Missouri Wall of Fame** which occupies a 500-foot-long stretch of the Mississippi River Flood Wall, itself a fascinating feat. Some 45 famous Missourians are honored in this colorful mural. Included are – in no particular order – Scott Joplin, Harry S Truman, Calamity Jane, Burt Bacharach, Walter Cronkite and Joseph Pulitzer. Another mural, this one at 535 Broadway, depicts the musical history of Cape Girardeau; public concerts are part of the town's tradition.

The **Cape River Heritage Museum** (☎ 573-334-0405; Wed, Fri, Sat 1-4pm; $1) at 538 Independence Street explains the battle Cape Girardeau has fought – and sometimes lost – against the Mississippi River.

Old St Vincent's Church at the corner of Main and William Streets is a mock-Gothic structure built in 1853 and now placed on the National Register of Historic Places.

The 1868 **Opera House** at 300 Broadway, now the Royale N'Orleans Restaurant, is another of the Cape's architectural gems.

Where to stay

The outstanding *Trail of Tears State Park* (☎ 573-334-1711; ❶), with some of the most scenic camping in Missouri, is near Jackson and just a short drive north from Cape Girardeau.

Cape Girardeau boasts four excellent bed and breakfasts. *Neumeyer's* (☎ 573-335-0449; ❸-❹) at 25 South Lorimer Street is well-placed for getting around downtown. The rooms are elegantly furnished and all have private bathrooms.

River Walk Bed & Breakfast (☎ 573-334-4611; ❸) at 444 Marie Street is a newer property dating back to 1924. Breakfasts here are very good and there's a whirlpool.

Cape Girardeau — chain hotels

- *Super 8 Motel* (☎ 573-339-0808) at 2011 North Kingshighway
- *Budget Inn* (☎ 573-334-2828) at 1448 North Kingshighway
- *Holiday Inn* (☎ 573-334-4491) at the junction of the I-55 and Route K
- *Drury Lodge* (☎ 573-378-7946) at the same junction
- *Hampton Inn* (☎ 573-651-3000) again, at the intersection of the I-55 and Route K.

Right downtown at 536 Broadway, *Annie's Cottage* (☎ 573-339-1301; ❷-❸) is a tiny two-room place with helpful owners. For more old fashioned elegance, however, try the *Bellevue Bed & Breakfast* (☎ 573-335-3302; ❸-❹), 312 Bellevue Road, an 1891 property with well-appointed rooms, gourmet breakfasts and even business facilities.

Where to eat

Broussard's (☎ 573-334-7235) at 120 North Main is a great Cajun restaurant decked out in New Orleans trinkets and souvenirs of Bourbon Street. The menu is as much Creole as Cajun – there's Gumbo, red beans and rice and etouffe – and includes such strange delights as gator's ribs and fried frog's legs. Expect to pay around $9 for a dinner entrée. Broussard's is a lively and justifiably popular place.

Other good restaurants include: *Mudsuckers* (☎ 573-335-7270), 2 North Main Street, for cheap but filling fare; *Port Cape Girardeau* (☎ 573-334-0954), 19 North Water Street, a slightly posher and reliable place overlooking the flood wall; *El Chico* (☎ 573-334-1707), 202 South Mt Auburn Road, a decent Mexican; *Mollie's* (☎ 573-339-1661), 11 South Spanish Street, a fairly upscale place with good French-influenced cuisine; and *Royale N'Orleans Restaurant* (☎ 573-335-8191), 300 Broadway, Cape Girardeau's best and oldest restaurant with an extensive wine list, an excellent New Orleans-style menu and a jazz band on Friday nights.

Where to find live music

There's almost no chance of finding live music on a weeknight in Cape Girardeau and even weekends are a lottery. *Jeremiah's* (☎ 573-334-0508) at 127 North Water Street sometimes has live bands on a Friday night and *Broussard's* (☎ 573-334-7235) at 120 North Main sometimes presents blues, rock and cover bands on Friday and Saturday nights.

Moving on — Cape Girardeau to Ste Genevieve

Still hugging the Mississippi River, Highway 61 continues north from Cape Girardeau for around 100 miles before it crawls into the quaint river-town Ste Genevieve. Along the way the road passes through some of Missouri's most beautiful farmland; lush, colorful crops and carefully-plowed fields climb away from the road to the west while the Mississippi River, the source of all this obvious fertility, washes towards the Gulf of Mexico to the east.

This stretch of Highway 61 winds past some of the smallest and most picturesque communities on the Blues Highway; Old Appleton, population 87, is a quaint town. Longtown, with a population of 121, is in comparison a raging metropolis while Perryville, a larger town again, is lined with antique stores selling old cartwheels and other farm-related flotsam.

Ste Genevieve

A charming small town with conspicuous German and French pedigree, Ste Genevieve has become a popular weekend getaway for St Louis' upwardly mobile. St Louis is just 60 miles to the north but the quiet streets of Ste Genevieve could be in another state. Bed and breakfasts, restaurants, bars and rows of antique shops have sprung up to meet the demands of weekenders. There's a frequent ferry service across the Mississippi from Ste Genevieve to Modoc in Illinois.

For **tourist information** visit the office at 66 South Main Street; the helpful staff here will be able to furnish you with a map and some friendly advice about where to stay.

What to see

The few **attractions** in Ste Genevieve include: the Ste Genevieve Museum (☎ 573-883-3461), on the corner of Merchant Street and Dubourg Square, which was founded in 1935; the Bolduc House Museum (☎ 573-883-3105), 125 South Main, which has been restored to its 1770 appearance; and the charming Ste Genevieve Winery (☎ 573-883-2800), 245 Merchant Street, where free tastings and nibbles might encourage you to pick up a few bottles. The wine is not quite in the same league as, say, the great California labels of Napa but it's not bad and a case of Chateau Ste Genevieve makes a good souvenir.

Where to stay

Campers should head for Hawn State Park (☎ 573-883-3603; ❶) about 10 miles west of town. With new showers and thickly shaded campsites, this is one of Missouri's best parks for campers. Other **budget** options include: *Microtel Inn & Suites* (☎ 1 888-771-7171; ❸) at 21958 Highway 32; the *Family Budget Inn* (☎ 573-543-2272; ❸) near the I-55 intersection; and *Triangle Inn Motel* (☎ 573-883-7191; ❷-❸) out on Highway 61.

Moving upscale there are several good bed and breakfasts. The *Southern Hotel Bed & Breakfast* (☎ 573-883-3493; ❹), 146 South Third Street, is a 200-year-old building and a pleasant place to stay. *Inn St Gemme Beauvais* (☎ 800-818-5744; ❺), 78 North Main Street, has rooms with canopy beds and jacuzzis. *Steiger Haus* (☎ 800-814-5881; ❹-❺), 1021 Market Street, specializes in murder mystery nights. *Main Street Inn* (☎ 573-883-9199; ❹), 221 North Main Street, was built in 1882 and was restored in the early nineties. Set in 2.5 acres of grounds, the *Creole Inn* (☎ 800-275-6041; ❺), 339 St Mary's Road, is another good choice as is *Annie's* (☎ 573-883-2001; ❸-❹), 207 South Main Street, run by the helpful Annie and Fred Fellion.

Where to eat

Places to eat include: *Sarah's Ice Cream*, 132 Merchant Street, a wonderful old-time ice cream parlor with a soda fountain and coffees for 10 cents (the price of coffee hasn't gone up here since they opened in 1986); the *Bogy House Restaurant*, 163 Merchant Street, with a vast menu mixing Cajun, Italian and down-home cooking; the *Old Brick House*, corner of Third and Market Street, a 1785 property which claims to be the first brick building built west of the Mississippi and which has also earned fame for its 40oz steaks; and *La Fete Landing Riverboat Restaurant*, Third and Merchant Street, where diners are entertained by cabaret acts.

Moving on — Ste Genevieve to St Louis

Soon after Ste Genevieve the landscape morphs into an increasingly industrial scene as farms give way to malls and out-of-town distribution centers. From here it's a fast drive along Highway 61 or the I-55 to the southern reaches of St Louis where the roads become tangled in the city's suburbs.

St Louis

Straddling the crossroads of the Blues Highway north and the Mother Road, Route 66, west, St Louis is used to people passing through. Jazz and bluesmen were among those who came by as they made their way north. St Louis learned from these musicians and added a few of its own ingredients to the musical melting pot of Highway 61.

The result is a city rich in jazz and blues history – a city which has been deeply influenced by the music of the South and, through a handful of bright luminaries, a city which has made its own mark on American music. Scott Joplin, Miles Davis, Clark Terry and Chuck Berry are just a few of the great names to have grown up in St Louis. This is a spirited, congenial city and a place where the musical contributions of its own people are widely recognized and cherished.

History

In 1764 French fur trader Pierre Laclede founded a small community, named St Louis after Louis IX (St Louis, the Crusader king), south of the confluence of the Mississippi and Missouri Rivers. Before this time Indians had occupied the area on which the city is now built. They constructed huge burial mounds and cultivated the fertile floodplains. Evidence of that time can still be found in the area. After 1764, St Louis began to build its fortune on the back of its thriving fur trade. That trade grew still further when, in 1803, the United States bought the American West from Napoleon in the Louisiana Purchase. Keen to explore the new frontier, US President Thomas Jefferson dispatched explorers Lewis and Clark to discover the region.

The two men set off from St Louis and in doing so pioneered the great westward expansion of the United States. They returned two years later having charted the immense lands. The much-admired Arch which now dominates the St Louis skyline was built in 1965 to commemorate their achievement and to symbolize the city's position as the gateway to the American west.

At the time of the Lewis and Clark expedition, St Louis was a growing community of around 1000 people. That number began to soar as St Louis became a key staging post on the route west. As more and more frontiersmen and fortune-seekers moved west, so St Louis became richer and bigger. Later a mass of families would rumble west through St Louis on Route 66, the American 'mother road'. St Louis also found itself on a south-north line of migration and trade. River transport and, later, rail freight further boosted the local economy.

St Louis was split bitterly during the Civil War but rifts were repaired relatively quickly over subsequent decades. Industry and transport continued to boom and, in 1904, the city was recognized as a world player when it hosted both a World's Fair and the Olympic Games. Today St Louis is a city of 2.5 million people and a major industrial and transport hub.

History of music in St Louis

St Louis lay at the crossroads of nineteenth century westward migration and the northward drift of the twentieth century. A major center for transportation by covered wagon, steamboat, rail and road, St Louis was an obvious stopping-off point, not least for those north-trekking jazz and blues musicians seeking their fortunes in northern cities.

Jazz

Although relatively few chose to settle here, St Louis has always been something of a jazz city, particularly, of course, in the field of ragtime. Scott Joplin, who lived in St Louis in the early 1900s, remains the undisputed king of ragtime piano and penned classics such as *Maple Leaf Rag*, *The Entertainer* and *Easy Winners* while living in St Louis.

The city is immortalized in jazz music in the title of one of the best-known works of cornet-player, bandleader and composer W C Handy. *St Louis Blues* has probably been played more often, in more arrangements and by more jazz musicians than any other tune. As arranged for the Glenn Miller Orchestra of the forties, it even acquired the status of a military march.

Two years before that, Louis Armstrong had realized a lifetime's ambition when he and his 'All Stars' had played *St Louis Blues*, accompanied by 88 members of the New York Philharmonic Orchestra conducted by Leonard Bernstein, at a Guggenheim Concert in New York. In the audience that night

(**Opposite**) The elegant curve of the Gateway Arch (see p203) dominates the St Louis skyline and stands as a symbol of westward expansion.

St Louis — events and festivals

Reflecting the city's importance to both jazz and blues, St Louis hosts festivals for each. The **Juneteenth Heritage Jazz Festival** takes place every June at various venues across town. Call ☎ 314-367-0100 for more information. The **Missouri Botanical Garden** presents a series of outdoor jazz concerts throughout June and July. Call ☎ 314-577-9400 for information. Blues lovers should look out for the annual **Big Muddy Blues & Roots Music Festival** which is staged every Labor day weekend around Laclede's Landing. Call ☎ 314-436-9420 for information.

was W C Handy himself – 83 years old and blind. At the end of the number, with the crowd in rapturous applause, Handy removed his hat to reveal a neatly folded white handkerchief with which he proceeded to wipe his eyes.

Handy was not a native of St Louis but a number of jazz luminaries were able to count St Louis as their birthplace. Chief among these are trumpet players Miles Davis and Clark Terry. With Louis Armstrong and Dizzy Gillespie, Davis is one of the most influential trumpeters jazz has known. His constant innovation allowed him to set the standard for four decades. Although born in Illinois, Davis moved with his family to East St Louis in 1927. He met and was influenced by Clark Terry, the other great St Louis trumpeter who worked with bandleaders Count Basie, Duke Ellington and Quincy Jones. Davis would later move to New York where he developed his sound with the likes of Charlie Parker. Other local trumpet stars included Harold 'Shorty' Baker, whose career highlights include service under bandleaders Fate Marable and Duke Ellington.

The pianist, organist and occasional vibes-player Milt Buckner was another St Louis local. A former member of the well-known McKinney's Cotton Pickers, he graduated in 1941 to the ranks of the newly-formed Lionel Hampton Orchestra – a band which was later to break all records as the longest-lived in the history of jazz.

Another great St Louis jazz musician was the vocalist and kazoo-player William 'Red' McKenzie, co-founder of the once popular Mound City Blue Blowers. A slightly upscale version of the comb and paper, the kazoo was unlikely ever to propel McKenzie to the very heights of musicianship. However, for a brief period, he did manage to join the ranks of the sophisticated Paul Whiteman Orchestra. During the late twenties he graduated to the occupation of musical talent scout, where he was successful in arranging a recording contract for the legendary Bix Beiderbecke.

(Opposite) Top: Downtown St Louis seen from the top of the Gateway Arch.
Bottom: Louis Armstrong, whose statue stands in Congo Square, New Orleans (see p42), and Charley Patton, whose grave marker lies in Holly Ridge in the Mississippi Delta (see p111), are two of the most influential musicians of the twentieth century. Armstrong defined the classic era of jazz; Patton shaped the Delta blues.

An even more untimely end befell another St Louis musician, the vocalist Velma Middleton. Once unkindly described as looking like 'a sequined football', she was more of an entertainer than a top-rank jazz singer. But she did attract the attention of Louis Armstrong with whom she remained throughout the glory days of the 'All Stars'. Featured on a number of his records, Middleton was to die of a stroke while on tour with the band in, of all places, Sierra Leone.

There were, needless to say, many other jazz musicians from St Louis but the majority were distinctly less prominent. Many of them were involved on and off during the twenties with the famous riverboats – the *JS*, the *Capitol* and the *St Paul*. Two more who did achieve wider recognition were the clarinet and tenor-sax player Eugene Sedric, for some time a regular with 'Fats' Waller, and the pianist Elmer Schoebel – actually born in East St Louis – composer of jazz standards *Nobody's Sweetheart* and *Farewell Blues*.

Blues

Opposite St Louis on the other side of the river is East St Louis which features in the title of one of Duke Ellington's earliest compositions – *East St Louis Toodle-oo* – but is better-known for its reputation as a cauldron of blues and, later, rock & roll. East St Louis has been a black ghetto since the earliest years of the century and, along with the so-called 'Deep Morgan' area of town, a potent blues scene.

Chicago-bound bluesmen contributed to that scene as they passed through town and some, like Henry Townsend, stayed. Along with Roosevelt Sykes, Lonnie Johnson and Big Joe Williams, Henry 'Mule' Townsend was and still is a central figure in St Louis blues. Now in his nineties, Townsend is still recording. As a young man, Townsend helped many bluesmen on their way to Chicago from the South – including one Muddy Waters.

Albert King became another key figure in St Louis blues when he moved to nearby Lovejoy, Illinois in 1956. For years he played the St Louis circuit before Memphis-based Stax Records transformed him from a locally famous musician to an international star.

Ike Turner moved to St Louis in 1954 where his band found considerable success and Turner himself found a wife, Annie Mae Bullock, who took the name Tina when she joined the band. Ike Turner made a considerable impression on the development of blues and rock & roll. But the contribution of another St Louisian, Chuck Berry, would be difficult to beat.

In 1952 Berry began playing with Sir John's Trio, led by St Louisian pianist Johnnie Johnson, which through his guitar style he gradually molded into what

KEY – ST LOUIS (MAP OPPOSITE)

⌂ **WHERE TO STAY**
1 La Quinta Inn
2 Econo-Lodge Airport
3 Congress Inn
4 Oakwood Cottage
5 Holiday Inn Forest Park
8 Lister House
12 Fleur-de-Lys Inn

○ **WHERE TO EAT**
6 Meriwhether's (in the Missouri History Museum)

♫ **LIVE MUSIC VENUES**
7 Turvey's on the Green
9 Moose Lounge

10 Powell Symphony Hall (St Louis Symphony Orchestra)
11 Jazz at the Bistro

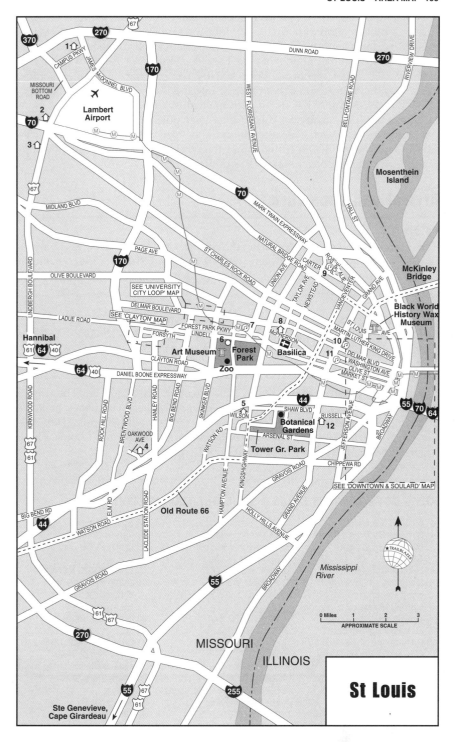

was essentially an early rock & roll band. Berry's legendary guitar work, a fusion of blues, country and R&B, and Johnson's equally impressive piano virtuosity created a sound which played as important a role in the birth of rock & roll as any other musician in America. Hits like *Maybellene*, *Johnny B Goode* and *Roll Over Beethoven* displayed Berry's witty songwriting and guitar genius. Berry was the first person to be inducted into the Rock & Roll Hall of Fame.

St Louis certainly has its place in the history of jazz – and perhaps more famously of blues – however it has never been able to claim recognition on a par with New Orleans, Chicago, Memphis or New York. Indeed it might be said to have been influenced by, rather than to have influenced, the development of twentieth century American popular music.

Arrival and departure

By air
The **Lambert-St Louis International Airport** (☎ 314-426-8000) is 12 miles north-west of downtown between the I-70 and the I-270. Carriers serving St Louis, an important hub, include TWA, Delta, USAirways, Continental, American and United.

Airport transfers Expect to pay between $18 and $25 for a cab downtown. Minivan services are provided by Airport Express (☎ 314-429-4950), $10 one way, and Exit Express (☎ 314-646-1166), $15 round trip.

By train
The Amtrak station is at 550 South 16th Street (☎ 800-872-7245). The *City of New Orleans* Amtrak service from New Orleans to Chicago and back makes a stop at Carbondale from where a bus service connects with St Louis. The *Texas Eagle* service from San Antonio to Chicago stops at Dallas and St Louis. There are five passenger services in and out of St Louis everyday.

KEY – DOWNTOWN ST LOUIS & SOULARD (MAP OPPOSITE)

⌂ **WHERE TO STAY**
1 St Louis RV Park
3 Hampton Inn Union Station
4 Courtyard by Marriott
6 Drury Inn
7 Hyatt Regency
9 Holiday Inn Select Downtown
10 Embassy Suites Hotel
13 Ramada Inn at the Arch
14 Mayfair Wyndham Grand Heritage Hotel
15 Omni Majestic
16 Radisson Hotel & Suites
17 Adam's Mark Hotel
18 Marriott Pavilion Hotel

22 Park Avenue
23 Lehmann House
25 Napoleon's Retreat
26 Lafayette House
31 Brewer's House
32 Somewhere!
36 Lemps Landing

○ **WHERE TO EAT**
2 St Louis Brewery & Tap Room
5 Harry's
8 Tangerine
19 Tony's
20 BB's Jazz, Blues and Soups
21 Broadway Oyster Bar
24 Arcelia's

33 Sydney Street
34 Venice Café
35 Lynch Street Bistro

♪ **LIVE MUSIC VENUES**
11 Lafitte's Restaurant & Nightclub
12 Hannegan's
20 BB's Jazz, Blues and Soups
21 Broadway Oyster Bar
27 Great Grizzly Bear
28 Mike & Min's
29 1860s Hard Shell
30 Molly's
34 Venice Café
37 Off Broadway

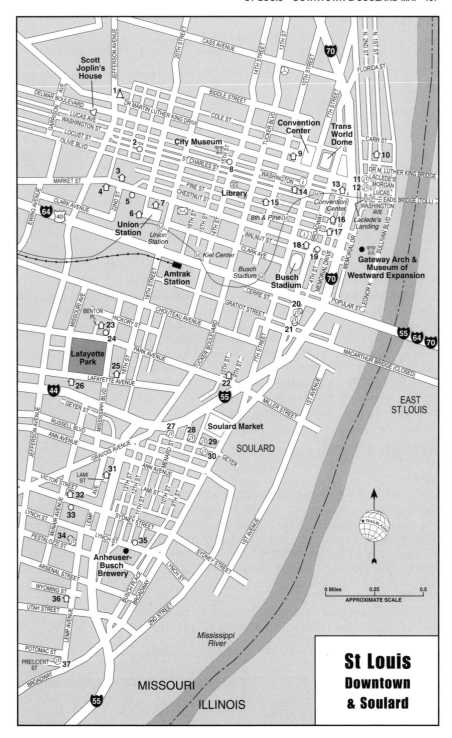

St Louis
Downtown
& Soulard

By bus

Greyhound buses use the terminal at 1450 North 13th (☎ 314-231-4485). There are three services a day to Davenport, Iowa and five services a day south to Memphis, a five- or six-hour journey.

By car

St Louis is a major US crossroads straddling important north-south and east-west trails: the I-55 and Highway 61 lead south to Memphis and north to Chicago; the I-64 runs east to Louisville, Kentucky; the I-70 races west to Kansas City and north-east to Indianapolis, Indiana; and the I-44 leads south-west to Oklahoma City, Oklahoma.

Orientation

Downtown St Louis stretches west from the banks of the Mississippi River between the Poplar Street and Martin Luther King Bridges. Despite its towering scale, downtown St Louis is fairly easy to navigate – if you get lost just head for the giant arch which shapes the St Louis skyline.

Soulard, the funky part of town with a reputation for good jazz and blues, is south of downtown near the river. Laclede's Landing, just north of downtown along the riverfront, is an area of restored warehouses, bars and loft apartments which has seen its fortunes improve over the nineties.

Another entertainment district, the University Loop, is some way west of downtown just north of Forest Park. East St Louis, the original home to the St Louis blues scene, is opposite downtown on the other side of the Mississippi River in Illinois. Today East St Louis is a run-down and semi-deserted suburb with nothing like the music scene it once enjoyed.

Getting around

By car

For a city of 2.5 million people, St Louis is surprisingly straightforward for drivers. Parking is easy and downtown, with a system of alternating one-way streets, is rarely over-crowded although those same one-way streets which ease traffic flow can be immensely irritating if you do get lost. Car rental firms in St Louis include: Avis (☎ 314-426-7766); Budget (☎ 314-423 3000); Enterprise (☎ 314-534-4440) and National (☎ 314-426-6272).

By cab

For some absurd reason cabs aren't supposed to stop when hailed in St Louis. Try calling Harris Cabs (☎ 314-535-5087), Laclede Cabs (☎ 314-652 3456) or Yellow Cabs (☎ 314-361-2345).

By bus

The Bi-State bus system is of limited use to visitors; its service is city-wide but can be slow and a little impractical. Fares are $1.25. Call ☎ 314-231-2345 for schedule information and maps.

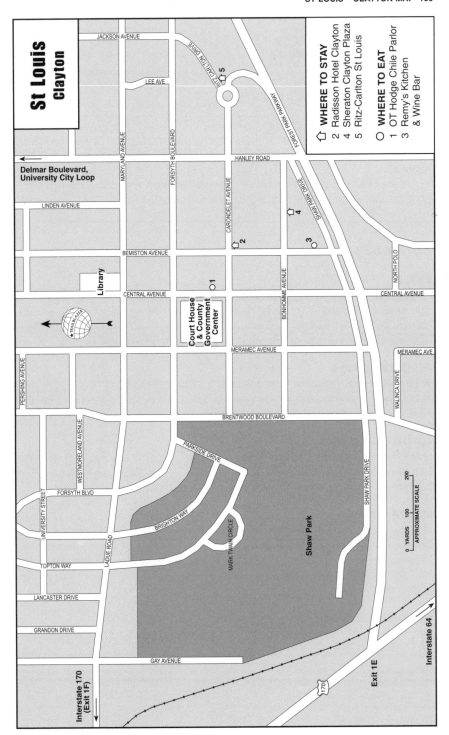

St Louis Clayton

⌂ **WHERE TO STAY**
2 Radisson Hotel Clayton
4 Sheraton Clayton Plaza
5 Ritz-Carlton St Louis

○ **WHERE TO EAT**
1 OT Hodge Chile Parlor
3 Remy's Kitchen & Wine Bar

JACKSON AVENUE
LEE AVE
Delmar Boulevard, University City Loop
LINDEN AVENUE
BEMISTON AVENUE
CENTRAL AVENUE
MERAMEC AVENUE
BRENTWOOD BOULEVARD
HANLEY ROAD
CARLTON DRIVE
FORSYTH BOULEVARD
MARYLAND AVENUE
FOREST PARK PARKWAY
CARONDELET AVENUE
SHAW PARK DRIVE
BONHOMME AVENUE
NORTH POLO
CENTRAL AVENUE
MERAMEC AVE
WALINCA DRIVE
Library
Court House & County Government Center
PERSHING AVENUE
WESTMORELAND AVENUE
PARKSIDE DRIVE
BRIGHTON WAY
MARK TWAIN CIRCLE
FORSYTH BLVD
UNIVERSITY STREET
LADUE ROAD
TOPTON WAY
LANCASTER DRIVE
GRANDON DRIVE
GAY AVENUE
Shaw Park
SHAW PARK DRIVE

0 YARDS 100 200
APPROXIMATE SCALE

Interstate 170 (Exit 1F)
Exit 1E
Interstate 64

By metro

More useful than the buses, St Louis's 17-mile 'mass transit system', Metro Link, coincides with many of the city's attractions. Head for Delmar for the University Loop, Forest Park for the park and its zoo and museums, Laclede's Landing for the Arch and the warehouse district and 8th and Pine for central downtown. Fares are $1.25 one-way.

By tour

The Greater St Louis Black Tourism Network (☎ 314-865-0708) offers comprehensive and eye-opening tours of St Louis from the point of view of black history.

Gray Line Tours (☎ 314-421-4753) in association with Vandalia Bus Lines provide more general tours as does Tour St Louis Inc (☎ 314-241-1400) which also provides a black history tour.

Services

Banks

ATMs and foreign currency exchange services are, of course, easy to find in downtown St Louis. If you're stuck, there are Bank of America branches on the corners of 10th Street and Market and 4th and Pine. You will find Firstar Bank branches on the corners of 7th Street and Market and 7th and Locust.

Communications

● **Post** The main US Post Office is at 1720 Market Street.
● **Internet** Free Internet access is available at the St Louis Public Library at 1301 Olive Street.

Tourist information

Head for the visitor information centers at 7th and Washington Avenue, Lambert-St Louis International Airport or in Keiner Plaza. Otherwise call ☎ 800-916-0092 or log on to 🖳 www.explorestlouis.com.

Record stores

Vintage Vinyl (☎ 314-721-4096) at 6610 Delmar Boulevard in the University Loop neighborhood is probably the best record store in St Louis and certainly the place to go for jazz and blues. Local artists are well represented and the staff here know music. Don't be fooled by the name; music is sold in all formats, not just vinyl.

Medical emergencies

One of the biggest healthcare providers in the area is SouthPointe Hospital (☎ 314-268-6000) at 2639 Miami Street.

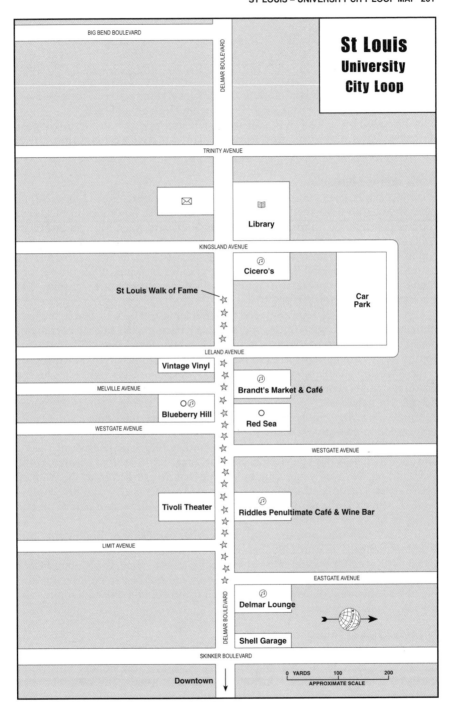

What to see

Given the contribution St Louis has made to jazz, blues and rock & roll, there are surprisingly few landmarks of note still surviving. The neglected East St Louis suburb is itself a landmark in that the local blues scene of the twenties, thirties and forties grew from here. The **Lincoln High School** on Bond Avenue, once attended by Miles Davis, still sees a few jazz pilgrims drive slowly past its gates. Davis played his first trumpet here and credited his former tutor, Elwood Buchanan, with getting him started along the musical track.

Scott Joplin's house

Scott Joplin's house (☎ 314-340-5970; Mon-Sat 10am-4pm, Sun 12-6pm; $2) at 2658 Delmar Boulevard is the best-maintained music landmark in St Louis. Joplin moved to the apartment on Delmar Boulevard, then Morgan Street, in 1900 after his *Maple Leaf Rag* had become the *fin de siecle* equivalent of a hit. Joplin's publisher, Stark, sold sheet music as fast as a modern record label could hope to sell discs. While living in St Louis, the King of Ragtime wrote many more of his most famous and complicated compositions including *The Entertainer* and *Ragtime Dance*.

During this time Joplin enjoyed national fame and became one of the first African-Americans whose music crossed racial barriers. His rags were enjoyed as much in white living rooms as in black honky-tonks. By 1907, however, Joplin wasn't doing so well. Convinced his compositions were as worthy of critical acclaim as any opera – and he could well have been right – Joplin set out to prove his genius. He moved to New York but his fame was fading and he quickly exhausted his once considerable funds trying to stage his most complex work, *Tremonisha*. Joplin died in 1917 in a mental home aged 49 and was buried in an unmarked grave.

In 1976 the house was placed on the National Register of Historic Places and in 1984 it was donated to the Missouri State Parks system. At that point the building was barely standing but significant investment from the State of Missouri saved the landmark. Now decorated with period furniture, Joplin-related artifacts and a working piano, the house-museum tells a critical part of the story of African-American music.

The next-door property, on the corner of Delmar Boulevard and Beaumont Street, is currently being transformed into the 'Rosebud Café' which will open for special musical events. In Joplin's time, the Rosebud Café was the center of the ragtime scene in St Louis. Other plans to improve the site include the planting of every species which features in the title of a Joplin rag, the maple taking pride of place.

St Louis Walk of Fame

Over in the University Loop district, set in the sidewalk of the 6200-6600 blocks of Delmar Boulevard, the St Louis Walk of Fame honors illustrious locals from every discipline – including, of course, music. The Walk of Fame was established in 1989 by the colorful owner of Blueberry Hill (see p210), Joe Edwards. Every year on the third Sunday in May an induction ceremony is

Highway 61 meets Route 66

The two most culturally significant routes in the United States, the Blues Highway and Route 66, cross in St Louis. Route 66 became the motor road of choice for families heading west across America in search of better lives on the new frontier. Locals will tell you to drive down Watson Road from Hampton Avenue to Ted Drewe's Frozen Custard store – itself a Route 66 landmark since 1929 – to say you've driven a genuine stretch of America's 'Mother Road'.

held at 6500 Delmar Boulevard to add to the list of local luminaries declared fit to join the Walk of Fame.

Current members of the Walk of Fame inducted for their contribution to music include (addresses on Delmar in brackets): Albert King (6370); Miles Davis (6314); Chuck Berry (6504); Tina Turner (6378); Scott Joplin (6510); Henry Townsend (6610) and Clark Terry (6623). Notable St Louisians from other fields include TS Eliot, William Burroughs, Tennessee Williams, Joseph Pulitzer and Ulysses S Grant.

Black World History Wax Museum

The Black World History Wax Museum (☎ 314-241-7057; Wed-Sat 10am-5pm; $4) at 2505 St Louis Avenue might be of passing interest to music lovers; wax figures include local music legends like Clark Terry.

Other highlights

One could hardly fail to notice the most obvious attraction in St Louis, the **Gateway Arch** (☎ 877-982-1410; daily, 8am-10pm; trams $6) which overlooks the city from 630 feet. This sublime structure is one of the most beautiful monuments in the country. Designed by Finnish architect Saarinen and built in 1965 the Arch was chosen to represent the point of America's westward expansion and to honor Thomas Jefferson's brokering of the Louisiana Purchase in 1803.

Jefferson, himself a successful architect, would no doubt admire the stunning symmetry of the Arch and the way its smooth steel edges appear to improve the changing light which falls across it. But the Arch isn't just for looking at; mini-trams travel up each 'leg' daily, ferrying visitors to the top. It's a cramped ride, and not recommended for anyone who hates small spaces, but the view from the top is enough to draw gasps. The Odyssey Imax theater at the foot of the Arch shows films of related interest which change every six months. There's also an enormous **Museum of Westward Expansion** which charts the journey of Lewis and Clark and explains the history behind a continental United States.

Forest Park, a 1370-acre expanse west of downtown, provides a refreshing oasis amid the clamor of the city. Apart from the miles of cycle tracks, forest and fields, Forest Park hides a zoo and outstanding art museum, both of which make enjoyable diversions. The **St Louis Zoo** (☎ 314-781-0900; daily

9am-5pm; free) is a comfortable home to some 6000 animals including big cats, primates and elephants. The **St Louis Art Museum** (☎ 314-721-0072; Wed-Sun 10am-5pm, Tues 1.30-8.30pm; free) is a wonderful, airy construction built for the 1904 World's Fair which attracted some 19 million visitors to St Louis and its Forest Park location. The collection includes a number of modern masterpieces from a diverse range of artists.

If Forest Park fails to sate your desire for the natural world, head for the **Missouri Botanical Garden** (☎ 314-577-9400; daily 9am-8pm; $5) at 4344 Shaw Boulevard. The impressive site includes a Japanese Garden and the 'Cimatron' rainforest. A series of jazz concerts are held here throughout June and July every year. Created by millionaire Englishman Henry Shaw in 1859, the Gardens were influenced by those at Kew in London. Like all true Englishmen, Shaw spent his retirement improving his garden.

Other notable attractions in St Louis include the **St Louis Cathedral Basilica** on the corner of Lindell Boulevard and Newstead Avenue, which houses the world's largest collection of mosaics, and the **City Museum** (☎ 314-231-2489) at 701 North 15th Street. Contrary to its staid name, the City Museum is a chaotic world of weirdness stuffed into a disused warehouse. With a brief to 'reawaken the childlike imagination', the museum has a license to do almost anything – and it does. A school bus teeters on the edge of the roof while inside kids play amid a labyrinth of salvaged building parts, caves and tunnels. There's also a 'Museum of Mirth, Mystery and Mayhem' and the famous 'puking pig'. Strange as it sounds, the City Museum is the most enjoyable public attraction in town.

Home of Budweiser and other beer brands, the **Anheuser-Busch Brewery** (☎ 314-577-2626; Mon-Sat 9am-4pm; free) at the junction of the I-55 and Arsenal Street is something of a Mecca for beer-lovers and a prized St Louis enterprise. Anheuser-Busch is the world's largest brewer; the massive complex in St Louis is the nucleus of the operation. Visitors see how the beer is brewed and bottled and are presented with a plastic cup full of beer and a bag of pretzels at the end of the tour. The whole thing is really little more than an extended commercial for Bud but the sheer scale of the business is interesting.

Where to stay

A look at the St Louis skyline gives the impression of a Marriott- and Hyatt-strewn city and, as an important business hub, St Louis does offer all the usual corporate hotel brands. But there are also some interesting places to stay, including a good number of **bed and breakfasts**. Bed and breakfast accommodations in St Louis are relatively expensive however – particularly after the good value places found scattered around more rural stretches of the Blues Highway.

Budget options

This isn't the easiest city in which to find a cheap place to sleep but if you're prepared to hunt around – particularly out towards the airport – you'll find somewhere.

St Louis — chain hotels

- *Courtyard by Marriott* (☎ 314-241-9111, 800-231-2211), 2340 Market Street
- *Drury Inn* (☎ 314-231-3900), 201 South 20th Street
- *Embassy Suites Hotel* (☎ 314-241-4200), 901 North First *Street*
- *Hampton Inn Union Station* (☎ 314-241-3200), 2211 Market Street
- *Holiday Inn Forest Park* (☎ 314-645-0700, 800-465-4329), 5915 Wilson Avenue
- *Holiday Inn Select Downtown* (☎ 314-421-4000), 811 North Ninth Street
- *Hyatt Regency* (☎ 314-231-1234, 800-233-1234), One St Louis, Union Station
- *Marriott Pavilion Hotel* (☎ 314-421-1776, 800-228-9290), 1 Broadway
- *Omni Majestic* (☎ 314-436-2355), 1019 Pine Street
- *Radisson Hotel & Suites* (☎ 314-621-8200), 200 North Fourth Street
- *Radisson Hotel Clayton* (☎ 314-726-5400, 800-870-6556), 7750 Carondelet Avenue
- *Ramada Inn* at the Arch (☎ 314-621-7900), 333 Washington Avenue
- *Sheraton Clayton Plaza* (☎ 314-863-0400, 800-325-3535), 7730 Bonhomme Avenue

Campers could check out the *St Louis RV Park* (☎ 314-231-3300, 800-878-3300; ❷) at 900 North Jefferson – a downtown location – or the *Casino Queen RV Park* (☎ 800-777-0777; ❷) at 200 South Front Street in East St Louis. Neither is particularly good; you might be better off parking the RV for a night or two and checking into a hotel.

Of the airport motels, the cheapest are usually *Congress Inn* (☎ 314-739-5100; ❷) at 3433 North Lindbergh Boulevard, *Econo-Lodge Airport* (☎ 314-731-3000, 800-446-6900; ❷-❸) at 4575 North Lindbergh Boulevard at the junction with the I-70 or *La Quinta Inn* (☎ 314-731-3881, 800-687-6667; ❸) at 5781 Campus Court.

Mid-range options ($50-120)
The best value of the area's bed and breakfasts is *Oakwood Cottage* (☎ 314-968-2434; ❸) a good 12 miles out of town to the west at 681 Oakwood Avenue in Webster Groves. It's a simple but attractive place away from the bustle of the city.

Brewer's House (☎ 314-771-1542; ❸) at 1829 Lami Street is much better placed for downtown and as such represents outstanding value by St Louis standards; it is, however, a specifically gay and lesbian establishment. *Lister House* (☎ 314-361-5506; ❸) at 4547 McPherson Street is another low-priced and perfectly adequate option.

The *Lehmann House* bed and breakfast (☎ 314-231-6724; ❹) at 10 Benton Place is a step up both in price and quality; the beautifully-decorated interior and antique furnishings mark the Lehmann House out as a well-maintained period property.

Another convenient and well-appointed choice is *Park Avenue* (☎ 314-241-6814; ❹) at 945 Park Avenue. The owners here make much of the fact that

---

Hotel price codes

Hotel and motels price bands used in this book reflect the range of prices charged for a double room.

❶ – $10-25　　　❷ – $26-50　　　❸ – $51-85　　　❹ – $86-120
❺ – $121-180　　❻ – $181-250　　❼ – $251+

See p22 for more information.

---

some rooms offer a 'jacuzzi by candlelight'. Sounds good. *Lafayette House* (☎ 314-772-4429; ❹) at 2156 Lafayette Avenue is fairly close to downtown and offers plush accommodation in a lovingly-maintained Victorian mansion.

High-end bed and breakfasts

Nudging up the price scale a notch, *Napoleon's Retreat* (☎ 314-772-6979; ❺) at – where else? – 1815 Lafayette Avenue is a beautiful bed and breakfast set back from a leafy suburban street of similarly imposing properties. The conscientious owners try hard.

If you're prepared to fork out still further for a bed and breakfast, there are still a few upscale places to explore. *Fleur-de-Lys Inn* (☎ 314-773-3500; ❺) at 3500 Russell Boulevard claims to be the 'city's most luxurious inn' and, in fairness, it is without doubt one of the best.

Competitors include *Lemps Landing* (☎ 314-771-1993; ❺) at 1900 Wyoming Street, which encourages its guests to enjoy a glass of champagne in the jacuzzi – candles are available if requested; *Parker Garden* (☎ 618-271-2005; ❺-❻), a luxurious townhouse incongruously located over the river in East St Louis; and the ever-trendy *Somewhere!* (☎ 314-664-4726; ❺-❻) at 2049 Sidney Street, a den of opulence and top notch food.

High-end hotels ($120-250+)

If you're really planning to splash out, St Louis also boasts a handful of first-rate hotels. The *Mayfair Wyndham Grand Heritage Hotel* (☎ 314-421-2500, 800-996-3426; ❺-❻) at 806 St Charles Street is one of these. The Mayfair Wyndham is indeed a grand affair and is unlikely to disappoint even the most particular visitors. Whether or not guests choose to believe that the Mayfair Wyndham was the first hotel to start the tradition of leaving a chocolate on guest pillows is another matter.

Adam's Mark Hotel (☎ 314-241-7400, 800-444-2326; ❺-❻) at the corner of Fourth and Chestnut is another memorable place which achieves high standards. The best of the bunch, however, is the *Ritz-Carlton St Louis* (☎ 314-863-8400, 800-433-6590; ❻-❼) in the Clayton neighborhood at 100 Carondelet Plaza. Like all hotels in this group, the Ritz-Carlton goes to a great deal of trouble to ensure its prestigious image is maintained; expect great service and attention to detail in the rooms and restaurants.

St Louis Symphony Orchestra

The Grammy Award-winning St Louis Symphony Orchestra was founded in 1879 and is the second oldest orchestra in the United States. It still ranks as one of the very best in the nation. If you like music, whether jazz, blues or whatever, you'll be gripped by an SLSO concert at its extravagant home, the Powell Symphony Hall.

Where to eat

Budget options

St Louis has as wide a range of restaurants as one would expect for a city of this size which is why, as in the New Orleans and Chicago chapters, this selection of restaurants is necessarily a rather personal and partial selection. That said, choose where you eat from this list and you won't be disappointed.

For a fattening feast at the cheap end of the scale, head over to the *O T Hodge Chile Parlor* (☎ 314-721-8880) at 6 South Central. This classic, popular diner serves fantastic breakfasts, burgers and meatballs for just a few dollars. You'll find the place packed with suits at mealtimes. Foreign visitors might benefit from the handy glossary of 'diner-speak' printed on the back of the menu. Don't forget to order some 'cow paste' with your toast and if you're in a hurry, 'let it walk'. There are several other franchises of this local chain dotted around St Louis.

Over in Soulard, a handful of the music venues listed later also serve reasonable food. The *Broadway Oyster Bar* (☎ 314-621-8811) at 736 Broadway offers Creole and Cajun classics like red beans and rice, gumbo and blackened fish. You can get your oysters prepared six different ways including the 'shooter' – oysters with horseradish, tomatoes and vodka. Expect to pay around $8-9 for an entrée.

Another New Orleans-inspired menu can be found at *BB's Jazz, Blues and Soups* (☎ 314-436-5222) at 700 South Broadway which sells bowls of gumbo for $5.15, red beans and rice for $6.75 and pizzas from around $8. *Venice Café* (☎ 314-772-5994) at 1901 Pestalozzi Street on the corner of Lemp Avenue, also featured in the live music section, has a menu almost as eclectic as the decor. More or less Caribbean in style, it includes a calypso salad for $4.75 and Jamaican Jerk Chicken with sweet dumplings for just $6.

Mid-range and expensive restaurants

Soulard does boast one or two more upscale restaurants. One of the best of these is *Arcelia's* (☎ 314-231-9200) at 2001 Park Street. The predominantly Mexican menu includes a few surprises and is exceptional value; the food is good, the service excellent and the atmosphere enjoyable. Also try the *Lynch Street Bistro* (☎ 314-772-5777) which hides in the shadow of the Anheuser-

Busch brewery at 1031 Lynch Street. It's a touch more expensive than Arcelia's and the multi-national menu, which includes Thai, Cajun and American influences, is a touch more pretentious, but this is a likeable restaurant.

Blueberry Hill (☎ 314-727-0880) at 6504 Delmar Avenue, again featured in the live music section, is known as much for its food as for its music. The menu is simple, diner fare but the quality is a clear step up from most diners. The burgers are perfect and the breakfasts awesome. Expect to gorge yourself for around $5. While you chomp through your plateful of fries and dips, don't forget to admire the weird and slightly obsessive collections of twentieth-century trinkets which occupy every shelf in the building.

Opposite at 6513 Delmar, *Red Sea* (☎ 314-863-0099), an Ethiopian restaurant, has earned a reputation in St Louis for quality. In fact, the menu borrows heavily from North Africa and Turkey and the food is excellent. Try the chicken with brandied bananas for $9.

Less exotic but strangely satisfying meals can be found at the *St Louis Brewery & Tap Room* (☎ 314-241-2337) at 2100 Locust Street. With its own-brewed ales and English pub food like 'ploughman's lunches' and salmon sandwiches, the Tap Room isn't the height of St Louis cuisine but does offer good value, good quality meals in an easy-going environment. There's live music here most weekends, too.

Downtown at 1405 Washington Avenue, *Tangerine* (☎ 314-231-7007) is a great value place to go for healthy and unusual food designed by chef-owner Blake Brokaw. The emphasis is on vegetarian fare but even committed carnivores will find something satisfying among the meatless offerings. Expect to pay a little under $10 for an entrée. Also try *Harry's* (☎ 314-421-6969) at 2144 Market Street, with great views over the downtown area and simple but effective Italian and American entrées. Since Harry's relies on businessmen on expense accounts, it's not cheap. Expect to pay $20 for an entrée. Good value but only if someone else is paying.

Over in the hotel- and office-crammed Clayton district, *Remy's Kitchen & Wine Bar* (☎ 314-726-5757) at 222 South Bemiston is a tucked away restaurant with exquisite food served in an overly ostentatious style. Diners choose wines in 'flights' – groups of four types to sample. The menu, which is a mix of tapas-style Mediterranean food with a hint of American cuisine, is then divided into large plates ($12-17) or small plates ($4-8) which tables share. The striking modern interior is perhaps the restaurant's most appealing asset.

A vaguely similar style of European-influenced cuisine is available at *Meriwhether's* (☎ 314-746-4599) in the Missouri History Museum in Forest Park. Meriwhether's is an orgy of light, delicious food, attentive waiting staff and giant cakes for dessert. The building itself, all steel and glass, adds to the refined feel of the place. Expect to pay a very reasonable $8 for an entrée at lunchtime. The restaurant is also open for early dinner.

Soulard's best restaurant, *Sydney Street* (☎ 314-771-5777) at 2000 Sydney Street, is also one of its most expensive. Still, you get what you pay for and in Sydney Street what you get is some of the simplest and most exquisite cuisine in St Louis. The succulent raspberry pork, for example, wouldn't embarrass any chef. Also try the blue cheese tarts for starters.

Sydney Street is an exceptionally good restaurant and, as such, the $20-25 tab for an entrée isn't overpriced. The lovely, candlelit room and discrete service helps the occasion.

Ask a St Louisian cab driver to take you to the best restaurant in town and chances are he'll put his foot on the gas and whisk you straight to *Tony's* (☎ 314-231-7007) at 410 Market Street. Once voted the best Italian restaurant in America, Tony's has a national reputation which it works hard to maintain and improve. The meals are, of course, faultless and the service, carefully overlooked by the convivial owner Vince Bommarito, is outstanding. Don't expect much change when the check comes; diners dig deep to bask in the gastronomical glory of a table at Tony's.

Where to find live music

Musicians to look out for in St Louis include bluesmen Henry Townsend, Tommy Bankhead, Gus Thornton, Kenny Rice and Bennie Smith, saxophonist Oliver Sain and rock & rollers Chuck Berry and Johnnie Johnson – although you're more likely to find Johnson playing a jazz set these days. For listings, pick up a free copy of the *Riverfront Times* or buy Thursday's *St Louis Post-Dispatch*.

East St Louis is the real home of St Louis blues but there's little there now for music lovers. This leaves the trendy Soulard neighborhood free to claim to be the home of blues in St Louis. Soulard is indeed home to a string of music venues; most are within walking distance of one another.

Soulard

BB's Jazz, Blues and Soups (☎ 314-436-5222) at 700 South Broadway is perhaps the most respected of Soulard's joints. Now in its third reincarnation on the same site since 1976, BB's regularly hosts the best blues and jazzmen in St Louis. Henry Townsend and Oliver Sain play here often while Tommy Bankhead plays every Tuesday night. Expect a steady stream of St Louis bluesmen to drop in to watch Bankhead play. Owner Mark O'Shaughnessy has made BB's a St Louis institution by serving coffee and beignets to early morning motorists as they drive by and by staging an outdoor barbecue after every Cardinals home game.

Just along Broadway at number 736, the *Broadway Oyster Bar* (☎ 314-621 8811) is another first-rate blues club. The Oyster Bar has the appearance of a tidied up Delta juke joint; fairly lights are hung across the trees and barbecues are cooked outside. Bennie Smith plays here often, as do several other top-flight St Louis bluesmen. The Broadway Oyster Bar also benefits from a relaxed and friendly feel; people come here for a good time.

The *1860s Hard Shell* (☎ 314-231-1860), formerly the 1860 Saloon, at 1860 South Ninth Street is another well-known St Louis blues joint which attracts some of the best local acts. One side of the property is a restaurant specializing in seafood, the other a bar and club. There's music every night and no cover charge.

Mike & Min's (☎ 314-421-1655) at 925 Geyer Avenue has blues or cover bands Wednesdays to Saturdays wedged into a small stage by the window.

> # St Louis — radio stations
>
> Tune in to KATZ 1600 AM for blues or WSIE 88.7 FM for jazz and you can't go too far wrong.

Again, there's no cover charge. *Great Grizzly Bear* (☎ 314-231-0444) just up the street at 1027 Geyer Avenue is another music venue worth checking out. Like Mike & Min's, the music isn't always top notch but it's a fun place where people like to dance till late. There's music Thursday to Saturday nights and a small cover. Doors open at 8pm. *Molly's* (☎ 314-436-0921) at 816 Geyer Avenue is less a music venue than a large and boisterous bar but there is, sometimes, live music here. Set in a rambling New Orleans-style house with iron balconies and a courtyard lit by flaming torches, Molly's is a great place for a night of drinking with a young and lively crowd.

A short drive away towards the Anheuser-Busch brewery, the *Venice Café* (☎ 314-772-5994) at 1901 Pestalozzi Street on the corner of Lemp Avenue is by far the coolest bar in Soulard. Weird mirrors, mosaics and courtyards make this an attractive and funky place. The music's good too; Bennie Smith regularly electrifies the young crowd. There's music here every night except Sunday; expect to pay a small cover charge.

University Loop district

Once you've exhausted Soulard, the University Loop district, west of downtown, is home to another clump of live music venues. The regeneration of the Loop was led by Joe Edwards and his bar-restaurant *Blueberry Hill* (☎ 314-727-0880) at 6504 Delmar Avenue.

Opened in 1972, Blueberry Hill has gone on to become a must-see St Louis institution, not least because Chuck Berry plays here regularly in the 'Duck Room', just one of several stages, named after his famous 'duck walk'. Blueberry Hill is crammed full of pop culture memorabilia from Elvis dolls to Simpsons posters to Beatles records.

It would be easy to write the place off as a den of pointless kitsch but that would be a mistake. Meet Joe Edwards and you realize that Blueberry Hill has, in its own inimitable way, done more for the preservation of St Louis music than any other venue in town. After all, nowhere else can claim regular visits from the great Chuck Berry. Edwards has made his mark on several other areas of the Loop, too. The Walk of Fame is his creation, the wonderful Tivoli Theater has been refurbished and reopened at a cost of $2 million and Edwards is soon to open the *Pageant*, also on Delmar, a new nightclub and music venue which will hold 2000.

Other live music venues in the Loop include *Cicero's* (☎ 314-862-0009) at 6691 Delmar Boulevard, a restaurant with a separate nightclub area out back, *Brandt's Market & Café* (☎ 314-727-3663) at 6525 Delmar Boulevard, a slightly strange grocery-restaurant with jazz or folk music every night, *Riddles*

Interview — Johnnie Johnson

How did you get together with Chuck Berry?
One night, when I had a band here in St Louis, my sax player got sick and couldn't make it. So I called Chuck Berry. I'd met him previously and I asked him if he would sit in for one night. That one night lasted the thirty years we stayed together. He was on a rockabilly kick and so I started to play that kind of stuff because I played with Chuck so long. It never affected the little bit I knew about jazz and blues has always been my main thing. It's just recently, in these last ten or twelve years, that I really got the chance to play some blues.

Why did you decide to stay in St Louis when so many other musicians moved on?
Because to me St Louis is the place with the most opportunities. I've lived in Chicago, in West Virginia, in Pittsburgh and none of them compare to St Louis. When I came here I could almost walk out on the street and get a job. It's the most progressive place and I have no intention of ever leaving until my time is up.

Do you think the St Louis music scene is healthy?
Yes, there's always some place to play. There's no real record industry here but there are gigs and there's studio work to do. In St Louis you can look in the paper every week and every night of the week there are people playing. St Louis is a fine town; we have some of the best musicians in the world right here.

Johnnie Johnson formed a 30-year musical partnership with Chuck Berry in 1952 and continues to record.

Penultimate Café & Wine Bar (☎ 314-725-6985) at 6307 Delmar Boulevard, with jazz, blues or funk music every night except Mondays, and the *Delmar Lounge* (☎ 314-725-6565) at 6235 Delmar Boulevard, a restaurant-club with live jazz till 3am every night.

Other venues

There are a number of other music venues scattered across St Louis which don't fall into the brackets of either Soulard or the Loop. Chief among these for blues lovers are *Off Broadway* (☎ 314-773-3663) at 3509 Lemp Avenue, a true blues club hidden at the industrial end of Broadway, and the *Moose Lounge* at 4571 Pope on the corner of Rosalie Street in north St Louis, a small, dark place in a residential suburb.

Jazz aficionados might try *Turvey's on the Green* (☎ 314-454-1667) at 255 Union Boulevard, an upscale place with regular live jazz including a Sunday jazz brunch, *Jazz at the Bistro* (☎ 314-531-1012) at 3536 Washington Avenue, perhaps the best jazz venue in St Louis, *Hannegan's* (☎ 314-241-8877) at 719 North Second Street in the Laclede's Landing area, with jazz at weekends, and the nearby *Lafitte's Restaurant & Nightclub* (☎ 314-241-5722) at 809 North Second Street, another occasional jazz venue.

Moving on — St Louis to Hannibal

Highway 61 weaves north from St Louis and quickly shakes off the city's grip. The gentle fields seem flatter and somehow harder than the pretty farmland further south. This expansive landscape creates the impression of an enormous sky which leaves the small towns en route seem exposed and open.

The first of these small towns, Troy, holds little interest for visitors but the second, Bowling Green, has a certain appeal. Bowling Green is quintessential small town America; a frail collection of stores built around a square and courthouse. Your very arrival will be an exciting event for the residents of Bowling Green. Further north, New London is another eminently forgettable place which soon fades in the rear-view mirrors of motorists on the Mark Twain trail to Hannibal.

Hannibal

If Mark Twain had never lived, Hannibal would be an unusually pretty town surrounded by jungly bluffs and overlooking the Mississippi River with a clear view across to Illinois unobstructed by levees. But Mark Twain, real name Samuel Langhorne Clemens, did live and he lived in Hannibal. The result is that Hannibal has been entirely absorbed by the legend of the American writer. From the actors who wander the streets in period costume to the Huckleberry Finn giftshops, there's no escape.

There's no particular music legacy in Hannibal, although it sits on the Mississippi so must have played at least some part in the Great Migration north. If you're passing by, however, it would be a shame to miss what is one of the more attractive towns along this stretch of the river.

Twain grew up here until he left to work as a riverboat pilot, plowing up and down the Mississippi River learning its every nuance and the character of each of its towns. When he began to write, Twain used Hannibal for the setting of some of his best-loved works – *The Adventures of Tom Sawyer* (1876) and *The Adventures of Huckleberry Finn* (1885). Both were written in dialect and captured perfectly the speech and mood of people who lived along the banks of the Mississippi at the end of the nineteenth century.

Orientation

Downtown Hannibal is wedged against the riverside east of Highway 61. If you're arriving from the south, cross the railroad tracks and go right on Market Street all the way into downtown. Most places of interest are on or within walking distance of Main and Third Streets.

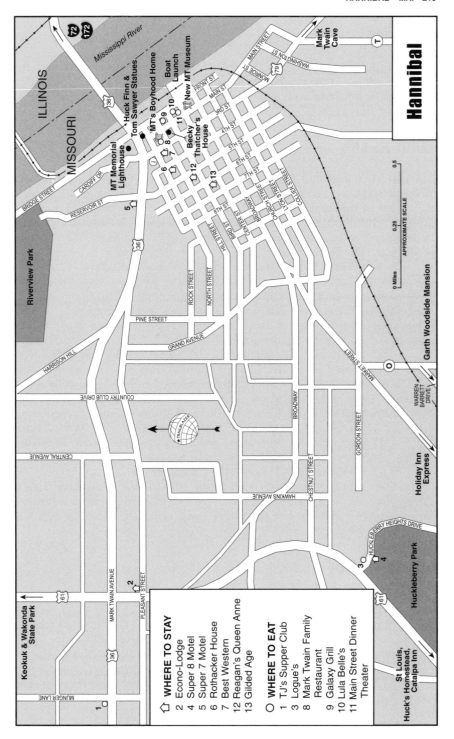

Hannibal

WHERE TO STAY
1 Econo-Lodge
2 Super 8 Motel
4 Super 7 Motel
6 Rothacker House
7 Best Western
12 Reagan's Queen Anne
13 Gilded Age

WHERE TO EAT
1 TJ's Supper Club
3 Logue's
8 Mark Twain Family Restaurant
9 Galaxy Grill
10 Lula Belle's
11 Main Street Dinner Theater

Services

Banks with ATMs include the Roosevelt Bank at 666 Broadway and the Commerce Bank in the Huck Finn Shopping Center.

Tourist information is available from the helpful staff of the Convention & Visitors' Bureau (☎ 573-221-2477) at 505 North Third Street.

What to see

Mark Twain's boyhood home (☎ 573-221-9010; daily 8am-6pm) at 208 Hill Street provides an interesting if anaesthetized glimpse of Samuel Clemen's early days in this simple two-story, whitewashed home. An annex houses a more insightful museum which charts Clemen's career as a riverboat pilot, inventor and author. It also explains the origin of his pen name, Mark Twain, which was a call of riverboat pilots.

The **New Mark Twain Museum**, affiliated to his boyhood home and covered with the same admission fee, is two blocks away on Main Street. The pride of the new museum is 15 original Norman Rockwell paintings used to illustrate the Huckleberry Finn stories. Rockwell spent a good deal of time exploring Hannibal relating Twain's stories to the local geography in an attempt to create accurate illustrations.

Another of Twain's best-known characters, **Becky Thatcher**, is believed to have been based on Laura Hawkins, Samuel Clemen's childhood sweetheart, who lived at 221 Hill Street. Her home is also now a museum and a bookshop. Other Mark Twain points of interest include the **Huck Finn and Tom Sawyer statues** at the foot of Cardiff Hill. The statues were created by Frederick Hibbard and presented to Hannibal in 1926. The **Mark Twain Memorial Lighthouse** which sits atop Cardiff Hill was dedicated in 1935 – the 100th anniversary of Mark Twain – and has since been renovated and rededicated by John F Kennedy in 1963 and Bill Clinton in 1994.

About a mile south of Hannibal, off Highway 79, the **Mark Twain Cave** is thought to be the cave so admired by Tom Sawyer in his adventures. Visitors are invited to explore this rather tenuous literary attraction on hourlong guided tours.

Where to stay

Budget choices are limited. **Campers** should drive 20 miles north to *Wakonda State Park* (☎ 573-655-2280; ❶). Others should try the *Super 8 Motel* (☎ 573-221-5863; ❸) at Highway 61 South and Huckleberry Heights, *Econo-Lodge* (☎ 573-221-0422; ❷-❸) at 3604 McMasters Street or the endearingly but unwittingly retro *Super 7 Motel* (☎ 573-221-1666; ❸) at 612 Mark Twain Avenue.

Main chains in Hannibal include the new *Holiday Inn Express* (☎ 573-406-0300; ❹) at 4000 Market Street and the ugly but convenient *Best Western* (☎ 573-248-1150; ❹-❺) at 401 North Third Street.

As you might guess, quaint Hannibal boasts several good **bed and breakfasts**. The *Catalpa Inn* (☎ 573-221-4053; ❸), seven miles south of Hannibal on Apache Drive off Highway 61, is a friendly and good-value country retreat where owners Jim and Barb Eddy go to great lengths to make guests welcome. In the same price range, *Rothacker House* (☎ 573-221-6335; ❸) at 423 North Fourth Street is a centrally-located 1847 Greek Revival property with a couple of quaint rooms.

Another central option is the *Gilded Age* (☎ 573-248-1218; ❸-❹) at 215 North Sixth Street. The 'flying' staircase is a prized feature and the breakfasts are hard to beat. *Reagan's Queen Anne* (☎ 573-221-0774; ❸-❹) at 313 North Fifth Street is perhaps the best of the downtown bed and breakfasts with a number of tastefully themed rooms; the clawfoot bath in the 'Captain's room' is a nice touch.

Each of these bed and breakfasts has its own charm but without doubt the best place to stay in Hannibal is the impeccable *Garth Woodside Mansion* (☎ 573-221-2789; ❹) at 11069 New London Road. One of the most elegant bed and breakfasts in Missouri, the Garth Woodside Mansion is a real treat. Owners John and Julie Rolson have maintained the property with considerable care.

Where to eat

For a budget buffet big enough to fill any belly try the predictably-named *Huck's Homestead* (☎ 573-985-5961) four miles south of Hannibal on Highway 61. The food could more or less be described as down-home – catfish, meatloaf and shrimps feature heavily.

The *Galaxy Grill* (☎ 573-248-3312) at 117 Hill Street is a diner-esque restaurant with burgers under $4 and plates of mashed potato, grilled chicken and gravy for just over $4; it's excellent value.

The *Mark Twain Family Restaurant* (☎ 573-221-5300) at Third and Hill Streets was established during the war and is something of a Hannibal stalwart. With a cheap but extensive menu of burgers, seafood dinners and sandwiches, this is another good value option which won't make much of a dent in your bank account.

A similar claim can be made for *Logue's* (☎ 573-248-1854), at the junction of Highway 61 and Huckleberry Drive, another carnival of fried food coated in bread crumbs.

Arguably a step up in quality – and certainly a step up in strangeness – is the *Main Street Dinner Theater* (☎ 573-231-0746) at 200 North Main Street. Meat and three veg dinners are dished up while diners are entertained by singing, dancing and general 'fun'.

TJ's Supper Club (☎ 573-221-5551) at the intersection of Munger Lane and Highway 36 is a rib specialist serving good quality food in a fairly functional setting. Apart from the ribs, which sell for $14 for 10oz, TJ's does a good line in seafood with grilled halibut for $13.95 and bronzed salmon for $10.95.

By far the most interesting restaurant in town, however, is Pam and Mike Ginsberg's *Lula Belle's* (☎ 573-221-6662) at 111 Bird Street. Lula Belle's doubles

Situated in the geographic center of the country, Iowa represents the very essence of serene, small town life. Nearly 95 per cent of the state is farmland and even Des Moines, the capital, is a tame place. Given its single-minded purpose, vast tracts of seemingly empty space and lack of gritty urban sprawl, Iowa has difficulty projecting much in the way of an exciting image for itself.

For many people, however – and in particular for readers of this book who will be heading towards St Louis or Chicago – Iowa's charm is derived from its sincere, rural beauty, inoffensive towns and exceptionally friendly people. What's more, Bix Beiderbecke, one of the brightest stars to burn in the jazz firmament, is a product of Davenport, perhaps the most enjoyable city in Iowa and an important Mississippi river-town.

Keokuk

Often thrown together with Fort Madison as the 'River Bend' towns, Keokuk overlooks the Des Moines river as it flows into the Mississippi. Said to be the first white settlement in what is now the state of Iowa, Keokuk is today a rather ordinary town with no discernable musical pedigree. It is, in truth, little more than a convenient place to grab a coffee on the drive between Hannibal and the Quad Cities.

What to see

If you do choose to explore the town, however, you might stumble across one or two points of interest. Between November and March, the Keokuk area is home to the largest number of **bald eagles** anywhere along the Mississippi River as they make their southern migration from Canada. A dam, lock and **hydroelectric power station**, built in 1913 and an engineering feat in its day, controls the powerful waters where the Mississippi and Des Moines rivers converge. Tours are available at 11am daily.

You might also choose to explore the **George M Verity steamboat**, permanently moored near the lock and dam, which is now a museum telling the story of the importance of river traffic and steamboats to the town. The steamboat moved barges between St Louis and St Paul and was donated to the town of Keokuk by the Armco Steel Company in 1960. Wander down to the Keokuk **Convention & Visitors' Bureau** (☎ 319-524-5599) at 329 Main Street for information on these and other local attractions.

Where to stay

Mainstream accommodation options are the *Holiday Inn Express* (☎ 319-524-8000; ❹) at Fourth and Main Streets or *Fairfield Inn* (☎ 319-524-9000; ❺-❻) at 3404 Main Street. Budget choices are *Super 8 Motel* (☎ 319-524-3888; ❷-❸) at 3511 Main Street or *Chief Motel* (☎ 319-524-2565; ❸) at 2701 Main Street. Keokuk's two bed and breakfasts are *Grand Anne* (☎ 319-524-6310; ❸-❹) at 816 Grand Avenue, an 1897 property overlooking the Mississippi, or the nearby *River's Edge* (☎ 319-524-1700; ❹) at 611 Grand Avenue, a 1915 mock-Tudor pile with a pool, library and patio which, again, looks out across the Mississippi.

Where to eat

Of Keokuk's few **places to eat**, *Chuck Wagon* (☎ 319-524-5916) at 706 Main Street is perhaps the most engaging. With booth seats polished to a high sheen by generations of Keokuk's buttocks, the Chuck Wagon is a real old-time eating house. The restaurant's slogan says it all: 'To a hungry cowhand, the Chuck Wagon is a welcome sight'. A typical and recommended lunch is baked ham, candied yams and beans – all for just $4.75. The Chuck Wagon is closed on Tuesdays and Wednesdays.

Other eating possibilities include: the self-explanatory *Sirloin Stockade* (☎ 319-524-5283) at 3461 Main Street; *Fort Worth Barbecue* (☎ 319-524-9880) at 526 South Fifth Street; Mexican *Papa Chico's* (☎ 319-524-7300) at 2528 Main Street; and the marginally more upscale *Hawkeye* (☎ 319-524-7549) at 105 North Park Drive.

Fort Madison

The second of the 'River Bend' towns, Fort Madison is a more interesting and, frankly, more attractive town than its sister Keokuk. There's a beautiful, uninterrupted view over the Mississippi to the thickly-forested Illinois side from the town's quaint streets.

Fort Madison does offer a number of useful **services**. **Banks** can be found at 25th Street and Avenue L, 1910 Avenue H and Seventh Street and Avenue G. **Car rentals** are available from Just Ask Rentals (☎ 319-372-3515) at 1904 Avenue H. There's even an **Amtrak** passenger terminal (☎ 319-372-3142) at

1601 20th Street and a Burlington Trailways **bus** station (☎ 319-753-2864) at Second Street and Avenue G. **Tourist information** is available from the Fort Madison CVB (☎ 319-372-5471) at 933 Avenue H.

What to see

Despite this wealth of convenient utilities, however, Fort Madison is still a quiet community which, like Keokuk, has little to detain visitors for long. The showpiece of the town's points of interest is the reconstruction of **Old Fort Madison** which occupies a precarious position down by the riverside. Used by the 1st Regiment US Infantry from 1808 to 1813, the fort is today peopled with locals dressed in period costume. A great deal of effort has gone into bringing the history of the fort to life. Bread is baked, cannons are fired and cartwheels fixed.

Other attractions, such as they are, include the **Santa Fe Swing Bridge** which leads across the Mississippi from the end of Second Street. This is apparently the longest double-decker swing span bridge in the world at an impressive 525 feet. You might also want to pay a visit to the **Catfish Bend Riverboat Casino**, moored alongside Riverview Park, which competes for attention with Old Fort Madison. More interesting perhaps – on the rare occasions it's open, at least – is the **Flood Museum** which is housed in the old Atchinson, Topeka & Santa Fe Passenger and Freight Complex building which dates back to 1910. The station was closed in 1968 but the building is now used to tell the story of Fort Madison's frequently unsuccessful attempts to tame the Mississippi River. The town was flooded as recently as 1993 but better flood defenses have since been built.

Where to stay

The least expensive options are: *Super 8 Motel* (☎ 319-372-8500; ❷-❸) on Highway 61 West; *Santa Fe Motel* (☎ 319-372-1310; ❸) at 2639 Avenue L; and the *Best Western Iowan Motor Lodge* (☎ 319-372-7510; ❹) also on Highway 61 West. Bed and breakfasts include: the good value *Coffey House* (☎ 319-372-1656; ❹) at 1020 Avenue D; *Kountry Klassics* (☎ 319-372-5484; ❸-❹) which, despite its terrible name, is also reasonable; *Mississippi Rose and Thistle Inn* (☎ 319-372-7044; ❸-❹) at 532 Avenue F, a step up from Kountry Klassics; and best of the lot, though more of a hotel than a bed and breakfast, *Kingsley Inn* (☎ 319-372-7074; ❹) overlooking the river from 707 Avenue H.

Where to eat

There are a handful of reasonable **places to eat** in town. Listed from the least expensive upwards, choose from the following: *Easter Foods and Deli* (☎ 319-372-5151) at 1802 Avenue H; *Ivy Bake Shoppe & Café* (☎ 319-372-7380) at 622 Seventh Street; *Hillside Inn Restaurant and Bar* (☎ 319-372-8676) at 1135 Avenue E; *Alpha's on the Riverfront* (☎ 319-372-1411) at 709 Avenue H; and *Fort Madison's Country Club* (☎ 319-372-1765) at 140 High Point.

Moving on — Keokuk and Fort Madison to Burlington

From Fort Madison, Highway 61 continues to wind north for a further 20 miles into the town of Burlington. Few could deny that the landscape along this stretch of the Blues Highway lacks the rich, fertile beauty of Missouri. If you're travelling from the south, the feeling of entering the colder, more business-like north is tangible. People speak faster, service is quicker; that Southern sleepiness is wearing off.

Burlington

The largest town between Hannibal and Davenport, a community has existed at Burlington since 1805. In 1938 blossoming Burlington became the first Territorial Capital of Iowa. Although political prominence was short-lived, Burlington is still a likeable and relatively lively backwater. For Burlington **tourist information**, head for 807 Jefferson Street.

Burlington even hides a little **jazz history**. As a river-town, Burlington was used to paddlesteamers chugging past. In the early years of the twentieth century, of course, many of those paddlesteamers had onboard jazz bands led by the likes of Fate Marable. Many of New Orleans' brightest jazz stars, including Louis Armstrong, played on the riverboats.

Years later Satchmo took part in the 1964 Burlington Jazz Festival organized by local jazz enthusiast Dan Beid. Beid was also successful in wooing several other legendary names in jazz to what was, in fairness, a rather low-key event. They included Al Hirt, Art Hodes – who had jammed with the greatest Iowan of all time, Bix Beiderbecke – and Lionel Hampton.

What to see

The **Jazz Festival**, now named in Beid's honor, takes place every year in mid-June on the eve of the **Steamboat Days Festival** which showcases a number of musical styles.

Beyond the festival, Burlington doesn't offer music lovers a great deal except, that is, for a **blues joint** – the Blues Shop (☎ 319-758-9553) – at 320 North Fourth Street. Owned by David Hazel, whose father Pat is a well-known local bluesman, the Blues Shop is a snug, neat place which features live music most weekends. Bring your own liquor.

There are very few 'attractions' in Burlington worth stopping to explore. **Snake Alley**, for example, is pushed by the town as 'the crookedest street in the world' but is, in reality, nothing more than a zig-zag path. Like Fort Madison, Burlington benefits from an annual influx of **bald eagles** but unless you're here for the music festival, there really is nothing else worth stopping for except, perhaps, a bite to eat or a night's sleep.

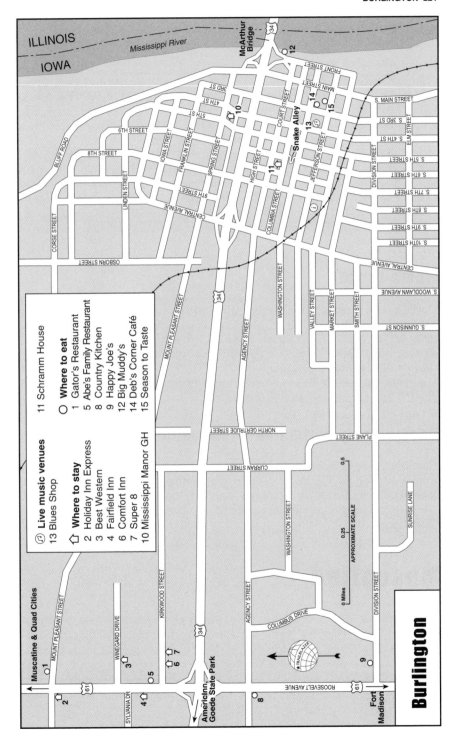

Burlington

Live music venues
13 Blues Shop

Where to stay
2 Holiday Inn Express
3 Best Western
4 Fairfield Inn
6 Comfort Inn
7 Super 8
10 Mississippi Manor GH

11 Schramm House

○ **Where to eat**
1 Gator's Restaurant
5 Abe's Family Restaurant
8 Country Kitchen
9 Happy Joe's
12 Big Muddy's
14 Deb's Corner Café
15 Season to Taste

Where to stay

Reasonable value places to stay are easy to find in Burlington. The four main chain options are: *Best Western* (☎ 319-753-2223), 3001 Winegard Drive, where kids under 18 stay free; *Holiday Inn Express* (☎ 319-752-0000), 1605 Roosevelt, with a heated pool; *Comfort Inn* (☎ 319-753-0000), 3051 Kirkwood Street, also with a pool; and *Fairfield Inn* (☎ 319-754-0000), 1213 North Roosevelt, with an indoor pool and, again, where kids under 18 stay free.

Budget choices include the *AmericInn* (☎ 319-758-9000; ❷) at Gear Street and Highway 34 and the *Super 8* (☎ 319-752-9806; ❷-❸) at 3001 Kirkwood Street. There are two **bed and breakfasts** in town, the *Mississippi Manor Guest Inn* (☎ 319-753-2218; ❸) at 809 North Fourth Street and *Schramm House* (☎ 319-754-0373; ❹) at 616 Columbia Street. Both are conveniently located and good value. **Campers** could try *Goede State Park* just 10 miles west of town.

Where to eat

Places to eat, in approximately ascending price order, include: *Abe's Family Restaurant* (☎ 319-752-7117) at 1220 North Roosevelt; *Big Muddy's* (☎ 319-753-1699) at 710 North Front Street; *Country Kitchen* (☎ 319-753-2853) at 3313 Agency Road; *Deb's Corner Café* (☎ 319-753-1190) at 320 North Third Street; *Gator's Restaurant and Lounge* (☎ 319-753-2534) at 2750 Mount Pleasant Street; *Happy Joe's* (☎ 319-753-1665) at 3110 Division; and *Season to Taste* (☎ 319-753-2345) at 218 Jefferson Street.

Moving on — Burlington to Muscatine

The 50-mile drive from Burlington to Muscatine follows an almost perfectly straight stretch of Highway 61 through Mediapolis, which sounds like a comic-book city but is, in fact, tiny, Newport, Wapello and Fruitland before rolling into Muscatine – the last town of any size before Davenport and the Quad Cities.

Muscatine

Overlooking a 90-degree bend in the Mississippi, Muscatine is a comfortable river-port which claims a 'small town feel, big city attitude'. Muscatine also labels itself the 'Pearl of the Mississippi' because at the turn of the last century this was the center of the world's pearl button industry – a slightly esoteric claim to fame, admittedly, but one of which Muscatine is proud. Modern Muscatine is quietly welcoming and a pleasant enough place to break one's journey.

What to see

Not surprisingly, local points of interest include a **Pearl Button Museum** at 206 West Second Street. The museum charts the rise and fall of Muscatine's button industry from the 1890s, when German immigrant John Boepple started making buttons from clam shells, to the forties. Some might rather spend an afternoon at the **Muscatine Art Center** at 1314 Mulberry Avenue, however, where the impressive permanent collection includes works by Chagall, Renoir, Matisse and Degas.

Other attractions are more rural. A few miles south of town on Highway 61, **Muscatine Island** is a particularly fertile stretch of land where a number of markets sell high quality, fresh produce such as melons, cantaloupes, tomatoes and sweetcorn. If this taste of Iowan farming leaves you keen to find out more, agricultural tours can be arranged through the Convention & Visitors' Bureau (☎ 319-263-8895) at 319 East Second Street. The helpful CVB staff can also provide general **tourist information**.

Where to stay

Options include a *Comfort Inn* (☎ 319-263-1500; ❸) at 115 Cleveland Street, a *Fairfield Inn* (☎ 319-264-5566; ❹) at 305 Cleveland Street and a *Holiday Inn* (☎ 319-264-5550; ❹) at-2915 Highway 61 North. **Cheaper** possibilities are a *Super 8 Motel* (☎ 319-263-9100; ❷-❸) at 2900 Highway 61 North, an *Econo-Lodge Motel* (☎ 319-264-3337; ❷) at 2402 Park Avenue or the *Muskie Motel* (☎ 319-263-2601; ❸) at 1620 Park Avenue.

Muscatine has just one **bed and breakfast**. It's *Strawberry Farm* (☎ 319-262-8688; ❹) at 3402 Tipton Road, a lovely place run by Karl and Linda Reichert. **Campers** will find *Fairport State Park* five miles east of Muscatine. It's a small site wedged between the road and river but it has full hook-ups.

Where to eat

With some 60 restaurants and fast-food joints crammed into a relatively small area, there are plenty of **places to eat**. In approximately ascending price order, try: *Snackers* (☎ 319-264-8059) at 206 East Second Street, serving lunch and shoeshines; *Mary's Downtown Café* (☎ 319-263-9813) at 220 Walnut Street with good lunch specials; *Dillons Bar-B-Que* (☎ 319-262-8838) at 1109 Grandview Avenue; *MataMoro's Mexican Restaurant* (☎ 319-263-3188) at 114 East Second Street; *Country Kitchen* (☎ 319-263-8832) at 2406 Park Avenue; *Bootleggers* (☎ 319-264-2686) at 214 Iowa Avenue with 'beer and wing' specials on Saturdays; *Missipi Brewing Company* (☎ 319-262-5004) at 107 Iowa Avenue; *Golden Corral* (☎ 319-263-1740) at 2300 Park Avenue for steaks; *Good Earth* (☎ 319-288-9626) at 5900 Grandview Avenue; or *The Elms* (☎ 319-263-8123) at 2108 Grandview Avenue.

Moving on — Muscatine to Davenport (Quad Cities)

From Muscatine it's an easy 30-mile drive through Sweetland and Pleasant Prairie into Davenport and the Quad Cities. If you're heading north, Davenport marks the spot where the Blues Highway leaves Highway 61 and the Mississippi River. Both the river and 61 continue north into Wisconsin and on to the source of the Mighty Mississippi. Blues and jazzmen, of course, made Chicago their goal. If you're heading south, Davenport marks the point on the Blues Highway where you'll get your first glimpse both of the great river and Highway 61, which will lead you all the way south to the Gulf of Mexico.

Davenport and the Quad Cities

Davenport, Iowa is the largest of five towns which make up the 'Quad Cities'. The others are Bettendorf, Iowa and Rock Island, Moline and East Moline, Illinois. When seen on a map these five towns create a quadrangle bisected by the Mississippi. The Quad Cities form a lively, accommodating and memorable place. Imposing brick buildings, cold streets and noisy industry make it a sort of miniature Chicago. And as the home of Bix Beiderbecke, one of the brightest stars to grace the American musical stage, Davenport's place both in jazz history and on the Blues Highway is assured.

History

Long before European settlers first gazed across the central Mississippi valley, Sauk Indians had established Saukenuk, the largest Indian settlement in North America, on the site which would become Rock Island.

When Europeans did come, however, their arrival meant catastrophe for the Indians. In 1789 American troops destroyed Saukenuk because its people had shown loyalty towards British traders. One young Indian, Black Hawk, refused to accept the appropriation of his people's land and grew up to lead a series of revolts against settlers. In 1832 Black Hawk became the only man in US history to have a war named after him when, with 1000 warriors, he fought back against the frontiersmen. Outnumbered and ill equipped, Black Hawk soon conceded defeat and surrendered all the Sauk and Mesquakie lands, some six million acres, to the United States in what was labeled the 'Black Hawk Purchase'.

The same period saw the Quad Cities experience a mass influx of immigrants from Germany, Holland, Belgium, Britain and Ireland. Many of the German settlers came from Schleswig-Holstein where a border dispute with

(Opposite) BB King's club in Memphis (TN) is a Beale Street stalwart and a showcase for local blues stars. See p158.

Denmark had made life increasingly difficult. With a growing number of capable workers, steamboat transportation and the arrival of the 'iron horse', industry grew apace in the Quad Cities. Lumber, mining and agriculture all became major employers.

Many more were employed by either the steamboat or railroad industries which were locked in fierce competition. That competition often grew ugly. In one instance a young Abraham Lincoln represented the railroad in a case against a steamboat company which had allegedly used one of its tugs to ram a railroad bridge. Those bridges, incidentally, are themselves of historical interest. The bridge between Rock Island and Davenport, built in 1856, was the first railroad bridge to span the Mississippi.

One young entrepreneur, John Deere, moved his new plow business to Moline against this backdrop of industrial growth. Deere's invention, a self-cleaning plow, was the first product of Deere & Company which has, of course, gone on to become a major multinational corporation and one of the world's leading manufacturers of agricultural machinery.

Another aspect of Quad Cities history also deserves a few lines. The Rock Island Arsenal was built as a fort in 1817 but became an arsenal towards the end of the nineteenth century. By the time of the Second World War, it employed 18,000 people and produced tanks, ordinance and guns. Today the arsenal is still an important military installation. The five towns which comprise the Quad Cities have a combined population of 400,000 and remain centers for industry, agriculture and river transportation.

History of jazz music in Davenport

The Rock Island Line is no more, the Company having been liquidated in the eighties, but the name lives on in the eponymous title of a well-known 'skiffle' ballad. Skiffle music is almost forgotten but it did enjoy a fairly significant cult following in the fifties and early sixties as a collective derivation of blues, ragtime and folk music often played on home-built or improvised instruments.

Rock Island itself is today a center of US military activity with few, if any, musical pretensions although, over the years, the town has produced a number of blues musicians who have achieved at least local fame. Some miles to the north-west, up the Rock River, lies Rock Falls. In 1924 Rock Falls was the birthplace of Louis Balassoni who, as jazz drummer Louis Bellson, achieved great fame from the forties onwards with the bands of Benny Goodman, Tommy Dorsey, Harry James and Duke Ellington. He later married singer Pearl Bailey, toured with the excellent Jazz at the Philharmonic and was successful as a musical director, composer and teacher. However, his lasting claim to fame remains as one of the foremost big band drummers of his generation.

(Opposite) A tug captain prepares to negotiate the bridges of the Quad Cities. The Blues Highway traces the Mississippi River from New Orleans to Davenport (IA) before racing east to Chicago. Migrant musicians would take the river, road or train to leave the South.

Davenport will forever occupy a prominent place in the history of jazz – and for one specific reason. On 10 March 1903 Leon Bix Beiderbecke (see box p233) was born to one of the many Iowan families of German descent.

Arrival and departure

By air

Quad Cities International Airport (☎ 309-764-9621, 🖳 www.qcairport.com), 2200 69th Avenue, is close to downtown Moline just south of the Rock River. Follow the I-74 south to junction 18 to find it. The airport is served by several major carriers, United, TWA, Northwest and Midwest, but the 'international' tag seems to be something of a misnomer. To get beyond America you'll need to fly TWA to St Louis or AirTran to Atlanta and then connect from there.

By bus

Greyhounds use the terminal at 304 West River Drive (☎ 309-326-5127). There are around six services a day to Chicago, a four-hour journey, and three a day south to St Louis, a journey of between six and ten hours.

By car

Highway 61 is the main north-south route through the Quad Cities on the Iowan side; on the Illinois side I-74 runs south to Galesburg. Interstate 80, an important east-west artery, connects the Quad Cities to Des Moines, Omaha and, eventually, San Francisco to the west and passes south of Chicago to the east. Interstate 88 is the recommended connection between Chicago and the Quad Cities.

Orientation

Getting orientated here isn't immediately easy. For a start, there are five cities in the Quad – not four as one might be forgiven for assuming. Each is technically separate but visitors would be wise to think of the Quad Cities as one place. Two of the five are on the Iowan side of the Mississippi, Davenport and Bettendorf, while three are on the Illinois side, Rock Island, Moline and East Moline. People get confused because the lack of bridges across the Mississippi can force drivers to follow fairly complicated routes to get somewhere which one might imagine to be easy. Use the map on p227 and you'll be all right. *(Continued on p230).*

KEY TO MAP BELOW

⇧ **WHERE TO STAY**
1 Comfort Inn
2 Best Western Steeplegate Inn
3 Super 8 – Davenport
4 Days Inn – North
5 Holiday Inn
6 Courtyard by Marriott
7 Jumer's Castle Lodge
8 Hampton Inn
9 Fairfield Inn
10 Days Inn – East
11 Econo-Lodge
12 Holiday Inn
17 Fairfield Inn
18 Comfort Inn
19 La Quinta Motor Inn
20 Holiday Inn Express
21 Hampton Inn
23 Super 8 – East Moline
24 Super 8 – Le Claire

🎵 **LIVE MUSIC VENUES**
15 O'Meara's
22 The Palace

OTHER
13 Rock Island Military Museum
14 Confederate Cemetery
16 Black Hawk State Historic Site
25 Buffalo Bill Cody Museum

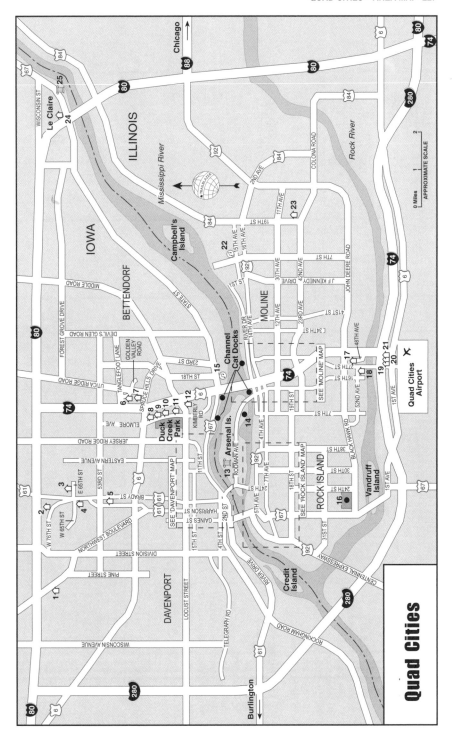

Quad Cities

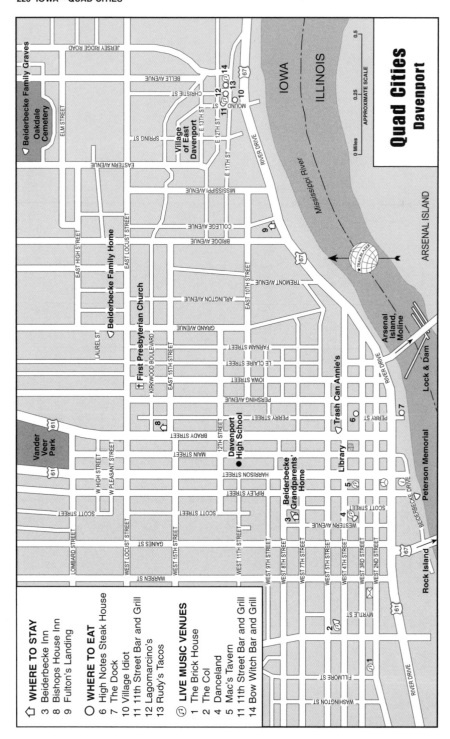

Quad Cities
Davenport

WHERE TO STAY
3 Beiderbecke Inn
8 Bishops House Inn
9 Fulton's Landing

WHERE TO EAT
6 High Notes Steak House
7 The Dock
10 Village Idiot
11 11th Street Bar and Grill
12 Lagomarcino's
13 Rudy's Tacos

LIVE MUSIC VENUES
1 The Brick House
2 The Col
4 Danceland
5 Mac's Tavern
11 11th Street Bar and Grill
14 Bow Witch Bar and Grill

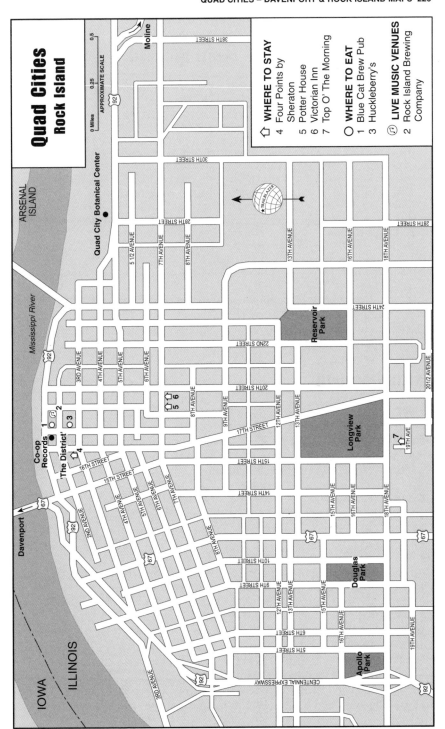

Quad Cities
Rock Island

APPROXIMATE SCALE

0 Miles   0.25   0.5

Moline

Davenport

Mississippi River

ARSENAL ISLAND

Quad City Botanical Center

IOWA
ILLINOIS

Apollo Park

Douglas Park

Longview Park

Reservoir Park

Co-op Records

'The District'

WHERE TO STAY
4 Four Points by Sheraton
5 Potter House
6 Victorian Inn
7 Top O' The Morning

WHERE TO EAT
1 Blue Cat Brew Pub
3 Huckleberry's

LIVE MUSIC VENUES
2 Rock Island Brewing Company

Quad Cities — events and festivals

● **May** – Quad Cities Jazz Festival. For more information on this three-day event held every year in mid-May, call ☎ 319-391-0459.

● **May** – Hornucopia Music Festival. Any band which features a horn player qualifies to participate in this two-day music and hot food festival in Rock Island's entertainment district. Call ☎ 309-788-6311 for details.

● **June** – Mississippi Valley Blues Festival. See p239.

● **July** – Rock Island Summerfest.

Another three-day event designed to lift the District, Rock Island, the Summerfest features food, games and some 30 bands. Call ☎ 309-788-6311 for information.

● **July** – Bix Beiderbecke Memorial Jazz Festival. See p239.

● **August** – Great Mississippi Tugfest. A giant tug-o'-war contest between Illinois and Iowa in which ten teams compete takes place every year during mid-August.

(Continued from p226). Davenport is the largest of the Quads and, for jazz lovers, the most significant area. The 'Village of East Davenport' is a lively entertainment hub. Rock Island has another vibrant entertainment area labeled simply 'the District'. Moline is home to the John Deere empire.

Getting around

By car

For car rentals try **Avis** (☎ 309-762-3605) at the airport and at 430 West 76th Street, Davenport, **Budget** (☎ 309-762-4110) at the airport and 612 Kimberley Road, Bettendorf or **Enterprise** (☎ 319-398-000) at 4437 North Brady Street, Davenport and 2001 State Street, Bettendorf.

By cab

Call Metro Cabs (☎ 309-787 1500), Lucky Cabs (☎ 319-381-8182) or Buddy Bo Cabs (☎ 309-755-5266).

By bus

Local buses are of limited use for visitors but for information on the Davenport Citibus and the Quad Cities Metrolink call ☎ 309-788-7515.

By water taxi

'Quad Citians', as they like to be called, have overcome their watery divide with the help of the popular **Channel Cat** water taxi which runs between Leach Park, Bettendorf, the Village of East Davenport, John Deere Commons, Moline and Celebration Belle Landing, Moline everyday except Mondays. Fares are $3.50 for adults and $1.50 for children. The boat stops in Bettendorf at 15 minutes past the hour and reaches each subsequent stop at 15-minute intervals.

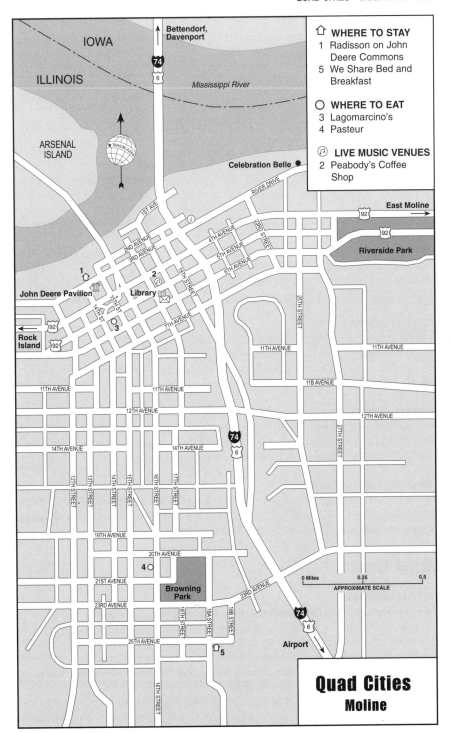

Quad Cities
Moline

By tour

Prominent tour outfits include **Parsall Tours** (☎ 309-935-6024), **Tri-State Tours** (☎ 319-359-1682), **Quad Cities Tours** (☎ 309-762-9665) or **Red Carpet Enterprises** (☎ 309-534-8380). MetroLink offers historical **tours by trolley** from Thursdays to Sundays for $8 per person. The trip takes in Arsenal Island, Rock Island and Moline. Call ☎ 309-764-4257 for more details.

Services

Banks

If you're having trouble finding an ATM, head over to Metrobank at 1313 East River Drive, Northwest Bank and Trust at 100 East Kimberley Road or Midwest Bank at 3637 23rd Avenue in Moline.

Communications

● **Post** Main post offices are located at 514 17th Street in Moline and 933 West Second Street in Davenport.
● **Internet** Libraries with Internet access can be found at 504 17th Street in Moline and 321 Main Street in Davenport.

Tourist information

Quad Cities CVB keeps offices on both sides of the river. On the Illinois side you'll find them at 2021 River Drive in Moline. On the Iowan side, head for 102 South Harrison Street in Davenport. The number for either office is ☎ 309-788-7800.

Record stores

Co-op Records, a local chain, has a number of outlets in the Midwest including a large store on 18th Street, Rock Island, in the heart of the District. Co-op Records stocks a reasonable collection of jazz and blues.

Medical emergencies

If you need medical help head for the **Genesis Medical Center** (☎ 319-421-1000) at 1227 East Rusholme Street in Davenport or the **Trinity Medical Center** at 500 John Deere Road in Moline.

What to see

Jazz landmarks

Bix Beiderbecke's father built the **Beiderbecke family home** at 1934 Grand Avenue in 1894. The Beiderbecke's were a prosperous middle-class family of German descent and the substantial house reflects their relative wealth. Bix was born in the house on Grand Avenue on 10 March 1903 and as a small boy was sent over the road to the Tyler Elementary School. His mother nurtured the young Bix's interest in music in the front room.

In 1990 the house was bought by Italian film makers Pupi and Antonio Avati. After using the property for their film on Bix the Avatis kept the house which they now use as the US office of their film company. The office is managed by the colorful Marilene McCandless. Marilene is happy to show interested visitors around the property. Call her on ☎ 319-324-4308 to make an appointment. Despite its office status, the house has changed little since it was restored for filming in 1990. Marilene will point out the room in which Bix was born and the cupboard where, after his parents deaths, a cache of unopened Bix records was found.

In life Bix's pursuit of jazz forced him apart from his disapproving family but in death the Beiderbeckes were reunited; the family is buried together in the **Oakdale Cemetery** (☎ 319-324-5121) at 2501 Eastern Avenue. Follow the main road through the cemetery till it reaches a small hill; the Beiderbecke family graves are on the left. On the Saturday of the Bix Fest Jazz Festival (see p239) a memorial is held at the grave.

Devoted fans might also want to pay a visit to the **First Presbyterian Church** on Iowa Street where the Beiderbecke family worshipped and where, on Sunday during Bix Fest, services are held at 8.30am and 10.30am which feature Bix's music. **Davenport High School** on Main Street, now Davenport Central, is the school Bix attended until he was sent to the Lake Forest Academy near Chicago. Trash Can Annie's, an antiques clothes store at 421 Brady Street, was once the **Haynes Dance Studio** where, aged 18, Bix began his performing career. The **Peterson Memorial**, on Beiderbecke Drive between

---

Bix Beiderbecke

Bix's mother was an accomplished pianist and, from his earliest years, the young Bix showed genuine musical talent, initially on the piano. Throughout his tragically short life Bix Beiderbecke retained a deep interest in the piano. It's said that at less than two years old he was able to pick out his first popular tune with unerring accuracy, although sight-reading was to escape him until his early twenties. He seemed to have been gifted with perfect pitch. As a composer he fell, like others of his generation, under the influence of Claude Debussy. His best-known works – notably his haunting *In A Mist* – clearly exhibit his interest in the impressionist harmonic language of music.

But it is as a jazz cornet player that Bix Beiderbecke will forever be remembered. Legend has it that the young Bix first heard jazz music being played on those famous riverboats of the Streckfus Line as they plied their trade from New Orleans, Memphis and St Louis towards the upper reaches of the Mississippi. Indeed, Beiderbecke himself attested to hearing no less a role-model than Louis Armstrong on one of those boats. One story has it that a young Bix, lying in bed, heard Armstrong's unwavering notes float all the way across from the river.

He also claimed to have been greatly influenced by one Emmett Hardy, New Orleans-born and a trumpet-player on the steamship *Capitol* which he first joined in Davenport. Since Hardy died of tuberculosis at the age of 22 without ever having recorded, it's now impossible to assess the degree to which the young Beiderbecke was indebted to him.
(Continued on p234)

Bix Beiderbecke (cont'd)

(Continued from p233) What is common knowledge is that the youngster was also greatly impressed by the early recordings of the Original Dixieland Jazz Band and its trumpet-lead, Nick LaRocca, another New Orleanian.

From his very early teens, Beiderbecke's innate musical talent took control of his whole life and by the age of 19 he had dropped out of the prestigious Lake Forest Academy to which his relatively well-heeled parents had dispatched him the previous year. They were less than pleased. But for Bix the place was just too near Chicago's South Side where the opportunities to hear and play jazz were too many and too tempting. Almost everyone who was anyone in the jazz world of the twenties found his or her way to Chicago.

From clubs to outdoor festivities in Chicago's many parks or the summer season's excursions on Lake Michigan, Beiderbecke lost no opportunity to play. Indeed, it was on one of those excursions that he came across a budding prodigy of jazz clarinet; Chicago-born Benny Goodman, then a mere 14-year-old and still in short pants.

Bix graduated through a string of Midwest bands to wider attention. His first recordings were made with the young all-white Wolverine Orchestra in 1924. From that point till his early death from alcoholism and consequent pneumonia a mere seven years later, he played and recorded almost continuously with such famous names as Frankie Trumbauer, Jean Goldkette, Paul Whiteman and Glen Gray's Casa Loma Orchestra.

Fully appreciated in life by only a relatively small number of fellow musicians and jazz enthusiasts, his name began to acquire almost legendary status with the publication of Dorothy Baker's novel *Young Man with a Horn* in 1938. The book was only loosely based on Beiderbecke's life but, according to the definitive *New Grove Dictionary of Jazz*, it: 'soon came to symbolize the "Roaring Twenties" in the popular imagination. Only in recent years have legend and fact become separated and Beiderbecke's career and achievements been seen in a true perspective'.

In contrast to that restrained epitaph are the almost poetic descriptions of his musical style by contemporaries. One early admirer described Beiderbecke's cornet playing as 'like shooting bullets at a bell'. Composer and pianist Hoagy Carmichael came up with a similar comment of 'a chime struck by a mallet', while Eddie Condon slightly lowered the tone but arguably made a more memorable statement when he reflected that Bix's sound 'came out like a girl saying "yes"'.

Although he made a conscious break from the place of his birth (and, indeed, from his family), it's obvious that Bix recognized the debt he owed to both. One of his most famous compositions – indeed one of the finest jazz melodies – remains the poignant *Davenport Blues*. And Davenport, in turn, has recognized the importance and enduring popularity of its most famous son. But for all the adulation that has surrounded the name of Bix Beiderbecke over the years, perhaps the saddest commentary of all is that, after their deaths, there were found among his parents' effects copies of every one of Bix's records, proudly and lovingly sent to them as they were produced. Not one had even been unwrapped.

the Freight House and the river, is a memorial to Bix and a permanent stone stage which is used for outdoor concerts. In his earliest years, Bix spent a good deal of time at his **grandparents' home** at 532 West Seventh Street on the corner of Western Avenue. That property is now a bed and breakfast (see p237).

Two of the Quad Cities most cherished music landmarks, the great **Col** and **Danceland** ballrooms, are drenched in music history. Since both are still going strong, however, they are described in more detail on p239 as part of the section on live music venues.

Other highlights

Given the importance of local Indian nations the Sauks and the Mesquakie to the history of the central Mississippi valley, it would be a shame to miss the **Black Hawk State Historic Site** (☎ 309-788-0177; donations) which sprawls over 208 acres of south Rock Island overlooking the Rock River. Indians occupied this site for thousands of years until 1832 when the Black Hawk war was lost. Black Hawk himself earned a reputation as a fearless warrior and champion of the Sauks. A small museum on the site tells the story of the Sauk and Mesquakie peoples.

John Deere's is one of the most famous names to have come out of the Quad Cities. Today the John Deere Company dominates the agricultural equipment business and it all started with a plow factory in Moline, Illinois in 1848. If you've traveled north to the Quad Cities along the Blues Highway, you'll already have seen countless distinctive green John Deere tractors plowing flat Delta fields and farmers in bars with weather-worn Deere caps perched on the backs of their heads.

The Deere name is important in country bordering the Mississippi which is why huge numbers flock to see the **John Deere Pavilion** (☎ 309-765-1000; Mon-Fri 9am-6pm, Sat 9am-5pm, Sun 12.30-5pm; free) at 1400 River Drive, Moline. The Pavilion, a glass and copper barn-shaped building, houses a collection of Deere machines from past and present. The thought of spending a morning looking at tractors might not appeal immediately, but the Deere display is well worth exploring. The simple childish fun to be had from clambering inside a massive harvesting machine surprises most visitors.

Arsenal Island occupies much of the Mississippi between Rock Island and Davenport and is home to the Rock Island Arsenal military horde. The Rock Island Arsenal Military Museum (☎ 309-782-5021; free) has a vast collection of small firearms for anyone interested in weaponry.

Visitors can also gasp at the scale of the Commanding General's house, the largest Government-owned home in the States after the White House. One can also tour the Confederate Cemetery; the island was a prisoner of war camp during the Civil War during which time many captured Southern soldiers died from wounds or disease. Apart from that grisly thought and its destructive role, Arsenal Island is a pleasant and green part of town used by locals for its parkland.

The *Celebration Belle*, a mock-paddlesteamer, offers lunch, dinner and day-long cruises on the Mississippi. Buffet-style food is served to the sounds of a cover band while passengers admire the view from the sundeck. It would be difficult to recommend the Celebration Belle on gourmet or even musical grounds but the views are outstanding. The boat is moored at 2501 River Drive (☎ 309-764-1952). Lunch cruises cost $20.00, day-long 100-mile cruises cost $125.00.

Of the other main attractions, the **Quad City Botanical Center** (☎ 309-794-0991; Mon-Sat 10am-5pm, Sun 1-5pm; $3.50) at 2524 Fourth Avenue in Rock Island is perhaps the best. A 6444 square foot 'sun garden' conservatory showcases plants from over 100 tropical destinations.

You might also like to check out the **Buffalo Bill Cody Museum** (☎ 319-289-5880) in Le Claire, Iowa, just a couple of miles east of Bettendorf. Bill Cody was born here and the house now displays various Buffalo Bill-related artifacts. Bill Cody earned his catchy moniker because he was employed by a railroad company to slay buffalo to feed thousands of hungry railroad workers. He was extremely good at his job; he killed over 4000 buffalo and no doubt perfected his aim in the process.

Where to stay

Accommodations are easy to find and, with an average room rate of $46, fairly cheap. Many of the main chains are here, some more than once, and there are several excellent bed and breakfasts.

Budget options
Cheap motels include three branches of *Super 8* (❷-❸) at 410 East 65th Street, Davenport (☎ 319-388-9810), 2201 John Deere Road, East Moline (☎ 309-796-1999) and 1522 Welcome Center Drive, Le Claire (☎ 319-289-5888) just east of Bettendorf.

Other low-cost motels include *La Quinta Motor Inn* (☎ 309-762-9008; ❸) at 5450 27th Street and the *Econo-Lodge* (☎ 319-355-6471; ❷-❸) at 2205 Kimberley Road, Bettendorf.

Mid-range options ($50-120)
The best of the bed and breakfasts are the Italianate 1871 mansion *Fulton's Landing* (☎ 319-322-4069; ❹) at 1206 East River Drive, Davenport, with impressive views over the Mississippi, and the *Victorian Inn* (☎ 309-788-7068; ❸) at 702 20th Street, Rock Island.

The two largest places in town, both with six well-appointed rooms and both in Rock Island, are *Potter House* (☎ 309-788-1906; ❸) at 1906 Seventh Avenue and *Top O' The Morning* (☎ 309-786 3513; ❸) at 1505 19th Avenue.

Hotel price codes

Hotel and motels price bands used in this book reflect the range of prices charged for a double room.

❶ – $10-25	❷ – $26-50	❸ – $51-85	❹ – $86-120
❺ – $121-180	❻ – $181-250	❼ – $251+	

See p22 for more information.

Otherwise you might try *We Share Bed and Breakfast* (☎ 309-762-7059; ❸-❹) at 1860 25th Avenue in Moline or *Bishops House Inn* (☎ 319-322-8303; ❸-❹) at 1527 Brady Street, Davenport, another 1871 mansion similar in style to Fulton's Landing. Fans of Bix might prefer to stay at the *Beiderbecke Inn* (☎ 319-323-0047; ❹), 532 West Seventh Street, a grand Victorian 'painted lady' which once belonged to Bix Beiderbecke's grandparents.

High-end options ($120-250)

Jumer's Castle Lodge (☎ 319-359-7141; ❹-❺) at 900 Spruce Hills Drive, Bettendorf is one of the Quad's best large hotels. Management, staff and decor conspire to create a mock-Bavarian atmosphere and German cuisine is a specialty. Another of the better big hotels is the *Radisson on John Deere Commons* (☎ 309-764-1000; ❺) at 1415 River Drive, Moline where you'll find all the amenities and the high standards of service you would expect from a hotel of this stature.

Where to eat

For cheap snackfood the two **Lagomarcino's** restaurants – one at 1422 Fifth Avenue, Moline (☎ 309-764-1814) the other at 2132 East 11th Street, Davenport (☎ 319-324-6137) – are hard to beat. A local favourite for years, the Lagomarcino restaurants are an hybrid of an ice cream parlor, a confectionery store and a café. For those without a sweet-tooth the menu offers sandwiches – including an excellent peanut butter and jelly sandwich for $2.50 – and soups.

A more substantial plateful can be found at *Huckleberry's* (☎ 309-786-1122) at 223 18th Street, Rock Island. Huckleberry's specializes in folded 'calzone' pizzas. Another pizza joint, *Village Idiot* (☎ 319-326-1532) at 1029

Quad Cities — chain hotels

- *Best Western Steeplegate Inn* (☎ 319-386-6900), 100 West 76th Street, Davenport
- *Comfort Inn* (☎ 319-391-8222), 7222 North West Boulevard, Davenport
- *Comfort Inn* (☎ 309-762-7000), 2600 52nd Avenue, Moline
- *Courtyard by Marriott* (☎ 319-355-3999), 895 Golden Valley Drive, Bettendorf
- *Days Inn – East* (☎ 319-355-1190), 3202 East Kimberley Road, Davenport
- *Days Inn – North* (☎ 319-388-9999), 101 West 65th Street, Davenport
- *Fairfield Inn* (☎ 319-355-2264), 3206 East Kimberley Road, Davenport
- *Fairfield Inn* (☎ 309-762-9083), 2705-48th Avenue, Moline
- *Four Points by Sheraton* (☎ 309-794-1212), Third Avenue and 17th Street, Rock Island
- *Hampton Inn* (☎ 319-359-3921), 3330 East Kimberley Road, Davenport
- *Hampton Inn* (☎ 309-762-1711), 6920 27th Street, Moline
- *Holiday Inn* (☎ 319-355-4761), 909 Middle Road, Bettendorf
- *Holiday Inn* (☎ 319-319-1230), 5202 Brady Street, Davenport
- *Holiday Inn Express* (☎ 309-762-8300), 6910 27th Street, Moline

Interview – Michael 'Hawkeye' Herman

What part have the Quad Cities played in the development of jazz and blues?

The first tune on my CD *Blues Alive* is called *Great River Road*. There was a time when the Mississippi River was the road. The steamboats took people to this part of the country from New Orleans. The music on the boats influenced all of the river towns all the way up.

Michael 'Hawkeye' Herman, originally from Davenport, Iowa, is a leading blues performer and blues educator.

When you leave New Orleans you travel through Vicksburg, Clarksdale, Memphis, St Louis and the Quad Cities. All the way up the river, for five or ten miles on either side, jazz and blues music influenced the population. The best examples are the two most influential early jazz trumpet players, Louis Armstrong and Bix Beiderbecke. Bix was born and raised here in Davenport – not what one would consider a hotbed of jazz. But Bix came down to Davenport and listened to the music that was coming off the steamboats that docked here. As a result of Bix hearing people like Louis Armstrong and 'King' Oliver on those boats, he became influenced by the music and so became one of the greatest, sweetest cornet players that America's ever produced. That's a classic example of how river travel and rail travel moved the music of all the communities along the Mississippi River all the way from New Orleans to the north. The same is true in blues.

There's never been a large black community here in the Quad Cities but blues has always been available. I remember Muddy Waters saying he remembered playing in Rock Island in 1961. I'm back here today because, although I left to be in the thick of blues on the West Coast, I found out in 1985 that there was a blues festival here in Davenport. I got in touch with the Mississippi Valley Blues Society here and asked to come back and play. One of the greatest Blues festivals in the world is right here.

Mound Street in the Village of East Davenport, serves reasonable value 'Wise Guys' pizzas which are nothing if not filling. Another Village of East Davenport restaurant, the **11th Street Bar and Grill** (☎ 319-322-9047) at 2109 East 11th Street and featured in the live music section, serves good sandwiches and boasts the 'best onion rings in town'. Nearby, and a break from American fare, **Rudy's Tacos** (☎ 319-322-0668) at 2214 East 11th Street serves decent Mexican cuisine.

Over in the District, Rock Island the **Blue Cat Brew Pub** (☎ 309-788-8247) is a step up. Entrées here are pretty good; the ribeye steak ($16.95) and grilled pork tenderloin ($6.95) can be excellent. There are also six home-brewed beers to choose from. If it's steaks you're after, you could try the **High Notes Steak House** (☎ 319-328-6000) at 200 East Third Street, Davenport which dishes up enormous and high quality steaks to tables packed with eager carnivores. For something very different, **Pasteur** (☎ 309-797-6336) at 2035-2037 16th Street,

Blues and Bix

The **Bix Beiderbecke Memorial Jazz Festival** has been held in Davenport every year since its foundation in 1972. This outstanding musical event features the famous 'Bix Bash' party in the Col Ballroom on the eve of every festival, a jazz liturgy in the church where the Beiderbeckes worshipped, a Bix Youth Band made up of talented young performers drawn from Quad Cities high schools and, of course, hours and hours of quality swing and jazz music. The festival is organized by the Bix Beiderbecke Memorial Society and is held in July. To contact the BBMS call ☎ 319-324-7170 or write to Box 3688 Davenport, Iowa 52808.

Another highly active local music organization, the Mississippi Valley Blues Society, has been presenting the **Mississippi Valley Blues Festival** since 1984. Twice labeled 'Blues Organization of the Year' by the Blues Foundation, the MVBS event regularly attracts some of the greatest names in blues to its growing summer festival. In 2000 alone, featured acts included Bobby 'Blue' Bland, Snooky Prior, Roomful of Blues, Ruth Brown and Matt 'Guitar' Murphy. Most years will see a zydeco or gospel group as well. The festival takes place on the weekend before or after 4 July and is held on the riverfront in Davenport. For more information about the MVBS or the festival, call ☎ 319-32 BLUES or write to MVBS, 318 Brady Street, Davenport, Iowa 52801.

Moline serves outstanding Vietnamese cuisine at very reasonable prices. Expect to pay $7-9 for an entrée. The Nguyen family who owns the restaurant provide the best service in the Quads.

For a more upscale dining experience, head for *The Dock* (☎ 319-322-5331) at 125 South Perry Street, Davenport. Built right on the river, the Dock has great views, superb food and attentive service. The raspberry duck ($16.95) and salmon *en croute* ($18.95) are recommended. If you sit next to a river-view window you might find the fast-running water so close to eye level creates the sensation of moving downriver which is a little unsettling at first.

Where to find live music

The two Grand Old Ladies of the Quad Cities' music scene are the Col and Danceland dancehalls. These are vast, elegant rooms that have, over the years, witnessed performances by some of America's greatest musicians. Both are interesting to visit as music landmarks and live gigs are still presented at both so check out the latest *River Cities' Reader*, the Quad Cities best newsweekly with entertainment listings, to find out who's playing while you're in town.

Danceland (☎ 319-323-5500), Fourth and Scott Streets, has seen Bix Beiderbecke himself perform on its stage and is today, after extensive renovation, a fine dancehall with a capacity for 1000 people. Look hard and you can still make out the old 'Danceland' sign painted on the side of the building. The

Quad Cities — radio stations

WXLP 96.9 FM plays blues all day Sunday, WVIK 90.3 FM has late-night jazz on Saturdays and Mix 96 at 96.1 FM has a Sunday 'jazz brunch'.

Col (☎ 319-322-4431), 1012 West Fourth Street, Davenport, was opened in 1914 and has hosted, among many others, Duke Ellington, Louis Armstrong, Glen Miller, Count Basie, Jimi Hendrix, BB King and Jerry Lee Lewis. During the evenings the Col is lit only by chandeliers and a disco ball.

One of the Quad's most popular venues for rock, blues and jazz is the **Rock Island Brewing Company** (☎ 309-793-1999), 1815 Second Avenue, Rock Island, in the District. 'Ribco' is open every night till three am with live music on Tuesdays, Thursdays, Fridays and Saturdays. It's a lively place with a massive range of beers and a young crowd keen to sample them. Over in Bettendorf, *O'Meara's* (☎ 319-359-7888), 1733 State Street, is a no-frills Irish bar with an outstanding open mic blues jam on Tuesday nights. Live music is often presented at weekends, too. There are quite a number of talented blues musicians in the Quads but the best, Michael 'Hawkeye' Herman, now lives in California. Hawkeye does make regular trips back to Davenport, however, so look out for him.

Scattered around town are a number of other bars and pubs which present live blues more or less regularly. *The Palace* (☎ 309-755 2157), 701 15th Avenue, East Moline, has a good Sunday night blues jam session with no cover charge. Expect to see some of the same faces from O'Meara's. Another bar, *The Brick House* (☎ 319-323-9212) at 1334 West Second Street, Davenport opposite the Kraft factory, presents regular blues to an enthusiastic blue-collar crowd. *Mac's Tavern* (☎ 319-322-9487), 316 West Third Street, Davenport, is an evocative and unpretentious Irish pub which occasionally hosts live music, particularly at festival times. You might also check out *Peabody's Coffee Shop* (☎ 309-794-5282), a funky little place at 1711 Fifth Avenue in Moline, which has good jazz on Tuesday nights.

The Village of East Davenport, a trendy collection of stores, bars and restaurants overlooking Arsenal Island, has at least two bars worth checking out for live music. The **11th Street Bar and Grill** (☎ 319-322-9047), 2108 East 11th Street, has cover, rock or blues bands every Friday and Saturday night. Nearby, the **Bow Witch Bar and Grill** at 2228 East 11th Street is a snug and cozy bar with blues, jazz or folk bands on Saturday nights.

Illinois was for Southern African-Americans something of a promised land. Beyond the reach of the forces of discrimination which dogged life south of the Mason-Dixie line, this vast northern state offered a new start.

Chicago dominates Illinois completely; the rest of the state is a sleeping giant stirring only to heap produce and wealth into the trading centers of the Windy City from where this enormous yield is distributed across America. It is a beautiful state and, in Chicago, it has a city as exciting and rich in music history as any in the world.

Davenport (Quad Cities) to Chicago

Chicago is a 175-mile drive across Illinois on Interstate 88 from the Quad Cities. This final leg of the Blues Highway races through Dixon and Rochelle past broad and rich farmland and the seemingly endless prairie of the Midwest.

Chicago, the end of the long migration for so many jazz and bluesmen in the twentieth century, is a sprawling city. The vast majority of the state's population live in or near Chicago and its lounging suburbs will slow traffic on Interstate 88 long before you can make out the towering and instantly recognizable Chicago cityscape.

Aurora

The first of those outlying 'burbs on I-88, Aurora, is a town worth exploring in its own right. Before RCA Records built a studio in Chicago in 1940, Aurora's downtown **Leland Hotel** on Stolp Avenue was used as a temporary recording venue. John Lee 'Sonny Boy' Williamson, Tampa Red and Big Joe Williams all recorded at the Leland – indeed Sonny Boy Williamson recorded over 40 sides here.

Aurora is also home to the **Blues on the Fox Blues Festival** every July. The organizers, the Fox Valley Blues Society (⌨ www.fox valleyblues.org), usually attract an impressive line-up. In 2000 Bobby Rush, Shemekia Copeland, Shirley King and Bernard Allison played. Beyond the festival and the historic presence of the Leland Hotel, there's not a great deal to keep visitors in Aurora for long.

NORTH
61

Chicago

For hundreds of thousands of African-Americans who joined the Great Migration north along Highway 61, the Mississippi River or the Illinois Central railroad line, Chicago was both the end of a journey and the start of a dream. This powerhouse of the Midwest offered jobs, relative freedom from persecution and, for jazz and blues musicians, a new scene to conquer. For readers of this book, Chicago is the beginning or end of the Blues Highway. Either way, the city deserves to be understood in its own right, not just in the context of the Blues Highway as a place where jazz came of age and where bluesmen allowed their raw country sound to develop, but as one of the most exciting metropolitan areas in the US. With its scores of great clubs, wealth of musical history and irrepressible vibe, however, Chicago is not just one of the great cities of the world but is, for jazz, blues and gospel lovers, home.

History

Origins
Chicago's transformation from swampland to one of the world's greatest cities has been fast and colorful.

By the early eighteenth century the region was home to a number of Indian tribes and in 1673 French pioneers Jacques Marquette and Louis Jolliet came upon the site that became Chicago on the banks of Lake Michigan.

The area quickly became something of a thoroughfare for early frontiersmen and, in 1779, an Afro-Caribbean Frenchman named Jean Baptiste Point du Sable set up a fur trade business at the mouth of the Chicago River. When the government erected Fort Dearborn the seeds of a city were sown. The population began to grow despite ugly skirmishes between Indians and settlers. In 1830 construction began on the ambitious Illinois and Michigan Canal which lured hundreds more workers and accelerated the city's immediate growth and its future potential.

Boom town
By 1837 there were 4170 Chicagoans and the town was declared a city. After one or two economic hiccups the canal was completed in 1848 and Chicago was well on the way to becoming the pivotal Midwestern metropolis. Within years train tracks reached the city, first from the Galena and Chicago Union Railroad and later from other lines which radiated out from Chicago across America. With the lake, canal and railroad, Chicago became the most important transport hub in the States. The amount of freight passing through Chicago grew rapidly as Chicagoans began to exploit, sell and ship produce from across the Midwest. Industry boomed and immigrants poured in.

After the Civil War, during which Chicago prospered, the city built its famous Union Stockyards which for 100 years processed, packaged and supplied meat for the entire country. All this industry and activity left Lake Michigan and the Chicago River appallingly polluted and workers were forced to accept harsh conditions. But millions were being made and nothing, it seemed, could reverse the city's fortunes.

Even a colossal fire, which in 1871 destroyed vast areas of the city, was somehow used as a catalyst for growth. Some 18,000 buildings had been lost and their subsequent replacement caused a great building boom which brought some of the world's finest architects to Chicago and allowed city planners to organize development. Chicago was, second time around, a carefully planned city.

Towards the end of the nineteenth century, Chicago's armies of workers began to agitate for better working conditions. Jobs were plentiful in the Windy City – so named, incidentally, because of the city's blabbering politicians – but workers' rights barely existed. Life for the blue-collar class was tough. Strikes and protests led to bloody clashes with the police who quickly gained a reputation for protecting the rich at the expense of the poor. Those early riots heralded a long period of labor unrest in Chicago.

Immigration and prohibition

Immigrants continued to arrive, despite such problems, and somehow Chicago's reputation as a city of freedom and opportunity remained intact. European and Jewish immigrants flooded into the city and, in the first half of the twentieth century, they were joined by hundreds of thousands of African-Americans from the South who traveled north to escape the prejudice and hardship of life south of the Mason-Dixie Line. With them came jazz and blues musicians who delivered to Chicago the best of the South's musical heritage.

A rough and hard-working town, Chicago reacted badly to the Prohibition law of 1920 which banned alcohol. 'Speakeasies' sprang up to meet the needs of drinkers and these illegal gambling and drinking dens were controlled by gangsters. The best-known leader of organized crime was, of course, Al Capone, who took control of gangs on the South Side and gradually in the whole city. Inter-gang rivalry made twenties and thirties Chicago a violent place (see p245).

Chicago today

The mid-fifties saw Richard J Daley elected mayor, a feat he repeated a further five times. His reign wasn't easy – police corruption was rife, the march of the civil rights movement led to bitter and murderous conflict in Chicago and the city's industry virtually collapsed during the seventies – but Daley clung on to power until 1976 when he died in office. After Chicago's first female mayor and then first black mayor, the city fell under the spell of Richard M Daley, son of Richard J Daley, who has so far been successful in prolonging the family dynasty.

Today Chicago has recovered from the industrial slump which bankrupted many of its businesses and rendered obsolete so much of its mighty infrastructure. White-collar commerce has, to some extent, replaced blue collar labor and Chicago is now a sophisticated and prosperous place – at least for some. The South and West continue to stagger on in relative poverty.

Indeed the naked disparity between rich and poor still shocks. But history would appear to show that no problem is insurmountable for this thick-skinned and towering city which, incredibly, was no more than a swamp just 200 years ago.

History of jazz, blues and gospel in Chicago

Jazz

Many of the early masters of New Orleans-style jazz traveled hopefully to Chicago in the middle years of the twenties in search of opportunity. These musicians, some of the earliest pioneers of the 'Great Migration' north to Chicago, made this city a pivotal place in the development of the genre.

During the twenties and thirties Chicago built a somewhat shady reputation as a place where 'anything goes'. Its heavy involvement in organized crime, violence and corruption was to tarnish its image in the eyes of many Americans. But the criminal and illegal activities that then flourished in Chicago ensured there was a bountiful supply of available wealth – albeit usually in the 'wrong' hands. And such money was there to be spent carelessly and lavishly on music and entertainment.

Beyond the relatively confined areas in which organized crime was able to flourish were found hard-working 'blue collar' areas. Many Southern blacks found homes on the South and West Sides in such working-class neighborhoods. 'Bronzeville', a South Side area roughly bound by 31st and 47th Streets to the north and south and Lake Park Avenue and the expressway to the west and east, became the major black ghetto in Chicago and a hotbed of jazz innovation during the twenties and thirties.

So from the early twenties there was developing in Chicago a sub-culture that was to prove something of a magnet to young black musicians from the South. Not only did the city offer prospects of relatively well-paid work, it was also a place in which many of their forebears had already settled. Even by the end of the First World War, Chicago was gaining a reputation as a center of ragtime jazz and it was the exponents of this music who paved the way for the northern migration of many others.

A decade or more before that migration became fully established, pianists as influential as **'Jelly Roll' Morton** and **Tony Jackson** had been performing in Chicago – the latter with a reputation as 'the greatest single-handed entertainer in the world' (which could not have endeared him to 'Jelly').

It is said that black jazz musicians first hit the Chicago Loop when **Bill Johnson's Original Creole Band** played the North American Restaurant. Soon after, a group of white jazz musicians – all from New Orleans – hit town when cornet-player Nick LaRocca appeared at the Casino Gardens with what was to become **The Original Dixieland Jazz Band**. As the good times in New Orleans drew to a close, more and more of the best of that first generation of jazz musicians traveled to Chicago.

In their essay on *Chicago Jazz History* in the 1947 edition of *Esquire's Jazz Book*, Paul Eduard Miller and George Hoefer describe how 'with the arrival of New Orleans jazzmen on a large scale...the Chicago Negro reacted quickly,

Cops and robbers

The image of a Chicago rocked by drive-by shootings, mob bosses and speakeasies has been forever branded on the minds of the world by the legend of one man, 'Scarface' Alphonse Capone, who controlled Chicago's underworld throughout the twenties and thirties. Capone's main income came from supplying illegal booze during the years of Prohibition. His cruel violence and shrewd business sense helped him to amass an estimated $30 million every year.

On 14 February 1929, Capone's gang, disguised as cops, shot seven members of their rival Bugsy Moran's gang in what was labeled the 'St Valentine's Day Massacre'. Despite these and countless other murderous sprees, Capone was eventually convicted for income tax fraud thanks to 'the Untouchables', a group of lawmen led by Elliott Ness who were said to be impossible to bribe. Since hundreds, if not thousands, of Chicago's cops and officials during the twenties and thirties were in the pay of the mob, the Untouchables were an unusual breed.

Ironically, perhaps, this background of prostitution, law-breaking and organized crime did much to foster jazz in Chicago. Speakeasies, illegal bars where alcohol was served, employed many of New Orleans' best jazzmen after they meandered north to Chicago. Indeed, the free-wheeling sound of jazz seemed an appropriate score for these illegal dens. Musicians had to be discreet, however, if they were to survive the mob's employment. When singer Joe E Louis left his regular gig at the Green Mill – then owned by Capone henchman 'Machine Gun' Jack McGurn – he had his vocal chords sliced.

absorbed the spirit and feeling of jazz, until soon the merging of talents and ideas expressed itself in more than a score of jazz organizations which were playing all over the city'.

The two go on to describe how 'being a direct, concise expression of the times, jazz appealed not only to the Prohibition gangsters, but to other Chicagoans who were caught up in a whirl of protest against a law [Prohibition] which they did not like. Biting and incisive, jazz personified this protest'.

The roll-call of great jazz names found in the cafés, clubs, theaters and ballrooms of the Chicago Loop and the South Side is staggering. This entertainment boom was fuelled in part by rich gangsters who were prepared to fund the jazz craze with, for Southern black musicians, previously hard-to-imagine sums. One New Orleanian to get caught up in the Chicago jazz explosion was **Louis 'Satchmo' Armstrong** who had traveled north to answer the call of his mentor **Joe 'King' Oliver** at the Sunset Café. Armstrong soon branched out as a bandleader in his own right and recorded, with his Hot Five and Hot Seven, one of the most treasured series of masterpieces in the history of jazz.

Merely to note the names of those joining Louis in those remarkable demonstrations of mature New Orleans music is to list some of the very greatest names in jazz. Among them were that still youthful veteran of tailgate trombone, **'Kid' Ory**, the **Dodds brothers** and **Johnny St Cyr**; with **Earl Hines**, on piano, eventually replacing **Lil Hardin**, Armstrong's second wife, who was to make her own mark on the music as pianist, singer and composer.

At venues such as Lincoln (later Royal) Gardens and Dreamland, from the Vendôme Theater to the Sunset Café nestling, like a score of others, between South Side's 26th and 39th Streets, Oliver, Armstrong and the rest were to be heard nightly performing to audiences both black and white. On any given night during Chicago's 'Roaring Twenties' could be heard jazz by the likes of **Erskine Tate** at the Vendôme, **Lovie Austin** at the Monogram, **Jimmy Noone** at the famous Apex Club or the **Fletcher Henderson Orchestra** at the Congress.

Chicago was also the birthplace of a surprising number of important white jazzmen including clarinetist **Benny Goodman**, trumpeter **Francis 'Muggsy' Spanier** and drummer **Gene Krupa**. Others, like **Lawrence 'Bud' Freeman**, **Jimmy McPartland**, **Charles 'Pee Wee' Russell**, **William 'Red' McKenzie** and **Eddie Condon** based themselves in Chicago where they helped to develop the distinctive and generally joyous style of 'Chicago Jazz'. Still others, the foremost among them **Bix Beiderbecke**, **Frankie Trumbauer**, **Joe Sullivan** and **Dave Tough**, were also associated with the 'Chicago school'.

But just as the closing-down of New Orleans' Storyville District had precipitated a move north to Chicago, so the enforced decline of the 'speakeasy' and the first serious moves to end Prohibition saw a significant scaling-down of available entertainment, of all types, in the Windy City. By the end of the twenties it was time for the next migration of jazzmen towards the West Coast and, predominantly, to the already-thriving jazz environment of New York City. In Chicago, however, jazz lived on – indeed, it still thrives today and the city will always hold an honored place in the history of jazz music.

Blues

As the heyday of Chicago jazz began to fade, black migrants from the rural South continued to pour into the city where they crammed into the tenements of the 'black belt'. With these migrants came a new musical authority: blues.

With hindsight it's easy to see why so many African-Americans chose to travel north. Plantation workers were kept in a state of perpetual debt by unscrupulous landowners. Living conditions were basic. The black and white populations were growing more polarized; southern police discriminated without reproach. Add to that the threat of mechanization of farms and its effect on the labor market. In contrast, Chicago was seen as a free and fair place where jobs were plentiful. This rather rosy view was encouraged by the *Chicago Defender*, a leading black newspaper, which distributed pro-migration editorials across the South. In *Deep Blues* Robert Palmer notes that between 1940 and 1950 alone the State of Mississippi lost a quarter of its already depleted population to Chicago.

Although the Chicago blues sound came of age after World War Two, blues had been played in West and South Side clubs since the twenties. While the jazz craze roared, pioneers like **Big Bill Broonzy** and **Papa Charlie Jackson** honed their craft in relative obscurity. Country migrants from the

Chicago — events and festivals

Chicago's summers are set to the soundtrack of a series of free, world-class music events sponsored by the City, The Blues Festival is, famously, one of America's very best but there are a several other major cultural celebrations, including the Jazz Festival, which are growing in stature year on year. For more information about any of these events, call ☎ 312-744-3315.

● **June** – Gospel Music Festival. Founded in 1985, Chicago's Gospel Festival is an entertaining three-day celebration of gospel music in its widest sense; expect singing groups from across the States

● **June** – Blues Festival. The most important musical event in the Midwest, and one of the world's great blues festivals, the Chicago Blues Fest is well worth visiting Chicago for, even if you don't stay long enough to see anything else

● **July** – Country Music Festival. A buzzing two-day showcase of country music with plenty of Nashville types venturing north to participate

● **August** – Latin Music Festival

● **August** – Jazz Festival. Since 1978 the Chicago Jazz Festival has built on its reputation for presenting great jazz stars to become one the most enjoyable jazz festivals in the States

● **September** – Celtic Fest

● **September** – World Music Festival

Delta school of blues, Broonzy, Jackson and a handful of others were the first to move their music towards what became 'Chicago Blues'. More refined than Delta Blues, the Chicago sound is the result of a sort of musical urbanization.

Illinois Central railroad carriages continued to deposit gifted bluesmen from the South onto Chicago's streets and many would, like Broonzy, contribute to the ever-more apparent transition from Delta to Chicago blues. Among them were: **Tampa Red**, a gifted slide guitarist whose style was smoother than that of Delta bluesmen even before he arrived in Chicago in the twenties; **John Lee 'Sonny Boy' Williamson**, whose blues harp became a key ingredient in the Chicago sound; and **Lonnie Johnson**, a guitar giant who allowed jazz to influence his polished style. **Lester Melrose**, once the godfather of Chicago blues, recorded these and other blues legends for Columbia and Victor. This clique of musicians began to adapt to the changing needs of the audiences, mixing jazz, folk and novelty songs with the blues.

In 1943, **Muddy Waters** was one of thousands of Southern blacks to take the 12-hour train ride to Chicago. Like so many others, Muddy was tempted by the thought of freedom and well-paid work rather than the idea of achieving fame as a musician. Indeed, he had been convinced of the fact that the urbane Chicago scene had no use for a down-home Delta bluesmen like himself. He found a job in a paper factory the day he arrived in Chicago. Despite his doubts about the currency of his blues, Muddy supplemented his income playing at house parties and, occasionally, at the Maxwell Street Market. He quickly found that his Delta reputation had traveled with him to Chicago; people knew him and they wanted to hear him play.

Jump blues, or R&B, and amplification had added a more aggressive sound and a driving beat to old-style Chicago blues by the mid-forties. This new and much-admired form competed with traditional Chicago blues as performed by the likes of John Lee 'Sonny Boy' Williamson – with whom, incidentally, Muddy Waters played from time to time. So when in 1946 **Sunnyland Slim**, a prolific recording artist who also arrived in Chicago in the forties, invited Muddy Waters to join a recording session for Columbia, Muddy assumed he should abandon his raw Delta blues in an attempt to emulate the more urban style. The result, an under-par performance, failed to impress Melrose.

One year later two Polish-born brothers, **Leonard and Phil Chess**, founded a record label, Aristocrat, with another partner. The Chess brothers already owned clubs in Chicago and so understood the popularity of blues. Their first releases were jump blues but in the same year Sunnyland Slim organized a session for Aristocrat and, again, he invited Muddy Waters to play guitar. Again, Muddy failed to deliver his potential but the record was released, albeit without enthusiasm, in 1948.

Muddy was invited to record again and this time he allowed himself to play vigorous Delta blues infused with a little of the Chicago sophistication he had picked up. He laid down *I Feel Like Going Home* and *I Can't Be Satisfied*. On the first day of the record's release it sold out. Muddy was a new Chicago star and his blues, though loud, amplified and confident, wasn't so far removed from the Mississippi Delta.

By the early fifties Muddy Waters was a nationally known bluesman. With **Little Walter** carving a fine reputation of his own on harp, and Vicksburg-born blues composer **Willie Dixon** penning hit tunes like *Hoochie Coochie Man* for Muddy – and sometimes joining him on bass – the Waters-Chess partnership was changing the face of blues with its confident but subtle style, stop-time riffs, booming beats and amplification.

While Muddy Waters' name is now synonymous with mature Chicago blues, many other talented musicians made colossal contributions to the Chicago sound of the fifties, even after Muddy had begun to dominate the genre. **Elmore James** redefined the slide guitar, **Howlin' Wolf** was a master of electric blues throughout the fifties and sixties, **Bo Diddley** brought a touch of funk to Chess Records (renamed from Aristocrat after the Chess brothers bought out their partner in 1950) and **James Cotton** and **Junior Wells** made the blues harp their own.

Such was the depth of the talent pool in Chicago, the list of other legends playing the circuit reads like a blues roll of honor. The raw, acoustic Delta sound found a niche in Chicago thanks to Robert Johnson contemporary **David 'Honeyboy' Edwards** (interviewed for this book on p273) while old-time master **Hound Dog Taylor**, genius modern blues guitarist **Buddy Guy**, **Koko Taylor**, the current Queen of Blues, Louisiana-born **Lonnie Brooks** and many more achieved fame on the Chicago circuit.

Blues in the Windy City remains healthy despite a decline in interest from younger blacks, many of whom consider blues to be old-fashioned, perhaps even an embarrassing reminder of a time when the place of blacks in America was considerably more subservient than it is today. During the seventies Bruce Iglauer founded Alligator Records which he used to maintain,

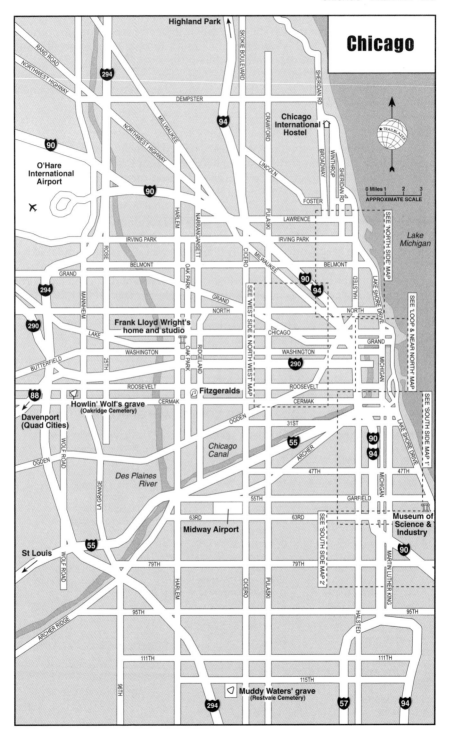

Chicago

Highland Park ↑

SKOKIE BOULEVARD

RAND ROAD

NORTHWEST HIGHWAY

294

DEMPSTER

MILWAUKEE

NORTHWEST HIGHWAY

94

CRAWFORD

SHERIDAN RD

Chicago
International
Hostel

90

O'Hare
International
Airport

90

LINCOLN

BROADWAY

WINTHROP

SHERIDAN RD

★ TRAILBLAZER

0 Miles 1   2   3
APPROXIMATE SCALE

FOSTER

HARLEM

NARRANGANSETT

PULASKI

LAWRENCE

CICERO

IRVING PARK

Lake
Michigan

SEE 'NORTH SIDE MAP'

294

ROSE

IRVING PARK

MILWAUKEE

BELMONT

SEE 'LOOP & NEAR NORTH' MAP

GRAND

BELMONT

OAK PARK

90

HALSTED

290

MANNHEIM

GRAND

94

Lake Shore Drive

NORTH

LAKE

OAK PARK

NORTH

SEE 'WEST SIDE & NORTH WEST MAP'

CHICAGO

GRAND

Frank Lloyd Wright's
home and studio

25TH

WASHINGTON

RIDGELAND

WASHINGTON

290

MICHIGAN

BUTTERFIELD

ROOSEVELT

ROOSEVELT

SEE 'SOUTH SIDE MAP 1'

88

CERMAK

🅟 Fitzgeralds

CERMAK

Davenport
(Quad Cities)

Howlin' Wolf's grave
(Oakridge Cemetery)

OGDEN

31ST

LAKE SHORE DRIVE

OGDEN

WOLF ROAD

Chicago
Canal

55

ARCHER

90

LA GRANGE

Des Plaines
River

47TH

94

47TH

MICHIGAN

55TH

GARFIELD

Museum of
Science &
Industry

St Louis

55

63RD

63RD

Midway Airport

SEE 'SOUTH SIDE MAP 2'

90

WOLF ROAD

79TH

HARLEM

CICERO

PULASKI

79TH

MARTIN LUTHER KING

ARCHER RIDGE

95TH

95TH

HALSTED

111TH

111TH

96TH

115TH

◁ Muddy Waters' grave
(Restvale Cemetery)

294

57

94

promote and even resurrect the ailing careers of many of Chicago's best blues musicians. In stark contrast to the early labels, Iglauer prides himself on treating bluesmen fairly and his label has done much to keep blues in general and Chicago blues in particular vibrant. Blues does still have a following in Chicago where clubs continue to play the real thing night after night for appreciative audiences. And Chicago, rightly, seems proud of its remarkable musical heritage.

Gospel

Aside from great jazz and blues legacies, Chicago also had a major impact on gospel music thanks, in part, to one man's career. **Tom Dorsey**, a blues pianist who moved to Chicago from Georgia in 1916, first made himself felt as one half of a famed double act with Tampa Red. The duo's biggest hit, *It's Tight Like That*, is a bawdy blues number loaded with sexual overtones. Dorsey also worked for a spell with legendary blues singer **Ma Rainey**.

In 1930, however, Dorsey found religion and became absorbed in the then embryonic gospel music genre. Bringing his vast and popular musical talent to gospel, Dorsey did much to make it the music so loved today. He wrote gospel standards *Precious Lord* and *Peace in the Valley* and, despite concerns from more conservative members of the congregation, was invited to become music director at the Pilgrim Baptist Church on Chicago's South Side by the Reverend JC Austin Sr. There he worked with the New Orleans-born great **Mahalia Jackson** to create a sound and style which defined gospel music.

KEY – CHICAGO: THE LOOP & NEAR NORTH (MAP OPPOSITE)

⌂ **WHERE TO STAY**
1 The Drake
2 The Seneca Hotel
4 HoJo Inn
9 Best Western River North
13 Hampton Inn & Suites
15 Radisson Hotel & Suites
16 Omni Chicago
17 Cass Hotel
18 Lenox Suites
21 Inter-Continental
22 Holiday Inn City Center
23 Sheraton
25 Courtyard by Marriott
28 House of Blues Hotel
30 Renaissance Chicago
31 Hotel Monaco
32 Hyatt Regency
33 Fairmont
37 Quality Inn Downtown
39 Hyatt on Printer's Row
40 Hostelling International
43 Hilton and Towers
44 Essex Inn

○ **WHERE TO EAT**
3 Centro
7 Gino's
8 Rock & Roll McDonalds
12 Frontera Grill
14 The Rosebud (720N Rush)
19 Pizzeria Uno
20 Heaven on Seven (600 N Michigan)
27 Harry Caray's
34 Heaven on Seven (111 N Wabash)
35 Nick's Fishmarket (One First National Plaza)
36 Blackbird
38 Berghoff

♫ **LIVE MUSIC VENUES**
5 Blue Chicago (736 N Clark)
6 Famous Dave's
10 Blue Chicago (536 N Clark)
11 Jazz Showcase
24 Joe's Be-Bop Café
26 Andy's Live Jazz
29 House of Blues
41 Hot House
42 Buddy Guy's Legends
45 Koko Taylor's Celebrity

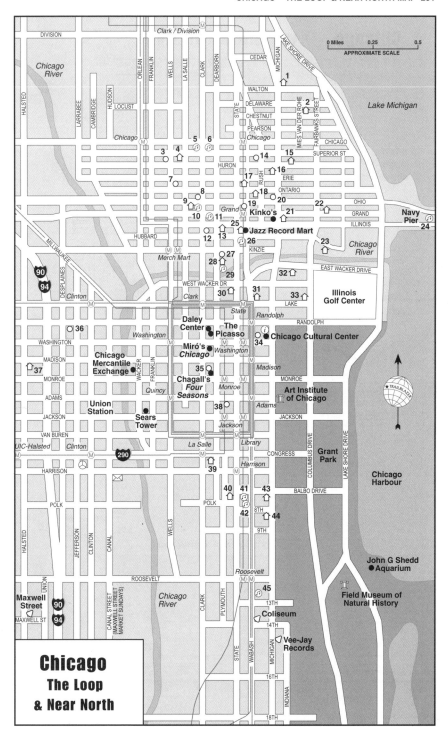

Chicago
The Loop
& Near North

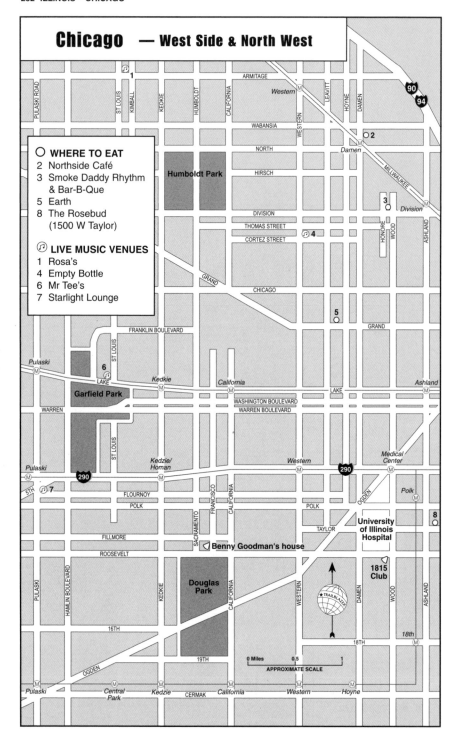

Chicago — West Side & North West

O WHERE TO EAT
2 Northside Café
3 Smoke Daddy Rhythm
  & Bar-B-Que
5 Earth
8 The Rosebud
  (1500 W Taylor)

♫ LIVE MUSIC VENUES
1 Rosa's
4 Empty Bottle
6 Mr Tee's
7 Starlight Lounge

Humboldt Park

Garfield Park

Douglas Park

University
of Illinois
Hospital

1815
Club

Benny Goodman's house

0 Miles   0.5   1
APPROXIMATE SCALE

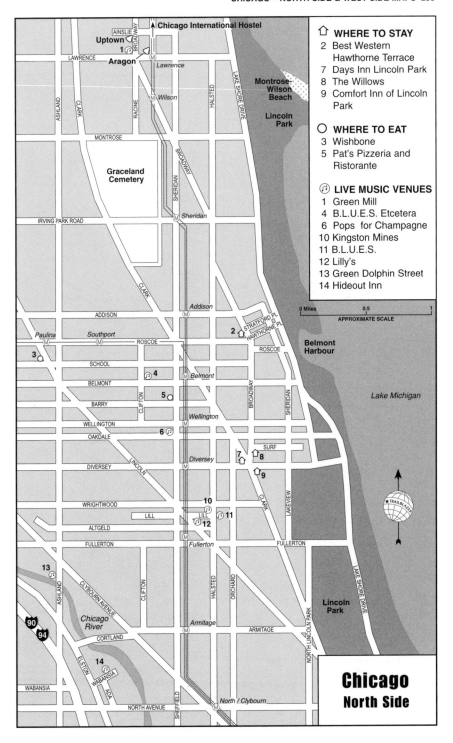

WHERE TO STAY

2 Best Western Hawthorne Terrace
7 Days Inn Lincoln Park
8 The Willows
9 Comfort Inn of Lincoln Park

WHERE TO EAT

3 Wishbone
5 Pat's Pizzeria and Ristorante

LIVE MUSIC VENUES

1 Green Mill
4 B.L.U.E.S. Etcetera
6 Pops for Champagne
10 Kingston Mines
11 B.L.U.E.S.
12 Lilly's
13 Green Dolphin Street
14 Hideout Inn

0 Miles   0.5   1
APPROXIMATE SCALE

Chicago
North Side

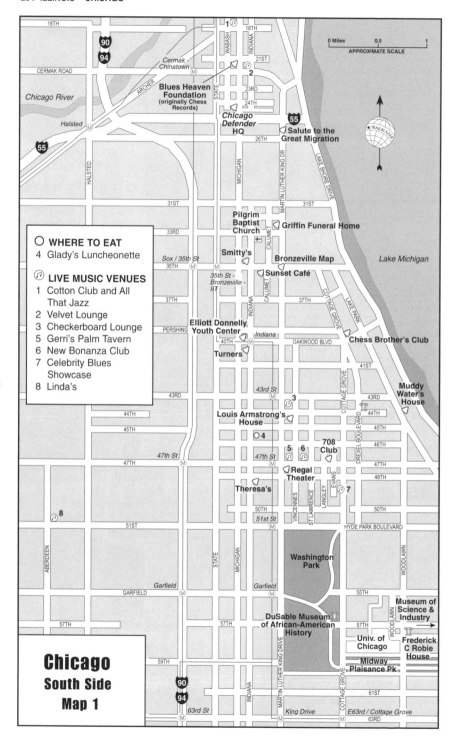

Chicago South Side Map 1

WHERE TO EAT
4 Glady's Luncheonette

LIVE MUSIC VENUES
1 Cotton Club and All That Jazz
2 Velvet Lounge
3 Checkerboard Lounge
5 Gerri's Palm Tavern
6 New Bonanza Club
7 Celebrity Blues Showcase
8 Linda's

0 Miles   0.5   1
APPROXIMATE SCALE

Chicago River
Cermak - Chinatown
Blues Heaven Foundation (originally Chess Records)
Chicago Defender HQ
Halsted
Salute to the Great Migration
Pilgrim Baptist Church
Griffin Funeral Home
Smitty's
Bronzeville Map
Lake Michigan
Sox / 35th St
35th St - Bronzeville - IIT
Sunset Café
Elliott Donnelly Youth Center
Chess Brother's Club
Turners
Muddy Water's House
Louis Armstrong's House
708 Club
Regal Theater
Theresa's
Washington Park
Museum of Science & Industry
DuSable Museum of African-American History
Univ. of Chicago
Frederick C Robie House
Midway Plaisance Pk

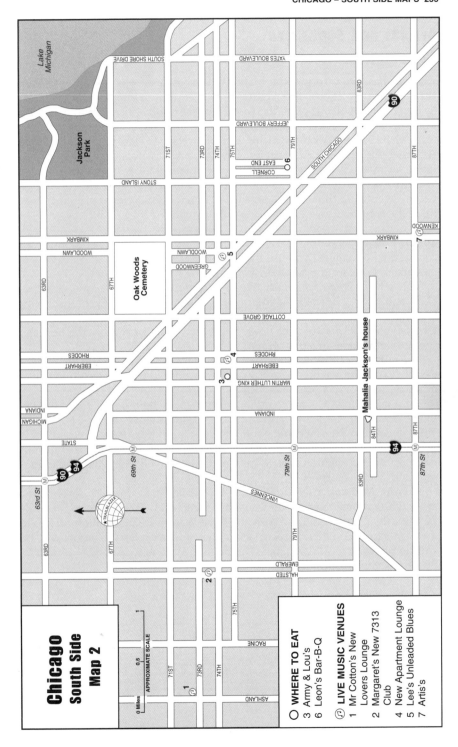

Chicago
South Side
Map 2

0 Miles   0.5   1

APPROXIMATE SCALE

★ TRAILBLAZER

Lake Michigan

Jackson Park

Oak Woods Cemetery

Mahalia Jackson's house

○ WHERE TO EAT
3 Army & Lou's
6 Leon's Bar-B-Q

ⓘ LIVE MUSIC VENUES
1 Mr Cotton's New Lovers Lounge
2 Margaret's New 7313 Club
4 New Apartment Lounge
5 Lee's Unleaded Blues
7 Artis's

Arrival and departure

By air

Chicago has two airports, the biggest and most useful of which is **O'Hare International** (☎ 773-686-2200) north-west of the city on Interstate 90. O'Hare is so big, in fact, it claims to be the world's busiest hub – the seemingly endless miles of corridor between check-in and gates confirm the scale of the place.

Many of the world's major carriers serve O'Hare including British Airways, Air Canada, All Nippon Airways, SAS, Swissair and most US airlines. Terminal Five is the international terminal; all the rest are domestic.

Midway Airport (☎ 773-838-0600), 20 minutes west of downtown on Cicero Avenue off the I-55, is a smaller, regional hub serving domestic routes. Budget airline Southwest Airlines uses Midway.

Airport transfers **From O'Hare** expect to pay up to $35 for the 30-minute **cab** ride to the Loop unless you use the 'Shared Ride' scheme which costs $15 per passenger. Look for the 'Shared Ride' sign.

The **El**, or **CTA**, runs every five or so minutes on the Blue Line, costs just $1.50 and takes a bearable 40 minutes. Actually finding the El station in this labyrinthine airport can prove tricky depending on where you leave customs. Unless your pockets are very deep, however, the El is probably the best and certainly most cost-effective option.

A company called Continental's Airport Express runs **shuttle buses** from O'Hare to downtown hotels for $17 or $30 for a round trip. Buses go every five minutes. To reserve a place call ☎ 312-454-7799.

Strange though it may sound, a **limo** could be a better value option. Limos hold four – at least – and can charge as little as $45 for an hour's ride. Since in good traffic you could get to the Loop in 30 minutes, you could face a modest $22.50 fee split four ways. You can contact limo companies at the airport; ask the information desk to put you in touch with companies with limos on standby at the airport.

From Midway, cabs downtown are quicker than from O'Hare so cost around $20; the shared ride flat fee is $10. The **El** takes 30 minutes to get to the Loop on the Orange Line and costs the same as from O'Hare. Follow 'Trains to the City' signs. Continental's Airport Express appear to hold the monopoly on **shuttle buses** from Midway, too. The price is $12 one-way or $22 round trip. Buses go every 20 minutes or so.

(Opposite) **Top:** The Maxwell Street Market, now on nearby Canal Street (see p265), has been the pulse of South Side Chicago since the early years of the 'Great Migration' and is the place where almost all Chicago bluesmen started out. **Bottom left:** Chicago's streets are crowded by high-rise architecture from great glass and steel towers to fume-blackened tenements. **Bottom right:** Picasso's sculpture in front of the Daley Center (see p260) has left locals scratching their heads for years.

By train

Every day, some 50 Amtrak passenger trains pull up to or pull out of Chicago's generously-proportioned **Union Station** at 210 South Canal Street. Of most interest to readers of this book, the *City of New Orleans* service rattles to and from New Orleans more or less following the route taken by so many African-Americans during the Great Migration. See p22 for more on this service. Other rail routes out of Chicago include the *California Zephyr* which races west, the *Lake Shore Limited* which heads for New York City and the *Southwest Chief* for dusty New Mexico and Arizona.

By bus

Greyhound buses use the main terminal at 630 West Harrison Street (☎ 312-408-5820). Buses from here connect Chicago to just about everywhere in America; name a city and Greyhound can get you there. Journeys are long and there are more salubrious ways to travel but at least tickets are cheap. Services to Davenport, Iowa and St Louis, Missouri – next stops on the Blues Highway south – leave several times a day.

By car

Look at any map of the US and you'll see that roads fan out from Chicago in every direction. Interstate 88 leads west to Davenport and Interstate 55 shoots straight down to St Louis. If you're planning to rent a car from here, see p258. The Auto-Driveaway Company, recommended in the New Orleans chapter, is a respected national network with a depot in Chicago. Call them on ☎ 800-720-2886 well in advance of your intended travel date to find out whether they happen to have a car due to be delivered south.

Orientation

A cunning system of street numbers prevents even the most navigationally-challenged from getting lost. The center of the Chicago compass, ground zero, is the intersection of State and Madison Streets. From here all streets travel north, east, south or west (even the few diagonals are labeled north and south) and numbers increase from zero. Every increase of 400 indicates a cross street. Increments of 800 indicate a mile in distance. Few streets are pre-fixed with 'East', of course, since these lead into Lake Michigan.

Chicago is divided into a myriad of neighborhoods from Andersonville to Wrigleyville. Boundaries are often blurred. Blues and jazz lovers will be most interested in the **South and West Sides**, both ominous ghettos where visitors will need to take care, **the Loop**, which is basically central downtown Chicago as defined by the El Loop, and **Lincoln Park**, a Northside suburb with a number of good clubs.

(Opposite) A mural at the Elliott Donnelly Youth Center on Chicago's South Side (see p266) tells the story of the 'Great Migration' from the South to Bronzeville. The Center was founded in 1924 as the South Side Boys Club.

Getting around

By car

Locals tell visitors not to mess with Chicago's drivers but if you plan to explore the South Side, you'll want a car. It's hard to get lost and the traffic generally flows quite well. Downtown parking, however, can be a nightmare. All the main car rental firms have offices in Chicago (see below). Be prepared to pay a stinging 18 percent state and city car rental tax. Tourists stick out in the South Side so if you hope to avoid too much attention, you might want to resist cruising down there in a flash or obviously rented car.

Car rentals Major rental firms have offices at O'Hare and Midway airports and in various downtown locations; call to find which branch is most convenient.
- **Alamo** (☎ 800-327-8017, 312-332-2908)
- **Avis** (☎ 800-327-9633, 773-694-5608)
- **Budget** (☎ 800-527-0700)
- **Enterprise** (☎ 800-867-4595)
- **Hertz** (☎ 800-654 3131, 773-735-7272)
- **Rent-a-Wreck** (☎ 800-535-1391)

By cab

If movies are to be believed, hailing a cab and then having someone else jump in before you is part of the big-city experience. In Chicago, however, cabs are everywhere and finding one is only difficult in residential suburban neighborhoods. Fares are relatively inexpensive and you can generally trust official taxis. To book ahead call American-United (☎ 773-248-7600), Flash Cabs (☎ 773-561-1444), Checker Taxis (☎ 312-243-2537) or Yellow Cabs (☎ 312-829-4222). Since the medallions which allow you to drive a cab in Chicago are in short supply and very expensive, most cab drivers are pretty experienced and won't need directing.

CTA – Bus and 'El'

The Chicago Transport Authority (CTA) operates the city's buses and El – or 'elevated' – railway. Visitors will find the El easier to use than the complex **bus system** for which there are no published schedules. Since the El is fairly comprehensive and simple, our advice would be to steer clear of buses altogether.

Fares are the same for both, however, just $1.50 for one ride plus 30 cents for transfers. Rather than fish for change, which in the case of most El stations would be useless anyway since there are no cashiers, buy a transit card from a vending machine. Turnstiles and bus machines will automatically deduct amounts from the card. Cards range in price from $1.50 to $91.

The **El** is divided into seven lines differentiated and labeled according to color. You will need to pick up a map from an information booth. Confusingly, different sections of different lines close at varying times so you'll need to check in advance if you plan to travel late. That said, late-night El travel isn't recommended; stations can be lonely and threatening after dark. Another hazard to note is the almost impossibly narrow platforms from which it feels all too easy to topple onto the tracks. These problems aside, and despite the grumbles of locals who love to diss the CTA, the El makes it easy for car-less visitors to get around town quickly and cheaply. For CTA information call ☎ 888-968-7282.

By tour

Chicago Neighborhood Tours (☎ 312-742-1190), affiliated to the Chicago Office of Tourism, offers fascinating, professional and insightful tours based on specific and carefully-researched aspects of Chicago's history. One tour focuses on Bronzeville and the South Side.

Their best tour, however, and perhaps the best in the City of Chicago, is the **Roots of Blues** tour which lasts five hours and takes in the Pilgrim Baptist Church, Gerri's Palm Tavern, Muddy Waters' home, Maxwell Street and a number of other key blues and gospel landmarks. Led by dapper blues guitarist and scriptwriter Fernando Jones, the tour gives a thorough introduction to Chicago blues. Admission to the tour is $56 per person but, since they are rarely scheduled, you will need to call ahead to find out when a tour's planned.

There are stacks of tours in Chicago. Those based on themes rather than general overviews are often more interesting. Other recommended companies include: **Black Coutours** (☎ 773-233-8907), a two-hour look at African-American history; the **Chicago Architecture Foundation** (☎ 312-922 TOUR), bus or walking tours taking in some of Chicago's many architectural gems; **Mercury Skyline Tours** (☎ 312-332-1368), the city's oldest boat trips along the lakefront; and the **Untouchables Tour** (☎ 773-881-1195), an amusing and colorful exploration of twenties and thirties gangland Chicago.

Services

Banks

There are more banks and ATMs in Chicago than you could ever need; there's no point listing them since, almost wherever you are in town, you're never more than a minute's walk from a 'cash station'. Don't just look for banks; they're in stores, malls and gas stations too.

Communications

● **Post** Chicago's main post office is located at 433 West Harrison Street but there are other, smaller offices dotted across the suburbs.

● **Internet** Kinko's 24-hour copy shops are probably the easiest places to find Internet access. There are branches at 540 North Michigan, 1201 North Dearborn, 444 North Wells, 55 East Monroe and 843 West Van Buren.

Tourist information

The **Chicago Cultural Center** at 78 East Washington Street (entrance on East Randolph) is the largest and most useful tourist information office in town. The CVB's website, 🖳 www.choosechicago.com, is a better place to start. Otherwise call for information on ☎ 312-567-8500.

Record stores

Without doubt the biggest and best jazz and blues record store in Chicago – perhaps the best in the States – **Jazz Record Mart** (☎ 312-222-1467) at 444 North Wabash is a treasure chest loaded with recent and rare LPs, CDs and tapes. It's something of a music landmark in its own right. This is another of Delmark Records founder Bob Koester's businesses. He can often be found here indulging customers with his vast knowledge of jazz and blues. You'll also find related books and magazines.

Consulates

- **Britain** (☎ 312-346-1810), 400 North Michigan Avenue
- **Canada** (☎ 312-616-1860), 180 North Stetson, Suite 2400
- **France** (☎ 312-787-5359), 737 North Michigan Avenue, Suite 2020
- **Germany** (☎ 312-580-1199), 676 North Michigan Avenue, Suite 3200
- **Italy** (☎ 312-467-1550), 500 North Michigan Avenue, Suite 1850
- **Japan** (☎ 312-280-0400), 737 North Michigan Avenue, Suite 1100
- **Mexico** (☎ 312-855-1380), 300 North Michigan Avenue, Second Floor
- **Spain** (☎ 312-782-4588), 180 North Michigan Avenue, Suite 1500
- **Switzerland** (☎ 312-915-0061), 737 North Michigan Avenue, Suite 2301

Medical emergencies

Chicago's main hospitals are the **University of Chicago Hospital** (☎ 773-702-1000) at 5841 South Maryland Avenue, **Northwestern Memorial Hospital** (☎ 312-908-2000) at 250 East Superior Street and **Columbia Michael Reese Hospital** (☎ 312-791-2000) at 2929 South Ellis Avenue.

What to see — highlights

Chicago is a colossal city which overwhelms first-timers. You could spend months exploring and still not see everything. This section presents a personal selection of highlights. For readers of this book, of course, the Checkerboard Lounge on the South Side is likely to prove more exciting than the Sears Tower. For music landmarks see p263.

Downtown

The Chicago Loop is named for the nineteenth-century cable car route which circled downtown. Today El tracks make the same circuit. Within the Loop one finds the commercial pulse of Chicago; harassed futures traders and tourists compete for space on the sidewalk. The scene is overshadowed by columns of skyscrapers. Works by a number of sculptors have been placed amid this frenzy – Picasso, Chagall and Miró among them.

'**The Picasso**' (it has no official name) stands outside the Daley Center which is on Dearborn between Randolph and Washington. Fans of the *Blues Brothers* might remember the duo used the Daley Center for the climax of their movie. As for the Picasso, well, make of it what you will. **Miró's** *Chicago*, a 40-foot metal-fest, is on Washington between Dearborn and Clark; **Chagall's** *Four Seasons*, a more conventionally appealing 1974 mosaic, is near the corner of Dearborn and Monroe.

Chicago architecture

When you're in the Windy City, don't forget to look up; Chicago built the first skyscraper at the end of the nineteenth century and the city continues its love affair with glass, steel and striking geometric patterns. These monolithic constructions are testament to the city's deserved high opinion of itself and are no less a statement than the vast temples or arenas of ancient Greece and Rome.

After the 1871 fire which destroyed so much of the then fledgling city, Chicago invited scores of eager, young and forward-looking architects to rebuild the city. This wave of innovation set the standard for big city American design and led to a new style of architecture, the 'Chicago School'. Pioneered by the likes of Louis Sullivan, the Chicago School placed function over form, creating buildings which allowed their very structure and purpose to define their shape and beauty.

As Chicago's reputation grew so it attracted many of America's most promising architects. Frank Lloyd Wright used Chicago to develop his organic 'prairie' style of architecture, noted for its sweeping horizontal lines, which catapulted him into the twentieth century's architectural élite. During the forties and fifties Chicago fuelled another architectural boom which saw Mies van der Rohe spearhead further refinement of Louis Sullivan's maxim.

For 23 years the 1450-foot-tall **Sears Tower** (☎ 312-875-9696; daily 9am-10pm; $10), 233 South Wacker Drive, was the world's tallest building. In 1996 Malaysia eclipsed it with the Petronas Towers in Kuala Lumpur. Still, the monumental building's reduced status has done little to dent its popularity: 1.5 million visitors continue to pour in every year. The reward for the long wait, 1600-foot-per-minute elevator ride and popped ears is a staggering view right across Chicago and beyond in every direction. An interpretation chart allows you to get your bearings, find your hotel and plan where you're going next.

Another famed piece of downtown architecture, albeit a very different one, is **Union Station** at 210 South Canal Street. Instantly recognizable thanks to *The Untouchables*, Union Station is a grand, ostentatious place which, like Sears Tower, reflects the optimistic mood of Chicago at the time of its construction. Few of the thousands of commuters who gush through the station everyday find time to admire the building but it is, in fact, one of the most elegant in town. Talking of commuters, the **Chicago Mercantile Exchange** (☎ 312-930-8249; Mon-Fri 7.30am-3.15pm; free) at 30 South Wacker Drive is the place where many of them go to buy and sell commodities on international markets with the help of archaic hand gestures and a lot of adrenaline. It's quite a spectacle.

Another landmark building but one with a less avaricious function is the **Chicago Cultural Center** (☎ 312-346-3278) at 78 East Washington Street. Built in 1897, this grand and attractive pile now presents changing exhibitions, concerts and displays relating to Chicago life. With a quiet coffee bar and a tourist information office attached, this is a convenient downtown hangout.

Art Institute of Chicago

Chicagoans are lucky to have one of the world's best art museums on their doorstep. The Art Institute of Chicago (☎ 312-443-3600; Mon, Tue, Wed, Thurs 10.30am-4.30pm, Tues 10.30am-8pm, Sat 10am-5pm, Sun 12-5pm; $8), 111 South Michigan Street, boasts an art collection spanning 5000 years. The more recent end of the timescale attracts most attention; Grant Wood's *American Gothic* is a must-see and Van Gogh, Picasso, Monet, Renoir and Gaughin are all well represented.

DuSable Museum of African-American History

The DuSable Museum of African-American History (☎ 773-947-0600; Mon-Sat, 10am-5pm, Sun, 12-5pm; $3), south of the Loop in the Hyde Park-Kenwood area at 740 East 56th Place, is perhaps a more relevant museum for jazz and blues aficionados. Opened in 1961 and named after Chicago's first settler, a black Frenchman, the DuSable Museum presents a frank depiction of the African-American experience from slave ships onwards. The often depressing story which the museum tells usefully places African-American music in its social context.

Museum of Science and Industry

At 57th Street and Lake Shore Drive, the Museum of Science and Industry (☎ 773-684-1414; Mon-Fri 9.30am-4pm, Sat-Sun 9.30am-5.30pm; $7, free on Thurs) is one of the most popular attractions in town. A huge, hands-on and brilliantly imaginative range of permanent and changing exhibits keep tourists and locals flocking back in massive numbers. Kids love it.

Field Museum of Natural History & John G Shedd Aquarium

The frighteningly vast **Field Museum of Natural History** (☎ 312-922-9410; daily 9am-5pm; $8) at 1400 South Lake Shore Drive has been improving its displays year on year since the eighties and now boasts a gripping and engaging range of exhibits including Sue, the world's most complete set of Tyrannosaurus Rex bones, a recreation of ancient Egypt and a lava flow.

Nearby at 1200 Lake Shore Drive, the **John G Shedd Aquarium** (☎ 312-939-2438; daily 9am-6pm; $13) is the world's largest fish tank with some 6000 sea creatures on view. The 90,000-gallon Caribbean coral recreation is home to an amazing and colorful collection of species. Make sure you're around at 11am or 2pm to see divers hand feed the sharks.

Lakefront area

Apart from the giant institutions above, the **lakefront** area is an attraction in its own right. After the fire which destroyed most of Chicago in 1871, planners were able to start afresh with a clear vision for the booming city. They decided to keep the lakefront uncluttered which is why, today, Chicagoans can enjoy miles of unobstructed beach as if this were a coastal town. **Navy Pier** at 600 East Grand Avenue, built in 1916 for shipping traffic, saw impressive regeneration throughout the nineties changing it from an almost abandoned piece of infrastructure into a key Chicago lakefront landmark with fairs, shops, restaurants and dinner cruises.

Frank Lloyd Wright buildings

Architecture buffs will know that Frank Lloyd Wright, one of the greatest American designers, refined his 'prairie school' style of residential architecture in Chicago. With its series of striking, low horizontal lines, the **Frederick C Robie House** (☎ 708-848-1976) at 5757 South Woodlawn Street, built in 1910, is Chicago's best example of Wright's work and, along with the more recent 'Falling Water House' in Pennsylvania, a key piece of 'prairie school' design.

Frank Lloyd Wright's home and studio (☎ 708-848-1976; daily 10am-3.30pm) at 951 Chicago Avenue in leafy Oak Park is another stunning example of Wright's work; he built this property aged 22 in 1889 with a loan from his boss. Self-guided audio tours are available. For more information about Chicago's architectural legacy, see the previous page.

What to see – jazz, blues and gospel landmarks

Most notable Chicago jazz, blues and gospel landmarks are on the South Side in the **Bronzeville** area simply because it was to cheap South Side tenements that so many migrating African-Americans flocked after jumping off the train at Union Station. The West Side also accommodated thousands of arrivals from the South but Bronzeville became the cultural and commercial heart of the black community in Chicago. Today the South Side remains a rundown and sometimes dangerous neighborhood. The West Side is worse. Visitors should be aware of the risks but not be put off. You simply need to show respect and be sensible. For more information on staying safe in dangerous neighborhoods, an occupational hazard for true jazz and blues lovers in America, turn to p24.

The origin of the phrase 'Bronzeville' is unclear but the area to which the term refers is not. A metal map imbedded in the ground at 35th Street and Martin Luther King Drive shows the boundaries to be roughly between 31st and 52nd Streets north and south and Lake Park Avenue and the Stevenson Expressway west and east. At the intersection of 26th Street and King Drive stands a statue made by Alison Saar in 1996 entitled a **Salute to the Great Migration**. The statue shows a weary but hopeful black traveler arriving in Chicago with a battered but empty suitcase. His suit and suitcase are made from thousands of soles, suggesting the long journey made by so many African-Americans.

Stars' homes

Of all the hundreds of musicians from journeymen to stars who lived across the South Side, just four **stars' homes** have been given historic markers by the City of Chicago.

Louis 'Satchmo' Armstrong lived on-and-off at 421 East 44th Street from 1925 throughout the turbulent years of his marriage to Lil Hardin. Louis first had his own place in Chicago at 459 East 31st Street. Surprisingly, given the stature of its one-time resident, 421 East 44th Street is a tumbledown heap surrounded by a wire fence and boarded up. It's difficult to tell whether anyone is living there now.

Muddy Waters' house

Muddy Waters' house at 4339 South Lake Park Avenue is in equally bad shape. Clearly at one time a large and imposing red-brick property, the house is now completely boarded up. It's shocking to find so little effort has been made to commemorate Chicago's most famous and influential bluesman. A marker confirms the fact that white clarinet star **Benny Goodman**, Chicago's 'King of Swing', lived at 1125 South Francisco Avenue. Sadly, however, South Francisco Avenue is one of the most threatening streets on the West Side – a feat in itself – so it's only worth driving past the place. Like the homes of Muddy and Louis, Goodman's old pad has been deemed worth a marker but not a makeover.

Mahalia Jackson's home at 8358 South Indiana Avenue has fared rather better. Jackson, the undisputed 'Queen of Gospel Music' and musical partner to Tom Dorsey, moved to Chicago from New Orleans in 1927 and bought the property on the relatively affluent South Indiana Avenue in 1956. In 1961 she sang at John F Kennedy's inaugural ball by which time her fame and reputation were assured. The neat, brick bungalow is immaculately maintained by its current owners.

Jazz landmarks

The golden age of Chicago jazz in the twenties and thirties was played out in a number of legendary **jazz venues**. Hardcore jazz fans will be interested to note that the **Coliseum**, a famous stage graced by almost all the jazz leaders of the 'Roaring Twenties', once stood at East 14th Street and South Wabash Avenue but there's nothing to see there now. Another great dance club, the **Regal Theater**, apparently stood on East 47th Street and King Drive although there are conflicting accounts about its exact location. Whatever the truth, that lot is now being developed into the 47th Street Cultural Center, an ambitious project to create new performance space on the South Side.

On a stiflingly hot day in New Orleans in August 1922 Louis Armstrong, having just played at a funeral in Algiers, received a telegram from his mentor, Joe 'King' Oliver. The telegram invited – instructed – the 21-year-old Armstrong to join Oliver's band in Chicago. During his career in Chicago, both with Joe Oliver and in other bands, he performed regularly at several long-gone jazz venues including **Dreamland**, **Lincoln Gardens**, **Plantation Café** and the **Vendôme**. Perhaps the venue most associated with Satchmo, however, was the **Sunset Café** which stood at 315-317 East 35th Street on the corner of South Calumet. The Sunset was managed by Joe Glaser, a shady figure linked to Al Capone who would become Armstrong's promoter. The site of the Sunset Café where, with Earl Hines and others, Armstrong ruled the Chicago jazz scene, is now an Ace hardware store.

Two uptown theaters, the **Aragon** and **Uptown**, hosted extravagant jazz events during the swing era. The Aragon, at 1100 West Lawrence Avenue, is now a rock venue but the Uptown, on North Broadway just north of Lawrence Avenue, is closed. Built in 1925 at a cost of $4 million, it was – and still could be – one of the finest and most elaborate theaters in Chicago. Duke Ellington played to a packed house here in 1931.

Blues landmarks

Many of the South Side's most important **blues venues** are described in the live music section on p272 since they're still open for business. Of the famous clubs which no longer exist, **Theresa's** at 4801 South Indiana and later at 411 43rd Street is most sorely missed by Bronzeville blues fans. Theresa ran her club for 44 years, during which time she regularly presented some of the most famous names in Chicago blues: Buddy Guy, Sunnyland Slim and Little Walter played here often. In 1986 Theresa was evicted. She moved her club to the 43rd Street location but it was never quite the same and she died two years later.

Smitty's at 35th Street and Indiana Avenue, another now defunct club, was Muddy Waters' regular gig throughout the fifties until he was projected onto the international stage. **Turners** at 4012 South Indiana, next to the El station, was frequently played by Little Walter and John Lee 'Sonny Boy' Williamson but, again, is now boarded up and closed. The same goes for the **708 Club** at 708 East 47th Street which is now Bud Marlow and Co selling electronics, furniture and clothing.

Despite an early nineties attempt to rekindle the club, the **1815 Club** at 1815 West Roosevelt Road, once home base to the great Howlin' Wolf, is another legendary name in ruins. Although there's nothing to see now, it's interesting to note that the Chess brothers owned a club at 3905 South Cottage Grove, on the corner with Pershing Road, before they founded their record label in 1947. Their experience of South Side club life made them realize how popular blues had become. Not all Chicago's clubs have gone, of course. The South Side still has a lot of great venues.

Maxwell Street

Maxwell Street, just a short way south of the Loop before 14th Street, is perhaps the most significant blues landmark in the city. The commercial pulse of the black community, Maxwell Street was lined with African-American businesses from the forties to the seventies. The vibrant Sunday street market which grew here is now held near Maxwell on Canal Street. Bluesmen hoping to make their mark in the Windy City would start out playing for tips on Maxwell. They all began here and even now the Canal Street market is conducted to a blues score provided by talented buskers. Sadly, Maxwell Street's days appear numbered. The university which owns many of the buildings around the area is planning to sell the space for so-called 'urban renewal'.

Honest trader,
Maxwell Street

Pilgrim Baptist Church

After the Canal Street market, the next most enjoyable music landmark with which one can get involved is the Pilgrim Baptist Church at 3301 Indiana Avenue. Here composer Tom Dorsey and singer Mahalia Jackson planted the seeds of modern gospel music as part of the church's much-admired choir. The congregation here is still strong and Sunday services have all the vigor and passion one would expect. While the music is wonderful, and visitors are made very welcome, if you're there out of curiosity you should perhaps sit in the balcony so you can slip out; services can last literally hours.

Record companies and other notable buildings

The stretch of South Michigan leading from the Loop into the South Side was once nicknamed **Record Row** because of the music business offices which sprung up here. **Vee-Jay Records** cut classic Jimmy Reed and Eddie Taylor tracks at 1449 South Michigan while at 2120 South Michigan **Chess Records** made its monumental contribution to blues music.

Leonard and Phil Chess ran their label here from 1957 to 1967 during which time they recorded, among many others, Willie Dixon, Muddy Waters, Howlin' Wolf, Chuck Berry, Bo Diddley, John Lee Hooker, Etta James, Buddy Guy and Aretha Franklin. The building was bought by Willie Dixon's wife, Marie Dixon, and donated to the **Blues Heaven Foundation**, an organization which Willie Dixon founded to look out for the 'welfare of the blues tradition'. When Dixon died in 1992 he left a songbook of over 500 numbers from *Back Door Man* to *Young Fashioned Ways*. Almost all have been covered many times in many countries. Tours of Chess Records are available daily between 12-2pm for $10. Call ☎ 312-808 1286 for more information.

Other notable buildings include the *Chicago Defender* **headquarters** on the corner of South Michigan and 24th. The *Defender*, an African-American newspaper distributed up and down the Illinois Central railroad line by porters working the trains, played an important role in encouraging blacks to join the Great Migration north. The **Griffin Funeral Home** at 3232 Martin Luther King Drive is said to have played an important role in blues; musicians would use space here to rehearse.

Elliott Donnelly Youth Center

Also consider swinging by the **Elliott Donnelly Youth Center** (☎ 773-268-3815) 3947 South Michigan Avenue. Founded as the South Side Boys Club in 1924, the center has a long and very distinguished history of helping kids from some of Chicago's least privileged neighborhoods. The center has an extraordinary mural depicting the Great Migration painted across the back of the building. It's well worth dropping in to see it; visitors are made welcome.

Grave of Howlin' Wolf (Chester Burnett)

Famous graves

Two of America's greatest bluesmen, Howlin' Wolf and Muddy Waters, are buried in Chicago and, naturally, their graves attract a steady stream of blues fans. **Muddy Waters' grave** is in the Restvale Cemetery in Alsip at 115th and Leamington. The **grave of Howlin' Wolf**, real name Chester Burnett, is in Oakridge Cemetery in Westchester on Roosevelt between Mannheim and Wolf Road.

Where to stay

Finding an inexpensive place to stay in Chicago can be extremely difficult – and, at times, impossible – despite the vast number of hotels and motels scattered around the city. Businessmen, weekenders and conventioneers flood the place, raising prices for future visitors. This guide to accommodations provides a range of recommended places across price categories. That said, it is, naturally, some way short of comprehensive. Contact the CVB if you're having trouble finding somewhere to slumber. Everywhere mentioned is located downtown close to the action; blues and jazz fans won't have much fun holed up in a motel by O'Hare Airport.

Budget options

Cheap rooms are rare in the Windy City; if your finances are running low a youth hostel might be the only solution. *Hostelling International* (☎ 773-327-5350; ❷) turns a Columbia University residence at 731 South Plymouth Court into a comfortable hostel over the summer months. Another hostel, *Chicago International* (☎ 773-262-1011; ❶-❷) at 6318 North Winthrope Avenue, is cheap, clean and lively thanks to its location near Loyola University. One of the cheapest hotel options is the *Cass Hotel* (☎ 312-787-4030, 800-787-4041; ❸) at 640 North Wabash Avenue. Considering its location, the Cass is a real bargain but don't expect too much from the rather down-at-heel rooms. The best of the budget options – and in any other city on the Blues Highway it wouldn't be labeled 'budget' – is *The Willows* (☎ 773-528-8400, 800-787-3108; ❸-❹) at 555 West Surf Street, an attractive neighborhood hotel with comfortable rooms, friendly staff and a good continental breakfast.

Mid-range options ($50-120)

Chicago has countless **bed and breakfasts** dotted about its 'burbs. Many compare favorably to larger hotels in terms of both price and comfort. *Bed and Breakfast Chicago* (☎ 312-951-0085) can arrange bookings.

The strange-looking *Essex Inn* (☎ 312-939-2800, 800-621-6909; ❸-❹) at 800 South Michigan – just across from Grant Park – is one of the better value downtown hotels with a reasonable level of comfort and quite good service. In a similar price bracket, *The Seneca Hotel* (☎ 312-787-8900, 800-800-6261; ❹) at 200 East Chestnut Street is a one-time apartment block which now houses some 50 rooms and at least as many suites. Some of the suites are fairly spacious so this is a good option for anyone hoping to bunk down in town for an extended stay. Far cooler – and a little cheaper – *HoJo Inn* (☎ 312-664-8100, 800-446-4656; ❸-❹) at 720 North LaSalle Street is an unashamedly retro motor inn which occupies a pretty handy location.

High-end options ($120-250+)

Heading up the plush scale a step or two, *Lenox Suites* (☎ 312-337-1000; 800-445-3669; ❺) at 616 North Rush has suites of varying size on offer just a short walk from the action on Michigan Avenue. Expect to find a good number of long-term residents. A more tourist-orientated set-up, the *Comfort Inn of*

Chicago — chain hotels

- *Best Western Hawthorne Terrace* (☎ 773-244-3434), 3434 North Broadway
- *Best Western River North* (☎ 312-467-0800, 800-727-0800), 125 West Ohio
- *Courtyard by Marriott* (☎ 312-329-2500, 800-321-2211), 30 East Hubbard Street
- *Days Inn Lincoln Park* (☎ 773-525-7010), 644 West Diversey Parkway
- *Hampton Inn and Suites* (☎ 312-832-0330), 33 West Illinois
- *Hilton and Towers* (☎ 312-922-4400), 720 South Michigan Avenue
- *Holiday Inn City Center* (☎ 312-787 6100, 800-465-4329), 300 East Ohio Street
- *Hyatt on Printer's Row* (☎ 312-986-1234; 800-233-1234), 500 South Dearborn Street
- *Hyatt Regency* (☎ 312-565-1234, 800-233-1234), 151 East Wacker Drive
- *Inter-Continental* (☎ 312-312-944-4100, 800-628-2112), 505 North Michigan Avenue
- *Quality Inn Downtown* (☎ 312-829-5000, 800-221-2222), One South Halsted
- *Radisson Hotel and Suites* (☎ 312-787-2900, 800-333-3333), 160 East Huron
- *Sheraton* (☎ 312-464-1000, 800-233-4100), 301 East North Water Street

Lincoln Park (☎ 773-348-2810, 800-228-5150; ❺) at 601 West Diversey is relatively good value given its pleasant position in the Lincoln Park neighborhood. There are few frills, however, and the rooms are fairly functional.

Taking a definite stride towards the more upscale end of the market, the new *Hotel Monaco* (☎ 312-960-8500; 800-397-7661; ❺-❻) at 225 North Wabash is a startlingly bright and expressive place where some lucky designer has indulged in art-deco fantasies seemingly without restraint.

The more sober *Omni Chicago* (☎ 312-944-6664, 800-843-6664; ❺) at 676 North Michigan is one of the more immediately likeable of Chicago's big business hotels; the staff seem a touch more sincere than in so many of these convention-dependent mega-hotels and the rooms are surprisingly cozy.

More in keeping with the theme of this book, if not necessarily with its author's budget, the *House of Blues Hotel* (☎ 312-245-03333; ❻) at 333 North Dearborn Street is an outlandish but beautifully-appointed pile with some fantastic rooms. The hotel's promotional literature claims the 'exotic decor performs backup to your individual style'. While it's perhaps best to assume this is some sort of attempt at satire on behalf of the House of Blues, full credit must go to the Loews hotel group which, working with the music club chain, has created a real gem in the heart of downtown.

A touch more traditional, perhaps, the *Fairmont* (☎ 312-565 8000, 800-527-4727; ❻-❼) at 200 North Columbus Drive is an elegant giant with all the amenities one would expect from such a prestigious establishment and many more besides – including singing waiters in the hotel's attached restaurant, the Primavera. The *Renaissance Chicago* (☎ 312-372-7200, 800-468-3571; ❻-❼) at One West Wacker Drive is equally impressive, although perhaps a touch less evocative. The exterior is ultra-modern but, incongruously, the interior is modeled on grand hotels of 100 years ago.

It would be hard to imagine anyone finding fault in either the Fairmont or the Renaissance but, if you're a truly discerning traveler, the only sensible option for you is the *Drake* (☎ 312-787-2200, 800-553-7253; ❼) at 140 East Walton Place. Every city has one great hotel which stands above the rest; in Chicago that place is the Drake. Built in 1920 at the height of Chicago's optimism, the Drake is an undeniably impressive place with palatial proportions and truly opulent rooms. The service reflects the hotel's status – and so do the prices.

Where to eat

Finding a restaurant in Chicago is difficult not because they're hard to find but because, on the contrary, there's too much choice; where do you start? This relatively brief guide is a hand-picked selection of great restaurants designed to give a range of prices and styles. Perhaps more than anywhere else on the Blues Highway, the proviso applies that this is necessarily a rather subjective and certainly not exhaustive list.

All restaurants described here, with the exception of a couple of classic South Side soul food joints, are located in or very close to downtown. As usual, restaurants are presented in approximate price order from the cheapest dive to the best places in town. In this section, however, that price scale operates within each cuisine type – American, soul food, Italian and pizza.

American

While local foodies trumpet the renaissance in modern American cuisine, a humble McDonald's franchise at 600 North Clark provides what is, arguably, the quintessential American dining experience. Labeled the *'Rock & Roll McDonald's'*, this particular branch of the global burger chain is distinguished by an interior plastered with fake plastic rock artifacts which are gawped at daily by legions of Big Mac-swilling visitors. The rock artifacts themselves are of little interest; what draws the crowds is the rumor that at 600 North Clark a McDonald's exists which isn't exactly like all the others. The food's the same, of course.

Wishbone, on the corner of North Lincoln Avenue and West School Street on the North Side, is a large, bright and busy neighborhood hangout which happens to serve some of the best breakfasts in Chicago. Their 'southern' eggs benedict, $6.25, have to be tasted to be believed. Back in the Loop, *Berghoff* (☎ 312-427-3170) at 17 West Adams Street has been peddling good value American-German cuisine since 1898. Despite its posh and ornate appearance, lunchtime snacks at the Berghoff aren't expensive. Interestingly, the Berghoff holds the city's liquor license number one; the first legal post-Prohibition pint was pulled here.

Heaven on Seven (☎ 312-263-6443) at 111 North Wabash, and its sister premises at 600 North Michigan Avenue (☎ 312-280-7774), is the place to go for Chicago's best Creole cooking. Anyone who's used this book to travel north from New Orleans will know that this is good Southern fare. All the classic dishes are on offer – jambalaya, red beans and rice and gumbo – and the prices are pretty reasonable; expect to pay around $9 for an entrée. The *Northside*

Café (☎ 773-384-3555), 1635 North Damen Avenue, is another cool place for cheaper than expected meals. While the menu is fairly standard – burgers, sandwiches and salads – the restaurant itself attracts an interesting crowd and the service is good.

During the eighties Chicagoans inexplicably fuelled a boom in tacky celebrity restaurants. Even the moderately famous attempted to associate their name with good food. Most failed – even the ever-popular Oprah – but one man, the late sportscaster Harry Caray, succeeded. *Harry Caray's* (☎ 312-828-0966), at 33 West Kinzie Street, has perhaps survived because the food is genuinely good – particularly the steaks. Expect to pay $10 upwards for an entrée. Health-conscious readers might prefer to abandon Harry's sportsman-sized steaks in favor of *Earth* (☎ 312-335-5475), an interesting organic restaurant at 2138 West Grand Avenue. Rather than rely on calorie-counters and vegetarians, Earth appeals to a broader range of gastronomes through an unusually creative approach to healthy cooking.

Blackbird (☎ 312-715-0708) at 619 West Randolph is a rare find; chef Paul Kahan applies the strictest standards to service, cuisine and presentation but the check won't leave you wishing you'd opted for a Happy Meal at the Rock & Roll McDonald's. Roasted sea bass is a favourite; also recommended is the wood-grilled sturgeon. The Blackbird's only flaw is the tightly-packed tables so if you hate being overheard you might want to go elsewhere.

Soul food

Moving on to soul food, a cooking genre more in keeping with the theme of this book, Chicago boasts some of the best down-home food on the Blues Highway. With few exceptions, however, you'll have to wander down to the South Side to find it. *Leon's Bar-B-Q* at 1640 East 79th Street, a carry-out only place where people eat in their cars, is a legendary rib-fest worth renting a car for.

Better still, *Army & Lou's* (☎ 773-483-3100) at 422 East 75th Street is a fine soul food restaurant serving up some of the best meals anywhere in Chicago; this is home cooking for the masses. Daily specials include 'meat and two veg' – the vegetables, as usual, have been boiled, steamed and candied until any hint of vitamins and minerals have long since evaporated – and prices rarely exceed $10 per head. Army & Lou's attracts a smartly-dressed post-church crowd on Sundays when the atmosphere and specials are at their best.

A similar style of place, though perhaps a little less plush, *Gladys' Luncheonette* (☎ 773-548-6848) at 4527 South Indiana Avenue is another respected soul food restaurant. Apart from the food – which is outstanding – Gladys' provides one of Chicago's best people-watching opportunities. On a good day, you'll see a dozen of the South Side's most interesting characters over the course of one meal. The whole thing is capped by the paying procedure; you hand your dollars to a fierce-looking old lady trapped behind a glass booth by the door.

For North Side food with a hint of soul, head for *Smoke Daddy Rhythm & Bar-B-Que* (☎ 773-772-MOJO) at 1804 West Division Street. Part blues joint, part restaurant, Smoke Daddy is well known for its cheap but mouth-watering barbecue. The tiny stage by the front window supports a blues band every night of the week.

Italian

As one might expect, Chicago is loaded with Italian restaurants and, equally predictably, many of them are blisteringly good. Small, café-style places litter the city but a good number of the Windy City's Italian restaurants are remarkably upscale affairs. The *Rosebud* (☎ 312-942-1117) at 1500 West Taylor Street, and its new sister at 720 North Rush Street (☎ 312-266-6444), is well known for its classic cuisine and exceptional pasta dishes. It's a noisy, lively place but few other establishments can match its reputation for authentic southern Italian specialties. Expect to pay anywhere from $15-25 for an entrée. A very different restaurant, *Centro* (☎ 312-988-7775) at 710 North Wells Street is a highly popular place where would-be movers and shakers clammer to be seen. If you're lucky enough to get a reservation, take it. Centro serves up consistently outstanding Italian classics with an emphasis on fresh, rural cuisine.

Still in an Italian vein, Chicago is, of course, home to its own particularly filling style of pizza. Years ago immigrant Italians, used to seeing pizza bases used as a thin and crunchy bed on which to place a pizza's ingredients, soon gasped in amazement as Chicagoans inflated the base of their pizzas till the crust eclipsed the topping. This 'deep pan' Chicago-style of pizza has since filled freezer compartments in supermarkets the world over. The place where it all started is said to be *Pizzeria Uno* (☎ 312-321-1000) at 29 East Ohio Street. Pizzeria Uno is now a chain but this first restaurant is a noisy, friendly place where Chicago-style pizza devotees will no doubt want to pay their respects.

Gino's (☎ 312-943-1124), 633 North Wells Street, is another deep pan institution which has been filling its customers to bursting point for 35 years and was apparently voted number one by *People* magazine. If all that crust gets the better of you and you long for a traditional Italian-style pizza, *Pat's Pizzeria and Ristorante* (☎ 773-248-0168) at 3114 North Sheffield is, without doubt, the place to go. Open since 1950, Pat's is a bastion of classic Italian-style pizzas and, more than that, a pleasant and likeable neighborhood restaurant.

Other food

Almost every other style of cuisine is represented somewhere, somehow in Chicago. The very best and most memorable restaurants from other cooking categories – and this really is difficult to distill – include Nick's Fishmarket, the Frontera Grill and Carlos'. *Nick's Fishmarket* (☎ 312-621-0200) at One First National Plaza on South Clark Street, a local favorite, has built a reputation for some of the best seafood in town served in a beautiful downtown restaurant with first-class service. The price reflects the quality.

Frontera Grill (☎ 312-243-6667) at 445 North Clark Street is famous for some of the best and most authentic Mexican cuisine this side of Tijuana. With entrées hovering around the $12 mark, the universally-applauded Frontera Grill represents exceptionally good value for money.

Carlos' (☎ 847-432-0770), at 429 Temple Avenue in the Highland Park area, is a place to take someone you really want to impress. The impeccable modern French cuisine and elegant setting – not to mention the steep prices – make this an exclusive and memorable restaurant.

Where to find live music

For jazz, blues and other entertainment listings, pick up a copy of the *Chicago Reader* which is published free every Thursday. The *Reader* is as complete a guide to Chicago life as one could imagine and an essential prop for music fans. Most clubs print schedules looking several weeks ahead so, one way or the other, it's easy to get a feel for what's on in Chicago despite the city's humbling size.

Local stars to watch out for include Delta bluesman David 'Honeyboy' Edwards (see opposite), guitar virtuoso Buddy Guy, 'Queen of Blues' Koko Taylor and jazz saxophonist Von Freeman. Also look out for Big Time Sarah, Willie Kent, Jimmy Burns, Son Seals, Jimmy Johnson and Liz Mandeville Greeson.

South Side

The thought of a trip to the South Side frightens many visitors and terrifies a good number of locals. Streets south of the Loop have a reputation for violence and crime. It is, however, easy to overstate the problem; be sensible and you'll have no reason to miss what is, for jazz and blues lovers, the most culturally and historically important district in Chicago.

At 423 East 43rd Street, the *Checkerboard Lounge* (☎ 773-624-3240), owned by LC Thurman, is currently one of the best-known South Side clubs. The Spartan interior has juke joint aesthetics but the Checkerboard is used to white visitors from the North Side and there's very rarely trouble here. Good live blues kicks off after 9.30pm every Friday and Saturday night till the small hours. Alma's Soul Food next door will cater for your late-night munchies when the music's over. Cabs will collect from outside the Checkerboard if you ask the bar staff to call one.

Lee's Unleaded Blues (☎ 773-495-3477) at 7401 South Chicago Avenue, formerly the Queen Bee, is an equally well-known establishment. The dim, red-lit interior oozes seventies American cool. Fake stone slabs on the outside of the building are an interesting touch. Design issues aside, Lee's Unleaded is a great club presenting top-flight blues and R&B acts every weekend to a friendly crowd.

After the Checkerboard and Lee's Unleaded, *Gerri's Palm Tavern* (☎ 773-373-6292) at 446 East 47th Street is perhaps the next most popular South Side music joint. Opened in 1933, Gerri's is a South Side survivor and a landmark music venue. In its early days the Palm Tavern was a well-known jazz hang out but these days the place is as much a blues club. There's live music from Wednesdays to Sundays. Gerri, who's owned the place since 1956, is usually perched behind the bar stroking an impossibly fat cat.

The *Velvet Lounge* (☎ 312-791-9050) at 2128 South Indiana is one of the few jazz clubs on the South Side still presenting regular sessions. It's a slightly odd place in that few concessions have been made to comfort but much effort has been put into promoting the joint and its brand of experimental jazz. More jazz can be heard at the *Cotton Club and All That Jazz* (☎ 312-341-9787) at 1710 South Michigan. This ultra-cool and upscale South Side jazz joint features some of the best local talent every weekend and frequently lures national acts.

Further south, the *New Apartment Lounge* (☎ 773-483-7728), 504 East 75th Street, is a mellow and likeable jazz club where pioneering Chicago saxophonist Von Freeman plays every Tuesday night. Freeman, born in 1922, is a veteran of the Chicago jazz scene. His son, Chico, another saxman, has forged an equally successful jazz career in New York. With its faded cocktail bar looks and sleepy staff, the New Apartment Lounge is one of the coolest clubs on the South Side.

Interview – David 'Honeyboy' Edwards

How did you finish up in Chicago?
I first came to Chicago in 1945 when I brought Little Walter. Then I went back to Mississippi in 1946 and then I went to Arkansas. I wanted to ramble through the country. I got my wife in 1947 and we started a family together. I bought me a car and we started to travel and play all through the country – New Orleans, Vicksburg, Louisiana, Texas and all through there.

David 'Honeyboy' Edwards, from Shaw, Mississippi, is a Delta bluesman and contemporary of Robert Johnson who settled in Chicago in the fifties.

We came back to Memphis in 1952 for Sam Phillips and after that I recorded with Chess. I then recorded in Houston for a recording company. By 1956 my brother had moved here while I was still out in Texas playing. I played a club there and I had a big write-up in the paper. I sent the paper to my brother, he looked at it and said 'Honey, you oughta come to Chicago where we is'. I've been here ever since and I've done a lot of recording and been to a lot of places since. It's got like I can't move, I go all over the world but I always come back to Chicago. I played on Maxwell Street with the rest of them. They all played there. We just played the blues all the time.

How have Chicago clubs changed since then?
Blues clubs mostly continue but they're playing a lot of rock & roll. The blues players play faster blues. They can play slow blues but they can't play the blues like we played them. But there's a lot of clubs in Chicago, they're pretty close to like it used to be. I don't care what you play all night so long as it's blues. When they put that expressway through here [the South Side] they tore up a lot of clubs and taverns and a few steel mills. They made a highway through here. Then white people moved clubs to the North Side. We got some clubs down here but we ain't got near as many as there used to be. People didn't have to leave the South Side to hear the blues because it was everywhere.

Do you have a favourite place to play here in Chicago?
Back in the old days I used play at Cadillac Davis' place. Me and Junior Parker used to play there on Dearborn. That was a nice place to play in, we played there a gang of times. We made records there with some of the guys like Magic Sam who was mostly a West Side player.

(Continued on p274)

Interview – David 'Honeyboy' Edwards (cont'd)

You've played with a lot of great blues stars over the years. Who do you think influenced you most?

Yeah I've played with a lot of people. But I liked to play with Robert Johnson. He and I were the same age. Robert used to go with my cousin. I went round there one day and she said, 'Honey, do you know Robert Johnson?'. 'No,' I said, 'I don't know him but heard a lot of talk of him'. She said, 'he's my boyfriend'. I finally met him about a year later in Greenwood. He was there with a little suit of clothes on and he had a little guitar. I was walking down the street with my guitar hanging on my back. I didn't know who he was, but I saw this little skinny guy standing there with a guitar. By the time I got there a woman walked up to him, she was half drunk. She said 'Mister, play me *Terraplane Blues* and I'll give you a dime'. He said, 'Miss, that's my recording'. She said 'I don't care, just play it'. He started playing and in about five minutes the street was crowded. We hooked up then. I knew every corner of Greenwood, where they sold white whiskey, every joint where they played music, every hot dog and hamburger stand. We played and made a few nickels and dimes. We stayed together all the fall and started playing for this man out at the Three Forks Club. I played with him sometimes, and sometimes Sonny Boy [Williamson II] went out there. Robert was the best guitar player around. He drew the crowds from the other clubs. People went where he played.

Do you still have ambitions in music?

Right now at my age I don't think I'll quit playing unless I get sick or something. That's the only thing keeps me going. I talked to Buddy Guy and told him a couple of weeks ago 'Man, if I'd made as much money as BB King I think I'd throw my guitar away'. He said, 'no man, keep on going'. I think that's about right.

Artis's (☎ 773-734-0491), at 1249 East 87th Street, is a low-key blues club with live bands on Wednesdays and Sundays. Most other nights this hidden-away neighborhood bar is filled with a young crowd pumping the juke-box for rap tracks so, if it's blues you want, choose your night carefully.

The *New Bonanza* club (☎ 773-538-3200) at 552 East 47th Street near Gerri's Palm Tavern is another place which regularly presents decent – and sometimes exceptional – blues acts. Look out for Elmore James Jr and the Broom Dusters. Not far away at 51st and Aberdeen, *Linda's* is a new and very small neighborhood joint which lays on blues most Thursday nights. At the time of writing Jerry Jones and the Night Owls were a regular and highly entertaining fixture.

Celebrity Blues Showcase (☎ 773-548-4812) at 4830 South Cottage Grove is a friendly club with live blues every weekend. If you're lucky, owner Fred Johnson and his band the Checkmates will be playing. Two other South Side clubs which might be worth checking out are *Margaret's New 7313 Club* (☎ 773-723-0592) at 7313 South Halsted, where LV Banks and the Swinging Blues Band play on Thursday nights, and *Mr Cotton's New Lovers Lounge* (☎ 773-488-9807) at 7251 South Ashland Avenue where there's live blues most Wednesday nights.

West Side

Most Chicagoans will tell you that the West Side is more dangerous than the South Side and there's usually something to be said for local advice. In practice, like everywhere else in the city, common sense will keep you out of trouble. Two West Side blues clubs frequented by hardcore music lovers are *Mr Tee's* on the corner of Lake and St Louis and the *Starlight Lounge* at 605 South Pulaski. Both are quite rough joints although Starlight is the better of the two. Live blues is played at weekends and the crowd is a pretty mixed bunch.

However the best blues club on the West Side, and another of Chicago's landmark clubs, is *Rosa's* (☎ 312-342-0452) at 3420 West Armitage. With some of Chicago's best artists providing music from Tuesdays to Sundays and an Italian-American history worthy of a soap opera, Rosa's shouldn't be missed. David 'Honeyboy' Edwards plays here often. Look out for the wonderful black and white blues prints around the walls.

Downtown and the Loop

Located just south of the Loop, or just north of the South Side depending on your point of view, two of Chicago's most successful blues stars own eponymous clubs.

Buddy Guy's Legends (☎ 312-427-0333) at 754 South Wabash, on the corner of South Wabash and Eighth, is several shades more sophisticated than most South Side clubs and the venue of choice for big names in blues. Big Bill Morganfield – Muddy Waters' son – Honeyboy Edwards, Son Seals and Buddy Guy himself all play here fairly regularly. Louisiana-born Buddy Guy began his Chicago blues career playing what would later be labeled 'West Side blues' with Magic Sam and Junior Wells. He has since become one of the most successful figures in blues. His club is a large and slick place with pool tables, good food and a large, mostly white, following.

Buddy Guy

'Queen of Blues' Koko Taylor has recently opened a new club, *Koko Taylor's Celebrity* (☎ 312-360-1558), at 1233 South Wabash Avenue. Managed by her daughter the club has so far presented an impressive series of blues acts although Koko herself rarely appears. Born near Memphis in 1935, Koko Taylor moved to Chicago at an early age. In 1966 her rendition of Willie Dixon's *Wang Dang Doodle* for Chess Records made her a star. She now records for Alligator. Koko Taylor's Celebrity is a snug and popular club although it doesn't look much from the outside. Amazing blues photographs adorn the walls.

Nearby at 31 East Balbo, *Hot House* (☎ 312-362-9707) is a rather self-consciously trendy place funded in part by the Illinois Arts Council. Its mission is to 'expose audiences to a wide range of cultural expression'. Blues and jazz are featured frequently so it's worth checking out the calendar. Comfy sofas and cozy booths make this a pleasant place; stars' guitars and photographs line the walls.

Moving north into the Loop, *Blue Chicago* has two clubs just a short walk apart; one is located at 536 North Clark Street (☎ 312-661-0100), the other at 736 North Clark Street (☎ 312-642-6261). One cover charge – usually $5 –

allows entry to both venues. There's good music almost every night. Blue Chicago's clubs are moody, atmospheric places but both are several steps more upscale than South Side clubs and so both attract plenty of visitors. *Famous Dave's* (☎ 312-266-2400), nearby at 739 North Clark Street, is a far more tacky and touristy place. There's music here every night, usually some form of blues or R&B, but musicians have to compete with giant sports screens.

If you've ventured into blues clubs on the South Side, you'll find the *House of Blues* (☎ 312-923-2000) at 329 North Dearborn to be a surreal experience. All the effort put into packaging and presenting this caricature of a blues club seems somehow superfluous when the real thing is available just a few miles to the south or west. In fairness, the management here book some fine musicians and the Sunday gospel brunch is a lot of fun. The standard of food served in the attached Cajun-orientated restaurant is pretty high, too.

Jazz in Chicago hasn't fared quite so well as the city's blues scene but there are a number of quality clubs worth checking out. The best of these is *Jazz Showcase* (☎ 312-670-BIRD) at 59 West Grand Avenue. Dark and candlelit like a jazz club should be, Jazz Showcase was opened in 1947 but has recently moved to its current location. Cover prices are usually high, perhaps $15-20, reflecting the stature of featured musicians. Sets are played at 8 and 10pm on Tuesday to Sunday nights. August is Charlie Parker month.

Another Loop jazz club, *Andy's Live Jazz* (☎ 312-642-6805) at 11 East Hubbard Street, is a thickly-carpeted, neon-lit place where mainstream jazz bands entertain hushed diners at 5 and 9pm most nights.

Joe's Be-Bop Café (☎ 312-595 5299) at Navy Pier, 600 East Grand Avenue, is a sprawling restaurant specializing in barbecue and jazz. There's music every night and a Sunday jazz brunch.

North Side

Some argue that in terms of clubs, rather than legend, Chicago's blues epicenter has shifted from the South Side to the Lincoln Park area. There is certainly a stack of great clubs on the North Side and the area is generally thought to be a lot safer.

B.L.U.E.S (☎ 773-528-1012) at 2519 North Halsted is the leading North Side blues club which has presented some of the greatest names in Chicago blues from Sunnyland Slim to Pinetop Perkins since it opened in the late seventies. B.L.U.E.S still hosts Chicago's best, night after night. The lively, enthusiastic crowd and tiny, close stage make this one of the most enjoyable clubs in town. In fact, the club's popularity led its owner to establish another venue, *B.L.U.E.S Etcetera* (773-525-8989), at 1124 West Belmont. This larger, less cozy club features bigger acts like Otis Rush and Magic Slim who can attract far larger audiences than the old club can handle.

Just a short stroll from B.L.U.E.S at 2548 North Halsted, *Kingston Mines* (☎ 773-477-4646) is an enormous club with two vast rooms each with its own stage. The stages are used alternately so one room is always music-free for people who want to chill. Kingston Mines has a license till four in the morning which might explain the club's slightly down-at-heel feel; it attracts a weird mix of desperate drinkers – very old or very young – and blues fans, who flock to the place because of its deserved reputation for great music. Some of Chicago's very best blues musicians have graced one or other of the two stages and the quality of bands presented here is always high.

Lilly's (☎ 773-525-2422), at 2513 North Lincoln Avenue, has blues, rock or folk music from Wednesday to Saturday nights. Although the music can be good, the club itself is a poor venue; unfriendly bar staff, incongruous European-style decor and weak acoustics work against the band. Lilly's location is convenient, however, so it's worth including on a North Lincoln bar crawl.

For jazz in this part of town, check out the seductively smooth *Pops for Champagne* (☎ 773-472-1000) at 2934 North Sheffield Street near the Wellington El station. Smooth-style dinner jazz is played here every night while discerning listeners indulge in glasses of champagne for $10 a throw.

Further north in the Uptown Andersonville area, near the Lawrence El Station on the Red Line, the *Green Mill* (☎ 773-878-5552) at 4802 North Broadway on the corner of West Lawrence Avenue is a legendary Chicago club which oozes thirties elegance and charm. This was one of Al Capone's favourite hangouts and the basement is said to lead into a series of tunnels used for escape and smuggling. The club still has the looks and even the atmosphere of an illegal speakeasy. Live jazz is performed nightly.

West of Lincoln Park at 1354 West Wabansia Avenue, the *Hideout Inn* (☎ 773-227-4433) is a great club buried in a quiet, blue collar industrial area. Exuberant owners Katie and Tim Tutan present blues and alternative bands to a mixed and friendly crowd. The Hideout has been open for business since 1934 but for years remained undiscovered by most Chicagoans. Since taking over in 1997, the new management has put the Hideout emphatically on the map of Chicago's best music venues.

Two other tucked away clubs which might be worth making the effort to find, depending on who's playing, are *Green Dolphin Street* (☎ 773-395-0066) at 2200 North Ashland, a plush restaurant with regular live music, and the *Empty Bottle* (☎ 773-276-3600) at 1035 North Western, a student hangout which tries hard to be trendy and sometimes hosts good bands.

If you've got a car and you're prepared to travel for your music, *Fitzgerald's* (☎ 708-788-2118) at 6615 Roosevelt Avenue in Berwyn is an interesting blues, roots and folk venue with an eclectic booking policy; it's well worth the excursion. Fitzgerald's organizes an annual 'American Music Festival' every July 4th weekend featuring two stages, over 30 bands and lots of good food. The line-up is mixed and impressive; expect anyone from CJ Chenier and the Red Hot Louisiana Band to the Chicago Jazz Orchestra or an Elvis cover band.

Chicago — radio stations

WNIB 97.1 FM has a regular morning blues slot; WBEZ 91.5 FM, a National Public Radio affiliate, has jazz most evenings. WNUA 95.5 FM plays what it describes as 'smooth jazz'.

Appendix

Who's who of Blues Highway musicians

Thousands of gifted musicians have contributed to the music of the Blues Highway; jazz, blues, soul, R&B, rock & roll, zydeco, Cajun, country and gospel music all owe their existence to this slice of America which is saturated in music history. This guide to some of the very greatest Blues Highway music legends includes only those who are mentioned frequently in the book. It is not an exhaustive list but one designed to help readers to piece together the story of the Blues Highway. Listed by the musician's name is the genre with which they are associated. Cross-referenced names are shown in SMALL CAPITAL LETTERS.

Armstrong, Louis (1901-1971) *Jazz*
Louis 'Satchmo' Armstrong grew up playing jazz on the streets and in the whorehouses of New Orleans and went on to become one of the very greatest names in the history of American music. His virtuoso trumpet playing, pioneering vocals and magnetic, embracing personality endeared Satchmo to millions around the world. Establishing himself first in New Orleans, then in Chicago and eventually in New York, Los Angeles and the world, it's impossible to over-estimate Louis Armstrong's influence on jazz both as a performer and as an ambassador for the music. Satch didn't invent jazz but he defined its classic era.

Bechet, Sidney (1897-1959) *Jazz*
Another product of the fledgling New Orleans jazz world, Bechet was a soprano saxophone player of immense stature who found a spiritual home in France where, in his later years, he was idolized. Bechet's musicianship was beyond reproach but his combative person-

ality led to a number of infamous jazz spats and some interesting collaborations. His legacy as a composer is one of the finest in classic jazz.

Beiderbecke, Bix (1903-1931) *Jazz*
Born into a prosperous middle-class family of German descent in Davenport, Iowa, Bix Beiderbecke first heard jazz from steamboats as they made their way up the Mississippi River. Despite strong opposition from his family, Beiderbecke developed a precocious jazz talent and recorded some of the most innovative cornet playing of the twenties. He was also a pianist and composer. Beiderbecke's early death – and the fact that his contribution to jazz was little understood in his lifetime – have created around his name one of the most enduring jazz legends.

Berry, Chuck (1926-) *Rock & Roll*
St Louis-born blues-influenced guitarist Chuck Berry is one of the great pioneers of rock & roll. His much-imitated guitar licks and wry

delivery made him a huge star in the fifties when trademark tunes like *Johnny B. Goode* and *Maybellene* dominated the charts and competed with ELVIS PRESLEY'S brand of rock & roll. Berry created his sound with pianist JOHNNIE JOHNSON and recorded many of his best-known hits for the Chess label in Chicago.

Bland, Bobby 'Blue' (1930-) *Blues*
A prolific recording artist and always on tour, Tennessean Bobby 'Blue' Bland has been in the blues first division since the fifties when he pioneered the soul-blues fusion in Memphis. Using big brass sections, gospel-inspired vocals and refined guitar licks, Bland created a string of hits for the Duke label. He continues to record with Malaco Records in Jackson, Mississippi, and frequently tours with BB KING.

Bolden, Buddy (1877-1931) *Jazz*
Often credited as the 'first jazz trumpeter', a great deal of myth surrounds the Bolden name. The facts would appear to be that Bolden was a highly charismatic and flamboyant character who played powerful early jazz in the clubs and parades of New Orleans where he inspired the subsequent generation of 'cornet kings' including JOE 'KING' OLIVER and Freddie Keppard. In 1906, however, he began a steady slide towards insanity and in 1907 was taken to a New Orleans' asylum where he remained till death.

Booker, James (1939-1983) *Blues*
A keyboards player of immense talent, Booker's musical progress was dogged by his drug habit for most of his life. He recorded briefly in the late fifties, including his 1960 hit *Gonzo*, before a spell in jail on drugs charges. Booker's career came close to resurrection when he played an inspired set at the New Orleans Jazz and Heritage Festival in 1975 and later recorded albums for Island and Rounder.

Brenston, Jackie (1930-1979) *Rock & Roll*
Composer of the 1951 hit *Rocket 88*, often described as the first ever rock & roll record, Brenston recorded at Sun Records with IKE TURNER'S band which was assembled in Clarksdale, Mississippi. Brenston's later career didn't live up to his early success but the legacy of *Rocket 88* is such that he succeeded in making his mark on American music.

Broonzy, Big Bill (1893-1958) *Blues*
Born in Mississippi but raised in Arkansas, Broonzy traveled to Chicago in the early twenties where he became a leading player on the burgeoning South Side blues scene. As the father of Chicago blues and a pioneer of the Chicago sound, Broonzy enjoyed a prolific recording career and considerable success as a composer. After World War Two, Broonzy became one of the first bluesmen to tour Europe where he was warmly received, stoking the European love affair with the blues.

Buckwheat Zydeco (1947-) *Zydeco*
Lafayette-born Stanley 'Buckwheat' Dural formed Buckwheat Zydeco in 1979 after playing with CLIFTON CHENIER in the Red Hot Louisiana Band. Previously, Dural played an R&B-soul hybrid in large bands. He allowed elements of R&B to influence his style of zydeco, creating a more mainstream sound which has significantly boosted the profile of zydeco music worldwide.

Cash, Johnny (1932-) *Country, Rock & Roll*
A witness to the birth of rock & roll in Sun Records, Memphis, where he recorded hits for SAM PHILLIPS and jammed with ELVIS PRESLEY and JERRY LEE LEWIS as part of the so-called 'Million Dollar Quartet', Johnny Cash – the 'Man in Black' – is perhaps best known for his considerable success in and profound influence on the Nashville music scene. Cash is one of the most important country-rock crossover musicians of the sixties and seventies and an accomplished songsmith and live performer.

Chenier, Clifton (1925-1987) *Zydeco*
The undisputed king of zydeco music, Clifton Chenier began his career playing R&B accordion rather than true zydeco. He recorded for several labels, including Chess, but his successes were patchy until, in 1964, he signed with Arhoolie Records and was persuaded to switch to straight

zydeco music. His excessive performances, joyous style and driving rhythm made him a star on the live stage. He toured continuously in North America and Europe, his reputation growing all the time. This frantic work schedule put zydeco on the musical map. He recorded the album *I'm Here* in 1982 for Chicago's Alligator label but poor health slowed his capacity to play live until his death in 1987.

Chess Brothers *Blues and Rock & Roll*
The Chess brothers, Leonard and Phil, were Polish immigrants who settled in Chicago in 1928. They became post-Prohibition club owners before establishing the Aristocrat label in 1947 to record the blues talent they had seen emerge on the South Side. MUDDY WATERS was one of Aristocrat's first artists. In 1950 the company changed its name to Chess and launched a subsidiary label, Checker. Throughout the fifties and sixties Chess and Checker recorded many of the best-loved names in Chicago blues and became synonymous with the Chicago sound.

Cropper, Steve (1941-) *R&B and Soul*
Born in Missouri, Steve Cropper moved with his family to Memphis at the age of nine and at 14 he bought his first guitar from a mail order catalogue. While still at school Cropper formed the Mar-Keys with whom he scored a top five R&B hit, *Last Night*. He went on to play a leading role in Memphis soul and R&B throughout the best years of the Stax and Hi labels. He worked with everyone from WILSON PICKETT to OTIS REDDING and, with Booker T and the MGs, helped define the Memphis soul sound both behind the scenes and on stage. Cropper is still a very active musician and a member of the made-for-movies band The Blues Brothers.

Davis, Miles (1926-1991) *Jazz*
St Louisian jazz trumpeter Miles Davis became one of the most influential figures in jazz during his long and inventive career. During the forties he was a key figure in the bebop movement along with Charlie Parker. He later led the 'cool school' style of jazz. Constant innovation and changes in style inspired a series of seminal recordings over four decades. His legendary quintets and sextets of the fifties, in particular, recorded some of the most influential jazz albums laid down including *Kind of Blue* with John Coltrane. Always looking to invent, later years saw Davis allow rock to influence his jazz – sacrilege to purists – and the addition of electric instruments to his band and even electric modification of his own trumpet.

Dixon, Willie (1915-1992) *Blues*
Born in Vicksburg, Mississippi, Willie Dixon made his name on the Chicago blues scene where he worked as a composer, arranger, session musician and talent scout for Chess Records as well as a recording musician in his own right. Dixon's influence was such that he became one of the most vital figures on the Chicago blues scene, writing hits for the likes of MUDDY WATERS and shaping the city's sound. A spell with the Cobra label saw him play a role in the West Side sound, too, working with BUDDY GUY, Magic Sam and Otis Rush. It was, however, as a composer that Dixon was at his best. His magnificent songbook contains hundreds of blues standards which have been covered by bands around the world.

Domino, Fats (1928-) *R&B and Rock & Roll*
Antoine 'Fats' Domino began recording New Orleans R&B in 1950 and enjoyed over 10 years at the top of the R&B charts with classic compositions like *Blueberry Hill* and *Whole Lotta Loving*. His exuberant recordings and live performances helped him cross over from R&B into rock & roll and his hits quickly climbed the pop charts. Fats Domino's success did much to fuel the New Orleans R&B boom which lasted well into the sixties.

Dorsey, Tom (1899-1993) *Blues and Gospel*
Often called the 'Father of Gospel', Dorsey, from Georgia, began his musical life as a blues pianist on Chicago's South Side playing and recording with the likes of Tampa Red. Ironically, perhaps, their biggest hit was the bawdy and innuendo-loaded *It's Tight Like That*. In the early thir-

ties Dorsey found religion and went to work as musical director at the Pilgrim Baptist Church. There he worked with MAHALIA JACKSON to define the modern gospel sound. Dorsey penned some of gospels finest standards, included *Precious Lord* and *Peace in the Valley*.

Edwards, David 'Honeyboy' (1915-) *Blues*
A Delta bluesmen from Shaw, Mississippi, 'Honeyboy' Edwards is one of the last of the originals. He began his career as a teenager playing juke joints with the likes of Big Joe Williams and ROBERT JOHNSON. In 1942 Alan Lomax recorded him for the Library of Congress. In the mid-fifties he settled in Chicago where he continued to play authentic Delta blues on the club circuit. The blues revival of the late sixties discovered 'Honeyboy' still playing his brand of Mississippi blues and he began recording again, first with Adelphi and later with Michael Frank's Chicago-based Earwig label. Edwards continues to perform in Chicago and at festivals in America and Europe.

Fountain, Pete (1930-) *Jazz*
A permanent fixture in New Orleans thanks to his eponymous club, Fountain and his Dixieland style of jazz clarinet achieved lasting fame through a long-running slot on ABC television and numerous high profile guest slots with stars like Bing Crosby and Johnny Carson. Fountain continues to perform in Las Vegas and at his club in New Orleans.

Frost, Frank (1936-1999) *Blues*
Predominantly a harp player but a talented multi-instrumentalist, Frost achieved blues fame with the Jelly Roll Kings which he formed with Sam Carr and Big Jack Johnson in Helena, Arkansas. The Jelly Roll Kings were much in demand in the Delta throughout the seventies and eighties. Frost's solo career was given a boost when he featured in the movie *Crossroads*.

Goodman, Benny (1909-1986) *Jazz*
Born in Chicago, Goodman took up the clarinet aged 11 and within a few years was using his exceptional talent to make a name on the professional circuit. Determined and ambitious, he was leading his own band at 25. Goodman was a perfectionist and an inventor who extended the scope of jazz clarinet and was one of the first great names to mix white and black musicians in his bands and orchestras. He was alleged to have been a harsh boss and a difficult man. But, whatever the truth, he carved a glittering career in jazz and brought on some great talents through his orchestra. Goodman continued to play right up until his death in 1986 when he was performing with small groups including Scott Hamilton and Warren Vaché.

Green, Al (1946-) *Soul and Gospel*
Brought up on a diet of church music in Grand Rapids, Michigan, Al Green signed to the Memphis-based Hi Records label after a chance encounter with producer Willie Mitchell in 1969. With his outstanding falsetto voice and perfect phrasing, Green became the biggest soul star of the seventies selling 20 million records on the back of hits like *Let's Stay Together*. In the eighties he returned to his gospel roots, found religion and became pastor of the Full Gospel Tabernacle in Memphis, Tennessee, where he preaches most Sundays.

Guy, Buddy (1936-) *Blues*
Originally from Louisiana, Buddy Guy found his musical home in Chicago in 1957 where he established himself as a pioneer of the 'West Side sound' and an innovator who helped move blues guitar forwards in the rock age. Throughout the sixties Guy worked as a session musician behind some of the greatest names in Chicago blues and slowly emerged as a guitar giant in his own right. His virtuoso style inspired both blues and rock musicians and has made him one of most admired guitarists in the world. He continues to perform and record, currently with the Silvertone label, and owns his own blues club in Chicago.

Handy, WC (1873-1958) *Blues and Jazz*
Described as the 'Father of the Blues', Handy, from Florence, Alabama, was a

composer and arranger who led bands in the South when, in 1903, he first heard proto-blues at a railroad station in Tutwiler, Mississippi. Intrigued and impressed, he began to incorporate blue notes into his own repertoire and was the first to use the term 'blues' in song titles. He penned classics such as *Memphis Blues, Beale Street Blues* and *St Louis Blues*. Many of these refined and brilliant compositions owed more to jazz than to blues. Whichever genre best fits the Handy songbook, however, there's little doubt that he was one of America's greatest composers. Handy set up his own music publishing business in New York, initially to look after his own work, and that company is still in the Handy family today.

Hines, Earl (1903-1983) *Jazz*
Born in Pennsylvania, Earl Hines relocated to Chicago at an early age where he shone as the pre-eminent jazz pianist in town, working for years with the great LOUIS ARMSTRONG. Hines and Armstrong shared a competitive relationship but their collaborations are the work of two undisputed geniuses. After a long residency with Armstrong at the Sunset Café Hines took center stage at the Grand Terrace for a 12 year run. By the late fifties Hines' career was faltering; jazz had moved on without him. The later sixties saw a change in fortunes, however, as the music rediscovered the amazing talent of Earl Hines and showered upon him the recognition he had long deserved. His reputation secure, he died in 1983 in the knowledge that he would be remembered as one of the very greatest pianists of the classic jazz age.

Hooker, John Lee (1917-2001) *Blues*
Growing up in Clarksdale, Mississippi, Hooker learned guitar from his stepfather, William Moore, and by 14 was wandering the South playing juke joints by night. He settled in Detroit and began to record his boogie guitar licks in 1948. Hooker's *Boogie Chillen* sold a million and from that point on Hooker's career soared. He was, without doubt, among the most successful bluesmen in history, with million-selling

albums released as recently as the nineties. Hooker's lean, simple but powerful delivery has been much imitated but never bettered.

House, Son (1902-1988) *Blues*
One of the original pioneers of the Delta blues sounds, Son House helped define the genre with other early legends CHARLEY PATTON and Willie Brown. By 20 Son House was a Baptist pastor but blues and its peripheral attractions, namely alcohol and women, overtook him. Throughout the thirties he played his intense and intuitive blues at juke joints and house parties and, in 1941, he recorded for Alan Lomax and the Library of Congress. Son House inspired, among others, ROBERT JOHNSON. During the fifties, he disappeared from the blues scene but was 'discovered' in time to enjoy the blues-folk revival of the sixties which turned him into a living legend.

Howlin' Wolf (1910-1976) *Blues*
SAM PHILLIPS at Sun Records in Memphis first recorded the legendary Howlin' Wolf, born Chester Burnett in West Point, Mississippi, in 1952. By that time, Howlin' Wolf was already a 42-year-old who had perfected his Delta blues over a long period of time. Phillips leased the tracks to Chicago's CHESS BROTHERS and Howlin' Wolf moved to the Windy City. There he developed an electric blues style which thrust him to the highest echelons of blues and sealed his reputation as one of the greatest ever live blues performers and MUDDY WATERS' chief rival.

Hurt, 'Mississippi' John (1893-1966) *Blues*
'Mississippi' John Hurt's gentle brand of blues made him locally popular in the Delta throughout the twenties but he remained unknown to wider audiences until the sixties, shortly before his death, when the folk-blues revival scooped him from the Delta and catapulted him into college campus fame.

Jackson, Mahalia (1911-1972) *Gospel*
Born in New Orleans, Mahalia Jackson already displayed an exceptional musical

talent when she moved to Chicago aged 16. Brought up in the Baptist church, but influenced by the blues and jazz she had heard both in New Orleans and in Chicago, Jackson developed a career in gospel music which was the most illustrious of any gospel singer before or since. Indeed, her powerful and immaculate delivery made her one of the most exceptional singers to record in the United States. Jackson worked with TOM DORSEY at the Pilgrim Baptist Church in Chicago to define the modern gospel sound.

James, Elmore (1918-1963) *Blues*
Like so many bluesmen, Elmore James learned his craft in Mississippi and perfected it in Chicago. He became the most important slide guitarist of the fifties and sixties, setting new standards and influencing a generation of rock musicians. While still in the Delta, James picked up strong elements of his technique from ROBERT JOHNSON and regularly played with SONNY BOY WILLIAMSON II. His classic hit *Dust My Broom*, based on a Robert Johnson number, is a seminal blues standard.

Johnson, Johnnie (1924-) *Rock & Roll*
After teaching himself piano while growing up in West Virginia, Johnson moved to Chicago where he played blues with MUDDY WATERS and then St Louis where he worked with ALBERT KING. He formed his own band and one night asked a young CHUCK BERRY to sit in with him. Their subsequent musical partnership played a leading role in the development of rock & roll. Johnson hasn't always enjoyed the recognition he deserves for his contribution to rock & roll but, in recent years, he has been recording solo albums to critical acclaim.

Johnson, Robert (1911-1938) *Blues*
Robert Johnson's life was steeped in blues mythology. He is said to have sold his soul to the devil to gain his phenomenal guitar style, which still amazes and inspire musicians today. His death was also surrounded by intrigue. The fact is that Robert Johnson was a blues guitar genius, gifted songwriter and outstanding

lyricist who, in just 29 recorded tracks, left ample evidence of his ability. Rather than sell his soul to the devil, chances are he practised hard. Whatever the truth, however, Johnson's name is probably the most revered in blues history.

Joplin, Scott (1868-1917) *Ragtime*
One of the true musical geniuses to come from the United States, Scott Joplin became an exceptional pianist at an early and went on to become the 'King of Ragtime' thanks to his complex compositions and agile piano playing. He wrote some of his best work in St Louis, although he was originally from Texas, including *Maple Leaf Rag*, *The Entertainer* and *Easy Winners*. Despite immense popularity among both blacks and whites, Joplin felt unappreciated and went broke in an attempt to stage an ambitious ragopera.

King, Albert (1923-1992) *Blues*
Like his namesake – but not relation – BB KING, Albert King was born in Indianola, Mississippi. There he learned guitar on a homemade instrument and set out to play the Delta circuit. At one time a fixture in Arkansas and later in St Louis, King honed a much-imitated, simple blues style using single strings to speak clear, soulful solos. Although King enjoyed a great deal of influence on other bluesmen for many years, he achieved real fame later in life after recording blues-soul crossover tracks for the Stax label in Memphis, Tennessee.

King, BB (1925-) *Blues*
Riley B King – 'BB' – has probably achieved more in his long career than any other bluesman and is, without question, the genre's most successful performer and admired ambassador. From his Mississippi roots he took an increasingly refined blues style to Memphis where he found a job as a disc-jockey, calling himself the 'Beale Street Blues Boy'. He did indeed play the blues on Beale Street and in time recorded for the Bullet label in Nashville then at Sun Records for SAM PHILLIPS. Immense success followed both in terms of record sales and concert sell-outs. A short-lived

dip in his popularity during the sixties inspired him to work harder and he has since gained a reputation, even now, for almost non-stop touring and recording. Today, King is the biggest star in blues and the man most responsible for taking blues to a worldwide audience.

Lewis, Jerry Lee (1935-) *Rock & Roll*
Piano virtuoso Jerry Lee Lewis was SAM PHILLIPS' answer to ELVIS PRESLEY after Sun Records sold Presley's contract to RCA. This 'new King of Rock & Roll' was a good-looking, flamboyant and electrifying musician when in 1957 he released smash hits *Great Balls of Fire* and *Whole Lotta Shakin' Going On*. His career at the top of charts was spectacular but short-lived, however, in part because of his controversial personal life. Lewis remains a living legend of rock & roll and occasionally performs to enthusiastic crowds.

Little Milton (1934-) *Blues*
A highly accomplished bluesman from Mississippi, Little Milton's satisfying soul-blues sound has for years been a precise and near perfect example of the smooth blues style. He recorded for Sun Records in the early fifties but failed to register a hit. Later, however, he recorded for Checker in Chicago – achieving considerable success in the sixties – and, back in Memphis, on the Stax label. Little Milton is a highly successful concert performer and a recording artist with the Malaco label in Jackson, Mississippi.

Little Walter (1930-1968) *Blues*
After growing up in rural Louisiana, where he learned to play the harmonica, Little Walter settled in Chicago in the mid-forties where he played with some of the South Side's finest, including BIG BILL BROONZY, and created a harmonica sound unlike any heard before him. His stunning solos and careful phrasing promoted him to the A-list of Chicago bluesman and, by the time he died in 1968, Little Walter had come to be considered one of the most influential and exciting harmonica players of the post-World War Two Chicago blues scene.

Marsalis, Wynton (1961-) *Jazz*
Son of jazz piano master Ellis Marsalis, Wynton Marsalis became first the most exciting musician in the New Orleans Marsalis family, almost every member of which is a prominent jazz musician, and then the most exciting young jazz musician in the world. His breathtaking trumpet playing has earned him almost every honor in jazz and many more in the field of classical music. He is artistic director of the Lincoln Jazz Orchestra and a prolific and exceptional recording artist on the Sony label.

Miller, Rice (see Williamson, 'Sonny Boy' II)

Morton, Ferdinand 'Jelly Roll' (1890-1941) *Jazz*
The self-proclaimed 'inventor of jazz', 'Jelly Roll' Morton was a tireless publicist and hustler who was also one of the most gifted early pianists in jazz. His spectacular small band shows and recordings helped shape jazz and add weight to the argument that jazz originated in New Orleans, Morton's home town. Despite his phenomenal talent and frequent successes, however, Morton's career ended in an unhappy and early fashion, the great man himself taking to the grave the conviction that his contribution to music went unrecognized.

Muddy Waters (1915-1983) *Blues*
Without doubt the leader of post-war Chicago blues and one of the most famous names in American music, Muddy Waters started life on a plantation in Mississippi. There he learned guitar and supplemented his living as a tractor driver playing local juke joints and parties. In the early forties he joined thousands of others and traveled north to Chicago where he began recording for CHESS and quickly notched up a string of hits. His urbanized Delta blues brought Waters fans around the world and he was a patriarchal figure in the blues-rock movement of the sixties when British bands looked to Chicago blues for inspiration. Waters' bands included many of the brightest stars in post-war blues and, in various incarna-

tions, continued to record and tour right up until Muddy Waters' death from heart failure in 1983.

Oliver, Joe 'King' (1885-1938) *Jazz*

Through hard work, talent and determination, Joe Oliver formed a reputation as one of New Orleans' great 'cornet kings' and formed a band which was constantly in demand. In 1919 he was quick to spot the trend jazz was following towards Chicago and he moved there, with his band, in an attempt to stay ahead of the times. He invited a young Louis Armstrong to join him and together they formed the King Oliver Creole Jazz Band, one of the greatest jazz ensembles to grace the stage. Armstrong saw Oliver as a father figure and in return for his mentoring was happy to play second cornet to a man who was, without doubt, his musical inferior. In time, of course, Armstrong moved on and despite often successful attempts to keep his band on the road, the once mighty Oliver saw out the end of his days working as a janitor in a pool hall.

Patton, Charley (1891-1934) *Blues*

The first true Delta bluesman, to whom all subsequent bluesmen and rock musicians owe at least some debt, Charley Patton defined the genre and the blues way of life. He learned guitar on the Dockery Plantation in Mississippi from Henry Sloan and began to sing about what would become classic blues themes – prison, women, hard work and travel. He indulged in all manner of histrionics on stage – a precursor to the most eccentric rock & roll performers – drank wildly, had several wives and was thrown in jail from time to time. He was also an itinerant musician, rambling from place to place. Standards like *High Sheriff Blues* and *Pony Blues* remain as artistically current as the day they were recorded.

Phillips, Sam (1923-) *Rock & Roll and Blues*

Like WC Handy, Sam Phillips was born in Florence, Alabama. Like Handy he made an immense and lasting contribution to American music. While working for a radio station in Memphis, Tennessee, Phillips scouted for talent and recorded a number of blues musicians – among them BB King, Howlin' Wolf and Jackie Brenston – for the Modern and Chess labels. In 1952 he set up his own label, Sun, where he recorded a steady stream of the most influential musicians in blues and, later, rock & roll. Phillips began looking for a white man who could sing with the spontaneity of black musicians and he found that artist in Elvis Presley whom Sun first recorded in 1954. After Presley, whose contract Phillips sold to RCA to fund further development at Sun, Jerry Lee Lewis, Johnny Cash, Carl Perkins, Roy Orbison and many other great names came to Phillips in search of a contract. Sam Phillips still lives in Memphis where he is treated like rock & roll royalty.

Pickett, Wilson (1941-) *Soul*

With a huge voice and an even bigger personality, Wilson Pickett, born in Alabama, is one of the greatest soul stars of all time. He recorded a string of seminal hits through the sixties and early seventies at Stax Records in Memphis. With the help of Stax stalwarts like Steve Cropper he bombarded the top of the charts with hits *In the Midnight Hour*, *Mustang Sally* and *I'm a Midnight Mover*. Wilson Pickett's career slowed in the eighties but he is currently enjoying something of a comeback and is recording and performing again.

Presley, Elvis (1935-1977) *Rock & Roll*

The 'King of Rock & Roll' needs little introduction. From his humble beginnings in Tupelo, Mississippi, Presley graduated to Memphis where he learned guitar and was influenced by the then flourishing blues scene on Beale Street. In 1954 he began recording for Sun Records where his fusion of gospel, blues and country music and his rich, distinct vocal style pioneered the rock & roll genre. At first a regional star, then a national star and, quickly, an international star on a scale not seen before or since, Elvis Presley became a cultural icon to millions around the world. At RCA Records, where he had behind him the sort of financial clout not available at Sun, Presley scored a steady stream of smash hits. His career dimmed towards the end of the sixties when he was forced to compete with bands like The Beatles but a subsequent comeback confirmed his place at the very pinnacle of the music industry.

Professor Longhair (1918-1980) *Blues*
A New Orleans legend and one of the Crescent City's favourite sons, Professor Longhair played an exuberant brand of piano R&B that prompted the New Orleans R&B boom and inspired, among many others, 'FATS' DOMINO. The Professor's career was rarely stable and, by the end of the sixties, he was working as a cleaner despite his early successes and local hits like the classic *Tipitina*. In the early seventies, Professor Longhair was 'rediscovered' and took his place as a legend of New Orleans music.

Redding, Otis (1941-1967) *Soul*
A country boy from Macon, Georgia, Otis Redding recorded enough material before his life was tragically cut short in a 1967 plane crash to make him a true giant of soul. Ironically, chart success during his lifetime was limited – despite the ground-breaking nature of his classic tracks *Try A Little Tenderness*, *Respect* and *Mr Pitiful*. The intense emotion in his outstanding voice was, perhaps, too soulful for many record buyers. His biggest hit, *Sittin' On (The Dock of the Bay)*, shot to number one after his death.

Smith, Bessie (1894-1927) *Blues*
Perhaps the greatest female blues singer of all time, Smith, from Chattanooga, Tennessee, exerted a strange hold over audiences who were seduced by her amazing presence and powerful voice. During the twenties she recorded some of the finest hits in blues including *Gulf Coast Blues* and *Taint Nobody's Bizness If I Do*. As her fame grew to big star status, she sold millions of records. Smith died amid controversy in Clarksdale, Mississippi, when she failed to receive adequate help after a car accident. Reports that she was refused admittance to the whites-only hospital are now considered by many to be false.

Taylor, Koko (1935-) *Blues*
Born to a farming family in Tennessee, Koko Taylor moved to Chicago at an early age where she forged a glittering career as a powerful and individual vocalist to become the unchallenged 'Queen of Blues' and the matriarch of the refined Chicago sound. Hit records on the Alligator label have kept her touring and, like another Chicago blues legend, BUDDY GUY, she owns a club bearing her name just south of the Chicago Loop.

Terry, Clark (1920-) *Jazz*
Trumpeter Clark Terry became a leading musician in his hometown St Louis – where he befriended and profoundly influenced a YOUNG MILES DAVIS – before national attention led to work with a string of great jazz orchestras including those of Count Basie, Duke Ellington and Quincy Jones. He has recorded widely in his own right and was responsible for introducing the flugelhorn as a jazz instrument. Terry's jubilant vocals and penchant for scat singing has also been a noted feature of his distinguished career. Terry continues to perform and record.

Thomas, Rufus (1917-) *Soul, Blues, R&B*
The self-proclaimed 'Funkiest Man Alive', Rufus Thomas has been a permanent and much-loved fixture on the Memphis music scene since the early fifties. He recorded Sun Records' first hit, *Bear Cat*, in 1953 and went on to score hits during the sixties and seventies with Stax. Inventing eccentric dances to go with his tongue-in-cheek tunes, many of which became standards of funk, Thomas registered high sales with *Walking the Dog* and *Do the Funky Chicken*. He is also a well-known disc jockey and all-round entertainer in Memphis where he continues to perform, often with his daughter Carla.

Thomas, Son (1926-1993) *Blues*
A gifted guitarist from Leland, Mississippi, James 'Son' Thomas failed to find fame until his forties and even then his gripping brand of blues reached a fairly limited audience. He learned to play the blues from listening to the radio and other local blues-

men and was a well-known musician in the Delta where he lived his whole life. Towards the end of his career he achieved some success in Europe and his album, *Highway 61 Blues*, is a classic.

Turner, Ike (1931-) *Blues and Rock & Roll*
Despite the controversy which has surrounded him in recent years, fuelled in part by the movie of his wife Tina Turner's life, Ike Turner's place as a central figure in the history of blues and rock & roll is unassailable. He formed his band, the Kings of Rhythm, while still at school and played with many of the greatest Delta bluesmen as they passed through his hometown of Clarksdale, Mississippi. In 1951, aged 20, he recorded *Rocket 88* for SAM PHILLIPS with JACKIE BRENSTON. That record is thought to be the first true rock & roll record laid down. Turner then worked as a talent scout in Memphis for the Sun and Modern labels, delivering future stars into the hands of Phillips, and later took his band to St Louis where he met Annie Mae Bullock – the soon-to-be Tina Turner. With his new wife and a fleet of backing singers, the Turner Revue became a major draw throughout the sixties until its eventual demise in 1974.

Wells, Junior (1934-1998) *Blues*
Growing up in Memphis, Junior Wells learned to play blues harmonica from the likes of Junior Parker before moving to Chicago after World War Two. There he carved a career as one of the great postwar Chicago harp players, continuing the tradition of JOHN LEE 'SONNY BOY' WILLIAMSON and LITTLE WALTER, whose position he took in MUDDY WATERS' band. Later forming a long musical partnership with BUDDY GUY, Wells recorded some seminal blues harp solos and a rich catalogue of classic blues records.

Williams, Hank (1923-1953) *Country*
The first artist elected to the Country Music Hall of Fame, Hank Williams, from Alabama, signed a record deal with MGM in Nashville and practically created modern country music with his legendary band The Drifting Cowboys. They were regular visitors to the top of the charts with hits like *Hey, Good Lookin'*, *Cold Cold Heart* and *Lovesick Blues*. Drink and drugs problems led to a premature death at 29 but Hank Williams paved the way for a host of subsequent stars who built on a genre he helped invent. His legend as musician and man is the most enduring in country music.

Williamson, John Lee 'Sonny Boy' (1914-1948) *Blues*
One of the most important harmonica players in blues history, John Lee 'Sonny Boy' Williamson, from Jackson, Tennessee, became a key figure on the early Chicago blues scene where he propelled the harmonica to the frontline of blues instruments. Where previously the harp had questionable stature as a solo instrument, Williamson's immaculate timing and searing phrases helped define the Chicago sound. His influence was such that the other great blues harp player of the time, RICE MILLER, assumed Williamson's name; Miller was often called SONNY BOY WILLIAMSON II. John Lee 'Sonny Boy' Williamson's career was cut short when he was attacked and killed while walking home from a club on Chicago's South Side.

Williamson, Sonny Boy II (1910-1965) *Blues* An odd, eccentric and difficult man, Sonny Boy Williamson II, real name Rice Miller, was without doubt . one of the greatest harmonica players to grace the blues stage and, many would say, the greatest of them all. He took the blues harp to new musical heights and recorded some of the most perfect blues ever cut. Born on a Mississippi plantation – the exact year is disputed – Williamson never strayed from the Delta for long, no matter how famous he became. He first attracted widespread attention as leader of the King Biscuit Time blues show on radio in Helena, Arkansas – the first ever blues radio show – and later cut sides for Trumpet Records in Jackson, Mississippi, and Checker in Chicago. His influence was enormous and his legacy is vast and lasting.

SOUTHERN
COMFORT.

Add Some Southern Spirit

Index

NORTH
US 61

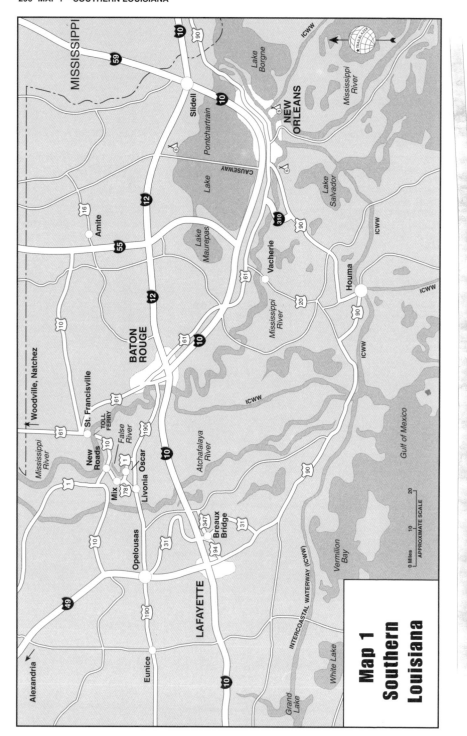

Map 1
Southern
Louisiana

MAP 2 – SOUTHERN MISSISSIPPI 297

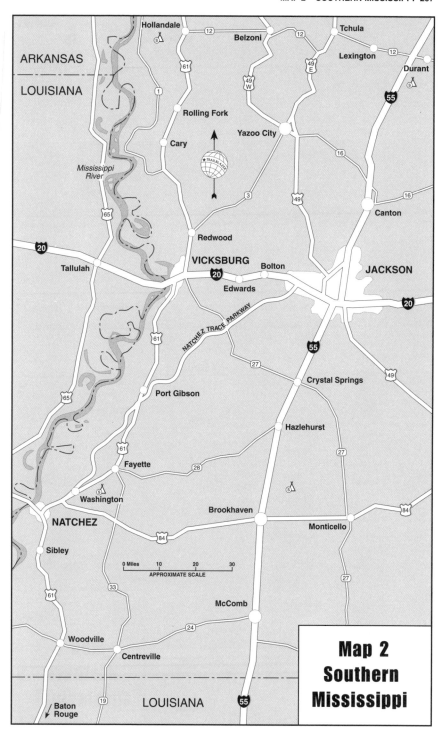

**Map 2
Southern
Mississippi**

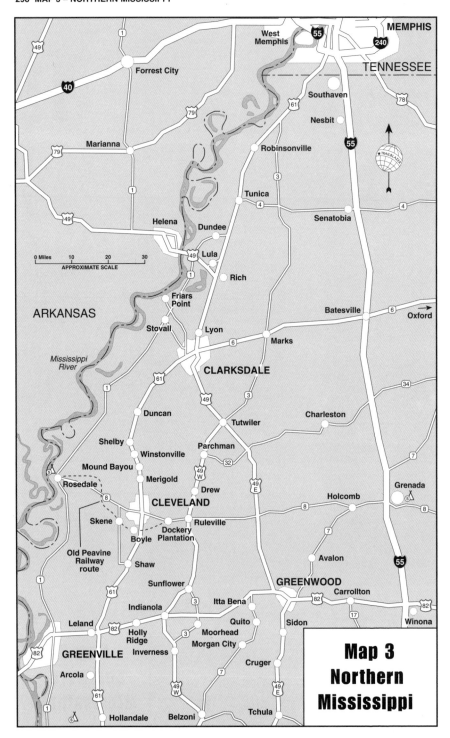

**Map 3
Northern
Mississippi**

MAP 4 – WESTERN TENNESSEE 299

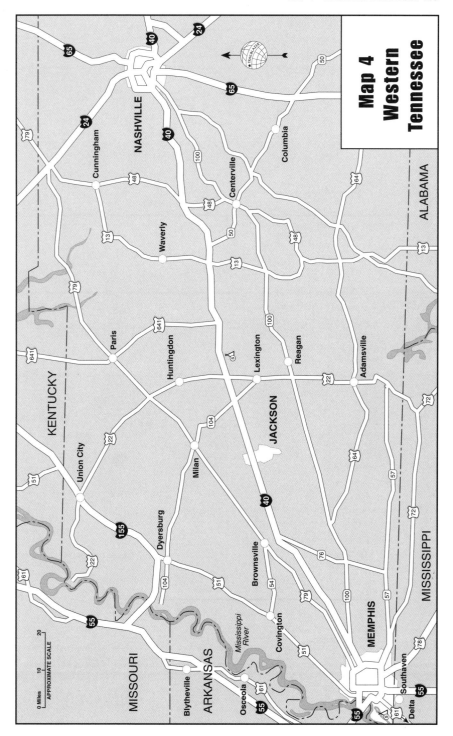

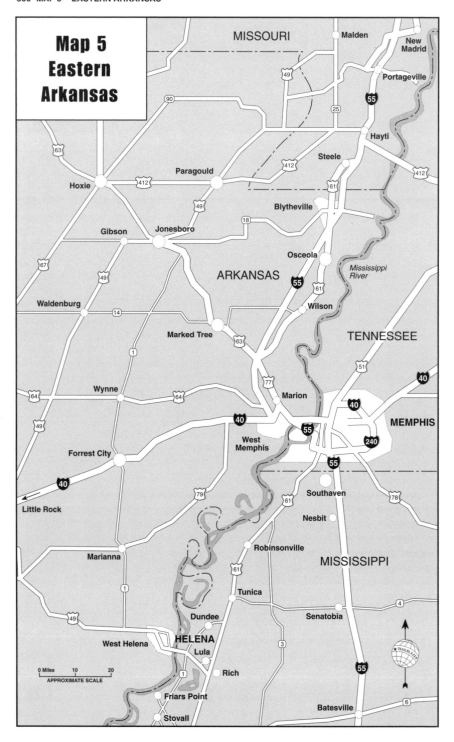

Map 5 Eastern Arkansas

MAP 6 – SOUTH-EASTERN MISSOURI 301

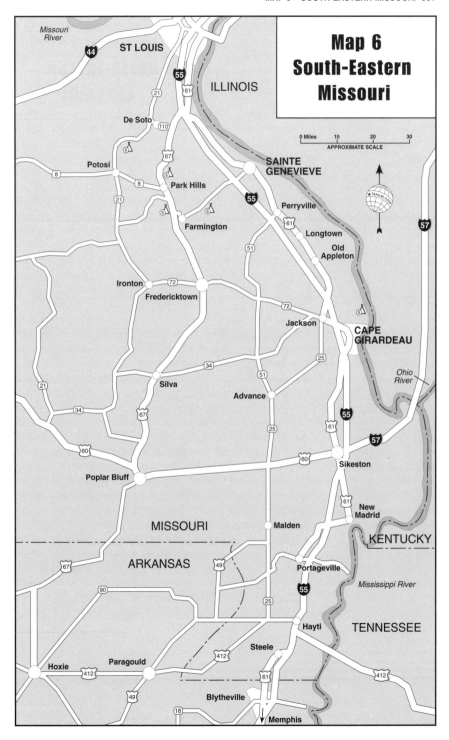

Map 6
South-Eastern
Missouri

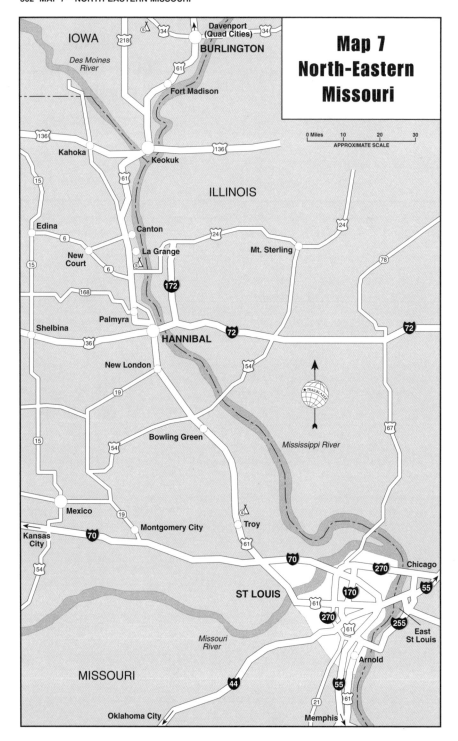

Map 7
North-Eastern
Missouri

IOWA

Des Moines River

Davenport (Quad Cities)

BURLINGTON

Fort Madison

Kahoka

Keokuk

ILLINOIS

Edina

Canton

La Grange

Mt. Sterling

New Court

172

Palmyra

72

Shelbina

HANNIBAL

New London

Bowling Green

Mississippi River

Mexico

Montgomery City

Troy

Kansas City

70

70

Chicago

270

ST LOUIS

170

270

East St Louis

255

Arnold

MISSOURI

Missouri River

44

55

Oklahoma City

Memphis

0 Miles   10   20   30
APPROXIMATE SCALE

MAP 8 – EASTERN IOWA 303

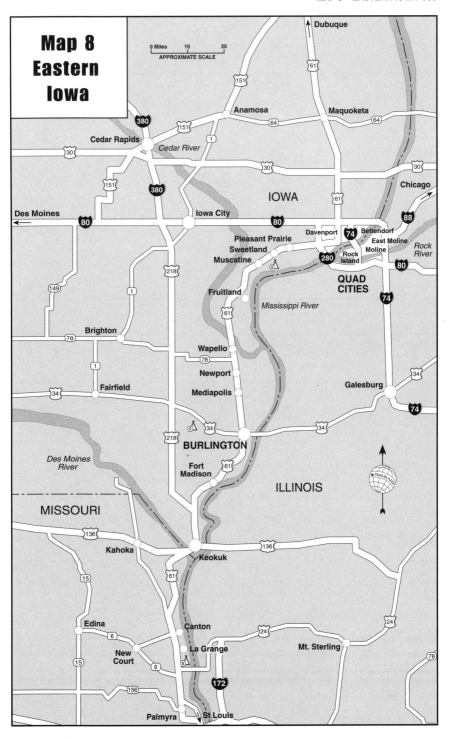

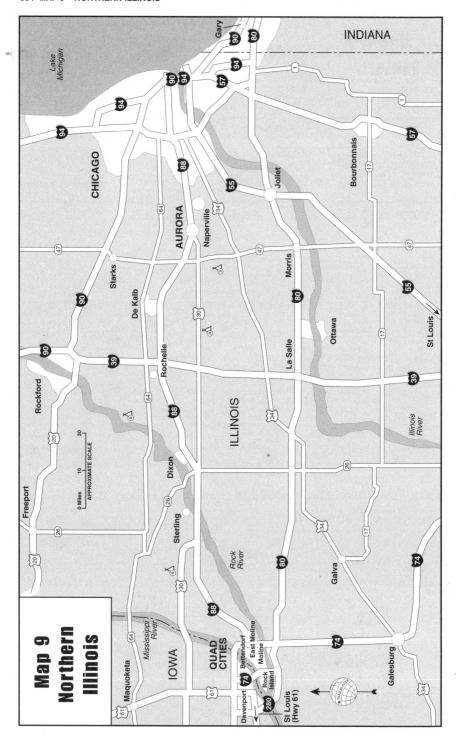

Map 9
Northern
Illinois